307.764 B72u 7053579
Bradbury, Katharine L.
Urban decline and the future
of American cities

URBAN DECLINE and the Future of American Cities

KATHARINE L. BRADBURY
ANTHONY DOWNS
KENNETH A. SMALL

URBAN DECLINE and the Future of American Cities

THE BROOKINGS INSTITUTION
Washington, D.C.

Library of Congress Cataloging in Publication data:

Bradbury, Katharine L.
Urban decline and the future of American cities.

Includes bibliographical references and index.
1. Cities and towns—United States—Growth.
2. Urban policy—United States. I. Downs, Anthony. II. Small, Kenneth A. III. Title.
HT123.B695 307.7'64'0973 82-70888
ISBN 0-8157-1054-2 AACR2
ISBN 0-8157-1053-4 (pbk.)

9 8 7 6 5 4 3 2 1

THE BROOKINGS INSTITUTION is an independent organization devoted to nonpartisan research, education, and publication in economics, government, foreign policy, and the social sciences generally. Its principal purposes are to aid in the development of sound public policies and to promote public understanding of issues of national importance.

The Institution was founded on December 8, 1927, to merge the activities of the Institute for Government Research, founded in 1916, the Institute of Economics, founded in 1922, and the Robert Brookings Graduate School of Economics and Government, founded in 1924.

The Board of Trustees is responsible for the general administration of the Institution, while the immediate direction of the policies, program, and staff is vested in the President, assisted by an advisory committee of the officers and staff. The by-laws of the Institution state: "It is the function of the Trustees to make possible the conduct of scientific research, and publication, under the most favorable conditions, and to safeguard the independence of the research staff in the pursuit of their studies and in the publication of the results of such studies. It is not a part of their function to determine, control, or influence the conduct of particular investigations or the conclusions reached."

The President bears final responsibility for the decision to publish a manuscript as a Brookings book. In reaching his judgment on the competence, accuracy, and objectivity of each study, the President is advised by the director of the appropriate research program and weighs the views of a panel of expert outside readers who report to him in confidence on the quality of the work. Publication of a work signifies that it is deemed a competent treatment worthy of public consideration but does not imply endorsement of conclusions or recommendations.

The Institution maintains its position of neutrality on issues of public policy in order to safeguard the intellectual freedom of the staff. Hence interpretations or conclusions in Brookings publications should be understood to be solely those of the authors and should not be attributed to the Institution, to its trustees, officers, or other staff members, or to the organizations that support its research.

Foreword

MOST LARGE CITIES in the United States have been losing population for at least two decades, some for much longer. Losses have occurred at precipitous rates in a few severely declining cities, where employment and local tax bases are also shrinking. Some of these cities contain large areas of abandoned buildings and neighborhood decay. Yet many other large U.S. cities are still gaining population, and the 1970s witnessed huge capital investments in downtown office buildings and neighborhood housing rehabilitation in nearly all big cities, including those whose populations are falling sharply.

This confusing combination of conditions and trends has caused urban observers to reach widely varying conclusions about the causes and nature of urban decline and what—if anything—should be done about it. Some, believing that large cities are obsolete in an age of automobiles and electronic communications, argue that public policies should help big cities decline gracefully and should not encourage their revitalization. Other observers claim large cities have already begun a renaissance that will reinforce their traditional roles as centers of cultural and economic dynamism. They think this is especially likely because of high energy costs and demographic shifts to smaller households. They want to encourage urban revival through public policies that bestow financial and other aid upon large cities. Still others favor federal aid to big cities to help them cope with disproportionate numbers of low-income households.

The myriad facts cited by proponents of these contrasting views have not been systematically related to explicit theories about the causes of urban decline. Hence urban policy debates usually revolve around fragmentary theories that have never been tested empirically. Decisions involving billions of dollars and affecting millions of households have been based on almost completely unverified propositions and assertions. The study reported in this book tackled the gigantic task of cataloging the various theories about why urban decline occurs and testing most of them against data gathered from 1960 to 1975 on the 153 American cities that contained 100,000 or more people in 1970. To explore other aspects of urban decline, the authors conducted several substudies: a review of general forces affecting the growth and decline of U.S. cities, an analysis of the nature and causes of neighborhood decline and revitalization within cities, a detailed simulation of possible policies to combat urban decline in one major metropolitan area, and a quantitative analysis of the effect of high energy costs on urban development. The authors' analysis required a four-year effort that perhaps constitutes the most comprehensive analysis of urban decline yet undertaken.

This study received support from the Ford Foundation, the Urban Mass Transportation Administration, the Federal Highway Administration, and the Brookings Institution. Katharine L. Bradbury is a research economist with the Federal Reserve Bank of Boston, a former research associate in the Brookings Economic Studies program, and coeditor (with Downs) of *Do Housing Allowances Work?* (Brookings, 1981). Anthony Downs is a senior fellow in the Brookings Economic Studies program and author of *Neighborhoods and Urban Development* (Brookings, 1981), another product of this study. Kenneth A. Small is assistant professor of economics at Princeton University and a member of the Brookings associated staff.

The authors are grateful to Robert Inman, Stephen Kennedy, Norman Krumholz, Edwin Mills, and Elizabeth Roistacher for reviewing the manuscript; to Edith Brashears, Mary Beth Burnham, Thea Lee, and Deborah Ramirez for research assistance; to Anita Whitlock for typing the many drafts; and to Diana Regenthal for preparing the index.

The views expressed in this book are solely those of the authors and should not be ascribed to the persons or organizations whose assistance is acknowledged above or to the trustees, officers, or other staff members of the Brookings Institution.

BRUCE K. MACLAURY
President

May 1982
Washington, D.C.

Contents

1. Introduction and Summary 1
The Basic Nature and Extent of Urban Decline *4*
The Causes of Urban Decline *8*
Decline at the Neighborhood Level *10*
How Future Trends Will Affect City Decline and Growth *11*
Future Impacts of Higher Energy Costs on Urban Development *12*
A Case Study of Anti-Decline Policies: Cleveland *13*
Public Policies Concerning Urban Decline *14*

2. What Is Urban Decline? 18
Social Functions and Differentiating Traits of Urban Areas *19*
Causal Relationships between Descriptive and Functional Decline *22*

3. How Extensive Is Urban Decline in the United States? 28
The Extent of Decline in Descriptive Terms *29*
The Extent of Distress and Decline in Functional Terms *42*
Intrametropolitan Disparity as an Element of Distress and Decline *61*
Conclusions *64*
Appendix: Descriptions of Indexes Used in This Chapter *65*

4. Causes of Urban Decline 68
Historic Trends and Their Influence *68*
Causes of Urban Decline in Individual Areas *77*
A Strategy for Empirical Testing *78*

5. Testing Theories of Urban Decline 84
Decomposition of Total City Population Change *84*
Testing the Theories *87*
The Growth and Decline of SMSAs and Cities to Their SMSAs *88*
Review of Implications for Theories of Decline *97*
Conclusion *107*
Appendix A: Regression Estimates and Discussion of Estimating Techniques *108*
Appendix B: Derivation of Testable Hypotheses from Density Gradient Analyses *123*
Appendix C: The Role of Industry Mix in Metropolitan Employment Change *126*

6. Anatomy of City Decline and Growth, 1960–75 132
Changes in City Population, 1970–75 *133*
Changes in City Per Capita Income, 1970–75 *139*
City Employment Growth, 1960–70 *149*
Conclusion *164*

7. Neighborhood Change and Urban Decline 165
How the American "Trickle-down" Process Copes with Rapid Population Growth *165*
What Happens When Metropolitan-Area Population Growth Slows or Stops *174*
Conclusion *177*

8. Forces Affecting the Future of Cities 178
An Approach to the Future of Urban Areas *178*
Assessment *190*
Appendix: Trends Relevant to the Future of Urban Areas *193*

9. General Conclusions about the Future of Cities 202
Dynamics of Urban Decline *202*
Self-Reinforcing Elements *205*
Self-Limiting Elements *208*
Is Decline Reversible? *211*
Neighborhood Decline and Revitalization *212*
Future Problems in Declining Cities *213*
Conclusions *215*

10. Energy Scarcity and Urban Development Patterns 217
Adjustment Mechanisms *218*
High-Cost Scenario *221*
Severe-Shortage Scenario *233*
Conclusion *236*

11. Alternatives for One Declining Area: Cleveland, Ohio 237
Recent Growth and Decline *238*
Future Trends: Base Case Projections *240*
Policy Impacts *243*
Results *247*
Conclusion *253*
Appendix A: Some Assumptions Underlying the Estimates of City-Suburban Cost Differentials *254*
Appendix B: Secondary Impacts *257*

12. Policies to Deter Urban Decline, Part One 258
Why Public Policies Should Respond to Urban Decline *258*
Removing Policy Biases against Big Cities *259*
Regional Impacts of Policy Choices *262*
Adapting to Lower Populations and Resources *265*
Big-City Poverty, Diversity, and Local Governments *265*

13. Policies to Deter Urban Decline, Part Two 278
Directly Empowering Individuals and Households *279*
Achieving Effective Scale for Recommended Policies *293*
Conclusion *295*

Appendix: Variable Definitions and Sources 297

Index 305

Tables

1-1. Cities by Population Group 6
1-2. Troubled and Healthy Cities 9
2-1. Specific Social Functions of Urban Areas 23
3-1. City and SMSA Population and Employment Changes 30
3-2. Cities in Each Cluster 36
3-3. Average Decline and Growth for City Clusters 38
3-4. Descriptive Characteristics of City Clusters 40
3-5. Trends in Distress and Decline Measures 43
3-6. City Distress and Decline Measures, by Region and City Size 44
3-7. SMSA Distress and Decline, by Region 46
3-8. City Decline Index: Cities Ranked from Worst Decline Rating to Least Decline Rating 51
3-9. City and SMSA Functional Index Values 52
3-10. Distributions of Distress and Decline Indexes 56
3-11. Population Changes and Functional Distress and Decline 58
3-12. Intrametropolitan Disparities, by Region and City Size 60
3-13. Distribution of Disparity and Divergence Indexes 63
3-14. Summary of Index Components 66

4-1. United States Population Growth, 1790–1980 70
4-2. United States Population, 1790–1980 71
4-3. Racial and Ethnic Characteristics of Cities 75
4-4. Theories Explaining Differences in Urban Growth and Decline 79
4-5. Strategy for Empirical Testing 82
5-1. Regression Estimates for Decomposition of City Growth for 120 Cities and SMSAs 85
5-2. Regional Differences in SMSA Growth and Suburbanization 97
5-3. Summary of Theories and Results 98
5-4. SMSA Population Change, 1970–75 109
5-5. SMSA Employment Change, 1970–75 110
5-6. SMSA Per Capita Income Change, 1970–75 111
5-7. City Population Change Relative to SMSA, 1970–75 112
5-8. City Real Per Capita Income Change Relative to SMSA, 1970–75 113
5-9. SMSA Population Change, 1960–70 114
5-10. SMSA Employment Change, 1960–70 115
5-11. SMSA Change in Real Per Capita Income, 1960–70 116
5-12. City Population Change Relative to SMSA, 1960–70 117
5-13. City Employment Growth Relative to SMSA, 1960–70 118
5-14. City Real Per Capita Income Change Relative to SMSA, 1960–70 119
5-15. Shift-Share Analysis for Cleveland SMSA 128
5-16. Shift-Share Analysis for San Jose SMSA 130
6-1. City Population Change, 1970–75: Combined City-Relative and SMSA Equations 134
6-2. Factor Contributions to Five Large Cities' Deviations from Average Population Growth, 1970–75 136
6-3. Factor Contributions to Four Medium-sized Cities' Deviations from Average Population Growth, 1970–75 137
6-4. Why Cities' Population Growth Rates Differed, 1970–75 140
6-5. City Per Capita Income Change, 1970–75: Combined City-Relative and SMSA Equations 146
6-6. Factor Contributions to Five Cities' Deviations from Average Per Capita Income Growth, 1970–75 148
6-7. Why City Income Grew at Different Rates, 1970–75 150
6-8. City Employment Change, 1960–70: Combined City-Relative and SMSA Equations 156
6-9. Factor Contributions to Five Cities' Deviations from Average Employment Growth, 1960–70 158
6-10. Why Cities' Employment Growth Rates Differed, 1960–70 159
10-1. Some Adjustment Mechanisms Available to Households for Reducing Energy Consumption 219
10-2. Percentage Distribution of All Workers Living and Working in Same SMSA and Not Working at Home, 1975 224
10-3. High-Energy-Cost Scenario: Work Travel, 1975 National Sample 225

10-4. Percentage Distribution of All Workers Living and Working in Cleveland SMSA, 1976 227
10-5. High-Energy-Cost Scenario: Work Travel, Cleveland SMSA 228
10-6. Some Determinants of Average Automobile Use for Nonwork Purposes per Driver 229
10-7. Housing Characteristics of Central City and Suburban Location, U.S. Metropolitan Areas, 1976 230
10-8. Upper-Bound Impacts of High-Energy-Cost Scenario 231
11-1. Cleveland Area Growth and Decline, Selected Years, 1940–77 239
11-2. Base Case Projections for the Cleveland Metropolitan Area, 1975, 1980, and 1990 242
11-3. Hypothesized Direct Impacts of Policy Packages after Ten Years 244
11-4. Impacts of Policy Packages on City of Cleveland, 1990 247
11-5. Comparison of Fiscal Effects of Policy Packages in 1990 249
11-6. Comparison of Travel Effects 251
11-7. Percentage Distribution of Indirect or Induced Jobs, by Location of Directly Affected Job or Residence 257

Figure

5-1. Schematic Representation of Model Interactions 121

1

Introduction and Summary

AFTER one hundred years in which increasing urbanization dominated U.S. settlement patterns, many large cities and even whole metropolitan areas have begun to lose population. If this dramatic turnaround continues, it will greatly affect the future quality of life in the United States. The growth of extensive urban settlements around big cities during the past century immensely influenced almost every aspect of modern life, from family structure to modes of industrial production. Reversal of that growth might have equally great impacts. Hence understanding the extent of current urban population losses, their causes, their effects, and whether they are likely to continue is vital to the formation of effective public policies.

Big-city population declines began to appear before World War II and became quite extensive after 1950. By the mid-1970s, 97 of the 153 U.S. cities containing 100,000 or more people as of 1970 were losing population. From 1970 to 1975, the average loss of population among these cities was only 0.8 percent, but 41 experienced declines of over 6.5 percent. In some cases these losses were accompanied by slow growth of employment or even falling job levels.

These declines have caused serious fiscal and other problems. The near-bankruptcy of New York City in 1975, and the subsequent default by Cleveland in 1978, dramatized a "fiscal squeeze" that has also forced other cities to cut service levels or capital-facility maintenance. In fact, large U.S. cities have become heavily dependent upon intergovernmental transfers, which accounted for over 40 percent of their general revenues in

1976.[1] Moreover, many cities contain decaying neighborhoods occupied mainly by poor households and devastated by housing abandonment, arson, vandalism, and high crime rates. Over one-fifth of all residents in some cities live on public assistance. Thousands of relatively affluent households—especially those with school-age children—have been moving to the suburbs. The resulting higher concentration of poor residents has burdened big-city governments with great needs for services, and low ability to pay for them. The additional concentration of minority and ethnic groups within large cities has intensified the economic and social problems found there.

These developments have led some observers to question the long-range viability of large U.S. cities. Some believe they no longer perform any productive social functions that cannot be better carried out elsewhere, except perhaps as "urban reservations" for people unable to conduct any economically useful activities.[2] Proponents of this view also argue that high-density settlements are obsolete in an era of instant electronic communications and tremendous mobility propelled by automotive vehicles. Indeed, recent population and economic growth have leapt outward beyond city and even suburban limits to locations along interstate highways or in isolated rural counties.[3]

Other observers claim that higher energy prices, rising housing costs, and the rapid increase in small households will reverse urban decentralization, sparking a revival of large cities. They cite booming downtown office-space markets, higher commuting costs, and spreading rehabilitation of older neighborhoods as evidence that an "urban renaissance" has already begun.[4] Some even believe modern societies cannot survive without strong high-density core settlements providing cultural and economic stimulation.

This debate is not just an academic argument: it has profound implications concerning how the United States should allocate its resources and shape other public and private policies. A recent study estimated that the federal government planned to spend about 18 percent of the total fiscal 1979 budget in the nation's central cities. That included both person-oriented

1. *Statistical Abstract of the United States*, 1979, p. 307.

2. See Norton E. Long, *The Unwalled City: Reconstituting the Urban Community* (Basic Books, 1972), and *The Polity* (Rand McNally, 1962).

3. See Peter A. Morrison, *Current Demographic Changes in Regions of the United States* (Rand Corp., 1977).

4. See Neal R. Peirce, "Nation's Cities Are Poised for Comeback," *Cleveland Plain Dealer*, July 7, 1977; T. D. Allman, "The Urban Crisis Leaves Town," *Harper's*, December 1978, pp. 41–56.

spending (such as social security and welfare) and place-oriented spending (such as community development block grants).[5] As these programs change, decisions must be made about whether to continue, increase, or decrease federal and state spending in large cities. Basic choices must be made concerning whether to invest billions of dollars in highways or in mass transit, whether to subsidize housing rehabilitation or new construction, loan guarantees for old factories or tax-exempt bonds to finance new ones.

These choices depend in part upon whether a primary goal is to recentralize urban settlements. Some current federal aid programs involve "targeting" assistance on large, older cities in which poor households are concentrated. Should such targeting be continued or used even more widely? Or should federal assistance be equally aimed at rapidly growing fringe and rural areas, even though they have lower fractions of poor residents? How to answer such questions depends on what posture society adopts concerning future urban decline.

Thus, it is vital that decision-makers understand urban decline and its implications. But there are conflicting views about almost every aspect of urban decline, including its extent, causes, effects, and likely duration. What is urban decline, anyway? Should every city with even a tiny fall in population be considered in decline, or is something more involved? How extensive has it been? Is it undesirable or really a good thing in disguise? What are its causes? Even if we want to do something about urban decline, can anything be done that will really alter its course? To what extent will it be reversed by higher energy costs? Given the nature of urban decline, what will happen to U.S. cities in the future?

This study tries to answer these questions. Chapter 2 analyzes the nature of urban decline as both a descriptive and functional concept. Chapter 3 describes the actual extent of such decline based upon empirical data for the 153 largest U.S. cities and their metropolitan areas. Chapter 4 sets forth some basic causes of urban decline and presents the most prevalent and plausible theories concerning why it has occurred. Chapter 5 tests those theories empirically through a regression analysis of data for 121 cities that are the largest in their metropolitan areas; chapter 6 then uses the results to evaluate the importance of various causes both in general and with respect to specific cities. Chapter 7 focuses upon the specific processes of decline and revitalization as they occur *within* metropolitan

5. See Anthony Downs, "Urban Policy," in Joseph A. Pechman, ed., *Setting National Priorities: The 1979 Budget* (Brookings Institution, 1978), pp. 182–87.

areas, emphasizing key relationships linking neighborhood change and overall urban development.

Part 2 then considers the likely future extent of urban decline in light of our analysis of its current nature and causes. Chapter 8 discusses the basic forces likely to affect urban decline and growth in the 1980s and 1990s, and how they will be influenced by general trends in our society. Chapter 9 draws some general conclusions about the future of U.S. cities. The possible effects of rising energy costs upon future urban settlement patterns are explored in chapter 10. Chapter 11 summarizes the results of simulating alternative futures for one declining city—Cleveland—in order to test possible policies designed to counteract urban decline. Finally, possible public policy responses to future urban decline *and* growth are discussed in part 3.

For convenience, we summarize our findings in the remainder of this chapter.

The Basic Nature and Extent of Urban Decline

We define urban decline in two ways. *Descriptive decline* is any loss of population or jobs in an urban area. *Functional decline* means changes that are socially undesirable because they reduce the ability of a city or metropolitan area to perform its social functions effectively. In this study we use many measures of decline (and its opposite, growth), particularly changes in population, employment, and per capita real income in the 153 largest cities in the United States (those over 100,000 as of 1970) and the 121 metropolitan areas in which they are located. Data for these measures are for the two periods 1960 to 1970 and 1970 to 1975.

The extent to which descriptive decline is undesirable is discussed at length in chapter 2. Declines in employment are usually injurious from the viewpoint of an area's residents. Declines in population can be desirable if the area is overcrowded to start with—as were most cities as late as 1950. But initial falls in population and employment often start self-reinforcing effects that tend to perpetuate them well beyond relief of overcrowding. For this and other reasons, the amount of decline in most large cities since 1960 has imposed net negative impacts upon their residents and upon the nation as a whole. Many of these impacts result from the disproportionate concentration of low-income residents that typically accompanies falling big-city populations. This concentration is not caused by pure market forces, but results from several types of "market failure," including externalities and deliberate local government policies.

The extent of recent urban decline is examined in chapter 3 by dividing large U.S. cities into five groups based on rates of population change in them and in their metropolitan areas. To analyze the latter, the most convenient geographic unit is the standard metropolitan statistical area, or SMSA, which is defined as the area around a large city that is economically integrated with it. Throughout this study we have used "SMSA" and "metropolitan area" interchangeably. The cities themselves are classified as growing, stagnant (falling in population but not in number of households), or severely declining (falling in both population and households).[6] The SMSAs are classified as either growing or declining. The resulting five combinations (one combination—growing cities in declining SMSAs—has virtually no members) are shown in table 1-1, along with the names of the cities in each category. The number, percent, and total population of these cities, as of 1970, were as follows:

	Number of cities	*Percent*	*Total city population (thousands)*	*Total SMSA population (thousands)*
In growing SMSAs				
Growing	44	36	11,869	25,126
Stagnant	32	26	9,109	22,188
Declining	19	16	9,208	25,129
In declining SMSAs				
Stagnant	11	9	12,746	23,179
Declining	15	12	8,206	25,038

In order to measure normative changes in cities, we developed indexes of *decline* (negative changes in key conditions), *distress* (relatively low-level conditions of desirability), *disparity* (each city compared to its SMSA), and *divergence* (changes in disparity). These were based upon changes in or levels of unemployment rates, violent crime rates, real income per capita, local tax rates, percentage of population in poverty, percentage of older housing (built before 1940), and city-SMSA tax disparity. When cities were ranked in accordance with their relative scores concerning decline, distress, disparity, and divergence, some cities consistently had very low desirability ratings, while others consistently had high ratings, as shown

6. Change in households is estimated. See chapter 3.

Table 1-1. *Cities by Population Group (Largest City in Each SMSA)*

Growing cities in growing SMSAs		*Stagnant cities in growing SMSAs*	*Severely declining cities in growing SMSAs*	*Stagnant cities in declining SMSAs*	*Severely declining cities in declining SMSAs*
Albuquerque, N.M.	Lubbock, Tex.	Albany, N.Y.	Atlanta, Ga.	Boston, Mass.	Akron, Ohio
Amarillo, Tex.	Memphis, Tenn.	Allentown, Pa.	Birmingham, Ala.	Columbus, Ga.	Bridgeport, Conn.
Anaheim, Calif.	Miami, Fla.	Baltimore, Md.	Canton, Ohio	Jersey City, N.J.	Buffalo, N.Y.
Austin, Tex.	Mobile, Ala.	Beaumont, Tex.	Chicago, Ill.	Los Angeles, Calif.	Cincinnati, Ohio
Baton Rouge, La.	Montgomery, Ala.	Cedar Rapids, Iowa	Flint, Mich.	New York, N.Y.	Cleveland, Ohio
Charlotte, N.C.	Newport News, Va.	Chattanooga, Tenn.	Gary, Ind.	Paterson. N.J.	Dayton, Ohio
Colorado Springs, Colo.	Omaha, Neb.	Columbia, S.C.	Hartford, Conn.	Providence, R.I.	Detroit, Mich.
Corpus Christi, Tex.	Phoenix, Ariz.	Columbus, Ohio	Kansas City, Kans./Mo.	Rockford, Ill.	Duluth, Minn.
El Paso, Tex.	Raleigh, N.C.	Dallas, Tex.	Louisville, Ky.	Stamford, Conn.	Newark, N.J.
Ft. Lauderdale, Fla.	Riverside, Calif.	Denver, Colo.	Milwaukee, Wis.	Topeka, Kans.	Philadelphia, Pa.
Ft. Wayne, Ind.	Sacramento, Calif.	Des Moines, Iowa	Minneapolis, Minn.	Wichita, Kans.	Pittsburgh, Pa.
Fresno, Calif.	San Antonio, Tex.	Erie, Pa.	New Haven, Conn.		St. Louis, Mo.
Greensboro, N.C.	San Diego, Calif.	Evansville, Ill.	Norfolk, Va.		Savannah, Ga.
Honolulu, Hawaii	San Jose, Calif.	Grand Rapids, Mich.	Portland, Oreg.		Seattle, Wash.
Houston, Tex.	Shreveport, La.				South Bend, Ind.
Jackson, Miss.	Spokane, Wash.				
Jacksonville, Fla.	Springfield, Mass.				

Knoxville, Tenn.	Springfield, Mo.	Huntsville, Ala.	Richmond, Va.
Las Vegas, Nev.	Stockton, Calif.	Indianapolis, Ind.	Rochester, N.Y.
Lexington, Ky.	Tampa, Fla.	Lansing, Mich.	San Francisco, Calif.
Lincoln, Neb.	Tucson, Ariz.	Macon, Ga.	Scranton, Pa.
Little Rock, Ark.	Tulsa, Okla.	Madison, Wis.	Syracuse, N.Y.
		Nashville, Tenn.	
		New Bedford, Mass.	
		New Orleans, La.	
		Oklahoma City, Okla.	
		Peoria, Ill.	
		Salt Lake City, Utah	
		Tacoma, Wash.	
		Toledo, Ohio	
		Trenton, N.J.	
		Washington, D.C.	
		Waterbury, Conn.	
		Worcester, Mass.	
		Youngstown, Ohio	

in table 1-2. However, similar ranking of *SMSAs* showed many more randomized patterns of normative change and status.

The Causes of Urban Decline

A certain amount of urban decline has been caused by basic society-wide forces, rather than by the traits of individual places. Among these forces are a sharp fall in fertility rates after the mid-1960s, an enormous drop-off in migration from farms to cities in the 1970s (including reduced migration of rural blacks), tremendous increases in the use of automobiles and trucks, the building of millions of new suburban housing units that attracted households out of older in-city neighborhoods, and increased air travel that made remote regions more easily accessible. These factors combined to slow the overall rate of metropolitan-area population growth in the 1970s compared to preceding decades. They also caused continued suburbanization within each metropolitan area.

However, other factors are required to explain why some cities continued to grow in the late 1960s and early 1970s, while others stagnated and still others declined. Chapter 4 discusses about forty theories of varying complexity that have been advanced as explanations. Chapter 5 tests many of these theories empirically through a set of regressions analyzing possible causes of changes in urban population, employment, and per capita real income. These changes were studied for the 121 cities of over 100,000 as of 1970 which were the largest in their SMSAs. We sought to separate the influences of changes occurring at the SMSA level—that is, among different SMSAs—from those related to the relative position of each city within its SMSA—that is, the amount of suburbanization there. Chapter 6 then combines these two influences to arrive at overall conclusions concerning the causes of growth or decline of cities. This analysis leads to the identification of certain factors that have affected big-city growth and decline in the past, and are likely to continue to do so. Detailed descriptions of the specific causal relationships are set forth in chapter 6.

Two overall conclusions about the causes of big-city *population* growth and decline can be drawn. First, we found that relatively rapid city population growth is associated with the following factors:

—fast SMSA employment growth;

—warm January temperature;

—low city-SMSA disparities concerning (a) the percentage of older housing in the total inventory; (b) the percentage of blacks in the total population; and (c) local tax rates;

Table 1-2. *Troubled and Healthy Cities*

City	*Among the 11 cities with worst distress*	*Among the 19 cities with worst decline*	*Among the 18 cities with worst disparity*	*Among the 11 cities with worst divergence*
Atlanta, Ga.	×	×	×	×
Boston, Mass.	×	×	×	×
Hartford, Conn.	×	×	×	×
Newark, N.J.	×	×	×	×
Camden, N.J.	×		×	×
Cleveland, Ohio	×	×	×	
Dayton, Ohio	×	×	×	
Paterson. N.J.		×	×	×
Trenton. N.J.	×	×	×	
Buffalo, N.Y.			×	×
Detroit, Mich.		×	×	
Miami, Fla.	×		×	
Oakland, Calif.			×	×
Philadelphia, Pa.	×	×		
	Among the 15 cities with least distress	*Among the 14 cities with least decline*	*Among the 11 cities with least disparity*	*Among the 12 cities with least divergence*
Virginia Beach, Va.	×	×	×	×
Livonia, Mich.	×		×	×
Parma, Ohio	×		×	×
Torrance, Calif.	×		×	×
Fremont, Calif.	×			×
Glendale, Calif.	×			×
Hampton, Va.	×	×		
Independence, Mo.	×			×
Lincoln, Neb.	×			×
Lubbock, Tex.		×	×	
Omaha, Neb.		×		×
Wichita, Kans.	×	×		

Source: See table 3-9.

—small total number of separate municipalities in the SMSA;
—low SMSA unemployment rate;
—high percentage of Hispanics in the SMSA and/or the city; and
—the extension of the city's public school district beyond the city limits.

Declining city population, or slow growth, is associated with conditions opposite those listed above.

Second, urban decline is not a homogeneous phenomenon. That is, the same symptom—declining city population—may be caused by any one of many different possible combinations of factors.

Decline at the Neighborhood Level

One widespread manifestation of urban decline is neighborhood deterioration, which involves both physical decay of structures and decreasing socioeconomic status of residents. Chapter 7 shows how neighborhood decline is an almost inevitable result of two factors: poverty and the way urban development operates in the United States.

Nearly all new housing is built on the urban periphery in accordance with high quality standards legally required there. Such housing can initially be occupied only by high- and middle-income households, since it is too costly for most lower-income households. In effect, the quality standards required legally exclude the poor from new-growth areas, which is one reason the standards are deliberately maintained at such high levels. This institutional arrangement has successfully provided the nonpoor majority of households in metropolitan areas with good-quality neighborhood environments. But it also compels most poor urban households to live in older neighborhoods close to the historic centers of large cities, and their concentration aggravates many social problems associated with extreme poverty. When poor households migrate into an SMSA, they usually enter such concentrated-poverty areas. This generates overcrowding, soon followed by a spilling over of poor households into other nearby neighborhoods. If the inmigration of the poor continues, this process of *overcrowding decline* can cause extensive transitions of inner-city areas to occupancy mainly by low-income households who cannot afford to maintain the housing there in its initial condition; hence that housing deteriorates. At the same time, the socioeconomic status of the neighborhood falls.

From the viewpoint of the initial residents of each neighborhood, such transition seems undesirable. But from the perspectives of the newcomers there and of the entire SMSA, this process is necessary to accommodate the rapid growth of the poor population—given society's refusal to allow the poor to move directly into new-growth areas.

Neighborhood decline can also take place after inmigration of the poor has slowed or stopped altogether. Such *emptying out decline* normally does not occur without high levels of new suburban housing construction in relation to net household formation. Institutional factors cause home builders to continue constructing new suburban units, which draw more middle- and high-income households out of older in-city neighborhoods. This kind of decline is thus part of an overall upgrading process that improves the environments of most SMSA residents. As moderate- and low-income households "filter up" through the inventory into units left behind by people moving into new homes, vacancy rates in the oldest, least desirable areas become high. This may lead to abandonment and further decay. The faster new peripheral home-building occurs relative to the growth of households in the SMSA, the more widespread such neighborhood decline is likely to be.

How Future Trends Will Affect City Decline and Growth

To determine how future trends are likely to affect urban decline, we examine in chapters 8 and 9 many such future trends and analyze their probable effects on the previously identified causal factors.

One overall conclusion reached in the analysis is that the net movement of population from metropolitan to nonmetropolitan areas will continue in the 1980s, and may accelerate. This will include both spillover growth into nearby counties—in spite of higher energy costs—and faster growth in more distant counties. Nevertheless, even though both fertility rates and migration from farms will remain low, natural increase and immigration from abroad will continue to cause substantial metropolitan-area population growth in the 1980s, probably slightly exceeding that of the 1970s. Most will take place in suburban areas, especially in fast-growing SMSAs in the South and West. These regions will continue to experience net inmigration from the Northeast and Midwest, partly because of lower nominal living costs and higher real incomes in the South. Most Northeastern and Midwestern cities that have recently been losing population will keep on doing so. However, Southern and Western cities that have grown through annexation will encounter increasing resistance to such expansion in the future.

The outflow of households from cities to their surrounding suburbs will also persist in most SMSAs, although probably more slowly. It will be accompanied by continuing office-space growth in big-city downtowns, plus expanding revitalization in many older neighborhoods. Yet neighborhood decline will not disappear from most large cities. It may even spread to a few more city neighborhoods and some suburban ones.

Once begun, big-city population decline sets in motion certain self-reinforcing forces likely to perpetuate it. These include the disproportionate withdrawal of high- and middle-income households from cities, rising local taxes and deteriorating public services there, city-suburban disparities in the percentage of older housing, losses of economies of agglomeration and scale as activities decrease, the tendency of physical deterioration to induce poorer maintenance by owners of surrounding properties, and the falling political power of cities within Congress and state legislatures. The impacts of these forces are likely to outweigh those of self-limiting forces initiated by decline, such as relative falls in big-city land and housing prices.

Moreover, population losses in large cities are rooted in certain persistent long-range social trends that many people regard as desirable. These include rising real incomes, greater use of cars and trucks, widespread desire for living in relatively new, low-density settlements, economic advantages of homeownership, and strongly entrenched tendencies for people to segregate themselves socioeconomically and racially by neighborhood.

As a result, continuing population declines in most large U.S. cities seem irreversible, at least in the near future. Hence public policies should not seek to reverse or even to halt such declines, but should aim at helping city governments and residents adjust to lower levels of population and activity, and at counteracting or offsetting any serious negative impacts of decline—especially upon the poor.

One of the continuing social functions of large cities—helping society cope with and upgrade its poorer citizens—will require sustained infusions of outside resources, especially from the federal government. Dealing with poverty requires income-redistributive policies, and such policies simply cannot be effectively carried out by local or even state governments.

Future Impacts of Higher Energy Costs on Urban Development

Recent and possible future increases in energy prices might affect urban settlement patterns by raising commuting and home heating costs, thereby influencing household locational decisions. To test this possibility, we analyze in chapter 10 the likely impacts of an increase in fuel prices of

$1.00 per gallon for gasoline and $.75 per gallon for fuel oil (in 1977 dollars). Even assuming no improvements in automobile fuel efficiency or driving patterns, the resulting increase in travel costs would create relatively minor incentives for suburban commuters to move into cities closer to their jobs. Including both work-oriented and nonwork travel, the total cost differential between living in the suburbs and living in the city would rise less than $200 per year per household, based upon national average commuting patterns. For home heating, the average city-suburban cost difference, given typical mixes of single-family and multi-family units in both areas, would rise only about $55 per year. Furthermore, most households are more likely to adjust to higher energy prices through means other than changing the locations of their homes or jobs, such as fewer trips, car pooling, more fuel-efficient cars, home insulation, and resetting thermostats.

Another reason that higher energy prices, or even intermittent shortages, will not greatly affect urban development is that changing settlement patterns takes many years. Changes must be made by altering the quantity or location of new construction, which has only marginal effects on the huge existing inventory of homes and other structures. The most likely effect of high energy prices on land use is greater nucleation of both city and suburban development, rather than any significant net shift from suburbs to cities.

A Case Study of Anti-Decline Policies: Cleveland

To test the possible effectiveness of policies aimed at counteracting urban decline, we made detailed quantitative simulations of how they would work if applied in the Cleveland metropolitan area. Cleveland was chosen because it is typical of many older declining cities and SMSAs, especially in the Midwest and Northeast. This analysis, presented more completely in another book, is summarized in chapter 11.

The first step was a "Base Case" analysis projecting what would happen to key variables if no major changes in current policies occurred. This revealed that a continuation of current trends from 1980 to 1990 would cause further falls in the city's population, number of households, and employment. Projections were also made of transit use, housing, and fiscal conditions—all of which would continue to deteriorate within the city.

Five individual "policy packages," focusing on jobs, housing rehabilitation, municipal finance, public transit, and suburban growth, respectively, were defined. The impacts of each were compared to the Base Case; then all five were combined into one "all-out revitalization package," and its effects also simulated. Both immediate, direct impacts and longer-range, indirect impacts of these policy packages were quantified, including multiplier effects upon household spending, job location, and household location.

Considered individually, none of the policy packages offset more than one-sixth of the loss of city jobs from 1980 to 1990 in the Base Case, or more than one-half the Base Case loss of households. Metropolitan transit subsidies are especially ineffective because they encourage residential suburbanization even while helping downtown businesses. When all five were combined, they reduced the city's Base Case job loss by about 50 percent, completely offset its loss of households, and cut its population loss by about two-thirds. That represents a generous maximum estimate of how much of the Cleveland area's future decline might be counteracted by public policies, especially since most help the city at the expense of its suburbs. They would therefore be politically controversial. However, many other possible responses to decline were not tested, including improvements in public schools and other social conditions.

One important finding concerned "targeting" aids to declining cities. In order to improve any particular condition such as unemployment or housing, it is much more effective to aim policies directly at that condition than to attack decline in general and hope the effects will "spill over" or "trickle down." This is especially true of fiscal distress, which is only slightly relieved by any of the nonfiscal measures considered.

Public Policies Concerning Urban Decline

Public policies should respond to decline when doing so improves society's equity, efficiency, or both. Such responses need not try to halt or reverse decline; many should aim at helping cities adapt to it, or counteract its most undesirable impacts. Many justifiable interventions seek to remedy problems caused by *externalities*—that is, direct relationships among persons that do not flow through markets. An example is air pollution in residential areas along expressways. Urban areas are permeated by externalities because people live and work so close together, but markets cannot handle such relationships in an equitable or efficient manner.

Solving urban problems in some ultimate sense would require radical changes in the existing institutions that generate those problems. We do not believe there are any major sources of political support for such radical policies since they would disrupt the benefits those institutions now provide to a majority of urban households. Therefore, we recommend relatively marginal changes in existing institutions and policies that deal with their effects.

Removing anti-city biases from federal policies. One set of fruitful policy responses to urban decline involves removal of several existing biases in federal policies that favor new construction in the suburbs over renovation, maintenance, or new construction in older cities. Much could be done to foster more evenhanded treatment of funding for highways, transit, and sewer and water systems; of depreciation of new and old structures for tax purposes; of location of federal jobs; and of tax benefits for housing.

Coping with regional biases in federal policies. Some Northeastern and North Central citizens believe certain federal biases against their regions encourage more rapid growth in the South and West and aggravate urban decline in Northern cities. However, most federal policies with varying regional impacts are aimed at goals other than achieving "regional neutrality." Examples are taxing incomes progressively, buying goods and services economically, and redistributing incomes to the poor. Any resulting regional biases are largely the accidental net outcomes of appropriately pursuing such goals. Thus, achievement of overall regional neutrality for total federal taxing and spending is not a legitimate objective, though assessment of how *changes* in existing federal behavior might affect regions is desirable.

Helping cities adapt to smaller populations and fewer jobs. A major strategy cities should use to cope with decline is adapting their behavior to lower levels of population and jobs. However, detailing that strategy is not within the scope of this book.

Effective forms of providing federal aid to cities. Most large cities need continuous infusions of federal aid because they provide services to a disproportionate share of the poor. Targeting federal aid to the neediest cities has been one way of providing such aid. But it is likely to be undermined by the weakening political power of big cities as their populations subside, and it has been greatly curtailed in recent years. Nevertheless the basic need remains and will increase in the future.

The enormous diversity of conditions both among and within large cities and SMSAs makes it difficult to develop effective uniform federal funding methods. Consequently, federal and state aid should take forms that allow tailoring detailed fund uses to each local situation as much as possible, while still pursuing national goals. Among existing forms of federal aid, revenue sharing and block grants are generally preferable to categorical funding arrangements. However, the latter can be adapted to diverse conditions by making local fund uses contingent upon certain local characteristics. Categorical funding should also be used for innovative or vital but unpopular programs.

We recommend development of a new "menu" approach providing local governments with more "consumer sovereignty." This would allow them greater freedom to choose how to allocate their federal funds among programs, while simultaneously giving federal officials considerable control over regulations for each program.

Coping with fragmented urban governments. Fragmentation of local governments helps worsen fiscal conditions in cities by depriving their governments of access to the expanding resource base in their suburbs. The most direct cure—consolidating city and suburban governments into one metropolitan government—has very little political support in the United States. Another approach is shifting some functions from city governments to regional, county, or state governments. Adoption of "power-equalizing" aid formulas by states can also help large cities capture some resources from nearby suburban tax bases. However, we recommend tax-base sharing at the metropolitan level as the best approach. It helps big cities fiscally without imposing any immediate costs upon suburban governments, and maintains complete local control over spending and land-use decisions.

Empowering individuals and households injured by decline. The persons most injured by various types of urban decline are residents of concentrated-poverty areas, including many low-skilled, unemployed workers. Public policies should try to stimulate employment and other improvements in conditions for such persons. A potentially effective general approach is *empowering needy households and individuals* to act for themselves in relevant markets. That means providing them with appropriate purchasing power, and letting them procure those goods and services themselves, rather than having public officials make such choices for them. The most comprehensive forms of such empowerment would be providing a combination of jobs and guaranteed annual incomes for unemployed or destitute households. Other, more limited forms involve voucher systems for particular purposes such as employment, housing, public transit, education, and health. However, consumer empowerment would probably not be effective at attacking the problems of concentrated poverty resulting from widespread socioeconomic and racial segregation in metropolitan areas. Such segregation is supported by institutional arrangements that benefit a majority of metropolitan-area citizens. One basic reform of these arrangements would be empowering poor households so they could move into more dispersed locations throughout each metropolitan area, or at least into moderate-sized clusters in most parts of each area. But any deliberate public policy of scattering poor households into predominantly nonpoor areas would arouse intense and widespread opposition from the nonpoor majority. In fact, strong opposition to any of the consumer empowerments suggested above would arise from many public officials and union workers. But their resistance might be mollified if these new programs were introduced as large-scale demonstrations with strong evaluative components to test the effects, as has been done recently with income support and housing programs.

Carrying out recommended programs on a sufficient scale. Certain policies cannot be effective unless they are carried out on a significant quantitative scale. However, Congress has a tendency to adopt myriad programs in response to every pressure to "do something"—but then to starve many of those programs for resources. To avoid such an outcome we recommend significant funding for certain high-priority programs. This can be made consistent with restricted overall federal domestic spending by reducing the total number of social programs attempted but focusing more adequate resources on those retained. Top priority, we believe, should go to programs that aid the residents of concentrated-poverty areas within big cities—especially the empowerment programs described above.

2

What Is Urban Decline?

THE TERM "urban decline" embodies the idea that declining cities are cities in trouble, cities not as economically or socially healthy as they used to be or as they should be. The most frequently cited *measure* of urban decline is population loss of a municipality or of an entire metropolitan area. Population loss is considered a measure of decline either because it actually detracts from the city's desirability, or because it is a symptom of broader difficulties. Why would more people be leaving a place than entering it if it weren't less healthy or attractive than other places?[1]

Thus, urban decline has both descriptive and functional meanings. In its *descriptive* sense, it refers to any decrease in such measures of size as population or employment. In its *functional* sense, urban decline means changes that somehow impair the functioning of a city or other urban agglomeration.

Not all descriptive declines are also functional declines. Population loss, for example, can be desirable: in areas that are extremely overcrowded, as were many U.S. cities right after World War II, some decrease in population may improve economic strength and quality of life. Conversely, cities can undergo functional decline while growing in population. For example, large influxes of refugees, especially if accompanied by physical destruction or supply curtailments as in Singapore in 1942, create changes that are undesirable from nearly every resident's viewpoint.

1. For a variety of views all embodying this general perspective, see *How Cities Can Grow Old Gracefully*, Subcommittee on the City of the House Committee on Banking, Finance, and Urban Affairs, 95 Cong. 1 sess., committee print (Government Printing Office, 1977).

This study postulates that every urban area has certain basic social functions that contribute to the well-being of its residents and of society in general. Any change that reduces its ability to perform these functions contributes to what we call "functional decline." Whether either descriptive or functional urban decline should be regarded as socially *undesirable* is yet another question. Shifts of activity that add to the health of an entire system of urban places considered as a whole may impair the functioning of any one of them. The recent report of the President's Commission for a National Agenda for the Eighties stresses this point, arguing repeatedly that attempts to slow these changes would detract from the common good.[2] Yet to assume that market forces by themselves will lead to an ideal outcome, even in terms of pure economic efficiency, is to ignore the many elements of externalities and other "market failures" inherent in urban areas. Indeed, the very existence of large urban areas depends on a degree of mutual interaction among people and firms which is known *not* to be efficiently mediated by a free market except in very special circumstances.[3] More specifically, much of the behavior and many of the policies that cause or aggravate urban decline violate the conditions under which economic theory predicts market outcomes would be optimally efficient. This implies that public intervention to influence these processes *may* be socially desirable. Many costs of urban decline are heavily concentrated upon particular groups, especially the poor. Society *may* decide to forgo some efficiency in order to ameliorate these inequitable effects. Thus, no valid theory justifies sweeping recommendations either for or against letting urban decline take its course; any policy recommendations must be based on a detailed understanding of the processes involved.

Social Functions and Differentiating Traits of Urban Areas

A *social function* of an urban area is an activity that provides important benefits to some local residents and to society as a whole. The activity can involve persons living, working, or visiting in the area, physical structures located there, or relationships among those persons and structures. Since

2. President's Commission for a National Agenda for the Eighties, *Urban America in the Eighties: Perspectives and Prospects* (GPO, 1980).

3. See Edwin S. Mills, *Urban Economics*, 2d ed. (Scott, Foresman, 1980), chap. 1; and Bruce W. Hamilton, "Indivisibilities and Interplant Transportation Cost: Do They Cause Market Breakdown?" *Journal of Urban Economics*, vol. 7 (January 1980), pp. 31–41.

urban areas perform hundreds of social functions, we concentrate upon those we regard as central to urban life. Our definitions of specific social functions primarily reflect the viewpoints of the residents of each urban area, either as consumers or as producers. Of course, divergences of interest arise among different groups of residents within each area concerning how some particular social function is performed. For example, high local government expenditures benefit municipal employees and recipients of subsidized city services; but they also contribute to high local tax rates that weaken the competitive position of local businesses, and make living there less desirable to those residents bearing the greatest tax burdens. However, the social functions used in this analysis have been broadly enough defined so that nearly every urban resident would agree they are desirable as stated.

Defining Traits of Urban Areas

It is useful to consider certain fundamental characteristics of urban areas that distinguish them from other settlements. An urban area has *mass* or *large scale* because it contains more inhabitants than typical of any other type of settlement. Large size is necessary to attain economies of scale in production, which also depend upon a large enough market to allow a highly specialized division of labor. However, degree of specialization does not always increase with population size: some very large urban settlements in nonindustrialized societies have relatively unspecialized divisions of labor. But in economically developed societies, specialization normally intensifies with the size of an urban area's population. Thus, the amazingly minute specialization in New York City's retail stores and restaurants is unmatched anywhere else in North America.

Geographic concentration means that urban inhabitants are located close together, primarily to reduce physical and other costs of interaction—especially travel time. Such concentration allows a large group of people to form a single market. Throughout most human history, people could sustain low interaction costs only by living very close together, since transportation was expensive in terms of both energy and time. As more efficient means of movement and communication developed, the fruits of geographic concentration became available without such close proximity. This is apparent from the way urban areas recently have spread over the landscape at much lower densities than nearly all past urban settlements.

Diversity of elements also differentiates urban areas from other settlements. Throughout history, cities have been where strangers from different cultures, ethnic groups, and classes of society came together to trade, argue, and stimulate each other's ideas. Hence they have always been less dominated by custom and tradition than villages, nomadic settlements, or rural areas. Diversity is also inextricably related to the other unique characteristics of urban areas. Intensive specialization of labor produces differentiation of roles in production processes, thereby generating social diversity of skills and ultimately of interests and viewpoints. Moreover, diversity stimulates innovations, which increase productivity. This allows higher living standards—thereby generating more diversity. Thus, the basic characteristics of urban areas are all closely interwoven and mutually reinforce each other.

The last defining trait is *intensive personal interaction* among the residents of an urban area, and between them and the numerous visitors it attracts. Such interaction is an essential part of the economic specialization inherent in urban settlements. If a large number of diverse persons lived in one spot, but were somehow constrained from interacting (as in a big prison camp), that settlement would not become a true urban area.

Basic Social Functions of Urban Areas

Urban areas can be seen as having four broadly defined social functions.

1. Large-scale production of goods and services.
2. Creative innovation.
3. Provision of a desirable residential environment.
4. Provision of a social support system for residents.

The first two functions are implicit in the defining characteristics of urban areas. Large-scale production follows from all four defining traits; innovation follows from diversity of elements and intensive personal interaction. The other two functions are common to all human settlements, though they may take rather different forms in urban places. Together they mean providing households with a safe residential environment in which they can live fruitful personal lives and pass cherished values on to their children. In most societies, effective performance of these functions has involved maintaining a certain degree of social homogeneity, so that the transmission of values and customs to children is not severely impeded by conflicting views. Thus, there is an inherent tension in urban areas between the degree of social homogeneity required to satisfy most people's idea of a good residential environment and social support system, and the degree of social diversity required for creative innovation and efficient large-scale production.

This tension is often partly resolved by two types of spatial separation. One is the separation of residences from most production activities (other than those carried on within the home or required to supply daily recurrent household needs). The other is the maintenance of separate neighborhoods for different ethnic, social, or economic groups—especially those with significantly different values. Despite these patterns of spatial separation, more mixing of ideas and values is likely in cities than in rural areas, so urban areas tend to generate faster changes in prevailing social values.

Specific Social Functions of Urban Areas

Certain specific social functions seem especially important in carrying out these mandates for a healthy urban area. In table 2-1 are listed those that we subsequently use in defining and measuring functional urban decline. These functions are organized in four groups, each pertaining to one of the basic functions discussed earlier, plus two groups that facilitate the operation of the urban area as a whole: urban governance and general supporting functions. Many of these functions are not unique to urban areas, but they summarize what a society can reasonably expect its urban areas to do.

Causal Relationships between Descriptive and Functional Decline

To what extent, or under what conditions, are descriptive decline measures also indicators of functional decline? In this section we consider the theoretical answer; in chapter 3 we examine the empirical relationships.

Employment Loss

Throughout this volume, we consider total employment as primarily a measure of urban size; therefore, we use employment change as a measure of descriptive decline. But employment is also related to some of the social functions listed in table 2-1. Jobs are sources of income and feelings of self-worth for an urban area's residents. They are also the primary input for

Table 2-1. *Specific Social Functions of Urban Areas*

Large-scale production of goods and services
1. Maintain and generate export (economic base) activities
2. Maintain and generate production for local use
3. Provide employment and earnings to residents and others in the region
4. Maintain, improve, and replace the stock of nonresidential structures
5. Maintain a labor pool of varying skills and specializations

Creative innovation
6. Stimulate innovations leading to higher productivity
7. Provide means for communications
8. Provide higher educational programs
9. Provide households with opportunities for upward mobility
10. Provide centralized facilities for face-to-face contacts
11. Provide opportunities for employment, education, and exercise of leadership for groups subjected to social or economic discrimination

Residential environment
12. Maintain, improve, and replace the stock of residential structures
13. Provide neighborhood amenities such as attractive appearance, safety, freedom from excessive noise, and social interactions
14. Provide retailing facilities for residents

Social support system
15. Provide educational programs for children
16. Provide cultural, recreational, religious, and entertainment services and facilities
17. Provide health care services and facilities

Urban governance
18. Provide an effective system of justice for settling conflicts and disputes
19. Maintain an efficient and equitable system of taxation to support governmental functions
20. Maintain government institutions for coping with changes in local conditions
21. Facilitate citizens' participation in local government decisions

Supporting functions
22. Provide public order and personal security
23. Provide and maintain transportation systems
24. Provide a system for collecting capital to finance consumer, business, government, and other activities
25. Provide and distribute the energy resources required for other activities
26. Maintain, improve, and replace physical infrastructure
27. Dispose of wastes and protect the environment

the production of goods and services. Therefore, only under extraordinary circumstances could a decline in an urban area's total employment be considered beneficial to its residents. Even if the area's labor force is falling faster than its total employment, causing unemployment to drop, some residents are forced to make difficult and often costly adjustments while the options open to those remaining are narrowed. Also, employment losses can weaken a city fiscally by reducing its tax base for financing local services, the need for which does not decrease enough to offset the resource loss. Moreover, outmigration by some firms makes the city less attractive to others that would otherwise benefit from proximity to them. Thus, loss of employment impairs the functioning of an urban area from the viewpoint of its residents, thereby causing functional decline by our definition.

Population Loss

The most readily available measure of descriptive decline is decrease in population. We focus here upon population decrease within a central city, but many of the same points apply to an entire metropolitan area. It is important to distinguish between losses of population and losses of *households*. The average number of persons per household fell 5.7 percent from 1960 to 1970, and another 12.4 percent from 1970 to 1980.[4] Consequently, in many cities, total population is falling but the number of households is rising. Some social functions of cities relate to population, but others—such as housing demand—relate to the number of households. This distinction should be kept in mind in the following discussion.

PRODUCTION OF GOODS AND SERVICES. Population loss tends to reduce production in two ways. Many jobs in urban areas are in local retailing and other household-supporting activities, so a population loss reduces these employment opportunities, which in turn produces the effects noted above. Second, the reduction (or slower growth) in housing demand tends to depress property values (in relative terms) in at least parts of the city. This adversely affects the nonlabor incomes of property owners as well as the local government's tax base.

CREATIVE INNOVATION AND SOCIAL SUPPORT SYSTEM. When large cities lose population, households moving out usually have higher average incomes than those moving in. For example, from 1975 to 1978, the median income of males over sixteen moving within the same metropolitan area was $12,411 for those moving *out* of central cities, but $10,240 (17 percent less) for those moving *into* central cities.[5] Similarly, net migration rates out of central cities are higher among whites than among minority groups.

4. Population per household was 3.33 in 1960, 3.14 in 1970, and 2.75 in 1980. Hence from 1960 to 1980, it dropped 17.4 percent. *Statistical Abstract of the United States, 1980*, p. 45; and Bureau of the Census, private communication.

5. Bureau of the Census, *Current Population Reports*, Series P-20, no. 331, "Geographical Mobility, March 1975 to March 1978" (GPO, 1978), table 33.

Among whites, the net migration rate from central cities to suburbs was 8.6 percent from 1970 to 1973, and 8.9 percent from 1975 to 1978. Among blacks, it was −0.3 percent from 1970 to 1973 and 2.9 percent from 1975 to 1978.[6]

The resulting concentration of poor and minority-group households in cities has several positive and negative effects. On the plus side, minority groups have been able to exert more political influence in such cities and to advance to higher positions in government and business than they probably would have under a local government more dominated by whites. Thus the roles of cities in providing upward mobility and leadership experience are enhanced. Also, city governments are probably more responsive to the needs of the poor when low-income households form relatively high fractions of their electorates.

On the negative side, the isolation of blacks and other minority groups tends to be increased, thereby reducing their mobility within the larger society.[7] Concentration of large numbers of poor households in a few deteriorating central-city neighborhoods tends to produce a "critical mass" of adverse conditions. Also, the higher proportion of children from less affluent households in the public schools creates difficult educational problems. Many of these children come from homes not strongly oriented toward education. Recent evidence suggests that such children can be taught effectively but that their concentration in certain schools often causes teachers and administrators to have low expectations concerning their performance.[8] This can be harmful both to these students and, by creating an unchallenging school environment, to children from middle- and upper-income households. In fact, recent evidence suggests that a high concentration of minority children often causes withdrawal of white (and frequently more affluent) children to suburban or private schools.[9]

RESIDENTIAL ENVIRONMENT. Severe population decline often results in housing abandonment. The owners of older, deteriorating units cannot obtain high enough rental revenues to cover costs. Abandoned units produce negative effects that reduce the attractiveness of the surrounding

6. Kathryn P. Nelson, *Recent Suburbanization of Blacks: How Much, Who, and Where?* (Department of Housing and Urban Development, 1979), p. 9.

7. National Advisory Commission on Civil Disorders, *Report* (GPO, 1968).

8. See the discussion of public school policies in chap. 13.

9. James S. Coleman and Sara D. Kelley, "Education," in William Gorham and Nathan Glazer, eds., *The Urban Predicament* (Urban Institute, 1976), pp. 234–55; and Charles T. Clotfelter, "Urban School Desegregation and Decline in White Enrollment: A Reexamination," *Journal of Urban Economics*, vol. 6 (July 1979), pp. 352–70.

neighborhood. For example, temporarily vacant apartment units in New York's South Bronx area often attract drug addicts and criminals. Such spillover effects drastically reduce the incentives of nearby owners to maintain their properties, thus generating the deterioration of whole neighborhoods.

However, when population loss is great enough to cause a drop in number of households too, it produces less crowding and lowers housing prices below what they would otherwise be. These benefits are often substantial and are enjoyed by a large part of the city's total population. This helps explain the paradox that some of the worst forms of functional decline occur in cities where rapid population growth increases crowding and housing prices. Much of the population decentralization out of cities after 1950 relieved severe overcrowding and housing shortages. However, by 1965 most cities losing population had already been relieved of the worst effects of overcrowding.

GOVERNMENT AND OTHER SUPPORTING FUNCTIONS. Local government fiscal difficulties frequently accompany population loss. Government revenues tend to fall at least proportionally unless tax rates are raised. If the local tax system is progressive, then when higher-income households leave, the remaining taxpayers have to pay even greater taxes. Yet the costs of certain local government activities do *not* decline proportionally with population losses. Examples include debt service on items that cannot be sold, like highways; operating costs that vary only slightly with usage, like those for libraries or parks; and wage costs of municipal workers whose organized bargaining strength may prevent proportionate cutbacks.[10] In addition, costly local services such as police and fire protection are concentrated among lower-income households. Thus, 1972–73 expenditures per capita on a group of common functions provided by virtually all city governments were $283 in cities of over a million population compared to $157 for cities in the 100,000 to 200,000 range. Among cities over 500,000 in population, those declining since 1960 (even excluding New York) had 35 percent higher per capita expenditures than those growing in 1973.[11] These opposite effects of population loss on revenues and service needs create a "fiscal squeeze" on local governments that forces them to reduce services, raise taxes, or seek additional aid from state or federal governments.

10. See George E. Peterson, "Finance," in Gorham and Glazer, *The Urban Predicament*, pp. 35–118. Also see Thomas Muller, *Growing and Declining Urban Areas: A Fiscal Comparison* (Urban Institute, 1975).

11. Peterson, "Finance," pp. 42, 48.

Other city functions need a "critical mass" of activity to operate efficiently, so falling city population leads to either higher per capita costs or cutbacks in services, or both. Examples are commuter railways, subways, bus systems, theaters, and specialized restaurants and retail outlets. If the level of patronage falls below that needed to sustain the activity economically, it will close entirely or require public subsidies to remain open. This effect is particularly likely to curtail activities used infrequently by most residents and thereby requiring a large total population to maintain efficient scale. Examples are higher education, health care, museums, and other cultural offerings.

Finally, if the population of a large city or metropolitan area falls substantially, its political representation in Congress and the state legislature is reduced at the next reapportionment. That decreases its representatives' ability to obtain or influence legislation favorable to its citizens. Corresponding increases in political representation elsewhere do not correct this negative result from the perspective of the city's residents.

The Net Effects of Central City Population Losses

When an overcrowded city loses population, the advantages of lower congestion and less crowded housing are likely to outweigh the other effects on city residents. However, when no residential overcrowding exists, these advantages are much less important than the disadvantages of population loss. Most U.S. cities currently losing population are clearly not crowded, since they exhibit one or more of the following signs of ample housing supply:

—Major housing abandonment.

—A large percentage decline from the city's historic peak population (for example, by 1980, St. Louis had lost about half its 1950 population).

—Large tracts of vacant residentially zoned land physically and environmentally suitable for housing.

—Many more new housing units built in the entire metropolitan area than new households added there each year, for a period of several years.

Therefore, we believe population losses in these cities are creating net losses of welfare for their residents.

The next four chapters further support this conclusion by providing quantitative evidence on the importance of the various links between descriptive and functional decline.

3

How Extensive Is Urban Decline in the United States?

ARE MOST U.S. cities declining or only a well-publicized few? Are problems of decline concentrated in a few cities? Do different cities show different types of decline? Is decline a metropolitan-area-wide problem as well as a central city problem? Are declining areas also in "distress," that is, worse off according to static indicators of conditions at a given time? This chapter attempts to answer these and other questions by analyzing data for 153 large U.S. cities and their metropolitan areas over the period 1960 to 1975.

The first part focuses on descriptive decline and growth by examining changes in population and employment in cities and SMSAs. The second part analyzes functional decline and distress. We examine patterns and trends in measures of cities' abilities to carry out their social functions, and we construct summary indexes of distress and decline for cities and SMSAs. Then we analyze the relationships among the functional and descriptive measures to discover whether cities losing population also display poor or deteriorating ability to perform their social functions.

The data in our analysis pertain to all cities in the United States with population greater than 100,000 in 1970. Of these 153 cities, 89 were in the 100,000 to 200,000 population range, 38 were between 200,000 and 500,000, 26 were larger, and only 6 had over a million inhabitants. The average population in the 153 cities was 422,628; the median was 172,106.[1]

Nearly every big city is part of a larger regional urban settlement that

1. These data reflect the well-known skewed shape of the city-size distribution in any large country. See Edwin S. Mills, *Urban Economics*, 2d ed. (Scott, Foresman, 1980), pp. 34–38.

forms a unified economic market. Neither current nor future changes in cities can be realistically considered apart from their relationships to these surrounding urban settlements. For example, possible public policy responses to decline in a large city surrounded by economically booming suburbs (like Atlanta's) may be quite different from those available to a city surrounded by relatively stagnant suburbs (like Cleveland's).

The 153 cities were contained within 121 SMSAs in 1975. Twenty-one of these SMSAs included more than one of the large cities, and 6 had 3 or more. Because the SMSAs were chosen on the basis of the largest *cities*, they include only 104 of the 121 largest *SMSAs* as of 1970.[2]

Some of the analysis examines only the 121 cities that were largest in each SMSA, excluding "satellite cities." (We refer to the 121 cities as "first cities.") Table 3-9, below, lists the 153 cities and indicates which are first cities and which are satellites.

The Extent of Decline in Descriptive Terms

The most commonly used indicator of decline is population loss. Employment changes are another useful measure of the health of the local economy. We begin our empirical examination of urban decline by describing the general trends in population and jobs in cities and SMSAs in the United States in recent years. We then look at individual cities and groups of cities to uncover descriptive patterns, in particular the relationships between city and SMSA changes and between employment and population changes.

Overall Urban Growth and Decline

Ninety-five of the 153 cities lost population between 1970 and 1975, compared to 59 during the previous decade. However, two of these (Chattanooga and Columbus, Georgia) grew in population only by annexing additional territory,[3] and 28 other cities engaged in annexation. The total population change for the cities (1975 boundaries) was a loss of almost 1.5

2. The biggest SMSA not included in our sample is Wilmington, Del.-N.J.-Md., which had a population of 499,493 and was the 66th largest U.S. SMSA in 1970. The smallest SMSA included in our sample is Amarillo, Texas. Its 1970 population was 144,396, and it was ranked 181st in size among U.S. SMSAs.

3. We use the term "annexation" to refer to all city boundary changes, including consolidation and mergers.

Table 3-1. *City and SMSA Population and Employment Changes*

Description	153 cities		121 first cities[b]		121 SMSAs		United States[c]
	Weighted[a]	Mean	Weighted	Mean	Weighted	Mean	
Percentage change in population							
1975–80 total[d]	−1.29	0.07	−1.62	−0.23	. . .	. . .	6.31
1970–80[e]	−2.51	2.12	−2.98	1.80	7.84	12.56	11.45
1970–75 in 1975 boundaries	−2.61	−0.44	−2.82	−0.84	3.33	5.58	4.56
1970–75 total[d]	−1.25	2.04	−1.38	2.13	. . .	. . .	. . .
1960–70 in 1960 boundaries	1.08	10.90	0.05	1.52	16.54	18.46	13.22
1960–70 in 1975 boundaries[f]	. . .	. . .	. . .	. . .	16.73	19.19	. . .
1960–70 total[d]	7.28	36.90	5.89	14.64	. . .	. . .	. . .
Percentage change in employment							
1970–77: Nonagricultural[g]	. . .	. . .	. . .	. . .	10.69	19.18	15.82
1970–76: Nonagricultural[g]	. . .	. . .	. . .	. . .	8.22	16.14	12.02
1970–75: Nonagricultural[g]	. . .	. . .	. . .	. . .	5.23	11.67	8.64
1970–75: Employed persons	. . .	. . .	. . .	. . .	. . .	. . .	7.83
1960–70: Nonagricultural[h]	. . .	. . .	. . .	. . .	26.24	34.16	30.77
1960–70: Employed persons[i]	2.16	27.11	1.10	10.96	13.68	19.28	19.53

a. Weighted figures are changes in sample mean *levels* and hence reflect aggregate changes; mean figures are unweighted sample averages of change measures.

b. First cities are those which had population over 100,000 in 1970 and were the largest in their SMSA as defined in 1975. (See table 3-2.)

c. U.S. figures calculated from *Statistical Abstract of the United States, 1978*, pp. 6, 399.

d. Total population change includes gains attributable to annexation and consolidation.

e. Total change (including annexation) for cities; change within 1980 boundary definitions for SMSAs.

f. SMSA data are for 122 SMSAs, as defined in 1960.

g. Nonagricultural wage and salary workers, from surveys of establishments; 120 SMSAs, 1975 definitions, Colorado Springs not available. Bureau of Labor Statistics, *Employment and Earnings, United States, 1939–74*, Bulletin 1370-11 (GPO, 1976); and *Employment and Earnings*, various issues.

h. 59 SMSAs with no boundary changes in BLS data 1960–70 and data available. Source: same as note g.

i. "Employed persons" refers to people *working in* the city or SMSA; *Census of Population, 1960: Journey to Work*, Subject Report PC(2)-6B (GPO, 1961); and *Census of Population, 1970: Journey to Work*, Subject Report PC(2)-6D (GPO, 1973). No correction has been made for unreported workplaces, which may bias the employment growth figures downward since there were more unreported workplaces in 1970 than in 1960. City data include jobs added through annexation; "153 cities" data are for the 110 cities for which 1960 data are available; "121 first cities" data are for the 87 first cities for which 1960 data are available. SMSA data are for the 90 SMSAs for which constant 1960-boundary employment data could be obtained.

million residents. It resulted from gains of 1.2 million people in the 56 growing cities offset by losses of 2.7 million in the 97 declining cities. The trend of falling city population has continued according to preliminary 1980 Census counts: between 1975 and 1980, the average rate of population growth of the cities was virtually zero—slower than the corresponding 1970–75 rate—and 86 of them lost population.

Table 3-1 reports population and employment changes for cities, SMSAs, and the nation. The "unweighted" figures are averages of individual percentage changes for the set of cities or SMSAs. The "weighted" figures give total changes in the population or employment of the whole set. The difference between the two implies that larger cities and SMSAs are declining more (or growing less) than smaller ones.

For the remainder of the analysis, we use fixed city boundaries whenever possible to examine the processes of growth and decline. Although annexation is an important means of combating the deleterious effects of population loss on city *governments*, it masks a more universal process involving changes in the relative attractiveness of parts of each metropolitan area, a process our analysis attempts to understand.

The same issue of changing boundaries arises in conjunction with SMSAs, which the Census Bureau periodically redefines to encompass all the counties that are economically integrated in the metropolitan setting.[4] When examining changes in SMSA variables over time, we use fixed boundaries (usually 1975) in order to encompass all metropolitan activity over the period. Twenty-six of our 121 SMSAs as defined by their 1975 boundaries lost population over the period 1970–75, whereas only four had lost population inside those boundaries during the 1960s.

These data show several trends. This set of metropolitan areas was growing *faster* than the nation as a whole from 1960 to 1970, but *slower* than the nation during the first half of the 1970s. The cities grew more slowly than the nation in *both* periods. Both the SMSAs and the cities experienced a decrease in population growth relative to the entire United States. Thus the overall slowdown in national population growth explains

4. SMSAs are made up of counties except in New England, where the units are cities and towns. We use "counties" as a shorthand reference for the actual building block geographic units. In addition to adding counties as the "market area" spreads, redefinitions may combine or separate areas around two major cities, or reallocate an intermediate county between two areas. There were three such "complicated" changes in SMSA definition in our sample over the period 1960–75: Anaheim-Santa Ana-Garden Grove split off from the Los Angeles-Long Beach SMSA in 1963, the Greensboro-High Point SMSA combined with the Winston-Salem SMSA in 1967, and the Dallas and Fort Worth SMSAs combined in 1973. Because of these changes, the 153 cities were in 122 SMSAs in 1960 and 1970 (rather than 121 as in 1975).

only part of greater city and SMSA decline. Finally, population loss is more prevalent for large cities than for the metropolitan areas in which they are located.

Data on employment in cities and SMSAs are less uniformly available than population data. However, we can look at employment patterns for some of the 153 cities and their SMSAs over the period 1960–70 using Census data, and we can examine SMSA changes in employment over the 1960–75 period with data from the Bureau of Labor Statistics (BLS).[5]

The number of jobs in the 110 cities for which 1960 Census employment data are available grew 2 percent between 1960 and 1970. However, employment in the entire nation grew almost 20 percent in the same period. So taken as a whole, these large cities sustained large *relative* losses, and 35 actually lost jobs.[6] In the 87 cities in the available sample that were the largest in their SMSAs, job growth was even slower.

Boundary changes make it difficult to compile consistent SMSA employment data. However, for the 90 SMSAs in our sample with 1960 data for which we could calculate 1970 employment inside 1960 boundaries, aggregate employment growth was 13.7 percent, considerably slower than the 20 percent national rate.[7] For the 59 SMSAs for which the BLS data are available within constant boundaries between 1960 and 1970, total nonagricultural job growth was 26 percent, compared to a national growth of 30.8 percent. Thus, SMSAs lost ground relatively in jobs as well as population in the 1960s.

There are no uniform data on city employment in 1975, so we cannot examine city job changes over the 1970–75 period.[8] For SMSAs, the patterns

5. Census employment data refer to employed persons by place of work, from household surveys; Bureau of Labor Statistics (BLS) figures are employees in nonagricultural establishments, from establishment surveys. BLS, *Employment and Earnings for the U.S. and Areas, 1939–1974*, Bulletin 1370-11 (GPO, 1976); Bureau of the Census, *Census of Population, 1960: Journey to Work*, Subject Report PC(2)-61B (GPO, 1961), and *Census of Population, 1970: Journey to Work*, Subject Report PC(2)-6D (GPO, 1973).

6. These data include jobs added through annexation. Note, however, that these figures do not adjust for unreported workplaces. This may bias the employment growth figures downward, because there were more unreported workplaces in 1970 than in 1960.

7. The average population of these 90 SMSAs was larger than the full sample average and grew more slowly than average; thus the *full* sample would probably show more than 13.7 percent employment growth.

8. A number of partial sources of city employment data exist in varying degrees of completeness and accuracy. The Travel-to-Work Supplement to the Annual Housing Survey provides data on the number of SMSA residents who worked in the central city for 41 large cities in 1976 or 1977, but these data are not comparable to the 1970 data due to definitional changes. A few cities coincide with counties or are treated by their states as county-equivalents,

are clouded by the national recession in 1975, so we report changes from 1970 to 1976 and 1977 as well as 1970–75. Fifteen SMSAs actually lost employment between 1970 and 1975, and another 35 SMSAs grew more slowly than the national average. Nonagricultural jobs in the entire United States grew four to five percentage points faster than in the 121 SMSAs over the periods 1970–76 and 1970–77, indicating these 121 SMSAs contained a declining share of U.S. employment. Comparison of weighted and unweighted figures implies that the smaller areas were growing faster than the largest, on average.

Patterns of Descriptive Decline

Is there any relationship between each city's growth and the growth of the metropolitan region in which it is located? One answer is provided by simple city-SMSA correlations in population and employment growth. Another answer that controls for differences along other dimensions is provided by the regression analysis of chapters 5 and 6.

The data show that a city's growth *is* closely related to the growth of its SMSA. In the 153-city sample, the correlation between city and SMSA population change over the 1970–75 period (inside 1975 boundaries) is .67.[9] For the 121 first cities, the correlation is .73 (it was .76 during the 1960s). City and SMSA employment growth are also positively associated in the limited data available, although more weakly: the correlation is .3 between city and SMSA *total* employment growth, 1960–70, and .57 for *manufacturing* job growth, 1967–72.[10]

Employment change is also strongly associated with population change; for 1970–75, the correlation for the set of 120 SMSAs with data is .78. SMSAs gaining population had over ten times the average employment growth rate of SMSAs losing population. The limited city data available

---

and therefore can be distinguished in the BLS data. Other cities have made employment estimates themselves. In addition, the quinquennial Economic Census provides data by city on four important sectors (manufacturing, retail trade, wholesale trade, and selected services).

9. The strength of this association is further demonstrated by the fact that there were only three growing cities inside SMSAs that were losing population, and those three were all satellite cities: Cambridge, Livonia, and Torrance. In fact, only 17 cities had faster growth, or slower decline, than their SMSAs. Nine of the 17 are satellite cities, and one was in a declining SMSA, so only 7 could be considered "boom towns" at the center of a growing SMSA: Amarillo, Colorado Springs, Corpus Christi, El Paso, San Jose, Springfield (Mass.), and Stockton.

10. Computed for the 87 cities and SMSAs in 1960–70, and 143 in 1967–72, having available data.

indicate a strong association between population and employment change for cities too.[11]

Intensive analysis of these data convinced us that they could be more meaningfully interpreted if cities and SMSAs were grouped into descriptive clusters. We began by defining three major groups of cities based upon 1970–75 population change: growing cities in growing SMSAs, declining cities in growing SMSAs, and declining cities in declining SMSAs (as already noted, there were no growing first cities in declining SMSAs). We further subdivided the declining cities into two groups, depending on their likely rate of change in households. Because average U.S. household size has been falling, cities losing zero to 6.5 percent of their population between 1970 and 1975 were probably gaining households in spite of their population losses. So we defined cities as "stagnant" if they lost zero to 6.5 percent of their population, and "severely declining" if they lost more than 6.5 percent. These definitions created five clusters of cities. The cities in each cluster are listed in table 3-2. Decline and growth characteristics of the clusters are shown in table 3-3.[12]

The average population and employment changes for each cluster shown in table 3-3 strongly imply that other conditions and trends—both past and present—are integrally related to the current population changes that form the basis for this clustering. Cities that lost population from 1970 to 1975 also did so on average between 1960 and 1970. While almost no SMSAs lost population during the 1960s, the average rate of population growth over that period was slower for SMSAs that subsequently lost population. The city-SMSA relationship also appears important. Even within the definitions of "stagnant" and "severely declining," cities in each cluster in declining SMSAs averaged more population loss than the cities in the corresponding cluster in growing SMSAs.

Employment growth was slower from 1960 to 1970 in cities that showed slower 1970–75 population growth, perhaps indicating that previous employment changes reflect the historic bases for current conditions. Furthermore, there is a suggestion that central city job losses presage subsequent SMSA population losses.

Although unavailability of 1980 data for most measures precludes their

11. Correlation between city population growth and job growth in 1960–70 is .62 (110 cities).

12. Several readers expressed surprise at seeing Seattle listed as a severely declining city. Seattle had lost an estimated 8.2 percent of its 1970 population by 1975. Between 1975 and 1980 (preliminary Census estimates) it gained about 4,800 people, for a net loss over the decade of 7.3 percent.

widespread use in this study, a comparison of 1970–75 and 1975–80 population growth rates seems to indicate that urban decline has slowed in recent years, even though the overall growth of large cities is lower. Specifically, intercity disparities in population growth rates appear to have narrowed: growing cities are growing more slowly, and most declining cities are declining more slowly, especially those severely declining from 1970 to 1975. Whether this trend will continue, and whether it will be mirrored in other decline indicators, can be known only from more recent data. However, one caution should be kept in mind—we do not know how changes in annexation affected these comparisons.

Other measures for these city clusters suggest that the clustering reflects, though imperfectly, both notable intragroup similarities and remarkable intergroup diversity among U.S. cities. In a later section, we examine the cluster differences along some functional dimensions; table 3-4 presents an elaboration of their *descriptive* differences. Highlights of the latter are as follows.

Regional differences in rates of growth and decline were quite large. Southern and Western cities showed population growth, on average, while those in the North lost over 5 percent of their 1970 population by 1975. Eighty-five percent of the declining SMSAs were in the North Central or Northeast regions, though fewer than half of all 121 SMSAs are in those regions. Even among the 35 cities in growing SMSAs in the North, only one-seventh gained population. Southern cities averaged 2 percent population growth from 1970 to 1975; Western cities averaged over 6 percent.

Growing cities and SMSAs generally had smaller initial populations than declining areas.[13] In spite of this apparent uniformity, it is worth noting that there were at least three cities with over 500,000 population in 1970 and at least one over 900,000 in each of the five clusters.

In both growing and declining SMSAs, severely declining cities were smaller in area than others, even though they contained more population. They also contained a smaller *share* of their SMSA's population.

Current growth patterns reflect cities' growth histories. Severely declining cities are the oldest, or have been large the longest, and cities in declining SMSAs are generally older than those in growing SMSAs. In addition, most cities that were severely declining in 1970–75 had slowed down at least three decades earlier.

13. In declining SMSAs, the pattern appears to be reversed: stagnant cities were larger than severely declining cities. However, this effect disappears when New York City is excluded from the average. Without New York, the average city population for this cluster is 485,010; the average SMSA population for the cluster is 1,320,550.

Table 3-2. *Cities in Each Cluster (Largest City in Each SMSA)*

Growing cities in growing SMSAs		*Stagnant cities in growing SMSAs*	*Severely declining cities in growing SMSAs*	*Stagnant cities in declining SMSAs*	*Severely declining cities in declining SMSAs*
Albuquerque, N.M.	Lubbock, Tex.	Albany, N.Y.	Atlanta, Ga.	Boston, Mass.	Akron, Ohio
Amarillo, Tex.	Memphis, Tenn.	Allentown, Pa.	Birmingham, Ala.	Columbus, Ga.	Bridgeport, Conn.
Anaheim, Calif.	Miami, Fla.	Baltimore, Md.	Canton, Ohio	Jersey City, N.J.	Buffalo, N.Y.
Austin, Tex.	Mobile, Ala.	Beaumont, Tex.	Chicago, Ill.	Los Angeles, Calif.	Cincinnati, Ohio
Baton Rouge, La.	Montgomery, Ala.	Cedar Rapids, Iowa	Flint, Mich.	New York, N.Y.	Cleveland, Ohio
Charlotte, N.C.	Newport News, Va.	Chattanooga, Tenn.	Gary, Ind.	Paterson. N.J.	Dayton, Ohio
Colorado Springs, Colo.	Omaha, Neb.	Columbia, S.C.	Hartford, Conn.	Providence, R.I.	Detroit, Mich.
Corpus Christi, Tex.	Phoenix, Ariz.	Columbus, Ohio	Kansas City, Mo.	Rockford, Ill.	Duluth, Minn.
El Paso, Tex.	Raleigh, N.C.	Dallas, Tex.	Louisville, Ky.	Stamford, Conn.	Newark, N.J.
Ft. Lauderdale, Fla.	Riverside, Calif.	Denver, Colo.	Milwaukee, Wis.	Topeka, Kans.	Philadelphia, Pa.
Ft. Wayne, Ind.	Sacramento, Calif.	Des Moines, Iowa	Minneapolis, Minn.	Wichita, Kans.	Pittsburgh, Pa.
Fresno, Calif.	San Antonio, Tex.	Erie, Pa.	New Haven, Conn.		St. Louis, Mo.
Greensboro, N.C.	San Diego, Calif.	Evansville, Ill.	Norfolk, Va.		Savannah, Ga.
Honolulu, Hawaii	San Jose, Calif.	Grand Rapids, Mich.	Portland, Oreg.		Seattle, Wash.
Houston, Tex.	Shreveport, La.	Huntsville, Ala.	Richmond, Va.		South Bend, Ind.

Jackson, Miss.	Spokane, Wash.	Indianapolis, Ind.	Rochester, N.Y.
Jacksonville, Fla.	Springfield, Mass.	Lansing, Mich.	San Francisco, Calif.
Knoxville, Tenn.	Springfield, Mo.	Macon, Ga.	Scranton, Pa.
Las Vegas, Nev.	Stockton, Calif.	Madison, Wis.	Syracuse, N.Y.
Lexington, Ky.	Tampa, Fla.	Nashville, Tenn.	
Lincoln, Neb.	Tucson, Ariz.	New Bedford, Mass.	
Little Rock, Ark.	Tulsa, Okla.	New Orleans, La.	
		Oklahoma City, Okla.	
		Peoria, Ill.	
		Salt Lake City, Utah	
		Tacoma, Wash.	
		Toledo, Ohio	
		Trenton, N.J.	
		Washington, D.C.	
		Waterbury, Conn.	
		Worcester, Mass.	
		Youngstown, Ohio	

Table 3-3. *Average Decline and Growth for City Clusters*[a]

Description	*All first cities (or all SMSAs)*	*SMSA grew, 1970–75*			*SMSA lost population, 1970–75*	
		City grew, 1970–75	*City stagnant, 1970–75*	*City severely declined, 1970–75*	*City stagnant, 1970–75*	*City severely declined, 1970–75*
Number of cities	121	44	32	19	11	15
Population change, 1975–80 (percent)						
Cities (total)[b]	−0.23	4.87	−1.96	−4.72	−2.07	−4.46
Population change, 1970–80 (percent)						
Cities (total)	1.80	19.14	−3.61	−12.50	−5.40	−14.10
SMSAs (1980 boundaries)	12.56	25.57	10.19	5.91	−1.14	−2.05
Population change, 1970–75 (percent)						
Cities (total)	2.13	15.01	−1.77	−8.14	−3.45	−10.25
Cities (1975 boundaries)	−0.84	8.11	−2.93	−8.61	−4.14	−10.37
SMSAs (1975 boundaries)	5.58	11.89	4.49	2.97	−2.18	−1.59
Net migration	1.60	6.75	0.60	−0.33	−4.53	−4.46
Natural increase	3.98	5.14	3.89	3.30	2.35	2.87

Population change, 1960–70 (percent)						
Cities (total)	14.64	31.31	16.26	−3.10	6.17	−9.00
Cities (1960 boundaries)	1.52	11.12	−1.48	−5.96	−0.69	−9.15
SMSAs (1975 boundaries)	19.19	27.81	17.30	15.65	9.57	9.47
SMSA employment change, 1970–75 (percent)[c]	11.67	20.62	11.17	6.42	1.10	1.47
Employment change, 1960–70 (percent)						
Cities, employed persons[d,e]	10.96	32.90	15.51	0.43	−5.22	−8.44
Number of cities with data	87	25	25	17	7	13
SMSA nonagricultural employees	34.16	49.79	29.55	29.70	22.50	17.47
Number of SMSAs with data and fixed boundaries	59	20	16	9	7	7
SMSA employed persons[e]	19.28	26.42	20.14	19.33	5.94	6.80
Number of SMSAs with data	90	29	26	17	6	12

a. Cities in each cluster are identified in table 3-2.
b. "Total" changes include population added through annexation.
c. Excludes Colorado Springs from columns 1 and 2.
d. Includes jobs added through annexation.
e. Employed persons refers to people *working in* the city or SMSA.

Table 3-4. *Descriptive Characteristics of City Clusters*[a]

Description	All first cities (or all SMSAs)	SMSA grew, 1970–75			SMSA lost population, 1970–75	
		City grew, 1970–75	City stagnant, 1970–75	City severely declined, 1970–75	City stagnant, 1970–75	City severely declined, 1970–75
Number of cities	121	44	32	19	11	15
Northeast	24	1	7	5	6	5
North Central	33	4	11	7	3	8
South	43	25	11	5	1	1
West	21	14	3	2	1	1
Average 1970 population						
City	422,630	269,760	284,669	484,650	1,158,700	547,050
SMSA	997,190	571,050	693,360	1,322,600	2,107,200	1,669,200
Average city area, 1970 (square miles)	96	107	107	75	103	61
Average city fraction of SMSA population, 1975	0.44	0.54	0.47	0.30	0.49	0.32
Average change in city fraction of SMSA population, 1960–75	−0.03	−0.02	−0.04	−0.10	−0.01	−0.10

Average city fraction of SMSA jobs, 1970[b]	0.59	0.67	0.60	0.54	0.52	0.49
Average year in which city reached 100,000 population	1923	1947	1922	1901	1909	1893
Fraction of cities in cluster growing faster than national population growth rate, 1940–50 (percent)[c]	55	83	52	28	50	29
Annexation, 1970–75[d]						
Number of cities annexing	27	19	2	3	1	2
Percent change in population[e]	12.5	14.7	19.6	3.3	8.0	1.0
Percent change in area[e]	50.0	52.9	61.2	6.8	188.6	6.7
Annexation, 1960–70[d]						
Number of cities annexing	81	37	22	12	5	5
Percent change in population[e]	20.7	23.9	29.6	4.9	16.1	0.5
Percent change in area[e]	112.5	131.8	164.6	25.6	60.5	0.9

a. Cities in each cluster are identified in table 3-2.
b. 1970 SMSA definition.
c. Data are available for only 105 cities, distributed across columns 2–6 as follows: 36, 29, 18, 8, 14.
d. Annexation refers to all city boundary changes, including consolidations and mergers.
e. These are average changes attributable to annexation for those cities that engaged in annexation activity.

Those cities that grew in fixed boundaries were also more likely to engage in annexation, and did so on a larger scale.

The Extent of Distress and Decline in Functional Terms

In chapter 2, we defined a reduction in an urban area's ability to perform its social functions as *functional decline*. An urban area may also have such a weak ability to perform one or more social functions that it cannot discharge them to a satisfactory degree, even if it is not experiencing negative change. We refer to this undesirable condition as *functional distress*. It is a static concept rather than dynamic like urban decline, but both terms refer to an urban area's ability to perform its social functions.

In this section, we apply the concepts of functional distress and decline to both cities and SMSAs to examine the prevalence of poor or decreasing ability to perform urban social functions. Measures of social functioning are not as easily agreed upon as descriptive measures; so it is appropriate to cast a wider net and include a greater number of individual variables. Ideally, individual variables would be chosen for each of the social functions listed in table 2-1. However, data limitations made this impossible; instead, we selected a few variables, attempting to represent most of the major groupings in that table.

The overall trends in such functional measures as unemployment rate, per capita income, poverty incidence, crime rate, percent of housing stock that is old, and tax effort provide initial information on the nature of functional distress and decline. We then construct simple summary indexes for cities and SMSAs to examine in more detail their extent in U.S. urban areas, and their relationship to the *descriptive* urban decline documented in the previous section.

Overall Trends in Functional Measures

Table 3-5 reports (unweighted) average levels of functional indicators in the 153 cities and 121 SMSAs, and U.S. averages for comparison. Because of a severe national recession, unemployment rates were considerably higher in 1975 than in 1970. The average unemployment rate in these cities was somewhat below the national rate in 1970 but slightly higher than the national rate in 1975. This worsening occurred partly because a

Table 3-5. *Trends in Distress and Decline Measures*

Description	*Average, all cities*	*Average, all first cities*	*Average, all SMSAs*	*United States*[a]
Number of areas	153	121	121	. . .
Unemployment, 1975 (percent)	8.9 (150)[b]	9.0 (118)	8.2 (117)	8.5
Unemployment, 1970 (percent)	4.6	4.7	4.2	4.9
Change in unemployment rate	4.3 (150)	4.3 (118)	3.9 (117)	3.6
Violent crime rate, 1975[c]	796	816	485 (120)	482
Violent crime rate, 1970[c]	561	590	352 (120)	364
Change in violent crime rate	236	226	135 (119)	118
Population in poverty, 1969 (percent)	13.6	14.5	11.7	12.1
Families in poverty, 1969 (percent)	10.4	11.1	9.2	10.7
Change in percent of families poor, 1959–69	−5.0 (72)	−4.9 (71)	−6.1 (117)	−7.7
Income per capita, 1974[d]	5,120	4,986	5,133	4,990
Income per capita, 1969[d]	4,742	4,614	4,690	4,579
Percent change in real income per capita[d]	8.2	8.3	9.9	9.0
Percent of 1970 housing stock built before 1940	41	44	34	41

a. U.S. figures from *Statistical Abstract of the United States, 1978:* unemployment from p. 398; violent crime rate from p. 179; poverty population from p. 465; change in percent of families poor from p. 470; pre-1940 housing from p. 789. Per capita income figures from *Statistical Abstract of the United States, 1977*, p. 478.

b. Figures in parentheses are number of observations when fewer than reported in column head.

c. Crimes per 100,000 population.

d. Per capita money income inflated to 1975 dollars using the consumer price index. For SMSAs, the per capita income figures use constant 1975 boundary definitions, except for the ten SMSAs in New England. In 1970 boundaries, the average 1969 SMSA per capita income was $4,737 (in 1975 dollars). For cities, per capita income for each year refers to the boundaries for that year.

few individual cities suffered from particularly high rates in 1975.[14] SMSAs fared better than the nation as a whole at both points in time, although their advantage decreased between 1970 and 1975.

Reported rates of violent crimes were substantially higher in large cities than in their SMSAs. In fact, only a quarter of the cities had crime rates below the nation's. Crime rates increased substantially between 1970 and 1975 on average, although they fell in fourteen cities including Washington, Baltimore, and Houston.

The nation's poverty became more concentrated in these cities during the 1960s, as evidenced by the smaller decrease in poverty concentration

14. Flint, Paterson, and Newark increased by over ten percentage points and had rates of 17 percent or higher by 1975. No other large city had over 15 percent.

Table 3-6. *City Distress and Decline Measures, by Region and City Size*

All figures except number of cities are averages

Description	*Northeast*		*North Central*		*South*		*West*	
	Under 200,000	*Over* 200,000	*Under* 200,000	*Over* 200,000	*Under* 200,000	*Over* 200,000	*Under* 200,000	*Over* 200,000
Number of cities	19	9	24	17	28	24	18	14
Poor population, 1969 (percent)	13.0	14.4	9.6	12.8	16.4	17.4	10.8	12.3
Poor families, 1969 (percent)	9.8	11.0	6.9	9.4	13.2	13.7	8.1	9.1
Poor families, 1959 (percent)	13.1 (7)[a]	14.1 (8)	12.4 (5)	13.5 (14)	27.2 (5)	22.1 (19)	13.3 (4)	11.8 (10)
Change in percent of poor families, 1959–69	−2.9 (7)	−2.3 (8)	−4.0 (5)	−3.7 (14)	−9.6 (5)	−8.3 (19)	−2.9 (4)	−3.1 (10)
Unemployment rate, 1975 (percent)	11.5	11.4	8.3 (22)	8.5 (16)	7.1	7.7	9.5	10.2
Unemployment rate, 1970 (percent)	4.5	4.7	4.3	4.7	3.8	4.0	6.1	5.9
Change in unemployment rate, 1970–75	7.0	6.7	4.0 (22)	3.8 (16)	3.4	3.7	3.3	4.2
Violent crime rate, 1975[b]	760	1,168	579	1,027	651	948	672	886
Violent crime rate, 1970[b]	445	814	382	754	465	807	374	633
Change in violent crime rate, 1970–75	315	354	197	273	186	141	298	253
Per capita income, 1974[c]	4,764	4,782	5,220	5,037	5,101	4,948	5,472	5,630
Per capita income, 1969[c]	4,659	4,695	4,844	4,724	4,466	4,419	5,171	5,282
Percent change in real per capita income, 1969–74	2.3	2.0	7.9	6.6	14.2	12.1	6.1	6.9
Debt burden, 1975	0.65	0.80	0.34	0.54	0.28	0.37	0.19	0.34
Debt burden, 1971	0.68	0.74	0.44	0.62	0.39	0.39	0.23	0.36
Change in debt burden, 1971–75	−0.03	0.07	−0.10	−0.08	−0.12	−0.02	−0.04	−0.02
Percentage of 1970 housing built before 1940	70	72	44	56	23	30	26	32
City/SMSA tax disparity, 1971	1.14	1.22	1.13	1.18	1.32	1.25	1.16	1.15

a. Figures in parentheses indicate actual number of observations when fewer than shown in column head.
b. Crimes per 100,000 population.
c. Income in 1975 dollars.

there than in the United States as a whole.[15] Cities ended the decade with a higher concentration of poor people than suburbs or nonmetropolitan areas.

Twelve cities, including Boston, Newark, Dayton, and Los Angeles, actually had lower real incomes per capita in 1975 than in 1970. This occurred during a period when U.S. real income per capita increased by 9 percent, despite inflation and a severe recession. However, within large cities as a whole, real per capita income rose during the period, a fact not widely appreciated. Real income per *household* grew also, but more slowly. The large cities and metropolitan areas began and ended the period with above average levels of income, but city incomes grew more slowly than the nation's.[16]

As expected because of post–World War II suburban development, cities contained a higher concentration of old housing than SMSAs. Nonmetropolitan areas contained an even higher concentration than did these large cities.[17] In nine cities, all in the Northeast, over three-quarters of the 1970 housing stock was more than thirty years old.

These overall trends show general worsening for cities and SMSAs (and the nation) in terms of crime and unemployment between 1970 and 1975 and an absolute improvement but relative worsening of poverty and real income levels in cities. Except for income levels and families in poverty, first cities were also more distressed than the nation.

Diversity in Functional Measures

This weakening of the *average* position of large cities resulted from diverse changes in individual areas. To examine them, we divided the city sample into eight groups on the basis of size and region and divided the SMSA sample into four regional groups. Tables 3-6 and 3-7 display the patterns of our functional measures.

In all regions, the largest cities had higher average poverty concentrations. Poverty incidence was highest in the South, which also showed the greatest reductions. To some degree, higher Southern poverty is illusory,

15. The figures are actually for 1959 and 1969. The measures of poverty incidence are based on poverty cutoffs varying by family size, age and sex of family head, number of children, and farm-nonfarm residence. The index is updated over time to reflect changes in the national price level, but it does not net out geographical price-level differences.

16. The per capita income figures for cities refer to current-year boundaries, while the SMSA figures use constant boundaries. Hence city changes over time reflect both changes in the incomes of residents within the initial area and changes from annexation/consolidation.

17. Forty-seven percent. *Statistical Abstract of the United States, 1978*, p. 789.

Table 3-7. *SMSA Distress and Decline, by Region*

Description	*Northeast*	*North Central*	*South*	*West*
Number of SMSAs	24	33	43	21
Poor families, 1969 (percent)[a]	6.6 (21)[b]	6.7	12.7 (42)	8.6
Poor families, 1959 (percent)	10.5 (21)	11.4	22.1 (42)	12.5
Change in percent of poor families, 1959–69	−3.9 (21)	−4.7	−9.4 (42)	−3.9
Unemployment rate, 1975 (percent)	9.8	7.8 (29)	6.9	9.5
Unemployment rate, 1970 (percent)	3.9	4.2	3.7	5.9
Change in unemployment rate, 1970–75	5.9	3.6 (29)	3.2	3.6
Violent crime rate, 1975[c]	389	439	541	557 (20)
Violent crime rate, 1970[c]	245	322	442 (42)	341
Change in violent crime rate, 1970–75[c]	144	117	106 (42)	214 (20)
Per capita income, 1974[d]	5,361	5,212	4,846	5,336
Per capita income, 1969[d]	5,138	4,808	4,247	4,900
Percent change in per capita income, 1969–74	4.7	8.5	14.2	9.1
Local tax effort, 1971	8.9	8.9	7.7	9.7
Local tax effort, 1962	7.7	7.5	6.5	8.0
Change in local tax effort, 1962–71	1.2	1.4	1.2	1.7
Local tax disparity between largest city and SMSA average, 1971	1.20	1.21	1.32	1.22

a. Families in poverty (percent) in 1969 in SMSA as defined in 1960.
b. Figures in parentheses indicate number of SMSAs for which data were available when fewer than indicated in column head.
c. Crimes per 100,000 population.
d. Per capita income is in 1975 dollars and uses 1975 SMSA boundary definitions except for the ten SMSAs in New England.

because the lower cost of living there is not taken into account. Per capita income in 1969 appears to follow the poverty incidence patterns. However, by 1974 (a year for which local area poverty data are not available), the income patterns had changed considerably, with incomes in Northeastern cities falling below those in all other regions. SMSAs in the Northeast also had slower income growth than in the other regions, but maintained a nominal lead.

Moreover, an important piece of information is missing from these tables: cost of living. We can obtain some idea of the effect from the thirty-three metropolitan areas in our sample for which cost-of-living data are published.[18] According to these data, the Northeast cities (six available)

18. "Annual Costs of an Intermediate Budget for a 4-Person Family," Bureau of Labor Statistics, press releases, selected years.

had the highest average cost of living in both 1970 and 1975, approximately 14 percent higher than the lowest region, the South (nine cities available). Areas in the West and North Central regions were the second and third most costly, respectively. Adjusting the per capita income figures by the relative cost of living allows us to make more accurate comparisons of economic well-being for these thirty-three areas. The six Western cities had the highest adjusted incomes in 1970 and 1975, and Northeastern cities the lowest. Southern cities had the second highest adjusted incomes, and by far the fastest adjusted income growth between 1970 and 1975—almost 10 percent, as compared with less than 1 percent for the average city in the Northeast. Regional patterns for SMSAs were similar to those for cities, except that the South (rather than the West) had the highest adjusted income by 1975. This was true even though Southern SMSA nominal incomes (shown in table 3-7) were the lowest!

Unemployment figures seem to indicate chronically high unemployment in Western cities and SMSAs, and cyclical unemployment in the Northeast and North Central manufacturing areas. Northeastern cities had the highest rates in 1975 and by far the largest increases in the preceding five years. Western cities had the highest rates in 1970, but showed less deterioration between 1970 and 1975. SMSA changes were similar to those in cities, although less precipitous.

Fiscal measures do not portray adverse trends in fiscal solvency, but they do suggest high and rising tax rates in cities. For all large cities, debt service costs fell from 46 percent of own-source revenues to 40 percent between 1971 and 1975; thus debt burdens actually declined.[19] The largest cities averaged higher debt service costs and smaller reductions. Local government own-source revenues, as a percentage of aggregate money income, in the 121 SMSAs rose from 7.3 percent in 1962 to 8.6 percent in 1971, on average. Increases occurred for all categories of SMSAs, but were greatest in the Western SMSAs with larger central cities—Sacramento, San Francisco, Seattle, and Tucson all had increases of more than two percentage points. Tax effort *fell* in only 11 SMSAs. Concerning city-SMSA *disparities* in tax rates, we find that city tax rates were *20 percent* higher than the SMSA average in 1971. Only 34 cities had lower tax rates than their SMSA average, whereas Cincinnati, Miami, Atlanta, and Chattanooga

19. Debt service costs include short-term debt outstanding (that which must be retired within a year), interest expense, and long-term debt retired. To smooth annual fluctuations in city budget data, these figures are actually two-year averages of fiscal years 1970/71–1971/72 and 1974/75–1975/76.

had rates twice as high as their SMSAs. The largest disparities appear in the South, but this may be partly a statistical artifact.[20]

The figures in tables 3-6 and 3-7 show severe and increasing urban problems in the Northeast region. This region's cities apparently suffered from the lowest adjusted real incomes and the highest debt burdens, unemployment, and crime rates, as well as the most disadvantageous changes in these four factors. Northeast *SMSAs* are not as uniformly afflicted, but they did experience the smallest income growth and greatest increase in unemployment, resulting in the highest 1975 SMSA unemployment rates. Cities over 200,000 population are also more troubled by poverty, crime, debt, and old housing than smaller ones, although their relative situation does not seem to be worsening.

Indexes of Distress and Decline for Cities and SMSAs

In this section, we summarize the data on social functioning by constructing indexes of distress and decline for cities and SMSAs. Because we cannot know the point at which "distress" truly sets in, these indexes are strictly relative measures, based on the relative rankings of cities and SMSAs in our sample and not on any absolute standards. However, because they combine several functional measures, they are useful indicators of how *concentrated* distress and decline are in individual localities or groups of areas. In addition, the indexes provide summary measures useful in examining relationships among descriptive decline, functional decline, and functional distress. However, because these indexes are based on only a few of the hundreds of factors relevant to each city's social functions, they should be considered suggestive rather than definitive measures.

CONSTRUCTION OF THE INDEXES. We constructed four indexes: two measuring distress and decline for cities and two for SMSAs. Each index includes information on three to five of the measures just discussed, as listed below:[21]

20. The disparity is measured by calculating the ratio of city tax effort to SMSA tax effort, where tax effort is municipal, township, and school own-source revenues as a percent of local resident income. Schools are excluded from both city and SMSA tax effort when school district boundaries extend considerably beyond the city's borders. County government is included in the SMSA figure only when the city has no overlying county government. Because city-suburban disparities in expenditures tend to be less for schools than other services, areas with schools excluded from our figures (of which many are in the South) may spuriously appear to have larger tax disparities.

21. Key to major urban functions represented (see chapter 2): P = large-scale production; I = creative innovation; R = residential environment; G = urban governance.

Components of Distress and Decline Indexes

SMSA distress (3)

Unemployment rate, 1975 (P)
Violent crime rate, 1975 (R)
Per capita income, 1974 (P)

SMSA decline (5)

Change in unemployment rate, 1970–75 (P)
Change in violent crime rate, 1970–75 (R)
Change in percent of families poor, 1959–69 (P, I)
Percent change in real per capita income, 1969–74, in 1975 boundaries (P)
Change in local government tax effort, 1961–72 (G)

City distress (5)

Unemployment rate, 1975 (P)
Violent crime rate, 1975 (R)
Percent of population poor, 1969 (P)
Percent of 1970 housing built before 1940 (R)
City/SMSA tax disparity, 1971 (G)

City decline (4)

Change in unemployment rate, 1970–75 (P)
Change in violent crime rate, 1970–75 (R)
Change in city government debt burden, 1971–75 (G)
Percent change in per capita income, 1969–74 (P)

In the appendix to this chapter, we describe the drawbacks of each variable used, and our reasons for selecting it nonetheless.

To construct the indexes, we ranked all cities or SMSAs in the sample on the basis of each component. We divided this distribution of values into thirds, giving a score of −1 to cities or SMSAs in the most disadvantaged third of the distribution (e.g., highest unemployment or lowest income), a score of +1 to the most advantaged third, and zero to the middle third.[22] We then added the scores for all the components of the index. Thus, for example, the city of Boston is in the highest third of all the large cities in unemployment rate, violent crime rate, poverty incidence, and percent old housing, and is in the lowest third in the per capita income ranking; so it has a score of −5 on the city distress index. That is the most distressed category. In contrast, the SMSAs of Duluth, Houston, and Raleigh ranked in the lower third of the 121 SMSAs in their increases in unemployment, violent crime, and tax effort, and in the third showing the greatest decrease in poverty and fastest increase in income. Hence their scores for the SMSA

22. All cities or SMSAs for which individual data were missing were assigned a zero for that element.

decline index are +5, the most favorable category. The maximum score for each index is the number of components that make it up, so the possible scores range from −3 (worst) to +3 (best) in the SMSA distress index, from −4 to +4 in the city decline index, and from −5 to +5 in the other two indexes.

HOW CONCENTRATED ARE DISTRESS AND DECLINE AND WHICH AREAS ARE SUFFERING? Table 3-8 reports the cities having each score for the city decline index. Table 3-9 lists the scores for each city or SMSA on all four functional distress and decline indexes (and two other indexes introduced later in the chapter). The most distressed and declining cities are familiar names: Atlanta, Boston, Cleveland, Dayton, Hartford, Philadelphia, Newark, Trenton.[23] Most have appeared on other lists of "troubled cities."[24] Boston and Cleveland are in the most disadvantaged third of all nine components of the city distress and decline indexes; Dayton, Hartford, Newark, and Trenton scored eight out of nine; and Atlanta, Jersey City, Paterson, and Philadelphia net seven negative counts. At the other extreme, the least distressed cities are Fremont, Hampton, Parma, Torrance, and Virginia Beach, none of which is the largest city in its SMSA. Five of the ten "+4" cities are also satellites.

The city of Boston provides an interesting example of both the limitations and usefulness of our indexes. Based on data from the early 1970s, Boston suffered from high and rising unemployment and violent crime rates; high percentage poor, old housing, and tax disparity; rising city government debt burden; and falling real per capita income. The entire metropolitan area also suffered from serious functional decline. Nevertheless, many people consider Boston a very attractive city, with excellent cultural, educational, and environmental amenities. This paradox implies both that a highly regarded city may still be suffering from serious underlying problems and that these problems do not necessarily make a city unlivable. Yet Boston's attractiveness was apparently not strong enough to overcome these underlying problems, since both the city and its SMSA lost population from 1970 to 1980.

23. These eight cities are in one of the two most disadvantageous categories on *both* city indexes.

24. See David T. Stanley, "Cities in Trouble," paper prepared for the National Urban Policy Roundtable, Academy for Contemporary Problems, December 1976. He compiles several authors' lists of problem cities. A widely cited distress index was developed by Paul Dommel at the Brookings Institution; see James W. Fossett and Richard P. Nathan, "The Prospects for Urban Revival," in Roy Bahl, ed., *Urban Government Finance: Emerging Trends* (Sage Publications, 1981), pp. 63–104.

Table 3-8. *City Decline Index: Cities Ranked from Worst Decline Rating (−4) to Least Decline Rating (+4)*[a]

−4
Boston, Mass.
Cambridge, Mass.
Cleveland, Ohio
Dayton, Ohio
Hartford, Conn.
Jersey City, N.J.
Las Vegas, Nev.
Paterson, N.J.
Trenton, N.J.

−3
Atlanta, Ga.
Detroit, Mich.
Gary, Ind.
Newark, N.J.
New York, N.Y.
Philadelphia, Pa.
Riverside, Calif.
Rochester, N.Y.
Springfield, Mass.
Worcester, Mass.

−2
Akron, Ohio
Anaheim, Calif.
Bridgeport, Conn.
Camden, N.J.
Canton, Ohio
Elizabeth, N.J.
Flint, Mich.
Garden Grove, Calif.
Indianapolis, Ind.
Long Beach, Calif.
New Bedford, Mass.
Oakland, Calif.
Oklahoma City, Okla.
Rockford, Ill.
San Bernardino, Calif.
Stamford, Conn.
Toledo, Ohio
Tucson, Ariz.
Waterbury, Conn.
Yonkers, N.Y.

−1
Albuquerque, N.M.
Berkeley, Calif.
Buffalo, N.Y.
Cincinnati, Ohio
Evansville, Ill.
Grand Rapids, Mich.
Hollywood, Fla.
Milwaukee, Wis.
New Haven, Conn.
Peoria, Ill.
Pittsburgh, Pa.
Portland, Oreg.
St. Petersburg, Fla.
Santa Ana, Calif.
Syracuse, N.Y.
Tampa, Fla.
Warren, Mich.
Youngstown, Ohio

0
Allentown, Pa.
Birmingham, Ala.
Cedar Rapids, Iowa
Colorado Springs, Colo.
Columbus, Ga.
El Paso, Tex.
Ft. Lauderdale, Fla.
Glendale, Calif.
Honolulu, Hawaii
Huntington Beach, Calif.
Kansas City, Mo.
Knoxville, Tenn.
Lansing, Mich.
Little Rock, Ark.
Los Angeles, Calif.
Memphis, Tenn.
Miami, Fla.
Minneapolis, Minn.
Norfolk, Va.
Pasadena, Calif.
Providence, R.I.
Sacramento, Calif.
St. Louis, Mo.
St. Paul, Minn.
San Diego, Calif.
Savannah, Ga.
Seattle, Wash.
Spokane, Wash.
Winston-Salem, N.C.

+1
Albany, N.Y.
Baltimore, Md.
Baton Rouge, La.
Charlotte, N.C.
Chattanooga, Tenn.
Chicago, Ill.
Columbia, S.C.
Columbus, Ohio
Dallas, Tex.
Dearborn, Mich.
Denver, Colo.
Des Moines, Iowa
Fort Wayne, Ind.
Fort Worth, Tex.
Fresno, Calif.
Hammond, Ind.
Hialeah, Fla.
Huntsville, Ala.
Jackson, Miss.
Jacksonville, Fla.
Kansas City, Kans.
Louisville, Ky.
Mobile, Ala.
Parma, Ohio
Phoenix, Ariz.
San Francisco, Calif.
Scranton, Pa.
South Bend, Ind.
Springfield, Mo.
Washington, D.C.

+2
Alexandria, Va.
Amarillo, Tex.
Beaumont, Tex.
Duluth, Minn.
Erie, Pa.
Fremont, Calif.
Greensboro, N.C.
Independence, Mo.
Lincoln, Neb.
Livonia, Mich.
Macon, Ga.
Madison, Wis.
Newport News, Va.
Portsmouth, Va.
Richmond, Va.
Salt Lake City, Utah
San Jose, Calif.
Shreveport, La.
Stockton, Calif.
Tacoma, Wash.
Topeka, Kans.
Torrance, Calif.
Tulsa, Okla.

+3
Austin, Tex.
Corpus Christi, Tex.
Hampton, Va.
Houston, Tex.
Lexington, Ky.
Nashville, Tenn.
New Orleans, La.
Omaha, Neb.
San Antonio, Tex.
Virginia Beach, Va.

+4
Lubbock, Tex.
Montgomery, Ala.
Raleigh, N.C.
Wichita, Kans.

a. Listed alphabetically within each rating group.

Table 3-9. *City and SMSA Functional Index Values*

Negative scores indicate the worst distress, decline, disparity, and divergence

City name	*City distress*	*City decline*	*SMSA distress*	*SMSA decline*	*Dis-parity*	*Diver-gence*
Akron, Ohio	−2	−2	−1	−3	−3	−1
Albany, N.Y.	+1	+1	+1	0	0	−1
Albuquerque, N.M.	+1	−1	−3	−4	+4	+1
*Alexandria, Va.	+3	+2	. . .	. . .	+4	+2
Allentown, Pa	+3	0	+1	0	0	0
Amarillo, Tex.	+4	+2	+1	0	+4	+1
Anaheim, Calif.	+2	−2	+1	−1	+1	−2
Atlanta, Ga.	−4	−3	0	−1	−5	−3
Austin, Tex.	+2	+3	+1	+4	+3	0
Baltimore, Md.	−3	+1	0	+2	−5	0
Baton Rouge, La.	0	+1	−1	+1	+3	+2
Beaumont, Tex.	0	+2	−1	+4	+1	−2
*Berkeley, Calif.	−3	−1	. . .	. . .	−4	−3
Birmingham, Ala.	−3	0	−1	+2	−3	−3
Boston, Mass.	−5	−4	0	−4	−5	−3
Bridgeport, Conn.	−1	−2	+1	−2	−4	0
Buffalo, N.Y.	−2	−1	−1	−4	−5	−3
*Cambridge, Mass.	−2	−4	. . .	. . .	−3	−1
*Camden, N.J.	−4	−2	. . .	. . .	−5	−3
Canton, Ohio	−3	−2	0	0	−4	−1
Cedar Rapids, Iowa	+4	0	+3	+2	+3	−1
Charlotte, N.C.	0	+1	−1	+1	+4	+3
Chattanooga, Tenn.	−2	+1	−1	+1	−4	+1
Chicago, Ill.	−1	+1	0	−2	−4	−1
Cincinnati, Ohio	−3	−1	0	0	−4	−1
Cleveland, Ohio	−5	−4	0	−4	−5	−2
Colorado Springs, Colo.	+2	0	−1	+1	0	−1
Columbia, S.C.	−1	+1	0	+2	0	−2
Columbus, Ga.	+2	0	−1	0	+5	+2
Columbus, Ohio	0	+1	0	−1	−1	+1
Corpus Christi, Tex.	+2	+3	−1	+3	+4	+1
Dallas, Tex.	+1	+1	+2	+1	+1	0
Dayton, Ohio	−4	−4	−1	−2	−5	−2
*Dearborn, Mich.	+1	+1	. . .	. . .	+5	+2
Denver, Colo.	−1	+1	+1	0	−3	−1
Des Moines, Iowa	+3	+1	+3	+1	0	−1
Detroit, Mich.	−3	−3	−1	−2	−5	−2
Duluth, Minn.	+2	+2	+1	+5	+3	−1
*Elizabeth, N.J.	−1	−2	. . .	. . .	−4	−3
El Paso, Tex.	+2	−0	−1	−2	+4	+2

Table 3-9 (*continued*)

City name	*City distress*	*City decline*	*SMSA distress*	*SMSA decline*	*Dis-parity*	*Diver-gence*
Erie, Pa.	+1	+2	0	0	+1	+1
Evansville, Ind.	−1	−1	−1	0	+1	−2
Flint, Mich.	−3	−2	−2	−4	−3	−1
Ft. Lauderdale, Fla.	−1	0	0	+2	+3	+2
Ft. Wayne, Ind.	0	+1	0	−1	0	−1
*Ft. Worth, Tex.	+3	+1	...	...	0	−1
*Fremont, Calif.	+5	+2	...	...	+3	+3
Fresno, Calif.	−1	+1	−3	0	+4	+1
*Garden Grove, Calif.	+4	−2	...	...	+1	−1
Gary, Ind.	−2	−3	−1	−3	−4	−2
*Glendale, Calif.	+4	0	...	...	+3	+3
Grand Rapids, Mich.	−2	−1	0	−3	−4	−1
Greensboro, N.C.	+1	+2	0	+2	+4	0
*Hammond, Ind.	+2	+1	...	...	+3	+1
*Hampton, Va.	+5	+3	...	...	+4	+1
Hartford, Conn.	−5	−4	+1	−3	−5	−3
*Hialeah, Fla.	+1	+1	...	...	+3	+2
*Hollywood, Fla.	+1	−1	...	...	+3	−1
Honolulu, Hawaii	+2	0	+2	0	+3	0
Houston, Tex.	+3	+3	+2	+5	+1	0
*Huntington Beach, Calif.	+3	0	...	...	+4	+3
Huntsville, Ala.	+3	+1	0	+1	+5	+1
*Independence, Mo.	+4	+2	...	...	+4	+3
Indianapolis, Ind.	+2	−2	0	−1	+2	0
Jackson, Miss.	+2	+1	+1	+4	+5	+2
Jacksonville, Fla.	+2	+1	−1	+4	+5	+2
Jersey City, N.J.	−3	−4	−2	−3	+1	+1
*Kansas City, Kans.	0	+1	...	...	−4	−1
Kansas City, Mo.	−1	0	+1	−1	−4	−2
Knoxville, Tenn.	−1	0	+1	+4	+2	−1
Lansing, Mich.	0	0	0	−1	0	+1
Las Vegas, Nev.	−1	−4	−1	−4	0	−2
Lexington, Ky.	−1	+3	0	+3	+2	+2
Lincoln, Neb.	+4	+2	+2	+2	+4	+3
Little Rock, Ark.	−1	0	−1	+2	+2	−1
*Livonia, Mich.	+4	+2	...	...	+5	+3
*Long Beach, Calif.	−1	−2	...	...	+4	+1
Los Angeles, Calif.	−2	0	−1	−4	−1	0
Louisville, Ky.	−3	+1	0	+3	−3	−1
Lubbock, Tex.	+3	+4	0	+4	+5	+2

Table 3-9 (*continued*)

City name	*City distress*	*City decline*	*SMSA distress*	*SMSA decline*	*Dis-parity*	*Diver-gence*
Macon, Ga.	0	+2	0	+2	+1	−1
Madison, Wis.	+4	+2	+3	+2	+3	0
Memphis, Tenn.	+1	0	−2	+1	+4	+1
Miami, Fla.	+4	0	−1	+1	−5	+1
Milwaukee, Wis.	+1	−1	+3	−2	−3	−2
Minneapolis, Minn.	0	0	+3	+1	−4	0
Mobile, Ala.	0	+1	−1	+3	+2	+3
Montgomery, Ala.	+1	+4	+1	+3	+4	0
Nashville, Tenn.	+2	+3	0	+2	+4	+2
New Bedford, Mass.	−1	−2	−1	−1	−1	0
New Haven, Conn.	−3	−1	+2	−3	−5	−2
New Orleans, La.	−1	+3	−2	+2	−2	+1
New York, N.Y.	−3	−3	−1	−5	−1	+1
Newark, N.J.	−5	−3	−1	−3	−5	−3
Newport News, Va.	+2	+2	+1	+2	+2	+1
Norfolk, Va.	−1	0	−1	+2	0	0
*Oakland, Calif.	−3	−2	. . .	. . .	−5	−3
Oklahoma City, Okla.	+1	−2	0	−1	+1	−1
Omaha, Neb.	+3	+3	+1	0	+2	+3
*Parma, Ohio	+5	+1	. . .	. . .	+5	+3
*Pasadena, Calif.	−1	0	. . .	. . .	+3	+2
Paterson, N.J.	−3	−4	−1	−4	−5	−3
Peoria, Ill.	0	−1	0	+1	−2	−2
Philadelphia, Pa.	−4	−3	0	−4	−4	+1
Phoenix, Ariz.	+1	+1	−1	+2	+3	+2
Pittsburgh, Pa.	−3	−1	+2	+1	−5	−2
Portland, Oreg.	−3	−1	−1	−2	−3	−2
*Portsmouth, Va.	0	+2	. . .	. . .	−1	0
Providence, R.I.	−2	0	0	+1	−3	−1
Raleigh, N.C.	+2	+4	+1	+5	+4	0
Richmond, Va.	−2	+2	+2	+1	−4	−1
Riverside, Calif.	+3	−3	−3	−2	+3	0
Rochester, N.Y.	−2	−3	+2	−1	−4	−2
Rockford, Ill.	+1	−2	+1	−2	0	−1
Sacramento, Calif.	−1	0	−1	−2	−1	−2
St. Louis, Mo.	−4	0	−1	−2	−4	0
*St. Paul, Minn.	+2	0	. . .	. . .	−3	−1
*St. Petersburg, Fla.	−3	−1	. . .	. . .	+1	−2
Salt Lake City, Utah	+1	+2	+1	+1	−2	+1
San Antonio, Tex.	+2	+3	−1	+2	+1	+1

Table 3-9 (*continued*)

City name	*City distress*	*City decline*	*SMSA distress*	*SMSA decline*	*Dis-parity*	*Diver-gence*
*San Bernardino, Calif.	−3	−2	. . .	. . .	−2	−1
San Diego, Calif.	+3	0	−1	−4	+2	+2
San Francisco, Calif.	−2	+1	0	−2	−4	0
San Jose, Calif.	+3	+2	+1	−1	0	+1
*Santa Ana, Calif.	+2	−1	. . .	. . .	−3	−1
Savannah, Ga.	−3	0	−2	0	−2	0
Scranton, Pa.	−2	+1	−1	0	+3	+1
Seattle, Wash.	0	0	+1	−2	−1	+2
Shreveport, La.	+1	+2	0	+2	+4	+2
South Bend, Ind.	0	+1	+1	−2	0	0
Spokane, Wash.	−1	0	−2	0	+2	+2
Springfield, Mass.	−3	−3	−2	−3	−4	−1
Springfield, Mo.	+2	+1	+1	+3	+4	+1
Stamford, Conn.	+1	−2	+3	+1	0	0
Stockton, Calif.	−2	+2	−2	0	0	+1
Syracuse, N.Y.	0	−1	0	−4	−3	−2
Tacoma, Wash.	−2	+2	−1	+1	−3	+2
Tampa, Fla.	−3	−1	−2	+1	−1	0
Toledo, Ohio	0	−2	−1	−1	0	−2
Topeka, Kans.	+2	+2	+1	+2	+2	+1
*Torrance, Calif.	+5	+2	. . .	. . .	+5	+3
Trenton, N.J.	−4	−4	+1	−2	−5	−2
Tucson, Ariz.	+1	−2	−2	−2	+2	+1
Tulsa, Okla.	+3	+2	+1	+2	+3	+1
*Virginia Beach, Va.	+5	+3	. . .	. . .	+5	+3
*Warren, Mich.	+4	−1	. . .	. . .	+4	+1
Washington, D.C.	−3	+1	+1	0	−5	−1
Waterbury, Conn.	+1	−2	0	−1	−3	0
Wichita, Kans.	+4	+4	+2	+3	+4	+2
*Winston-Salem, N.C.	−3	0	. . .	. . .	−1	+1
Worchester, Mass.	−1	−3	0	−1	−1	−1
*Yonkers, N.Y.	+3	−2	. . .	. . .	+5	+2
Youngstown, Ohio	−3	−1	0	+1	−5	−1

*Satellite city—not the largest city in its SMSA as defined in 1975. The 121 cities without asterisks are referred to as "first cities"; they are the largest in their SMSAs.

. . . SMSA index scores reported by largest city name.

Table 3-10. *Distributions of Distress and Decline Indexes*
Number of cities or SMSAs in each category

Description	Index[a]										
	−5	−4	−3	−2	−1	0	+1	+2	+3	+4	+5
City distress index											
Actual distribution	4	7	23	14	21	16	19	20	14	10	5
Expected distribution of 153 cities if five elements independently distributed	0.6	3.1	9.4	18.9	28.3	32.1	28.3	18.9	9.4	3.1	0.6
City decline index											
Actual distribution	n.a.	9	10	20	18	29	30	23	10	4	n.a.
Expected distribution of 153 cities if four elements independently distributed	n.a.	1.9	7.6	18.9	30.2	35.9	30.2	18.9	7.6	1.9	n.a.
SMSA distress index											
Actual distribution	n.a.	n.a.	3	10	35	32	26	9	6	n.a.	n.a.
Expected distribution of 121 SMSAs if three elements independently distributed	n.a.	n.a.	4.5	13.4	26.9	31.4	26.9	13.4	4.5	n.a.	n.a.
SMSA decline index											
Actual distribution	1	11	8	16	14	17	19	19	7	6	3
Expected distribution of 121 SMSAs if five elements independently distributed	0.5	2.5	7.5	14.9	22.4	25.4	22.4	14.9	7.5	2.5	0.5

n.a. Not applicable.
a. Most disadvantaged, −5; least disadvantaged, +5.

Table 3-10 summarizes the distributions of index values and provides a comparison with the distribution that would be expected if all the component variables were independently and randomly distributed. This comparison shows how distress and decline tend to "pile up" in a few places. City distress, city decline, and SMSA decline are much more concentrated than would occur at random.[25] For example, one would expect fewer than four cities in the worst two city distress categories, whereas we find eleven. The mirror image of this phenomenon is that signs of health also concentrate. SMSA distress, in contrast, is not nearly as concentrated in a few areas; only Albuquerque, Fresno, and Riverside had the combination of high unemployment, high crime rates, and low income qualifying them for the most distressed category.

The relationships among the various indexes may indicate underlying

25. A statistical chi-square test can indicate how likely it is that the actual distribution differs from the random one purely by chance. For SMSA distress, no such difference is indicated even at a 50 percent level of significance; for the other three indexes, in contrast, the differences are significant at well below the 0.01 percent level.

processes of interaction. The fact that several cities are high on both distress and decline indexes suggests that cities in trouble are also getting worse as confirmed by the simple correlation of .55 between these city indexes. In contrast, the correlation between SMSA distress and decline indexes is only .27. Many declining SMSAs—for example, Boston, Cleveland, and Syracuse—are not particularly distressed, and conversely Fresno, in the most distressed category, has a zero decline index.

Are declining or distressed SMSAs more likely to contain declining or distressed cities? Yes, for decline. The correlation between the city and SMSA decline indexes is about .7.[26] Ninety-four of the cities have the same signed decline index as their SMSAs.

In contrast, city distress and SMSA distress show only a weak (though statistically significant) correspondence, with a correlation of about .3. Only half (seventy-seven) of the cities have the same *signed* distress index as their SMSAs. With the exception of Jersey City, the SMSAs in the worst two distress categories are not commonly associated with severe problems; the three ranking worst are all in the Southwest and contain largest cities ranking −1, +1, and +3 on the distress index. Similarly, those cities and SMSAs appearing repeatedly in the worst categories on the other three lists—Boston, Cleveland, Philadelphia—do not have distressed SMSAs. This suggests that many "problem" cities are surrounded by suburbs in reasonably good shape, a hypothesis explored more deeply later.

POPULATION LOSS AND DISTRESS AND DECLINE. The next question is whether cities losing population are also more likely to suffer functional distress or decline than those not losing population. Table 3-11 displays the mean distress and decline index values for the five descriptive clusters. (The bottom two rows present similar values for two indexes introduced later in this chapter.)

Both city indexes imply that the healthiest cities, on average, are growing cities in growing SMSAs, followed by stagnant cities in growing SMSAs; the most troubled cities are severely declining cities in declining SMSAs. Overall, cities in shrinking SMSAs show the greatest functional *decline;* but cities declining severely in population are the most *distressed.* This suggests that *SMSA* population trends are an important factor in *changes* in city conditions (i.e., functional *decline*), while *city* population trends reflect or are a reflection of city distress conditions.

There are, however, some interesting anomalies. Duluth is the only

26. The exact correlation depends on whether 121 or 153 observations are included.

Table 3-11. *Population Changes and Functional Distress and Decline*

		SMSA grew, 1970–75			*SMSA lost population, 1970–75*	
Description	*All first cities (or all SMSAs)*	*City grew, 1970–75*	*City stagnant, 1970–75*	*City severely declined, 1970–75*	*City stagnant, 1970–75*	*City severely declined, 1970–75*
Number of cities	121	44	32	19	11	15
Mean value of city distress index (maximum value 5)	−0.35	+0.91	+0.06	−2.05	−0.73	−2.47
Mean value of city decline index (maximum value 4)	−0.02	+0.89	+0.22	−0.79	−1.18	−1.40
Mean value of SMSA distress index (maximum value 3)	−0.02	−0.39	+0.28	+0.37	+0.09	−0.13
Mean value of SMSA decline index (maximum value 5)	−0.02	+0.98	+0.41	−1.00	−1.36	−1.60
Mean value of disparity index (maximum value 5)	−0.32	+2.23	−0.72	−3.26	−0.27	−3.27
Mean value of divergence index (maximum value 3)	−0.14	+0.82	−0.34	−1.42	−0.09	−0.93

severely declining city in a declining SMSA that has a positive distress score, and is one of the only two in that cluster (along with South Bend) showing positive functional decline scores. (Recall that a positive score indicates a *lack* of distress or functional decline.) Conversely, a few growing cities show functional distress or decline: Miami is the most distressed growing city, and Las Vegas has the worst functional decline.

The same cluster patterns are apparent among SMSAs as among cities, but are less pronounced. The SMSA distress index, in particular, does not seem strongly related to population changes in the expected direction. The three most distressed SMSAs are growing ones in which the largest city is also growing: Fresno, Riverside, and Albuquerque. The SMSA decline index has a fairly strong association with population changes, but the distributions are quite spread.

Implications

What can we conclude about the extent of functional decline and distress and their relationships to descriptive decline? Our indexes are *relative* measures, but they do show the degree to which key unfavorable conditions or changes bunch together. If we assume functional distress or decline is shown by the *simultaneous* occurrence of several undesirable conditions or deteriorating trends, then the distribution of city and SMSA values on the indexes roughly indicates the extent of trouble. Like population loss, severe functional decline is somewhat more prevalent among cities than among SMSAs. The same is true of distress. In fact, SMSA distress does not really appear to be a problem on a national scale: there is little or no tendency for unfavorable conditions at the SMSA level to combine systematically.[27]

The index means for city clusters in table 3-11 clearly show that descriptive and functional decline of cities are positively associated. This result is consistent with the hypothetical relations between population loss and functional decline discussed in chapter 2, though it does not establish the direction of causality. However, not all cities losing population—even severely—show high distress or functional decline. This relationship is influenced by a third factor: population trends in each city's SMSA. In particular, stagnant or severely declining cities in growing SMSAs show considerably less functional decline and somewhat less distress (according to our measures) than their counterparts in declining SMSAs. Thus, population loss in an SMSA seems to be a strong indicator of likely problems for its largest central city.

We use changes in per capita income as our empirical measure of functional decline in chapter 5, and later focus on poverty concentration as a particularly troublesome companion of population loss; so associations between population loss and these two indicators are especially important. Cities that severely declined had slower growth in real income per capita over the same period (6 percent) than did stagnant or growing cities (8 percent and 11 percent, respectively). Severely declining cities also lagged the most behind the rate of real income growth in their SMSAs, and ended the period with the largest city-suburb income disparities. Similarly, cities that lost population during the 1960s had a full percentage point smaller reduction in family poverty incidence over the decade, and ended it with a higher percentage of population and families in poverty, than did cities which grew during the 1960s.

For SMSAs, connections between descriptive decline and functional conditions are more tenuous. True, areas losing population are likely to be deteriorating functionally as well, but there are numerous exceptions;

27. Because these indexes are *relative* measures, there are also relatively more cities than SMSAs with "good" distress scores, although less so with regard to functional decline.

Table 3-12. *Intrametropolitan Disparities, by Region and City Size*

All figures except number of cities are averages

Description	All cities[a]	Northeast		North Central		South		West	
		Under 200,000	*Over* 200,000	*Under* 200,000	*Over* 200,000	*Under* 200,000	*Over* 200,000	*Under* 200,000	*Over* 200,000
Number of cities	153	19	9	24	17	28	24	18	14
Unemployment rate (percent)									
City minus SMSA, 1975	0.58 (149)	1.72	1.56	−0.20 (22)	1.19 (15)	0.07	0.60	0.01	0.69
City minus SMSA, 1970	0.31	0.76	0.73	−0.07	0.71	0.11	0.33	0.02	0.40
Percent of population poor									
Ratio, city/SMSA, 1969	1.2	1.6	1.5	1.1	1.4	1.0	1.2	1.1	1.2
Violent crime rate[b]									
City minus SMSA, 1975	264 (152)	427	486	89	505	126	345	70 (17)	283
City minus SMSA, 1970	169 (152)	242	357	6	360	73 (27)	293	−11	203
Percent of housing old									
City minus SMSA, 1970	7.6	16.0	14.9	2.0	14.6	1.8	7.0	4.2	9.7
Per capita income, 1975									
Ratio, city/SMSA, 1974	.98	.89	.88	1.00	.93	1.05	.98	1.01	1.00
Ratio, city/SMSA, 1969[c]	.99	.91	.90	1.01	.94	1.06	.99	1.01	1.02

a. Figures in parentheses indicate actual number of cities when fewer than indicated in first row.
b. Crimes per 100,000 population.
c. Denominator is 1969 per capita income in SMSA as defined in 1975.

and distress at the SMSA level bears little relation to other factors. In general, central cities seem to bear the brunt of problems created by adjusting to a smaller metropolitan population and economy. That brings us to the next subject: city-SMSA disparities in ability to carry out urban social functions.

Intrametropolitan Disparity as an Element of Distress and Decline

Since many location and investment decisions are made at the local level, central cities often suffer in comparison to their surrounding suburbs, regardless of how they compare to other cities. For this reason, we examine disparities between cities and their SMSAs and changes in those disparities along several of the functional dimensions already discussed. An additional advantage of disparity measures is that they are *not* affected by regional differences in the particular variables used, such as unemployment rates, age of the housing stock, and cost of living. This resolves some of the interpretation problems discussed in the appendix to this chapter.

Trends and Patterns of Intrametropolitan Disparity

Table 3-12 shows average disparities between the 153 cities and their SMSAs with respect to several measures of social functioning, by region and city size. In general, cities were not doing as well as their SMSAs in 1970 and 1975. Even more troublesome, recent changes have *worsened* disparities in income, unemployment, and crime rates. As shown by tables 3-6 and 3-7, cities had more unemployment, poverty, crime, and old housing than their SMSAs, and lower per capita incomes.

Average disparities were larger for some measures than others: city unemployment in 1975 was about 7 percent (half a percentage point) higher than SMSA unemployment; poverty incidence was almost one-quarter higher, although per capita incomes were only 2 percent lower; violent crime rates were over 50 percent higher; and the fraction of housing built before 1940 was about 20 percent higher. Considerably larger disparities appear in certain regions. Especially notable is the increase in city-SMSA unemployment rate differences in the Northeast and larger North Central cities, and the resulting large differences in 1975 rates.

Disparities in average income are quite variable. Outside the Northeast, smaller cities generally had higher per capita incomes than their SMSAs, while the larger cities were poorer than their SMSAs. In fact, 71 of the 153 cities, and 55 of the 121 "first" cities, had higher per capita incomes than the rest of the SMSA in 1975. However, no group except the smaller Southern cities showed income per *household* to be higher on average in city than in SMSA (data not shown), and only 43 individual cities (including 11 satellites) showed higher per household income than their SMSAs; thus, many cities' favorable showing on per capita income is due to smaller family sizes. Furthermore, nearly all groups showed a deterioration of the city's relative income position over time, though by only one to two percentage points.

Indexes of Disparity and Divergence

In a manner similar to our indexes of distress and decline, we calculated a disparity index and an index of worsening disparity, which we labeled "divergence." The elements of each index (drawn from the measures just discussed) are listed below:

City-SMSA disparity

City minus SMSA unemployment rate, 1975
City minus SMSA violent crime rate, 1975
City/SMSA ratio of per capita income, 1974
City/SMSA ratio percent of population poor, 1970
City minus SMSA percent of housing old, 1970

City-SMSA divergence

Change in city/SMSA difference in unemployment rates, 1970–75
Change in city/SMSA difference in violent crime rates, 1970–75
Change in city/SMSA ratio of per capita income, 1969–74

The table in the appendix to this chapter also provides a summary of all six indexes, for easy reference.

Table 3-8 shows the disparity and divergence index values for the 153 cities, and table 3-13 summarizes the distributions. The most striking feature of these tables is the large number of cities with extreme index values, especially for the disparity index. There are 18 cities with high disparities on all five counts, and another 18 with four out of five. This is *ten times* the number that would be expected in those two groups if the five components were independently distributed. There are also many cities at the opposite extreme of low (or even favorable) disparity. These tend to be noncentral cities: over a third of the low-disparity cities (values 5, 4, 3) are in SMSAs that contain a larger city.

Table 3-13. *Distribution of Disparity and Divergence Indexes*
Number of cities in each category

	Index[a]										
Description	−5	−4	−3	−2	−1	0	+1	+2	+3	+4	+5
Disparity index											
Actual distribution	18	18	14	5	10	16	12	11	17	21	11
Expected distribution of 153 cities if five elements independently distributed	0.6	3.1	9.4	18.9	28.3	32.1	28.3	18.9	9.4	3.1	0.6
Divergence index											
Actual distribution	n.a.	n.a.	11	21	33	25	30	21	12	n.a.	n.a.
Expected distribution of 153 cities if three elements independently distributed	n.a.	n.a.	5.7	17.0	34.0	39.7	34.0	17.0	5.7	n.a.	n.a.

n.a. Not applicable.
a: Most disadvantaged, −5; least disadvantaged, +5.

Familiar names crop up at the top of the disparity list: Boston, Cleveland, Dayton, Hartford, Newark, Paterson, and Trenton. All were in the worst category of city distress or decline. Boston, Dayton, Hartford, Newark, and Trenton also reappear at the worst end of the divergence index. Such deterioration of a city's position relative to its SMSA is particularly disturbing in areas where the SMSA itself has a high decline index score. Examples are Boston, Hartford, Newark, Buffalo, Camden (Philadelphia SMSA), and Elizabeth (Newark SMSA). In contrast, other cities with fairly high divergence scores, such as Beaumont, Duluth, and Knoxville, are low-disparity cities in SMSAs with very little functional decline, a less worrisome combination.

Correlation coefficients indicate the degree to which decline, distress, disparity, and divergence occur in the same places. For the 153 cities, the correlation between the disparity and city distress indexes is strongly positive, +.77. This implies that cities suffering by comparison with the rest of their SMSAs also suffered by comparison with other cities. High-disparity cities are often also high-divergence cities; the correlation between the two indexes is +.71. These and other correlations reinforce the earlier finding of greater association between city and SMSA functional *decline* than *distress*. While many troubled cities apparently had reasonably healthy suburbs (thus disparities are high), *changes* in city and SMSA status tended to move in the same direction.

The bottom two rows of table 3-11 display the mean disparity and divergence scores for the five descriptive clusters of cities. The index means are zero in the 153-city sample (by definition), but are negative for these

121 cities that are largest in their SMSAs. Growing cities in growing SMSAs rated most favorably and severely declining cities least favorably, on both indexes.

Conclusions

Urban decline is widespread. We found evidence of population loss, employment loss, rising unemployment and crime rates, and stagnant incomes for cities and SMSAs, on both intermetropolitan and intrametropolitan scales. In addition to decline, we found distress and disparity—clear "troubles" measured at a point in time by comparing cities and SMSAs with other areas or with each other.

Urban decline and distress are mutually reinforcing, as shown by the "bunching" of undesirable conditions and changes in particular places. Distress is a static measure of relatively low-level performance of certain key social functions. The bunching of adverse measures can be seen in several ways. First, there are far more high-distress, high-decline, high-disparity, and high-divergence cities than one would expect if the individual impairments were randomly distributed.[28] Second, the same cities appeared over and over with extreme scores on the six indexes. For example, when all six scores were combined, the city and SMSA of Boston were in the most disadvantageous third of 22 out of 25 individual indicators. Cleveland, Newark, and Paterson all scored −20. Cities in trouble were often inside SMSAs in trouble, but doing worse than and sinking further behind their SMSAs. Third, cities displaying descriptive decline generally suffered more functional decline, and vice versa.

Cities in descriptively or functionally declining SMSAs tend to suffer more difficulties than those in growing SMSAs. These cities are more troubled than their suburbs and more troubled than other cities. This implies that central cities bear the burden of area-wide adjustments to changed conditions.

Urban distress is not very prevalent at the SMSA level, even though it is widespread among central cities.

A tremendous diversity of urban conditions exists across the United States. Some cities fit none of the above patterns—growing cities showing distress, troubled cities improving. Hence whatever processes generate "bunching" of conditions are neither inescapable nor universal. Enough

28. That is, distributed independently of one another.

surprises arise to give mayors and city residents hope and keep analysts wondering.

Appendix: Description of Indexes Used in This Chapter

The components entering each of the six indexes of functional decline, distress, disparity, and divergence are summarized in table 3-14. The following text describes the drawbacks of the individual measures and explains why they were included nonetheless.

1. Unemployment rates are chronically higher in some areas than others. The failure of migration to equalize them suggests that some areas with higher unemployment have other strong attractions (perhaps higher wages, perhaps other amenities). However, we do not believe this can account for all the interarea differences in unemployment rates, and recent econometric evidence supports us.[29] Overall, we believe higher or increasing unemployment indicates a city or SMSA is not performing its job-providing function well.

2. Per capita income and poverty incidence measures are distorted by cost-of-living differences. Because we lack data for most areas, we cannot "correct" local income figures for cost-of-living differences (as we did for the 33 cities for which data were available). However, relative cost-of-living rankings do not change much over time, so *changes* in income or poverty incidence should accurately indicate the direction of change in local well-being.

3. Crime rates may be distorted by variations in the fraction of actual crimes that are reported. Also, because some areas have considerably greater daytime population (commuters, tourists) than others, rates calculated on the basis of local *resident* population do not reflect the relative likelihood of experiencing a crime. We believe neither of these factors removes the (negative) association between reported crime rates and residents' perceived well-being, at least partly because residents may be as aware of the *reported* rates as of their actual risk of being victimized. Although we view crime rates as primarily a measure of residential quality, crime also affects production, particularly by small businesses.

4. Many old housing units are as sound and attractive as new ones.

29. William C. Wheaton, "Metropolitan Growth, Unemployment, and Interregional Factor Mobility," in William C. Wheaton, ed., *Coupe Papers on Public Economics*, vol. 2: *Interregional Movements and Regional Growth* (Urban Institute, 1979).

Table 3-14. *Summary of Index Components*[a]

Element	SMSA distress index	SMSA decline index	City distress index	City decline index	Disparity index	Divergence index
Unemployment rate	S_3	S_3-S_2	C_3	C_3-C_2	C_3-S_3	$(C_3-S_3)-(C_2-S_2)$
Per capita income	S_3	$(S_3-S_2)-1$	. . .	$(C_3/C_2)-1$	C_3/S_3	$(C_3/S_3)-(C_2/S_2)$
Poverty incidence	. . .	S_2-S_1	C_2	. . .	C_2/S_2	. . .
Violent crime rate	S_3	S_3-S_2	C_3	C_3-C_2	C_3-S_3	$(C_3-S_3)-(C_2-S_2)$
Percent of housing old	. . .	. . .	C_2	. . .	C_2-S_2	. . .
Government debt burden	. . .	. . .	. . .	C_3-C_2	. . .	. . .
Tax effort	. . .	S_2-S_1	C_2/S_2	. . .	. . .	. . .

a. C = city value; S = SMSA value; 1 = 1960 (or 1959, 1961); 2 = 1970 (or 1969, 1971, 1972); 3 = 1975 (or 1974). For example, S_3 in the first column, first row, indicates that the 1975 SMSA unemployment rate is one of the elements in the SMSA distress index; $(C_3/C_2)-1$ in the fourth column, second row, indicates that the percentage increase in city per capita income is one of the elements in the city decline index.

Thus the percent of a city's units built before 1940 may not indicate the quality of "protective shelter" there. However, even if individual units are well-maintained, cities with a predominance of older units are likely to be more *spatially* obsolete, that is, have densities appropriate to an earlier age of lower incomes and slower transportation. In addition, the *average* value and *average* gross rent of pre-1940 units are uniformly lower than those of units built more recently,[30] indicating that older units on average are smaller or of lower quality than new units.

5. A city's debt burden may rise when it embarks on a large capital improvement program or when it responds to fiscal stringency by funding a greater share of its budget through short- and long-term bonds. The latter is the difficulty we want to measure. We believe that few cities in the sample are involved in major first-time investment in infrastructure that would seriously distort this interpretation of measured debt burden changes.

6. A serious problem with tax effort measures is that the services provided by local governments vary widely among areas. Taxes may be higher in a city because more services are provided, or because of a weak tax base or inefficient government. Only the latter two causes are of concern in terms of weak performance of the city's social functions—citizens are paying "too much" for government services. The former presumably results from local citizen choice, or legal division of responsibilities between state and local governments. We have minimized this problem by using changes or ratios: for SMSA decline, we include the *change* in local government tax effort in the SMSA, while for city distress, we use the city effort expressed as a *fraction* of the SMSA average.

30. This is true for the United States as a whole, for SMSAs, central cities, and the balance of SMSAs. See Bureau of the Census, *Annual Housing Survey, 1975, United States and Regions, Part C: Financial Characteristics of the Housing Inventory* (GPO, 1977), tables A-1 to A-3.

4

Causes of Urban Decline

MOST LARGE American cities experienced uninterrupted population growth for so long that it came to be regarded as natural. In reality, there is nothing inevitable about urban growth or decline. This chapter discusses the two major factors that may cause urban growth changes: historic and society-wide trends affecting overall urban growth and forces affecting the relative growth and decline of individual areas.

Historic Trends and Their Influence

Large-scale historic developments bring about aggregate changes affecting all cities' growth, although they also have varying impacts on different areas. These important national factors include the determinants of total U.S. population growth, trends in urbanization, and influences on overall intrametropolitan location patterns.

Tables 4-1 and 4-2 present population data for the nearly 200 years covered by the U.S. Census. Total population growth has generally slowed since 1860. It ran slightly over a one-third increase per decade until 1860, between one-quarter and one-fifth per decade until 1910, and since then has averaged 14 percent per decade.

In 1790, about 95 percent of the population lived in rural areas—settlements containing fewer than 2,500 persons. These areas also experienced over two-thirds of the nation's population growth until 1860. Although urban areas were expanding faster in percentage terms, their growth did not exceed rural growth in absolute numbers until the Civil

War. Absolute urban growth reached a temporary peak of 14.8 million in the 1920s, suffered a sharp slowdown during the depression, more than doubled in the 1940s, and surged to all-time highs in the 1950s and 1960s. The share of total U.S. population in cities over 50,000 began to fall sooner, sometime before 1970. Provisional 1980 Census data indicate a possible reversal in these long-run pro-urban trends: between 1970 and 1980 the proportion of the population living in urban areas increased only one-tenth of 1 percent. Furthermore, the growth rate of nonmetropolitan population exceeded the metropolitan growth rate over the 1970–79 period, after at least two decades of lagging well behind metropolitan growth.[1]

Immigration from Abroad

Table 4-1 shows the significant degree to which this nation has drawn its population growth from immigration. Gross immigration as a percentage of total population growth by decades was never below 24 percent from 1840 through 1930. Over two million persons arrived per decade during that period, reaching a peak of 8.8 million from 1900 to 1910. A sizable fraction of these immigrants settled in urban areas, contributing to rapid urban population growth. From 1970 through 1977, the annual number of legally admitted immigrants averaged about 400,000—more than in any other decade since 1930—and in 1978, the figure jumped to 601,000. In addition, a large number of immigrants entered the United States illegally during the 1970s.

Fertility Rates

Dramatic changes in the number of live births per 1,000 women aged fifteen to forty-four (the general fertility rate) also contributed to changes in urban growth rates.[2] During the nineteenth century, the general fertility rate for white women (the only group for which there are continuous data) fell more than 50 percent, from 278 to 130. It continued dropping to a low of 76 (for all women) in 1936. However, there was a marked rise after World War II to a high of 123 in 1957, followed by a steady decline to 66 in 1976—the lowest ever up to now. A subsequent small rise, coupled with

1. *Statistical Abstract of the United States, 1980*, p. 18.
2. *Historical Statistics of the United States, Colonial Times to 1970*, p. 49; and *Statistical Abstract of the United States, 1980*, p. 62.

Table 4-1. *United States Population Growth, 1790–1980*

Decade ending in	Rural population growth		Urban population growth		Total population growth			Births (thousands)	Gross immigration	
	Thousands	Percent	Thousands	Percent	Thousands	Percent	Percent urban		Thousands	Percent of all growth
1800	1,258	33.7	120	59.4	1,378	35.1	8.7	n.a.	n.a.	n.a.
1810	1,728	34.7	203	63.0	1,931	36.4	10.5	n.a.	n.a.	n.a.
1820	2,231	33.2	168	32.0	2,399	33.1	7.0	n.a.	n.a.	n.a.
1830	2,794	31.2	434	62.6	3,228	34.5	13.4	n.a.	152	4.7
1840	3,485	29.7	718	63.7	4,203	32.7	17.1	n.a.	599	14.2
1850	4,424	29.1	1,699	92.1	6,123	35.9	27.7	n.a.	1,713	28.0
1860	5,579	28.4	2,673	75.4	8,252	35.6	32.4	n.a.	2,598	31.5
1870	3,429	13.6	3,685	59.3	7,114	22.6	51.8	n.a.	2,315	32.5
1880	7,370	25.7	4,228	42.7	11,598	30.1	36.4	n.a.	2,812	24.2
1890	4,815	13.4	7,976	56.4	12,791	25.5	62.4	n.a.	5,247	41.0
1900	4,994	12.2	8,054	36.4	13,048	20.7	61.7	n.a.	3,688	28.3
1910	4,138	9.0	11,839	39.2	15,977	21.0	74.1	n.a.	8,795	55.0
1920	1,580	3.2	12,159	28.9	13,739	14.9	88.5	28,995	5,736	41.7
1930	2,267	4.4	14,797	27.3	17,064	16.1	86.7	28,250	4,107	24.1
1940	3,426	6.4	5,469	7.9	8,895	7.2	61.5	24,315	528	5.9
1950	4,524	7.9	14,503	19.5	19,027	14.4	76.2	32,739	1,035	5.4
1950[a]	−3,016	−4.8	22,044	29.6	19,028	14.4	115.9	32,739	1,035	5.4
1960	−176	−0.3	28,801	29.8	28,625	19.0	100.6	41,167	2,515	8.8
1970	−322	−0.6	24,234	19.3	23,912	13.3	101.3	38,280	3,322	13.9
1980	5,885	11.0	17,384	11.6	23,269	11.4	74.7	30,567[b]	3,502[c]	30.7[d]

Sources: Calculated from U.S. Census Bureau, *Historical Statistics of the United States: Colonial Times to 1970*, pp. 8, 11–12, 49, 105; *Statistical Abstract of the United States, 1980;* and preliminary published 1980 Census estimates.

n.a. Not available.

a. New definition of "urban" includes all incorporated and unincorporated places above 2,500 in population.

b. Incomplete decade: April 1, 1970, to July 1, 1979. *Statistical Abstract of the United States, 1980*, p. 13.

c. Incomplete decade: 1971–78. Ibid., p. 93.

d. Gross immigration 1971–78 as a percent of estimated population growth 1971–78 (*Statistical Abstract of the United States, 1979*, p. 6). This is probably an overestimate of the actual percent of growth, because the 1980 Census revealed recent-year population totals to be underestimates.

Table 4-2. *United States Population, 1790–1980*

Year	Total population: Thousands	Total population: Percent urban	Rural population (thousands)		Population in cities of 50,000 or more: Thousands	Population in cities of 50,000 or more: As percent of total U.S. population
1790	3,929	5.1	3,728		0	0
1800	5,308	6.1	4,986		61	1.1
1810	7,240	7.2	6,714		150	2.1
1820	9,638	7.2	8,945		251	2.6
1830	12,866	8.8	11,739		425	3.3
1840	17,069	10.8	15,224		705	4.1
1850	23,192	15.3	19,648		1,459	6.3
1860	31,443	19.8	25,227		3,091	9.8
1870	39,818	28.0	28,656		4,898	12.3
1880	50,156	28.2	36,026		7,159	14.3
1890	62,947	35.1	40,841		11,726	18.6
1900	75,995	39.7	45,835		16,916	22.3
1910	91,972	45.7	49,973		24,481	26.6
			Farm	*Nonfarm*		
1920	105,711	51.2	31,359	20,047	33,055	31.3
1930	122,775	56.2	30,158	23,663	42,817	34.8
1940	131,669	56.5	30,216	27,029	45,333	34.4
1950	150,697	59.0	23,077	38,693	53,520	35.5
1950[a]	150,697	64.0	23,048	31,181	53,243	35.3
1960	179,323	69.9	13,475	40,567	64,849	36.2
1970	203,235	73.6	8,292	45,587	73,188	36.0
1980	226,505	73.7	n.a.	n.a.	n.a.	n.a.

Sources: *Historical Statistics of the United States: Colonial Times to 1970;* and preliminary published 1980 Census estimates. Rural from series A-69 (pp. 11–12); farm-nonfarm from series A-73 (p. 13); cities of 50,000 or more from series A-58-62 (pp. 11–12); total from series A1-5 (p. 8).

n.a. Not available.

a. New definition of "urban" includes incorporated and unincorporated places over 2,500 in population.

a substantial increase in the number of women of childbearing age, has made the absolute number of births rise since then.

Migration from Farms

The ascendency of urban growth after 1880 was caused in part by large flows of people from rural to urban pursuits, due both to high birth rates on farms and to technical improvements and capital accumulation in agriculture. The number of persons living on farms rose throughout the nineteenth century, peaked at 32.5 million in 1916, and then decreased slowly to 30.2 million in 1940. After that, farm population plummeted. Net migration from farms exceeded one million people annually between 1940 and 1960. By 1979, only 7.5 million people lived on farms; consequently, migration from farms to urban areas dropped sharply in the 1970s. These changes, prompted in part by rising urban wage rates, were until recently an important source of urban growth. For example, the mechanization of cotton harvesting in the South during the 1950s and early 1960s displaced millions of black sharecroppers, many of whom moved to large cities.

Wars

Three major wars in U.S. history have accelerated urbanization. Urban growth jumped to over half of all growth during the Civil War decade, fell back in the 1870s, and then exceeded 60 percent in every decade thereafter. In the decade of World War I, urban growth again escalated, and it remained high in the 1920s. After the depression slowdown, World War II renewed overall growth and stimulated urban growth, raising its share back to 76 percent in the 1940s.

National Economic Conditions

Aggregate levels of employment and unemployment in the national economy have strongly affected rates of growth and decline of large cities. During national recessions or economic slow-growth periods, unemployment rates tend to be higher in large cities than elsewhere. (See tables 3-5, 3-6, and 3-7.) During the depression, the nation's total population growth fell by almost half, and urban growth dropped over twenty percentage points to a 62 percent share. Conversely, during periods of prosperity when the national unemployment rate is low, local variations among unemployment rates become smaller, both regionally and between the city and suburbs within each metropolitan area.[3]

On the other hand, inflation has injured big-city governments by raising their costs faster than their revenues, especially in the 1970s, thereby putting them in a "fiscal squeeze."[4] By the early 1980s, inflation had also raised interest rates to high levels, reducing the ability of municipal

3. See Elizabeth A. Roistacher, Margaret C. Simms, and Andrea Mills, "Recession and the Cities: Metropolitan Structure and Unemployment over the Business Cycle," paper presented at the American Economic Association meeting in Chicago, August 30, 1978.

4. See U.S. Advisory Commission on Intergovernmental Relations, *State-Local Finances in Recession and Inflation: An Economic Analysis*, Commission Report A-70 (GPO, 1979).

governments to float long-term bonds at relatively low cost. But the advent of high *real* interest rates in the 1980s greatly increased the true cost of capital, which in turn provided several benefits to large cities. Construction of new housing slowed, and the economic attraction of existing structures increased, reducing the tendency of new suburban housing to draw households out of older in-city units. Higher capital costs motivated people to conserve space by occupying smaller units and accepting higher residential densities. Unfortunately, these conflicting impacts of inflation upon urban growth and decline have not been quantified. Nevertheless, it appears that severely declining cities are probably *relatively* better off during periods of prosperity—even including inflation—than during periods of recession or slow economic growth.

Transportation

The long-run shift to automobiles and trucks for transportation greatly affected urban growth and decline during the twentieth century, exerting a decentralizing influence on urban settlement. In 1945, there were 29.5 million cars, trucks, and buses in use in the United States—one for every 4.8 persons. By 1979, the number of such vehicles had soared to over 137 million, one for every 1.6 persons.[5] If trucks are included, about 50 percent of all households had more than one vehicle as of 1979, and only about one in six had no vehicle.

The resulting increase in mobility reduced the relative attractiveness, to both households and business firms, of large older cities. Older cities tend to have inadequate parking space and relatively narrow streets prone to congestion. Furthermore, one of their advantages over lower-density settlements—easier access on foot or by public transportation—has been rendered less important. An indication of this is the 72 percent drop in the number of passengers carried by public transit systems, from the all-time high of 23.4 million in 1946 to a low of 6.6 million in 1972. Massive federal and local subsidies were required to raise the number to 7.6 million in 1977.[6]

Another important change in transportation is the rise in air travel. The number of revenue passengers carried on scheduled airlines soared from 19 million in 1950 to 317 million in 1979. General use of private planes

5. *Statistical Abstract of the United States*, 1980, p. 651; and Anthony Downs, "The Automotive Population Explosion," *Traffic Quarterly*, vol. 33 (July 1979), pp. 347–53 (Brookings reprint 353).

6. American Public Transit Association, *Transit Fact Book*, various years.

increased even faster. From 1960 to 1977, the number of airports in the United States more than doubled; the number of active general aviation aircraft rose 141 percent; hours flown in general aviation (excluding major commercial carriers) increased 173 percent; and domestic air cargo revenue ton-miles flown rose 370 percent.[7] Major commercial airports require large amounts of space and create unpleasant noise. Though a few older airports near downtowns still function (as in Washington, Boston, and San Diego), the newest ones have been built in suburban areas many miles from existing downtowns (as in Dallas-Ft. Worth, Houston, and Kansas City). These sites have attracted other business activities, as did passenger stations in the era of rail travel. Hence their increased importance has exerted a decentralizing impact upon urban growth patterns. Air travel has also integrated many distant urban areas into the nation's mainstream both economically and socially.

Technological Change

Technological change rooted in the national economy has had important effects on urbanization. Almost universal access to telephones has been an essential ingredient permitting relatively low-density settlements to function efficiently. Industrial plant designs favoring one-story layouts, enclosed-mall shopping centers, increased use of computers, and other communication improvements have aided dispersal of economic activity from more densely developed cities.

Location and Status of Minority Groups

Racial segregation and discrimination have also influenced American urban development. Three trends have been especially significant: rapid urbanization of the black population since 1940, expanded civil rights for all minority groups after 1960, and large-scale immigration of Hispanics into big cities since 1960.

In 1940, 49 percent of all blacks lived in urban areas, compared to 57 percent of all other groups. From 1940 to 1960, many Southern blacks moved from farms to cities because of both wartime production needs and technological displacement of farm labor; this reduced the black farm population from 4.5 million to 1.5 million in twenty years, as the black urban population grew by 7.5 million.

7. *Statistical Abstract of the United States, 1980*, p. 669.

Table 4-3. *Racial and Ethnic Characteristics of Cities*

Description	*Number of cities*	*Percentage of city population black, 1970*	*Change in percentage of city population black, 1960–70*	*Percentage of city population Hispanic, 1970*
Cities by region				
All	153	17.1	2.7	6.3
Northeast	28	17.4	6.5	4.0
North Central	41	14.2	3.4	2.1
South	52	25.3	0.7	7.1
West	32	7.3	1.8	12.3
First cities by cluster				
All	121	18.7	2.8	6.1
Growing city in growing SMSA	44	14.5	−0.4	11.0
Stagnant city in growing SMSA	32	18.0	2.1	2.7
Severely declining city in growing SMSA	19	24.0	6.2	3.4
Stagnant city in declining SMSA	11	16.1	4.8	5.5
Severely declining city in declining SMSA	15	27.4	7.8	2.7

Blacks became more concentrated than whites in large central cities. In 1980, 58 percent of all blacks in the United States lived in central cities, compared to 25 percent of all whites. Consequently, the percentage of central-city black residents rose from 12.2 in 1950 to 22.5 in 1980. As shown in table 4-3, the 153 largest cities averaged 17.1 percent black in 1970, and even higher in the South (25 percent) and in cities over 200,000 population in the Northeast and North Central regions (22 percent, data not shown). In 1980, eight large cities—Atlanta, Baltimore, Birmingham, Detroit, Gary, Newark, New Orleans, and Washington, D.C.—had a majority of black residents.

Because most black newcomers were poor, they tended to settle initially in low-income neighborhoods and move to better-quality areas after they got jobs and higher incomes. After the Supreme Court ruled racially restrictive covenants unconstitutional in 1948, this movement occurred more rapidly. Furthermore, the urban black population experienced a baby boom like that of the rest of the nation. Effectively barred by continuing racial discrimination from many outlying areas, blacks expanded mostly along the edges of existing ghettos, causing a dramatic racial transition of many neighborhoods in the course of a few years. In Chicago during the late 1950s and early 1960s, as many as five blocks per week were shifting from mainly white to mainly black occupancy.

Because the black population on average was poorer, had larger families with more school-age children, suffered from higher unemployment, and had greater welfare dependency than whites, this shift in the racial composition of big cities had impacts upon their fiscal as well as social nature. Moreover, movement of whites away from areas of racial transition became a major source of suburban growth. Table 4-3 indicates that cities losing the most population averaged a higher percentage of blacks in 1970 than other cities. However, a recent shift in the location choices of black households may reduce black centralization. From 1970 to 1979, only 39 percent of all black population growth took place inside central cities, whereas over half occurred in suburban areas.

Accurate information about Hispanic movements into and among U.S. urban areas is not available. The Census Bureau has not been collecting such data for long, and some of those movements involve illegal immigration. The limited available data indicate that over half the estimated 12.1 million persons of Spanish origin in the United States in 1979 lived in central cities, and one-third lived in metropolitan suburbs. In 1976, about 42 percent lived in the Western region. For individual cities, the most recent data are for 1970. As shown in table 4-3, the large city average was about 6 percent, with greater Hispanic concentrations in Southern and Western cities. Hialeah, Miami, El Paso, Corpus Christi, and San Antonio all had more than 40 percent Hispanic residents in 1970. In cities where it is most pronounced, the Hispanic inflow often leads to overcrowding. Twenty-two percent of Hispanics were in poverty in 1976, a lower incidence than among blacks (31 percent) but almost twice the overall U.S. rate. The newest immigrants are even poorer and tend to fill available housing in the lowest-income neighborhoods.

Growth in Real Income

Real personal income per capita in the United States in 1979 was 2.6 times as large as that in 1929, indicating an average growth of 2 percent compounded annually.[8] As individuals' incomes rise, they consume more goods and services, including residential space and amenities. In the United

8. Data sources for real (constant dollar) per capita personal income are *Historical Statistics of the United States*, p. 225, and *Statistical Abstract of the United States, 1980*, pp. 440, 486.

States, such increases in housing consumption are usually accomplished by moving to a higher-quality or larger house and lot. Thus, as the average income of U.S. residents has grown, the average density of developed residential areas has fallen. Within metropolitan areas, such upgrading moves reduce the density of already-built areas—generally central cities—and extend the edges of development by stimulating new housing construction. Furthermore, the nature of the U.S. urban development process tends to concentrate low-income housing in the oldest areas within an SMSA. For both these reasons, city incomes have generally not risen as fast as the national averages (see table 3-5).

Moreover, the creation of low-quality housing for occupancy by the poor is a normal part of urban development, as discussed in chapter 7. Therefore, in spite of average income gains, the normal process of urban development has caused some urban decline in nearly every SMSA.

Causes of Urban Decline in Individual Areas

Although average levels of urbanization or suburbanization can largely be traced to national historic trends and forces, the experience of individual areas varies widely. These differences occur for several reasons. First, some national trends have varying impact across areas. For example, as national income growth has lowered average residential densities and augmented suburbanization, areas with faster income growth have suburbanized more than other areas. Second, given the average urbanization trends, additional factors have affected location choices of households and firms *among* specific metropolitan areas. Similarly, local attributes affect the choice between city and suburban locations differently within each metropolitan area.

Overall, the growth of individual metropolitan areas, cities, and suburbs depends on the interaction of many general trends with local characteristics. This section organizes and describes what we believe are the most important theories regarding these interactive processes. The theories were mainly synthesized from an abundant literature which we do not attempt to review here; additional details and references are provided elsewhere.[9]

By a *theory*, we mean any hypothesis about behavior patterns explaining

9. Katharine L. Bradbury, Anthony Downs, and Kenneth A. Small, "Explaining Urban Decline: Theories and a Proposal for Testing," working paper (Brookings Institution, March 1979).

how they might contribute to either descriptive or functional urban decline. Our focus is mainly on descriptive decline, both because it is easier to measure and because we have already shown that there are important causal links between descriptive and functional decline. The relevant behavior patterns are largely the location decisions of households (classified by income) and business firms. Thus, the theories are mainly about why these actors may find one location more attractive than another. We have sorted the theories according to the underlying forces motivating this behavior. Our approach produced six groups of theories, summarized below, and thirty-seven component theories described in table 4-4.

Disamenity avoidance theories assert that people or business firms are moving away from central cities to suburbs, or from certain metropolitan areas to others, to avoid negative characteristics such as crime and high energy costs. Every move away from a negative characteristic is also implicitly a move toward a positive one, but we perceive the theories in this category as chiefly emphasizing the negative factors.

Tax avoidance theories claim that households or firms move to the suburbs because various characteristics of large cities make local tax burdens (especially on households with high and middle incomes) heavier there than in many surrounding suburbs.

Positive attraction theories state that people or business firms are moving from central cities to the suburbs, or from some metropolitan areas to others, in order to obtain desired amenities. The amenities being sought range from lower density to better employment opportunities.

Economic evolution theories postulate that large urban areas, and specific activities within them, undergo definite stages of development. This evolution alters the optimal combination and location of activities in ways unfavorable to maintaining those activities within large cities.

Biased policy theories assert that certain government policies influencing the location of public and private investments, households, and economic activities are biased in favor of suburbs and against central cities, or in favor of some areas and against others.

Demographic trend theories state that certain population growth trends have impacts adverse to some cities and metropolitan areas.

A Strategy for Empirical Testing

The theories listed in table 4-4 encompass most hypotheses that have been offered to explain decline in the size and functions of cities and

Table 4-4. *Theories Explaining Differences in Urban Growth and Decline*

Disamenity avoidance theories

1. Households and firms avoid locating in cities with high crime rates and insecurity.
2. The "trickle-down" process of urban development leads to concentrations of low-income households within older portions of some large cities. The desire not to live in such neighborhoods causes high- and middle-income households to avoid or withdraw from those areas with the highest concentrations.
3. The poor quality of education offered by many public schools in large cities causes high- and middle-income households with children to avoid those cities.
4. Mandated racial desegregation of public schools in large cities causes many households with school-age children to leave those cities.
5. The desire of many households to avoid living in black neighborhoods causes significant withdrawal of white households from cities with large black populations.
6. Deteriorating public transit service from 1945 through 1975 removed much of the accessibility advantage of big city locations.
7. Cities with high levels of air pollution or other disamenities such as traffic congestion are less attractive to households.
8. Once decline begins, investors are afraid to put more funds into facilities in declining areas because they believe no one will purchase their properties when they want to sell.
9. Higher costs of living in certain regions—especially the Northeast and Midwest—encourage movement of households and businesses to lower-cost regions—especially the South.
10. Higher energy costs and a less certain energy supply availability in certain regions—notably the Northeast—encourage households and businesses to move to regions where energy is less expensive and more likely to be available without interruption.

Tax avoidance theories

11. The per capita cost of providing urban public services tends to rise with size and density; so many residents and firms reduce their tax burdens by moving to smaller communities.
12. Because of fixed costs in past public infrastructure investments and various forms of social overhead, the loss of population and jobs from a city does not proportionally reduce the costs of providing public services; so tax burdens on firms and households there will rise. This provides an incentive for firms and households to move elsewhere.
13. Central city governments' attempts to redistribute incomes by subsidizing services to the poor and more heavily taxing affluent households provide an incentive for the latter to move to suburban communities where high- and middle-income households are politically dominant, and the net burden of taxes minus services received is lower.
14. The inability of older cities in the Northeast and Midwest to annex growing suburban territories (as many Southern and Western cities do) prevents them from "diluting" higher per capita costs of providing service in inner-city areas with lower-density areas that have lower per capita public service costs. This raises relative per capita tax burdens in such cities and contributes to outmigration of households and firms.

Positive attraction theories

15. Americans prefer low-density residential living; so as their real incomes rise, they move away from higher-density cities. In technical urban economics terms, urban density gradients flatten as average incomes rise.
16. Many business firms also prefer low-density workplaces; so they choose locations where land is less costly and more easily available.

Table 4-4 *(continued)*

17. American households find it economically advantageous to upgrade by moving out of older structures and into areas where newer ones are available.
18. Many individual decisions to migrate are influenced by the relative economic opportunities available. Hence locations that offer relatively poor economic opportunities are likely to experience net outmigration, while those that offer better economic opportunities are likely to experience net inmigration.
19. Many workers want to live near their jobs, and some business firms want to be near the population from which they draw their workers or to which they supply goods or services. Therefore, as more jobs move to new locations, more workers do too—and as more people move there, so do more jobs.
20. Americans prefer temperate climates and enjoy outdoor recreation. As average incomes rise and technological advances, such as air conditioning, reduce the drawbacks, people locate in areas with warmer climates.
21. Long-term increases in automobile ownership favor residential and business choices of less densely developed locations.
22. Long-term declines in transportation costs reduce the advantage of central locations. In technical urban economics terms, transportation improvements and cost reductions flatten urban density gradients.
23. Newer cities and suburbs have been built to accommodate automobiles and automobile travel; hence they are attractive to persons who value the life-style associated with intense automobile usage.
24. Newer cities and suburbs have also been built to accommodate trucks and truck travel; hence they are more attractive than older cities to business firms that rely heavily on road transport.
25. For historical reasons, some areas have been a focus of migration for individual racial or ethnic groups. Once a concentration of a particular group occurs, it attracts additional members of that group to the area.

Economic evolution theories

26. New firms are more easily "incubated" in large cities where innovative stimuli are greatest and a diversity of ancillary services can be readily obtained. But once established, many firms move to smaller communities where labor and other costs are lower.
27. Some cities have heavy concentrations of industries that had their fastest-growth periods in the past, but now exhibit the slower growth typical of "mature" industries. Therefore, the particular mix of industrial activities in those cities causes them to have slower-than-average economic growth.
28. More jobs located in some cities are becoming white-collar jobs as office work replaces manufacturing—but a large fraction of the workers living in such cities are blue-collar workers. The resulting "mismatch" of jobs and workers produces slow growth of incomes there.
29. As suburban areas grow, they eventually become large enough to support production or distribution facilities that formerly were located in central cities and served suburbs as part of their overall markets. The establishment of those facilities within the suburbs reduces the markets remaining within the central cities, thereby decreasing employment there. (An example is the creation of outlying department store branches.)
30. As a metropolitan area's population and employment increase overall, the central city does not grow proportionally because it is already more densely developed. This and the preceding theory both imply that metropolitan areas tend to extend over a wider

Table 4-4 (*continued*)

area and display flatter density gradients as their total population and employment grow.

31. As population or employment decreases in an entire metropolitan area, the central city loses at a faster rate than the area as a whole because it contains the oldest capital stock (housing, sewer and water systems, streets, commercial and industrial buildings, etc.). So cities in declining SMSAs decline relatively faster.

Biased policy theories

32. Some federal policies and programs contain biases favoring new construction on vacant land over renovation or maintenance of existing structures in already-built-up areas. (This theory could be broken down into many separate theories, each focusing on one particular form of such bias.)
33. Large indirect subsidies to homeownership, built into the federal income tax system, encourage occupancy of single-family dwellings, which are more likely to be located in suburbs or new cities.
34. Some federal policies and programs contain biases favoring the South and West. The fractions of federal funds spent for those policies and programs in the favored regions are much larger than their proportional share of the nation's total population, employment, federal tax revenues, etc.
35. Federal income taxes do not have varied rates in different parts of the nation or otherwise recognize the wide variations in the cost of living. This produces higher effective tax rates (in relation to real incomes) in higher-living-cost areas, thereby encouraging high-income households and firms to move to places with lower living costs.

Demographic trend theories

36. The demographic composition of population in each metropolitan area—especially its age structure—has a big impact upon the rate of natural increase that population generates, and therefore upon its rate of growth.
37. Cities and metropolitan areas experiencing net outmigration are likely to lose more persons with relatively high skills and incomes than they gain because such persons tend to move more readily in response to opportunities. Thus, net outmigration may reduce the average skill and income level in areas experiencing it.

metropolitan areas in the United States. More broadly, they explain interarea *differences* in growth rates, so they are equally applicable in examining the experience of growing areas.

The observed net changes in city population, jobs, or income which cause concern are almost always the result of an imbalance between much larger gross flows. Inmigrants, births, deaths, and outmigrants contribute to population flows. Total employment changes as firms are created or die, move in or out of the area, or expand or contract in place. Changes in average resident income reflect the relative incomes of inmigrants and outmigrants as well as changes in the incomes of stable residents. Each force identified in the theories, by influencing one or several of these gross

Table 4-5. *Strategy for Empirical Testing*[a]

Theory	*Population*		*Employment*		*Income*	
	SMSA growth	*Suburbanization*	*SMSA growth*	*Suburbanization*	*SMSA growth*	*Suburbanization*
Disamenity avoidance						
1. High crime rates	?	X	...	X	...	X
2. Trickle-down	...	X	...	...	...	X
3. Low-quality education	...	X	...	...	...	X
4. School desegregation	...	X	...	...	...	X
5. Race	...	X	...	...	...	X
6. Deteriorating transit	...	X	...	X	...	...
7. Air pollution	?	X	...	...	...	...
8. Investor fears	?	?	?	?	...	...
9. Living costs	X	...	X	...	X	...
10. Energy costs	X	...	X	...	X	...
Tax avoidance						
11. Size and density	?	X	?	X	...	...
12. Fixed costs	?	X	?	X	...	X
13. Redistribution	...	X	...	...	...	X
14. Annexation	...	X	...	X	...	...
Positive attraction						
15. Low-density living	?	X	...	...	...	X
16. Low-density workplace	...	...	?	X	...	...
17. Move, not renovate	...	X	...	...	...	X
18. Economic opportunity	X	?	X	?	X	X
19. Jobs follow people and vice versa	X	X	X	X	...	...
20. Climate	X	...	...	...	...	...
21. Auto ownership	...	X	...	X	...	...
22. Transport cost declines	...	X	...	X	...	...
23. Auto life-style	X	X	...	...	...	...
24. Truck accessibility	...	...	X	X	...	...
25. Ethnic groups follow	X	X	...	...	...	...
Economic evolution						
26. Incubation	...	...	?	X	...	...
27. Industry mix	...	...	X	X	...	...
28. Mismatch	...	...	...	...	...	X
29. Suburban size	...	...	...	X	...	...
30. Central density	...	X	...	X	...	...
31. Obsolescence	...	X	...	X	...	...
Biased policy						
32. New construction	...	X	...	X	...	...
33. Homeownership	...	X	...	...	...	...
34. Federal funds location	X	...	X	...	...	...
35. Income taxes	X	...	...	...	X	...

Table 4-5 (*continued*)

Theory	Population: SMSA growth	Population: Suburbanization	Employment: SMSA growth	Employment: Suburbanization	Income: SMSA growth	Income: Suburbanization
Demographic trends						
36. Age structure	X	?	. . .	. . .	. . .	. . .
37. Selective outmigration	. . .	. . .	. . .	. . .	X	X

a. X = theory relates to this type of change; ? = theory may be relevant; . . . = theory not applicable.

flows even slightly, may substantially affect the net outcome. The actual strength of each such interaction, and thus the relative importance of these theories, can be determined only through empirical evidence. To facilitate the presentation of such evidence in the next chapter, table 4-5 lists the theories and indicates whether the hypothesized behavior in each primarily affects population, employment, or income; and whether at an inter- or intrametropolitan level. The empirical testing consists of a set of simultaneous equations, one for each column of table 4-5, intended to represent as many of the hypothesized influences as possible with available data.

5

Testing Theories of Urban Decline

THE preceding chapter presented hypotheses about the sources of urban decline. This chapter tests the validity and importance of some of them. First we present a simple decomposition of the sources of city population growth over the period 1960–75. The next section outlines the general framework in which the specific tests are undertaken—a set of simultaneous regressions—and briefly describes some of the methodological problems involved in such tests. Then we summarize the empirical results; the actual equation estimates are reported in appendix A to this chapter. The final section reviews the findings regarding individual theories.

Decomposition of Total City Population Change

The basic economic territory in which residents and businesses of an individual city operate is encompassed by the metropolitan area concept. Because of a policy focus on cities and an interest in the operation of city government and its effects, we retain our focus on what occurs within city borders. But it is folly to consider cities divorced from their metropolitan context; so we have separated city growth into two components: (1) the growth of the metropolitan area, which reflects its attractiveness relative to other metropolitan areas; and (2) the growth of the city relative to its metropolitan area, reflecting the city's attractiveness vis-à-vis its suburbs. There is a third component in the growth of some cities: population added through annexation of or consolidation with surrounding territory. Table 5-1 reports three ordinary least squares regressions that provide a simple

Table 5-1. *Regression Estimates for Decomposition of City Growth for 120 Cities and SMSAs*[a]

Independent variable	Period 1960–70	Period 1970–75	Period 1960–75
Constant	−11.51 (1.43)	−5.56 (0.64)	−16.87 (2.17)
SMSA population change in fixed boundaries (percent)	0.757 (0.058)	0.780 (0.069)	0.713 (0.060)
City annexation (percent increase in population)	0.891 (0.034)	1.178 (0.043)	1.011 (0.046)
R^2	0.8982	0.8918	0.8665
Standard error of the regression	10.3	5.66	16.5
$F_{2,117}$(F-statistic with [2, 117] degrees of freedom)	516	482	380
Addendum: Average contribution to total city population growth[b]			
Suburbanization (constant)	−11.5	−10.9	−11.6
SMSA growth	14.1	8.8	11.9
Annexation	11.7	6.7	10.8
Total city growth (percentage increase in a decade)	14.3	4.6	11.1

a. Dependent variables are total percentage change in city population for the periods shown. Standard errors are given in parentheses below the coefficients.
b. Estimated coefficients multiplied by sample mean values and expressed as decade rates.

breakdown of these basic contributors to city population growth over the period 1960 to 1975.[1]

The results indicate that if SMSA growth and annexation had both been zero, city population growth would still have been negative; that is, suburbanization of the (given) SMSA population occurred. Furthermore, the rate of this suburbanization was fairly constant over the period: 1.1 to 1.2 percent annually. The estimated coefficients on the SMSA growth rates indicate that cities received only about three-quarters of their "share," in percentage terms, of whatever metropolitan population growth (or decline) occurred. Annexation contributed population on about a one-for-one basis, as would be expected, suggesting that annexation simply added population without any strong feedback on the population within the original boundaries.[2]

1. Only 120 cities and SMSAs were used for this analysis because complicated SMSA boundary redefinitions eliminated one.

2. The annexation variable measures the population directly added through city boundary

In the lower panel of the table, the sample mean values have been multiplied by the estimated coefficients to provide an indication of the relative importance of the three components of the total change. In terms of annual rates, population growth for the average city slowed, from 1.3 percent per year in the 1960s to 0.4 percent per year in the early 1970s. But the nearly unchanged annual value of the suburbanization component shows that, contrary to popular belief, *the slowdown in average city population growth is almost entirely due to less metropolitan growth and fewer annexations, not to an increase in suburbanization.*

During the 1960s, annexations by city governments more than offset the underlying rate of suburbanization, on average. Between 1970 and 1975, annexation offset only 60 percent of the suburbanization. However, during both periods many cities had no annexation at all, while others had more than enough to offset local suburbanization. Because SMSA population growth slowed during the period, from an annual rate of 1.7 percent during the sixties to less than 1.1 percent during the first half of the seventies, its average contribution to city growth also lessened.[3]

These results are illuminating and appealing for their simplicity. However, we wish to understand the *processes* by which these changes, as well as changes in employment and income, occur. That is, we need to test the theories of decline presented in the previous chapters to see which offer viable explanations for the wide variation in growth and suburbanization.

---

changes as a percentage of the initial city population. The estimated coefficients are near one, although statistically the 1970–75 estimate is significantly greater than one and the 1960–70 coefficient is significantly below one, at the 0.01 level of significance. The full period 1960–75 coefficient is indistinguishable from one. These differences from one reflect the correlation in each period between annexation and growth in fixed boundaries. During the 1960s, the correlation was negative; during the 1970s, it was positive. Thus the annexation coefficient is picking up a small amount of the suburbanization and/or SMSA growth components.

3. R. D. Norton, in *City Life Cycles and American Urban Policy* (Academic Press, 1979), performed a similar analysis for the thirty largest cities (as of 1970), using data for the 1950–70 and 1970–75 periods. He used slightly different measures of metropolitan area growth and annexation: namely, urbanized area (not SMSA) growth rate, and the percentage increase in the city's incorporated territory (not population in that territory). Norton found that between 1950 and 1970, in the absence of metropolitan growth and annexation, the large cities on average would have lost 62 percent of their population. He estimated a one-for-one correspondence between city and urbanized area growth rates, and a small (but significant) effect of annexation. For 1970–75, he obtained results somewhat similar to ours, although with a higher suburbanization rate (8.6 percent over the five years), and lower capture rate (60 percent) of the urbanized area growth rate. When we re-estimated our version of the equation using his sample of thirty large cities, we obtained results for 1970–75 between those shown in table 5-1 and his. Even allowing for these differences, it appears there has been a substantial slowdown in the rate of suburbanization since the 1950s.

To do this, we estimated the much more detailed set of equations presented below.

Testing the Theories

The basic framework used to test the theories is a set of cross-section regressions performed on 121 cities and their metropolitan areas for the time period 1970 to 1975. The cities are the largest in their SMSAs (as defined in 1975).[4] We also estimated similar regressions on a smaller subsample of the cities (for which consistent data are available) for the 1960–70 period. To examine both functional and descriptive decline, we used three dependent variables: changes in population, employment, and per capita income. Employment and population are measures of *descriptive* decline or growth; per capita income change is a *functional* indicator.

Although our discussion focuses upon urban *decline*, most of the hypotheses can be construed more broadly as explanations of *changes* in conditions, whether positive or negative. Thus our sample includes cities that are gaining in population, jobs, or income per capita as well as cities that are "declining" along these dimensions. The regression framework allows us to evaluate the important causative differences between growing and declining areas. Decline is not a single uniform process even among declining cities, but rather the outcome of a variety of factors locally present. The regressions sort out the effects of these separate factors, and estimate the *independent* contribution of each, controlling for all the others.

One problem in measuring population, employment, and per capita income change in cities and SMSAs is that their boundaries change over time. SMSA boundaries change as the Census Bureau adds or subtracts counties (towns in New England) to reflect patterns of economic integration. We used a set of fixed boundaries in examining SMSA growth and decline—1975 boundaries for the 1970–75 analysis, and 1970 boundaries for the 1960–70 analysis.[5] For cities, the choice between actual and fixed boundaries is less obvious. As an indicator of the city's likely health, total change may be useful, but because we are attempting to understand household and business *location* decisions, fixed boundaries are more appropriate.[6]

4. See the list of first cities in table 3-9.

5. For 1960–70 SMSA employment growth, we used constant 1960 boundaries, since we could develop 1970 employment data for these boundary definitions but not vice versa.

6. Income data are not available for fixed city boundaries, so we used actual income change as the dependent variable and included estimates of the effect of annexation on city income as explanatory variables in those equations.

Thus of the three components decomposed by the previous equation, we restricted our attention to the "SMSA growth" and "suburbanization" components, and did not attempt to explain the annexation component.

To derive the two components from a city's constant-boundary rate of growth or decline, we used an additive decomposition. The percentage change in city population (jobs, per capita income) during a period can be expressed as:

$$\Delta C = \Delta M + (\Delta C - \Delta M),$$

$$\begin{matrix} \text{city} & & \text{SMSA} & & \text{city relative} \\ \text{growth} & = & \text{growth} & + & \text{to SMSA} \\ \text{rate} & & \text{rate} & & \text{growth rate} \end{matrix}$$

where C and M are city and SMSA population (or jobs or per capita income), and Δ indicates percentage change over a period of time.

An alternative approach would be to analyze the difference between city and suburban growth rates rather than city and SMSA rates. The two approaches are essentially equivalent, and differ only in convenience of presentation. The city versus SMSA distinction has the advantage that we need only sum the two parts to obtain the city growth rate. More important, we consider the SMSA the basic economic market area, and hence are interested in how well the city performs in maintaining its share of that area's economic activity.

Thus we planned to estimate, for each of the three measures, two equations: one explaining the metropolitan growth rate, the other explaining relative city growth. This would be six equations for each time period. Unfortunately, data on employment in cities are lacking for 1975, so we estimated only five basic equations for 1970–75:

Percent change in SMSA population;
Percent change in SMSA employment;
Percent change in SMSA real per capita income;
City minus SMSA percent change in population;
City minus SMSA percent change in real per capita income.

For 1960–70, we estimated these five equations plus the sixth:

City minus SMSA percent change in employment.

The Growth and Decline of SMSAs and Cities Relative to Their SMSAs

We tested so many hypotheses about what causes urban decline that we cannot concisely report the equations with all the relevant variables included. Instead, we present "pared down" versions in which variables that consistently showed no significant association with the dependent variables are excluded, provided doing so did not appreciably alter the other results.

The Growth and Decline of SMSAs

As described in chapter 3, the 121 SMSAs included in our sample experienced an average 1970–75 population growth of 5.6 percent inside 1975 boundaries.[7] Twenty-six of the SMSAs lost population over the period. The sample ranged from a 7 percent loss in Columbus (Georgia) to growth of 38 percent in Austin. For employment, the average five-year growth was 11.7 percent, and only 15 SMSAs showed declines; the range was wide, from −24 percent to +49 percent. Real per capita income growth[8] averaged 9.9 percent over the period 1969–74, ranging from a 2 percent loss in Stamford (the only SMSA to decline in real income) to 20 percent growth in Birmingham. During the 1960s, for 97 SMSAs,[9] average population growth was 18.6 percent over the ten years, employment growth averaged 19.3 percent, and real income per capita expanded by an average of 30.7 percent. These data suggest the wide variety of SMSA experiences, a variety our regression equations are reasonably successful in explaining.

We found the following to be the most important relationships in determining *SMSA population growth* (each statement should be read with the implicit qualification "holding all other factors constant"):[10]

7. Throughout this discussion, the percentage changes cited refer to the entire five- or ten-year period in question; they are not *annual* rates unless explicitly noted. Similarly, we use the term growth "rate" to refer to percentage changes over the entire period. The terms "average" and "mean" refer, unless otherwise noted, to a simple unweighted average of the SMSAs or cities in our sample.

8. We inflated all income figures to 1975 dollars using the national consumer price index, and refer to these figures as *real* income; they are *not* adjusted for interarea differences in price levels, mainly because data for the latter are more limited and less reliable than the income data.

9. The 97 SMSAs used in the 1960–70 analysis were those for which we could ascertain employment in 1960 boundaries for both 1960 and 1970.

10. In a regression framework, the *t*-statistic and beta coefficient are two different means to judge the importance of a particular explanatory variable or factor. The *t*-statistic provides a test of the hypothesis that the variable has no explanatory power at all: more precisely, that the true coefficient on this factor in the regression equation is zero. The regression coefficient itself is an estimate of the effect of a change in the explanatory factor on the dependent variable, and the *t*-statistic (or the standard error of the estimated coefficient from which it is calculated) also indicates how precisely this effect is measured and hence how much confidence one has in the specific estimate. The coefficient may be measured or estimated very precisely, that is, one has a great deal of confidence that the true effect of this variable

—Where SMSA employment was growing faster over the same period, so was population.

—Where the SMSA unemployment rate was initially higher or income initially lower, population growth was slower. The unemployment effect was important for 1970–75; whereas income served as the secondary indicator of economic opportunities available to migrants (the primary indicator in both periods being job growth) for 1960–70.

—SMSAs with warmer climates (mean January temperatures) grew faster.

—Areas where the percent of Hispanic population in the SMSA's largest city or the percent of black population in the SMSA (outside the South) was higher grew faster; migrants went to places peopled by others of similar race or ethnicity, and the dominant minority migrants were black in the 1960s and Hispanic in the early 1970s.

—During the 1960s, SMSAs with higher population density grew more slowly.

Thus each area's economy, climate, and ethnic composition were critical to households' choices among metropolitan areas. The first finding on the list means that people followed jobs. For both time periods, the estimated coefficient is less than one, indicating that labor force migration responds less than fully, within any fixed period, to changing employment opportunities. But in both periods, this was the most important source of differences among areas in population growth.

Because employment growth is such an important factor in population

---

is very close to the estimated effect, and at the same time, the effect may be very small. The beta coefficient, in contrast, measures the effect on the dependent variable of a standard deviation of change in the factor, divided by the sample variation in the dependent variable. Since the standard deviation of any factor is a characteristic of the *sample data* on that factor, this provides an indication of how big a change in the dependent variable a "reasonable" change in the factor would cause, with "reasonable" defined on the basis of the actual range of variable values that occur in the sample.

For our purposes, both these measures are relevant, so the lists of "important" factors that follow include only those satisfying both these criteria. In fact, we rarely found the two criteria in conflict, even regarding the ranking of important factors for each equation. We are interested in both types of "importance" because we use these results for several purposes. The beta coefficient provides a useful summary indicator of the major sources of variation across SMSAs in growth and suburbanization during the sample period. However, in analyzing the importance of likely future trends, the estimated coefficient itself and the confidence we have in it are more relevant. This is because the structural coefficients are used to *predict* the effect of hypothesized changes in the explanatory factors on SMSA growth and suburbanization, and the size of future changes may not be at all the same as the recently observed variations among SMSAs.

growth, the determinants of the former are of special interest. Our equations found the following relationships to be important in explaining variations in *SMSA employment growth* rates:

—SMSAs with greater population growth over the same period, through both natural increase and migration, gained more employment.

—SMSAs with high or increasing levels of real per capita income gained jobs more rapidly.

—SMSAs with favorable industry mix (a high concentration of industries with fast national growth rates or containing state capitals) grew faster.

—SMSAs with high or increasing cost of living[11] grew more slowly (data not available for the 1960s).

—Higher SMSA local taxes per capita were associated with slower SMSA job growth during the 1960s.

—SMSAs with greater urbanized area population density or a greater absolute number of jobs at the beginning of the period grew more slowly.

In sum, firms seemed to respond to the strength of local markets and costs of doing business in making decisions about location, relocation, expansion, and contraction. Just as people followed jobs, employment responded to growth in population. Presumably, this reflects an increase in local production to meet local consumption demands, as well as employer decisions to locate near available labor pools. Within each time period, the estimated response of jobs to population growth, in percentage terms, was greater than the response of population to employment growth. This indicates, in a sense, that jobs followed population more fully or instantaneously than vice versa during these two periods. For both population and jobs, the response is more complete over the entire 1960s than during the first half of the 1970s, probably because the time period is longer.

SMSA *growth in real per capita income* was best explained by the following relationships:

—SMSAs with faster-growing employment had faster growth in per capita income.

—Population growth, especially through natural increase, diluted per capita income growth.

—SMSAs with initially high per capita income or high cost of living had slower income growth (cost-of-living data not available for the 1960s).

—SMSAs with high unemployment rates had slower income growth.

11. Local cost-of-living data are available only for thirty-three large SMSAs. We assigned to each SMSA in our sample the cost of living for the nearest of these thirty-three. The result is probably not very reliable, which is why we did not deflate incomes by the local measure.

—SMSAs with a high fraction of jobs in construction, retail and wholesale trade, transportation, utilities, and mining had faster income growth for 1970–75, but slower income growth for 1960–70.

—SMSAs where the cost of living was rising were compensated somewhat by increases in per capita income (data not available for the 1960s).

—SMSAs with higher percentages of black population had greater per capita income growth during the 1960s.

Thus the ability of the local economy to support the population was the most important determinant of income growth, but was modified somewhat by local cost of living, industry mix, and population composition.

Suburbanization

We examined the processes of intrametropolitan decentralization using the *largest* city in each of our 121 SMSAs. The average such city's population growth lagged 6.4 percentage points behind its SMSA's growth, the percentage-point difference ranging from −27 in Ft. Lauderdale to +10 in San Jose. In addition to San Jose, only seven cities grew faster than their SMSAs: Amarillo, Corpus Christi, Columbus (Georgia), Colorado Springs, El Paso, Springfield (Massachusetts), and Stockton.[12] City real income growth was also generally slower than SMSA growth, but the difference was considerably smaller—less than 2 percentage points on average. Twenty-two cities gained more income, in percentage terms, than their SMSAs, but for over half these cases the difference was less than 1 percentage point.

During the 1960s, cities also grew more slowly in population and income than did the metropolitan areas in which they were located, by about 19 and 5 percentage points, respectively. The gap was slightly less for jobs (17 percentage points) than for population. Among the eighty-seven cities available for analysis,[13] two grew faster in population, nine had more job growth, and ten had more income growth than their SMSAs.

12. Columbus was the only one of these eight losing population (but its SMSA lost more rapidly).

13. These eighty-seven cities were those for which employment data were available for *both* city and constant-boundary SMSA, 1960–70. Because we could not obtain constant-boundary city employment data, we *estimated* the percentage effect of annexation on city employment as equal to the effect on population. The regression coefficients indicate that this *under*estimates actual constant-boundary city employment growth over the period, probably because annexed fringe areas were likely to contain relatively more population than jobs.

Just as for SMSA growth and decline, city changes relative to their SMSAs occurred in many forms. Although the equations we estimated for relative city growth, in general, do not "fit" the data as closely as the SMSA equations, they do pinpoint some important factors in suburbanization.

Many of the theories outlined in chapter 4 related most directly to the suburbanization of population within metropolitan areas. Our tests of these hypotheses indicated that the following relationships were most important for *relative population growth rate of cities* during the 1970–75 period:

—Cities with only a small share of SMSA population and in fast-growing SMSAs lagged further behind their SMSAs.

—Cities with a greater concentration of old housing than their SMSAs grew relatively more slowly.

—SMSAs with a higher percent of Hispanic population tended to experience less suburbanization.

—Except in the South, cities with a high percent of black population relative to that in the entire SMSA experienced more suburbanization.

—Cities whose school districts extended beyond their borders grew faster relative to their SMSAs than did cities in which the school district and city boundaries coincided.

—There was greater suburbanization in SMSAs containing a larger number of municipalities.

—Cities where local per capita taxes were high relative to the rest of the SMSA grew more slowly.

Some of these forces appear to have been at work in the 1960s as well. However, others had different effects in the two periods. For example, the SMSA growth rate and city share had no significant association with relative city growth in the 1960s. In addition, SMSA income growth, a suspected cause of suburbanization, was more important in the 1960s than in the early 1970s. Racial characteristics of city relative to SMSA had similar effects in both periods, as did the placement of school district boundaries serving the city, and the relative concentration of old housing in city and suburbs. The tax disparity measure was not available for 1960. Two additional factors emerged as important during the 1960s that were not detected for the early 1970s—excess new construction of housing in the SMSA and relative growth of city jobs. It appears that SMSA new housing construction (which, in an equation not reported here, was found to depend on more than just household location shifts) drew residents out of older housing in the city.[14] The employment finding (data not available for the 1970s)

14. In that equation, excess housing construction was treated as an endogenous variable.

indicates that where city jobs suburbanized faster, so did city population, although nowhere near one-for-one in percentage terms.

Thus intrametropolitan disparities in housing stock and racial composition, local governmental fragmentation, ethnic migration patterns, and job locations were critical to household choices between city and suburban residence.

We were able to examine the *difference between city and SMSA employment growth rates* only for the 1960s, and found the following relationships most significant:[15]

—Cities growing faster in residents (relative to SMSA population growth) were also doing so with respect to jobs.

—Cities in which income per capita was growing relatively more slowly than SMSA income showed slower relative job growth as well.

—Jobs suburbanized more in SMSAs in which unemployment was initially focused in the central city, apparently indicating that employers *avoided* high-unemployment areas within SMSAs.

—As in the population finding for 1970–75, cities with relatively higher shares of SMSA jobs and in SMSAs with slower job growth lagged less.

—Job suburbanization was greater in SMSAs with greater initial absolute employment.

Just as for choices among SMSAs, firms appear to be most responsive to the strength of the local market in choosing a specific location within a metropolitan area. Jobs follow people within as well as among metropolitan areas. Our results imply that a 10 percent decrease in city population (going to the suburbs) was associated with a 5 percent decrease in city jobs (choosing suburban locations instead). This is larger than the reverse association of only 2 percent population loss in response to 10 percent employment loss.[16] However, in contrast to the intermetropolitan case, local unemployment seems to set up a perverse reaction in which jobs move *away* from areas with high unemployment.

15. One additional variable appeared to be important in our estimated equation: the city population increase during the 1960s attributable to annexation. We believe this reflects not a real effect of annexation on employment growth, but rather a "correction" for our method of estimating constant-boundary city employment growth. The coefficient indicates that we overestimated the effect of annexation on city employment, and thereby underestimated constant-boundary employment growth (the dependent variable). Specifically, it appears that an average annexation adds only 62 percent as many jobs, proportionally, as population, while we had assumed 100 percent.

16. Donald N. Steinnes, "Causality and Intraurban Location," *Journal of Urban Economics*, vol. 4 (January 1977), pp. 69–79, is another study that found population rather than jobs to be the leading force in their simultaneous effects on postwar suburbanization.

The *relative income growth of a city* results from both changes in the incomes of initial residents and the relative incomes of new residents (either inmigrants or residents of areas annexed to the city), compared to changes in the SMSA. Our estimated equations indicate the following as important contributors to this process during the early 1970s:

—As would be expected, annexation raised or lowered average city income depending on whether the rest of the SMSA had higher or lower income than the city, and such changes were proportional to the magnitude of the annexation.

—Cities with faster population growth had relatively *slower* income growth for 1970–75, a result similar to that found for SMSAs.

—Cities with a high percentage of single-family homes compared to their SMSA attracted higher-income inmigrants.

—SMSAs with greater initial city-suburb income disparity showed less disparity in income growth rates.

—Cities with a relatively higher concentration of black population than their SMSAs showed slower relative income growth.

—Cities in SMSAs with faster employment growth lagged less behind the income growth of those SMSAs.

—Cities containing a greater share of the SMSA economic base—jobs—showed relatively greater income growth.

—Cities in fast-income-growth SMSAs lagged further behind those SMSAs, though on nowhere near a one-for-one basis.

During the 1960s, some of the same factors appear to have been important. However, the effect of city population growth was *opposite* that which prevailed in the early 1970s. That is, cities growing faster in the 1960s generally showed greater income growth, other things equal, although this effect is not very strong. In addition, relative city employment growth appeared to positively influence income growth; whereas for 1970–75, we found the opposite to be true (although the estimated effect was statistically weak) for employment growth in *manufacturing*. It may be that manufacturing employment creates disamenities for higher-income people, while total employment attracts them and also helps generate local incomes. SMSA economic growth and single-family housing in the city had virtually no effect in the 1960s.

These income results are not easily summarized.[17] The intrametropolitan

17. The explanatory power of the 1970-75 city relative income equation was the lowest of all eleven estimated equations. Probably even more telling, the dependent variable had a much smaller variance than any of the others—there simply was not much variation across cities in the relative rate of income loss.

location choices of higher-income households were apparently affected by the relative availability of single-family housing, and probably by relative racial composition and job availability in the city. SMSA income growth, through the upgrading process, also increased the suburbanization of higher-income households. The relative income growth of in-place city residents appears to have been affected by the SMSA's economic growth, and might also have been a function of both the racial composition of those residents and nearby employment opportunities.

Regional Differences

As shown in table 5-2, there were very sizable growth rate differences among the regions during the early 1970s. On an annual basis, differences of comparable magnitude existed in the 1960s as well, although all areas were growing faster. Our equations enable us to isolate some of the sources of these interregional differences as differences in the growth determinants just identified; for example, Northeastern SMSAs have a less favorable industry mix than Western SMSAs. Even after all these identified factors are accounted for, however, certain regional differences remain. We measured them by re-estimating all the equations including dummy variables representing the four regions. The most striking finding is that unexplained regional differences appear to be more important in the 1970s than in the previous decade, even though the list of other included variables is generally more complete for the more recent time period. The major sources of regional growth rate differences are summarized below.

For SMSAs between 1970 and 1975, both employment and income growth were slowest in the Northeast (as shown), and this was attributable both to the factors included in those equations and to unmeasured factors. Among the factors included in the income equation, regional differences in employment growth, initial SMSA income levels, and the cost of living were the most important explanations for the large gap between Southern and Northeastern income growth rates. The Northeast's lack of SMSA employment growth in the early 1970s, as compared to the fast growth in the West, appears to be attributable to several factors: slower population and income growth, and an unfavorable industry mix.

The slow rate of population growth in Northeastern SMSAs is largely accounted for by regional differences in employment growth. However, after controlling for employment growth and all the other factors in the population equation, residual population growth was greater in North-

Table 5-2. *Regional Differences in SMSA Growth and Suburbanization*

Description	*All*[a]	*North-east*	*North Central*	*South*	*West*
Number of cities or SMSAs	121	24	33	43	21
SMSA growth, 1970–75 (percent)					
Population	5.6	0.5	1.7	8.7	11.1
Employment	11.7	0.1	7.5	16.6	21.5
Real per capita income	9.9	4.7	8.5	14.2	9.1
Suburbanization, 1970–75 (difference between city and SMSA growth rates)					
Population	−6.4	−6.1	−7.1	−6.8	−5.0
Real per capita income	−1.6	−2.2	−1.3	−1.3	−1.9
City growth, 1970–75 (percent)					
Population	−0.8	−5.7	−5.4	1.9	6.1
Real per capita income	8.3	2.5	7.2	12.9	7.2

a. The sample is all 121 SMSAs or the largest city in each.

eastern SMSAs than elsewhere. This was the case for both 1960–70 and 1970–75. It probably means there are attractions in the Northeast which we have failed to capture in our variables, attributes that attract (or keep) population but not firms. One such attribute may simply be a reluctance to move as jobs leave the area.

Quite notable in table 5-2 is the fact that the regions did not differ greatly in rates of suburbanization, and varied hardly at all in city-SMSA relative income growth. This surprising result also holds if one looks at the coefficients estimated for regional dummy variables (which are indistinguishable from zero), or at the other factors included in the equations. *Most of the interregional variation in city population and income growth rates is attributable to differences in corresponding average regional growth rates for the SMSAs.*

Review of Implications for Theories of Decline

Having presented the regression results for each equation individually, we now recap and interpret the findings from a more unified vantage point. Chapter 4 listed specific theories of decline, some of which were tested within our regression framework. In what follows, we review the regression

Table 5-3. *Summary of Theories and Results*

Description of theory[a]	Results[b]: SMSA growth	Results[b]: Suburbanization
Disamenity avoidance theories		
1. High crime rates	−	−
2. Trickle-down	...	+
3. Low-quality education	...	+[c]
4. School desegregation	...	o
5. Race	...	++
6. Deteriorating transit	...	−[c]
7. Air pollution	−	−
8. Investor fears	o	+[c]
9. Living costs	++[d]	...
10. Energy costs	o	...
Tax avoidance theories[e]		
11. Size and density; 12. Fixed costs; 13. Redistribution; 14. Annexation	+[f]	+
Positive attraction theories		
15. Low-density living	+[f]	+[f]
16. Low-density workplace	+	−
17. Move, not renovate	...	+
18a. Economic opportunity for population	++	−[d]
18b. Economic opportunity for firms	++	++
19a. Jobs follow people	++	++
19b. People follow jobs	++	+
20. Climate	+	...
21. Auto ownership	...	−
22. Transport cost declines	...	o
23. Auto life-style	o	o
24. Truck accessibility	o	o
25. Ethnic groups follow	+	+
Economic evolution theories		
26. Incubation	o	o
27. Industry mix	+	o
28. Mismatch	...	+[c]
29. Suburban size	...	−
30. Central density	...	++[g]
31. Obsolescence	...	−
Biased policy theories[h]		
32. New construction	...	+
33. Homeownership	...	+
34. Federal funds location	o	...
35. Income taxes	+[c]	...

Table 5-3 *(continued)*

Description of theory[a]	Results[b]: SMSA growth	Results[b]: Suburbanization
Demographic trend theories		
36. Age structure	+[c]	−
37. Selective outmigration	+	+[f]

a. For more complete description of each theory, see table 4-4; the order is the same.
b. Results codes:
+ + = strongly supported hypothesis (an important factor)
+ = some support
− = no support
o = not tested
. . . = theory not applicable.
c. Indirect; see text.
d. See text.
e. In the equations reported here, we did not sort out the causes of higher taxes, but did find that residents avoid locations where taxes are relatively higher.
f. 1960–70 data supported the theory; 1970–75 data failed to.
g. Population suburbanization was in accord with the hypothesis during the early 1970s; so was job suburbanization in the 1960s.
h. We did not test whether the policies are biased, but we did attempt to trace out the direction of their effects *if* the biases exist.

results to highlight findings regarding those theories; table 5-3 contains a list of the theories and a summary of these findings. We also discuss versions of the equations not reported above; many of the theories shown in table 5-3 as receiving "no support" were tested using variables not included in the pared-down versions of the equations presented in the previous section.

Disamenity Avoidance

We lacked measures of school quality and the racial mix in schools, so we could not directly test the theories relating to avoidance of city schools. However, we found that less suburbanization occurred in areas where the school district serving the city extended beyond its boundaries. This may imply that any advantages of avoiding a city location were increased when that also entailed avoiding the central city school system, which in many cities was notoriously poor. On the other hand, it could be a response to school taxes or otherwise unrelated to school quality.

Lacking measures of transit service quality changes, we could not test whether deterioration in transit service contributed to net outmigration from cities. However, earlier we included seat-miles of transit service in a single year (1972) as a measure of service *level*, and found no effects on location decisions; automobile ownership (which is influenced by transit service quality) also had no effect.[18]

We found fairly consistent evidence that racial prejudice and/or discrimination played an active role in intrametropolitan location patterns. High concentration of blacks within a central city fostered suburbanization, except possibly in the South. This result may reflect avoidance of predominantly black schools or neighborhoods. Although we initially thought it might reflect class rather than racial avoidance, when we included a measure of the relative concentration of poverty population it showed no significant association with suburbanization rates.[19] Furthermore, cities with a higher percentage of black population than their SMSAs also tended to have relatively slower *income* growth, again with the exception of the South. This could be either because higher-income households were more likely to avoid living near predominantly black neighborhoods, or because the rate of income growth of central city blacks was slower than average. These results may also reflect a constellation of city traits associated with racial mix, or "white flight" in previous years, as well as racial concentration itself.

Avoidance of high crime rates appeared to play no role in either inter- or intrametropolitan location decisions, insofar as the FBI uniform crime reports accurately reflect differences in crime rates. In earlier versions, we included measures of local crime rates in the SMSA population growth equation and a measure of the city relative to SMSA violent crime rate in the suburbanization and relative income growth equations, but never found any significant effects.

We found evidence that the trickle-down process of urban development did concentrate lower-income people in central cities, but no evidence that upper-income groups avoided locating near lower-income neighborhoods once race is controlled for. Contemporaneous SMSA income growth favored suburbanization and slow city income growth.[20] Apparently, as

18. See Kenneth A. Small, "Transportation, Land Use, and Urban Decline," working paper (Brookings Institution, 1980), chap. 2.

19. David F. Bradford and Harry H. Kelejian, "An Econometric Model of the Flight to the Suburbs," *Journal of Political Economy*, vol. 81 (May/June 1973), pp. 566–89, tested some similar hypotheses. They found that "middle" income class location decisions were affected by the initial distribution of low-income people between city and suburb, and not by racial composition. This result is just the opposite of ours.

20. In another equation, not reported here, we found that SMSA income growth had a positive effect on the rate of new housing construction, given the SMSA population growth rate. Since most new construction occurred in the suburbs, this is another indication of the suburbanization bias of income growth.

households' incomes rose they were more likely to choose suburban locations and leave existing city housing units to lower-income groups. In addition, cities with a relatively greater concentration of old housing experienced more suburbanization, and for the 1960s, SMSAs with a greater excess of housing construction over population growth also experienced greater suburbanization. However, the income equations show that cities with lower relative incomes were *not* less attractive to higher-income SMSA residents and in fact showed greater subsequent relative income growth. This was an unexpected finding, and suggests that divergence in incomes between city and suburbs may tend to disappear in the absence of other conditions leading to slower city income growth.

We had no direct test of the theory that decline breeds further decline because of investor fears of capital losses. However, we do have indirect support for the hypothesis, since a city that has been losing population to its suburbs for several decades will tend to have a high proportion of old housing units relative to its suburbs, and we found that cities with relatively more old housing were more likely to lose population.

We found no evidence that air pollution was important in either intra- or intermetropolitan location decisions of households. In earlier versions of the equations, we found some effect of pollution levels on business location choices among metropolitan areas, but we believe this reflected an effect of industry mix on firm location and expansion, rather than an effect of pollution per se.

Finally, we did find some evidence that firms avoided SMSAs with high and rising living costs, presumably because they would have to pay higher wages for labor there. The negative effects of density or size on employment growth may also reflect cost factors. For the 1960s, higher local taxes also reduced net SMSA job growth. Estimates of the SMSA income change equation may indicate that higher-income households avoided higher living cost areas, other things equal. On the other hand, aside from its indirect effect through employment change, we found no evidence of an additional independent effect of living costs on aggregate population change. Presumably the reaction to energy cost differentials would be the same as to general costs, although we had no measures of either energy costs or differential availability.

Tax Avoidance

Our evidence implies that firms avoided higher tax areas when making intermetropolitan location choices in the 1960s, but we could detect no such effect in 1970–75. At the intrametropolitan level, the four tax avoidance theories are hypotheses about why city taxes are higher than suburban taxes, so we could not test them separately.[21] However, we did test the effect of city-SMSA tax disparities, whatever their cause. We found that tax disparity and other measures of the importance of the city governmental boundaries had negative effects on city population changes: the more *local* was local government, the more residents avoided living in the city.[22] In addition, suburbanization was greater where more suburban jurisdictional alternatives to the city existed. This is consistent with the view evolving from Tiebout's hypothesis that the existence of many separate jurisdictions in suburban areas offers a better selection of tax-service packages, which, along with freedom from the burden of taxes for redistributive expenditures, lures residents away from central cities.[23] We did not find that tax disparities had any effect on city income change, so we lack support for the hypothesis that the redistribution of benefits from upper- to lower-income taxpayers through city government services discourages higher-income households from living in the city. However, the relative amount of redistribution may not have been strongly related to tax disparities, so our test is only indirect.

Regarding the advantageous fiscal effects of annexation, we found no additional independent effect of annexation on the attractiveness of the city to additional population after including the tax disparity and other fiscal variables. Annexation, of course, directly added the residents of the annexed area to the population of the city; these new residents had higher or lower incomes, on average, than the previous residents of the city, and thereby changed average city income.

21. In an equation not reported here, we examined the determinants of 1971 city-SMSA tax disparities in a cross-section of our 121 cities and SMSAs. We found that the size of the city-SMSA tax disparity depended on the institutional structure in which the city government operated (e.g., presence or lack of an overlying county government), the relative costs of operating government in city and suburbs (e.g., relative pay scales), and the size of the tax bases available to city and suburb. We found no support for the hypotheses that disparities were an increasing function of the relative size and density of the central city, nor that they were higher where the city recently experienced population losses. We also found no effect of annexation over the period 1960–70 on the disparity measured in 1971. However, these (negative) findings may be a result of our attempt to explain the *level* of tax disparity, rather than changes in it.

22. In an equation not reported here, we found that a tax disparity more disadvantageous to the city was also associated with greater SMSA new housing construction. This implies that, given the other determinants of new construction included in that equation (including suburbanization of population), high city taxes may augment suburbanization and encourage earlier retirement of the city housing stock.

23. See, for example, Edwin S. Mills and Wallace E. Oates, eds., *Fiscal Zoning and Land Use Controls: The Economic Issues* (Lexington Books, 1975).

Positive Attraction

There is evidence that the attractions of certain environments drew households away from some cities as their incomes rose, or attracted firms as conditions changed. For example, we found that increases in SMSA per capita income contributed to greater suburbanization over both time periods; this implies that some suburban attribute was desired by households, and they purchased it as their incomes rose.[24]

We found no effect of city or SMSA residential density on residential or business location decisions, either within or between metropolitan areas in the 1970s. However, in the 1960s, higher density appears to have been associated with slower growth of both population and jobs at the metropolitan level. And cities in areas that were more densely developed by 1950 apparently grew more slowly relative to their SMSAs during the 1960s.

We found fairly strong support for the hypothesis that a predominance of old housing deterred subsequent city growth, in both the 1960s and early 1970s. We could not determine whether this was because of the economic difficulty of renovating the existing stock, a preference for newness, or an indication of previous decline.

The SMSA population growth equation indicates a strong effect of economic opportunity on household intermetropolitan location decisions. Employment growth was the predominant determinant of population growth. Furthermore, a high unemployment rate discouraged entry by additional households (perhaps especially higher-income households) during the early 1970s, which can be seen as a delayed response to changes in the availability of jobs before 1970. For the 1960s, real income per capita appeared to be a better indicator of local economic opportunity than the unemployment rate, perhaps because the latter was much smaller than during the 1970s. In contrast, at the intrametropolitan level, higher relative city incomes appeared to have negative effects on city population growth, although local job growth was an attractive force.

Firms were also responsive to the economic opportunities available in different locations. Three aspects of potential markets—population growth and the level and growth in SMSA income per capita—were apparently important attractions in intermetropolitan business location decisions. (Here, as before, we use the term "location decision" to include all in-

24. More precisely, either the demand for suburban amenities or the avoidance of city disamenities is income-elastic.

vestment decisions made by firms that affect their employment in any area; that is, we mean to include expansions, contractions, births, deaths, and moves.) Similarly, we found that intrametropolitan business location was quite responsive to population and income changes.

Thus the interaction of employment growth and population growth, when either people or firms were making location choices among metropolitan areas, was quite strong in both directions. On average, a 10 percent increase in SMSA employment was associated with a 5 percent increase in SMSA population during the first half of the 1970s, and an 8 percent increase in SMSA population during the 1960s; while a 10 percent increase in SMSA population educed about an 8 percent increase in SMSA employment in both periods (the response depended on whether the population increase was births or migration). Moreover, the 1960–70 intrametropolitan results suggest that jobs followed people quite strongly, and people followed jobs less completely. On the other hand, we failed to find any effect of manufacturing employment changes on population suburbanization in the early 1970s.

The estimates imply that climate also entered the location decisions of households. During both the 1960s and early 1970s, warmer areas attracted proportionally more migrants.

Just as for the "disamenity" theories regarding transportation, we could not satisfactorily test the several theories about the role of transportation cost and availability in our cross-section framework because they operated in all areas simultaneously. We did try, and failed, to find a substantial effect of automobile ownership on suburbanization; but cross-sectional variations in automobile ownership were quite small compared to the secular changes over the last few decades.[25]

We found that ethnic migrations appeared to operate as hypothesized. The typical migrant group followed previous migrants and, within a metropolitan area, chose central city locations. For the 1970–75 period, the urbanizing migrant group was predominantly Hispanic; during the 1960s, it consisted of blacks.

25. In a regression not reported here, we found that the most important *explanators* of cross-sectional variation in per capita automobile ownership were household size, income, city population density, and transit service. The latter three were also important in explaining transit modal share for work trips. Neither highway capacity nor highway expenditures contributed, but again the variations are far less than the secular changes in highway availability over the postwar period. See Small, "Transportation, Land Use, and Urban Decline," chap. 2.

Economic Evolution

The incubation process would lead to city decline if the births of new firms slowed down for some reason or if conditions changed in such a way as to cause new firms to choose suburbs (or other cities) as their incubation site. Lacking separate measures of births, deaths, and moves of firms, we could not determine whether the nature of the incubation process changed in recent years.

We did not find that larger absolute suburban population size encouraged suburbanization of jobs during the 1960s, although larger total SMSA population did.

We found strong evidence that for metropolitan areas growing in population during the 1970s, the suburbs grew proportionally faster than the city; and similarly for employment growth during the 1960s.[26] It is at least partly for this reason that so many well-known growth areas, such as Denver, Phoenix, Austin, Atlanta, and Ft. Lauderdale, showed large disparities between city and SMSA growth.[27] However, metropolitan *decline* had little effect on relative city-suburban growth rates. Thus, *the more-than-proportional impact of SMSA decline on central cities was largely attributable to specific disparities, not inherent in the process of population or employment loss.*

The results also offer some support for the hypothesis that industry mix helped to determine an area's employment growth (see appendix C to this chapter). In addition, we found that state capitals experienced less decline (or more growth) in employment than other cities over the 1970–75 period, probably because government employment was less vulnerable than other sectors in the 1975 recession.

Our lack of data on job types as well as any employment data for cities for 1975 limited our ability to examine the mismatch hypothesis. However, the negative effect of higher city unemployment on city job growth provides some indirect supporting evidence, since it indicates a lack of interest on the part of employers in tapping this underutilized labor pool.

26. In technical terms, this indicates that metropolitan growth was associated with a flattening of the overall density gradient, implying slower growth in the center than in the area as a whole. See appendix B to this chapter.

27. Austin was the fastest-growing SMSA in our sample at 38 percent, but the city grew only 18 percent. Denver and Atlanta, both in SMSAs growing by more than 12 percent, experienced sizable population *losses*. Ft. Lauderdale, the second most rapidly growing SMSA in our sample (36 percent) had the greatest city-suburb disparity (27 percent)!

Biased Policies

In general, we could not measure the actual application of policies taken by the federal government and others that are hypothesized to create biased location incentives for households and firms. Either they were national in scope and therefore did not vary across the sample (for example, subsidies to homeownership through the individual income tax), or we could not obtain data measuring "inputs" for individual SMSAs or cities (for example, the number of FHA mortgages). However, our equations do provide some indication of the *possibility* for such policies to operate with bias. For example, we found that during the 1960s excess SMSA new housing construction strongly influenced population suburbanization, and that households' intrametropolitan location decisions were sensitive to the age of the housing stock in city and suburb. These findings imply that a policy to encourage new construction would be likely to have adverse effects on the city, unless the new construction could be focused on city locations. In addition, single-family housing appeared to be more attractive to higher-income groups; thus policies encouraging expansion of the suburban single-family housing stock would tend to encourage selective high-income outmigration from central cities. We also found that areas with high cost of living (which includes federal taxes) had slower subsequent income growth; thus, any regional bias in federal tax laws might affect selective migration by different income groups.

Demographic Trends

In earlier versions, we included the percent of population over sixty-five years old in both the population and income change equations, and found no effect for SMSAs or cities. However, some effects of the age structure on growth may operate through natural increase, which had a small effect on SMSA population growth.

We were able to test the theory involving migrant characteristics only indirectly, because we lacked data on the skill levels and incomes of both migrants and "stayers." We found that within a metropolitan area, unemployment was ineffective in attracting firms; this suggests that the qualifications of the unemployed were not those sought by growing or relocating firms. For declining cities, those workers left behind may have been less skilled or for some other reason less employable.

More to the point, selective intrametropolitan outmigration would be confirmed by evidence that city population change had a positive effect on city income change. In chapter 3 we found a positive association between descriptive and functional decline—cities losing population were more likely to have declining relative incomes. Our relative income equation estimated for 1960–70 provides support for a causal interpretation of this: even controlling for other factors, both population and job loss in large cities tended to reduce their average incomes. However, the 1970–75 income equation, which lacks a contemporaneous employment change variable, implies just the opposite regarding population. This latter result may reflect a pattern of large-scale inmigration by groups who use the city for upgrading but enter with low incomes; but if so, the result for 1960 (when migrations were larger) should have been stronger in this direction, instead of the opposite. Alternatively, we may be tracking the recent trend of "revival" in a few cities (very few in the 1970–75 period) characterized by replacement of large low-income families by small high-income families. Or perhaps this intrametropolitan result is the parallel of our SMSA finding that population growth (especially through natural increase) dilutes real per capita income. We find none of these explanations very satisfactory.

Since we failed to uncover a consistent causal link between population loss and income changes, our focus later in this book on the concentration of poverty in cities as a particularly detrimental concomitant to population loss requires further discussion. First, as just noted, the results do support this interpretation for one of the two time periods. Second, the percent of population in poverty is not perfectly correlated with real per capita income. There are discrepancies because the poverty measure refers only to the low end of the income distribution, and because the amount of income per capita equivalent to the poverty line varies as a function of family size—larger families require less income per capita to achieve a given standard of living. Finally, and most important, there is a *simple* correlation between increased poverty and population loss, as documented in chapter 3. Even if the causation works indirectly through other factors such as the trickle-down urban development process, the result is no less difficult for the city government and its residents to deal with.

Conclusion

These analyses provide a fairly clear picture of the most significant factors in descriptive decline of cities and SMSAs. A key finding is that employment and population loss are closely intertwined, presumably in a causal way. Jobs followed people; people also followed jobs among SMSAs, but only slightly within SMSAs. This suggests that policies to counter descriptive decline of metropolitan areas, if desired, could be aimed at business firms *or* households, and both would probably respond in the long run. Suburbanization, in contrast, could be most effectively slowed by policies focusing on attractions for *households*. Retaining firms in central cities would probably not have commensurate effects on residential location choices—households wishing to live in the suburbs are clearly able and willing to commute to jobs, wherever located.

The analyses also shed some light on the relationships between descriptive and functional distress and decline. Some dimensions of distress appear to contribute to subsequent decline. For example, high SMSA unemployment slowed subsequent SMSA population and income growth, and city-SMSA disparities in taxes and concentration of old housing increased suburbanization. Functional decline, as measured by income changes, has inconsistent relationships with descriptive decline. We found no effect of functional decline on population change, but firms are more likely to locate (or stay) in an area with growing incomes. Also, job loss apparently contributes to income loss, as would be expected; whether population loss has similar detrimental effects is less clear.

We conclude that SMSA growth and decline depend importantly on the functioning of the area's economy—the interactions of residents and firms in labor and product markets. Suburbanization, on the other hand, seems to result more from local disparities in attributes. This is probably because the basic markets are area-wide and thus need not impose binding limitations on local site choices.

Appendix A: Regression Estimates and Discussion of Estimating Techniques

Tables 5-4 to 5-14 report the equation estimates for the various changes that affected urban decline in two periods: 1970–75 and 1960–70.

Table 5-4. *SMSA Population Change, 1970–75*

Dependent variable: Percent change in SMSA population inside 1975 boundaries, 1970–75

Independent variable	*Estimated coefficient*[a]
Constant	−1.31
	(1.97)
Percent change in SMSA population through natural increase, 1970–75	0.234
	(0.180)
Percent change in SMSA employment inside 1975 boundaries, 1970–75[b]	0.464
	(0.0579)
SMSA unemployment rate, 1970 (percent)	−0.849
	(0.322)
Percent Spanish population in SMSA's largest city, 1970	0.0998
	(0.0466)
Mean January temperature (degrees Fahrenheit)	0.0965
	(0.0425)
R^2	0.6656
Standard error of the regression	4.48
$F_{5,115}$	45.8
Number of observations	121

a. Asymptotic standard errors in parentheses.

b. Variable treated as endogenous in two-stage least squares estimation.

Table 5-5. *SMSA Employment Change, 1970–75*

Dependent variable: Percent change in SMSA nonagricultural employment inside 1975 boundaries, 1970–75

Independent variable	*Estimated coefficient*[a]
Constant	26.9 (17.4)
Percent change in SMSA population through natural increase, 1970–75	1.10 (0.220)
Percent change in SMSA population through migration, 1970–75[b]	0.614 (0.113)
Predicted employment growth rate based on SMSA 1970 industry mix and 1970–75 U.S. industry growth rates	0.746 (0.298)
Dummy variable indicating central city is state capital	2.29 (1.36)
Estimated SMSA cost of living (household budget in thousands of 1975 dollars)	−1.34 (0.827)
Percent change in real cost of living, 1970–75	−0.718 (0.280)
SMSA income per capita, 1970 (thousands of 1975 dollars)	2.95 (1.13)
Percent change in SMSA per capita income inside 1975 boundaries, 1970–75[b]	0.638 (0.259)
Logarithm of SMSA 1970 employment inside 1975 boundaries	−2.07 (0.653)
R^2	0.7409
Standard error of the regression	5.72
$F_{9,111}$	35.3
Number of observations	121

a. Asymptotic standard errors in parentheses.
b. Variable treated as endogenous in two-stage least squares estimation.

Table 5-6. *SMSA Per Capita Income Change, 1970–75*

Dependent variable: Percent change in SMSA real income per capita inside 1975 boundaries, 1970–75

Independent variable	*Estimated coefficient*[a]
Constant	31.4
	(6.81)
Percent change in SMSA employment in 1975 boundaries, 1970–75[b]	0.202
	(0.0640)
Percent change in SMSA population through migration, 1970–75[b]	−0.0850
	(0.0753)
Percent change in SMSA population through natural increase, 1970–75	−0.412
	(0.128)
SMSA unemployment rate, 1970 (percent)	−0.641
	(0.228)
Percent SMSA jobs in industries other than manufacturing, government, finance, and services, 1970	0.156
	(0.0641)
Percent SMSA jobs in durable manufacturing, 1970	−0.00286
	(0.0390)
Percent SMSA jobs in nondurable manufacturing, 1970	0.00319
	(0.0617)
SMSA 1970 income per capita inside 1975 boundaries (thousands of 1975 dollars)	−2.46
	(0.517)
Estimated SMSA cost of living, 1970 (household budget in thousands of 1975 dollars)	−1.01
	(0.383)
Percent change in SMSA real cost of living, 1970–75	0.446
	(0.152)
R^2	0.6569
Standard error of the regression	2.99
$F_{10,110}$	21.1
Number of observations	121

a. Asymptotic standard errors in parentheses.

b. Variable treated as endogenous in two-stage least squares estimation.

Table 5-7. *City Population Change Relative to SMSA, 1970–75*

Dependent variable: (Percent change in city population) minus (percent change in SMSA population), both inside 1975 boundaries, 1970–75

Independent variable	*Estimated coefficient*[a]
Constant	5.32
	(4.31)
Transformation[b] of SMSA population growth, 1970–75, and city population share, 1970, for growing SMSAs	0.907
	(0.129)
Transformation[b] of SMSA population growth, 1970–75, and city population share, 1970, for SMSAs losing population	0.218
	(0.771)
Percent change in SMSA real income per capita, 1970–75, inside 1975 boundaries	−0.127
	(0.106)
SMSA automobiles per capita, 1970	−9.88
	(9.88)
Percent Spanish population in SMSA, 1970	0.0995
	(0.0434)
City minus SMSA percent 1970 housing built before 1940	−0.224
	(0.0558)
City minus SMSA percent black population, 1970	−0.159
	(0.0748)
City minus SMSA percent black population, 1970 differential effect in southern region	0.134
	(0.101)
Dummy variable indicating city is in southern region	−2.14
	(1.24)
City minus SMSA local government taxes per capita, 1971 (thousands of dollars)	−9.92
	(5.59)
Dummy variable indicating school district serving city serves larger area as well, 1971	2.79
	(1.13)
Number of municipalities in SMSA, as defined in 1975	−0.0148
	(0.00622)
R^2	0.5636
Standard error of the regression	4.06
$F_{12,108}$	11.6
Number of observations	121

a. Asymptotic standard errors in parentheses.

b. Transformation is $-(1-p)\Delta M$, where p is city share and ΔM is five-year SMSA population growth rate. See appendix B for rationale.

Table 5-8. *City Real Per Capita Income Change Relative to SMSA, 1970–75*

Dependent variable: (Percent change in city real income per capita) minus (percent change in SMSA real income per capita inside 1975 boundaries), 1970–75

Independent variable	*Estimated coefficient*[a]
Constant	2.92
	(2.92)
Percent change in SMSA real income per capita inside 1975 boundaries, 1970–75	−0.124
	(0.0542)
Estimated percent change in city per capita income attributable to annexation, 1970–75	0.693
	(0.133)
Percent change in city population through annexation, 1960–70	0.0129
	(0.00711)
Percent change in city population inside 1975 boundaries, 1970–75[b]	−0.131
	(0.0372)
Percent change in SMSA employment inside 1975 boundaries, 1970–75	0.0571
	(0.0260)
City minus SMSA percent change in manufacturing employment, 1967–72	−0.0118
	(0.00950)
1970 city fraction of SMSA jobs	2.45
	(1.19)
City/SMSA ratio percent housing units in single-family structures, 1970	4.35
	(1.48)
City/SMSA ratio per capita income, 1970	−8.83
	(2.96)
City percent black population, 1970	−0.136
	(0.0365)
SMSA percent black population, 1970	0.173
	(0.0515)
R^2	0.4429
Standard error of the regression	1.98
$F_{11,109}$	7.98
Number of observations	121

a. Asymptotic standard errors in parentheses.
b. Variable treated as endogenous in two-stage least squares estimation.

Table 5-9. *SMSA Population Change, 1960–70*

Dependent variable: Percent change in SMSA population inside 1970 boundaries, 1960–70

Independent variable	*Estimated coefficient*[a]
Constant	−18.2
	(7.35)
Percent change in SMSA population through natural increase, 1960–70	0.181
	(0.144)
Percent change in SMSA employment inside 1960 boundaries, 1960–70[b]	0.744
	(0.0967)
Percent black population in SMSA, 1960	0.575
	(0.191)
Percent black population in SMSA, 1960, differential effect in South	−0.589
	(0.189)
Mean January temperature (degrees Fahrenheit)	0.256
	(0.069)
SMSA real income per capita, 1960 (thousands of 1975 dollars)	5.77
	(2.33)
Logarithm of SMSA population density, 1960	−2.03
	(0.813)
R^2	0.8909
Standard error of the regression	5.77
$F_{7,89}$	103.8
Number of observations	97

a. Asymptotic standard errors in parentheses.
b. Variable treated as endogenous in two-stage least squares estimation.

Table 5-10. *SMSA Employment Change, 1960–70*

Dependent variable: Percent change in SMSA nonagricultural employment inside 1960 boundaries, 1960–70

Independent variable	Estimated coefficient[a]
Constant	−11.0
	(12.4)
Percent change in SMSA population, 1960–70[b]	0.884
	(0.0563)
Predicted employment growth rate based on SMSA 1960 industry mix and 1960–70 U.S. industry growth rates	0.337
	(0.247)
SMSA income per capita, 1960 (in thousands of 1975 dollars)	2.18
	(2.28)
Percent change in SMSA per capita income inside 1970 boundaries, 1960–70[b]	0.238
	(0.146)
Urbanized area population density in 1950 (thousands of people per square mile)	−0.967
	(0.481)
SMSA local government taxes per capita, 1961 (thousands of dollars)	−0.0285
	(0.0127)
R^2	0.8786
Standard error of the regression	6.12
$F_{6,90}$	108.5
Number of observations	97

a. Asymptotic standard errors in parentheses.

b. Variable treated as endogenous in two-stage least squares estimation.

Table 5-11. *SMSA Change in Real Per Capita Income, 1960–70*

Dependent variable: Percent change in SMSA real income per capita inside 1970 boundaries, 1960–70

Independent variable	*Estimated coefficient*[a]
Constant	59.1
	(5.13)
Percent change inside SMSA employment inside 1960 boundaries, 1960–70[b]	0.492
	(0.0988)
Percent change in SMSA population through migration, 1960–70[b]	−0.327
	(0.0960)
Percent change in SMSA population through natural increase, 1960–70	−0.672
	(0.130)
Percent SMSA jobs in construction, retail and wholesale trade, transportation, utilities, and mining	−0.450
	(0.0731)
SMSA 1960 income per capita inside 1970 boundaries (thousands of 1975 dollars)	−3.86
	(1.10)
SMSA percent population black, 1960	0.320
	(0.0529)
R^2	0.6410
Standard error of the regression	4.11
$F_{6,90}$	26.8
Number of observations	97

a. Asymptotic standard errors in parentheses.
b. Variable treated as endogenous in two-stage least squares estimation.

Table 5-12. *City Population Change Relative to SMSA, 1960–70*

Dependent variable: (Percent change in city population inside 1960 boundaries) minus (percent change in SMSA population inside 1970 boundaries), 1960–70

Independent variable	*Estimated coefficient*[a]
Constant	59.7
	(14.3)
Difference between city and SMSA employment growth rates, 1960–70[b]	0.205
	(0.0732)
Transformation[c] of SMSA population growth, 1960–70, and city population share, 1960	−0.203
	(0.145)
Percent change in SMSA real income per capita inside 1970 boundaries, 1960–70	−0.300
	(0.151)
City/SMSA ratio per capita income, 1960	−43.6
	(12.3)
City minus SMSA percent 1960 housing built before 1930	−0.293
	(0.121)
City percent black population, 1960	−0.438
	(0.203)
SMSA percent black population, 1960	0.522
	(0.273)
Dummy variable indicating school district serving city serves larger area as well	8.44
	(3.17)
SMSA housing construction in excess of population increase[b]	−1.19
	(0.285)
Urbanized area population density, 1950 (thousands of people per square mile)	−0.828
	(0.579)
R^2	0.5479
Standard error of the regression	7.32
$F_{10,76}$	9.2
Number of observations	87

a. Asymptotic standard errors in parentheses.

b. Variable treated as endogenous in two-stage least squares estimation.

c. Transformation is $-(1-p)\Delta M$, where p is city share and ΔM is ten-year SMSA population growth rate. See appendix B for rationale.

Table 5-13. *City Employment Growth Relative to SMSA, 1960–70*

Dependent variable: (Percent change in city employment) minus (percent change in SMSA employment) inside 1960 boundaries, 1960–70

Independent variable	*Estimated coefficient*[a]
Constant	43.5
	(17.2)
Difference between city and SMSA population growth rates, 1960–70[b]	0.520
	(0.121)
Transformation[c] of SMSA employment growth, 1960–70, and city employment share, 1960	0.431
	(0.156)
Difference between city and SMSA growth in real income per capita, 1960–70[b]	0.712
	(0.254)
Difference between city and SMSA unemployment rates, 1960	−3.87
	(1.27)
Logarithm of SMSA employment, 1960	−3.06
	(1.38)
Percent change in city population through annexation, 1960–70	−0.381
	(0.0586)
R^2	0.6809
Standard error of the regression	9.37
$F_{6,80}$	28.4
Number of observations	87

a. Asymptotic standard errors in parentheses.
b. Variable treated as endogenous in two-stage least squares estimation.
c. Transformation is $-(1-p)\Delta M$, where p is city share and ΔM is ten-year SMSA employment growth rate. See appendix B for rationale.

Table 5-14. *City Real Per Capita Income Change Relative to SMSA, 1960–70*

Dependent variable: (Percent change in city real income per capita) minus (percent change in SMSA real income per capita inside 1970 boundaries), 1960–70

Independent variable	*Estimated coefficient*[a]
Constant	13.1
	(8.82)
Percent change in SMSA real income per capita inside 1970 boundaries, 1960–70	−0.0298
	(0.108)
Estimated percent change in city per capita income attributable to annexation, 1960–70	1.42
	(0.424)
Percent change in city population through annexation, 1960–70	−0.213
	(0.127)
Percent change in city population inside 1960 boundaries, 1960–70[b]	0.116
	(0.0756)
Percent change in SMSA population through migration, 1960–70	−0.108
	(0.0746)
Difference between city and SMSA employment growth rates, 1960–70[b]	0.129
	(0.0565)
1960 city fraction of SMSA jobs	5.89
	(3.49)
City/SMSA ratio per capita income, 1960	−16.7
	(7.40)
City minus SMSA percent population black, 1960	−0.329
	(0.166)
City minus SMSA percent population black, differential effect in southern region	0.427
	(0.192)
Dummy variable indicating city is in southern region	−5.15
	(1.87)
R^2	0.6478
Standard error of the regression	4.60
$F_{11,75}$	12.5
Number of observations	87

a. Asymptotic standard errors in parentheses.
b. Variable treated as endogenous in two-stage least squares estimation.

Estimation Techniques

Figure 5-1 diagrams the relationships allowed for in the equations we estimated. Reading from left to right, variables representing factors identified by the theories as likely to be important to SMSA growth and decline were included as explanators in the three SMSA equations. Some overlap among the three types of factors was expected. For example, the local cost of living might affect both household and business location choices, and hence both population and employment growth. The variable being explained by each of the three SMSA equations was also considered to be a factor influencing the other two;[28] for example, we were interested in the effect of metropolitan employment growth on population increase.

For the suburbanization equations, the theories suggest another set of exogenous factors, again with some overlap and also with some duplication of SMSA factors. For example, local tax disparities should affect both business and household location decisions; the presence of Hispanic residents was expected to affect city-suburb location choices as well as inter-SMSA migration. Just as for the SMSA equations, suburbanization rates for population, employment, and income growth were also expected to influence each other. In addition, several theories suggested that SMSA growth *itself* might affect the suburbanization rate.

Finally, after estimating these two blocks of equations, we can calculate how the SMSA factors and intrametropolitan factors together affect *city* growth and decline, by simply adding each SMSA growth equation and its corresponding suburbanization equation. This is indicated at the far right of figure 5-1, and is discussed in chapter 6.

We estimated the five equations relating to 1970–75 and the six equations for 1960–70 as simultaneous *systems*. We used two-stage least squares estimation techniques in order to account for the endogeneity of dependent variables when they enter the right-hand side of another equation. We did not, however, treat all the dependent variables as endogenous in all the other equations they enter. Instead, we estimated the equations in a block recursive framework, based on the assumption that relative city growth does not affect metropolitan growth, but that metropolitan area conditions and changes are important influences on the city's relative performance.

28. Because of the inclusion of these endogenous variables, two-stage least squares estimation was required. See below for a discussion of estimation techniques and the "identifying restrictions" making it possible to obtain distinct estimates for the three simultaneous equations.

Figure 5-1. *Schematic Representation of Model Interactions*

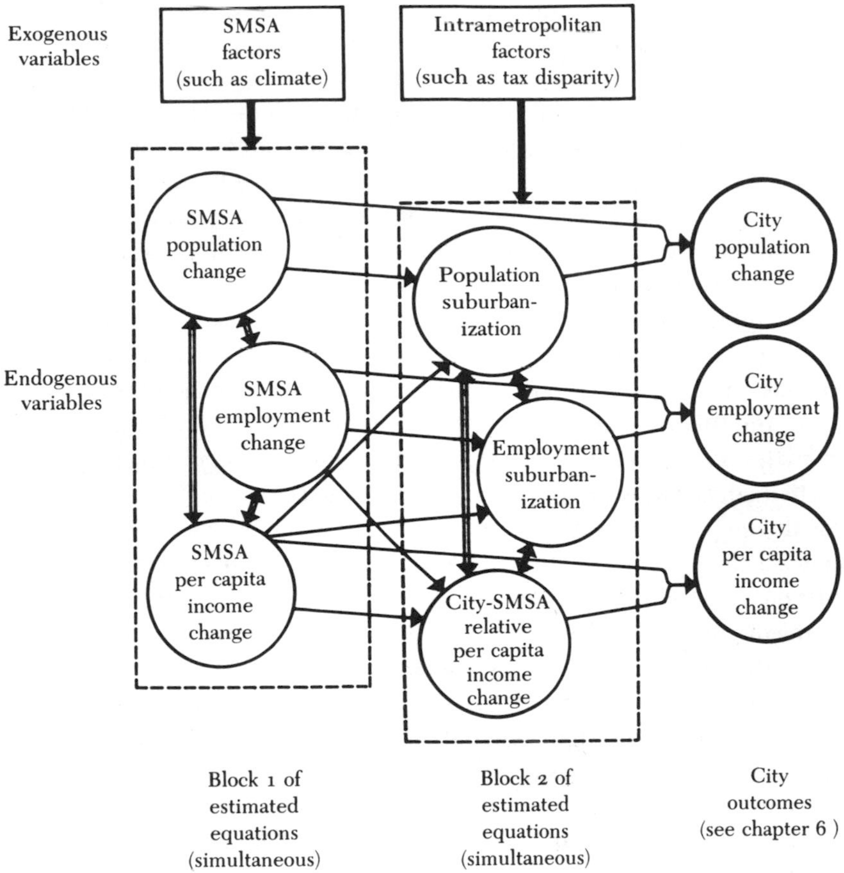

For each time period, the three SMSA equations were estimated as a block, with each dependent variable treated as endogenous whenever it appeared as an explanatory variable in another equation. The city relative equations were estimated as a second block, and the SMSA changes in population, employment, and per capita income were treated as exogenous (predetermined) variables in this block.

The identifying restrictions that permitted us to estimate the equations simultaneously were exclusion restrictions based on assumptions that certain factors important to one dependent variable had no theoretical relationship to another variable or variables. Table 4-5 in the last chapter provides some clues as to which variables (representing specific hypotheses) do not belong in other equations. In the SMSA block, we assumed climate had no direct effect on employment or income growth, percent Hispanic (or black for 1960–70) had no direct effect on employment growth, and predicted employment growth (U.S. national industry growth rates weighted by local industry mix) had no effect on population or income (although the fraction of employment in each industry group affects income growth). Other variables, such as unemployment rate, income level, cost of living, state capital dummy, size, and density, were believed to have possible relationships with all the dependent variables, and so were allowed to interact with them, but were found to have no consistent effects in several cases and therefore do not appear in the reported equations. These latter findings of zero coefficients were not, of course, used for identification, because that requires an a priori assertion that the coefficient is zero.

In the suburbanization block, the transformation of SMSA population growth was constructed especially to enter only the population suburbanization equation, as was the transformation of SMSA employment growth for the employment suburbanization equation. In addition, SMSA attributes including percent Hispanic population were expected to affect population alone. Population and employment were not expected to respond to the distribution of single-family housing units between city and suburb; population movements and income changes were assumed to be independent of city-suburb unemployment disparities; relative city income changes were assumed independent of SMSA automobile ownership rates; and intrametropolitan business location choices were assumed to ignore the racial or ethnic composition of the population, SMSA excess housing construction, and the distribution of old housing. On the other hand, local fiscal disparities and governmental fragmentation, annexation, overall SMSA growth, relative crime rates, and the initial distribution of people, jobs, and incomes between city and suburbs were thought to have potential effects on the suburbanization rates.

The system of equations is identified even without the restrictive block-recursive assumptions on the basis of the restrictions just discussed and the assumptions that (1) intrametropolitan disparities do not affect intermetropolitan location decisions and (2) certain metropolitan attributes such as climate, cost of living, and overall unemployment rate do not affect suburbanization rates. To test the sensitivity of the results, we later relaxed the computationally convenient block-recursive assumptions and estimated the same set of equations. These two-stage least squares regressions treated as endogenous any variables previously treated as endogenous in *either* block, plus any functions of those variables wherever they appeared. The estimates obtained in this way differed in no substantial respect from those reported.

Appendix B: Derivation of Testable Hypotheses from Density Gradient Analyses

From the literature analyzing the familiar urban population density function in the context of a monocentric urban model, we derived some hypotheses about the effect of metropolitan population growth and decline on suburbanization, which we then tested in the equations presented in this chapter. There is considerable evidence that density gradients have flattened concurrently with growth, but the question we are interested in is whether metropolitan growth itself—when other suburbanization factors are held constant—has an effect on a city's share of the economic activity in its metropolitan area.

Growth can be absorbed through either a rise or a flattening of the density function. Using the exponential representation of density functions,[29] we derived an expression which would be expected to obtain a coefficient of one in our suburbanization equation if metropolitan growth were entirely absorbed through flattening of the density function. A reasonable approximation to that expression is $-(1 - p)\,\Delta M$, where p is the city share of SMSA population, and ΔM is the rate of growth of SMSA population. In the absence of other changes, and assuming the central density does not increase, the difference between city and metropolitan growth rates would be proportional to $(1 - p)$; hence the greater the share of the metropolitan population inside the city, the smaller the difference between the two growth rates (this is obvious in the limit). The difference is also greater the faster the SMSA is growing.

On the other hand, if growth were absorbed entirely by a rise in the central density (that is, a proportional rise in the entire function), the growth rate would be uniform across the metropolitan area—metropolitan growth would have no effect on the difference between city and metropolitan growth rates.

29. See Edwin S. Mills, *Urban Economics*, 2d ed. (Scott, Foresman, 1980), chap. 6.

Testing the Hypotheses

For growing SMSAs, these two hypotheses seem to represent alternative extremes which can be tested by simply including the variable $[-(1 - p)\Delta M]$ in the suburbanization equation. A coefficient near one supports the flattening hypothesis; a coefficient near zero suggests a proportional rise in density everywhere. However, our sample contains SMSAs that were losing population as well as those that were growing. Since we did not expect decline to act just like growth in reverse, we developed the alternative flattening hypothesis that all metropolitan population *loss* occurs in the central city or cities. If this were the case, and no other influences were operating, the difference between city and metropolitan growth rates would be $[(1 - p)/p]\Delta M$. Thus, just as on the growth side, the difference in rates would be proportional to the metropolitan rate (ΔM), with the suburbanization rate getting larger as the city share shrinks.

Therefore, in estimating our suburbanization equation we included the following variables: for cities in growing SMSAs, we included the expression $-(1 - p)\Delta M$; for cities in declining SMSAs, we tested two alternatives, $[(1 - p)/p]\Delta M$, and the same variable as for growing SMSAs. In the 1960s there were so few declining SMSAs that we used the expression $-(1 - p)\Delta M$ for all cities. The results, summarized in the text, favored the flattening hypothesis for growing but not for declining areas in 1970–75; and perhaps for employment but not for population in 1960–70.

Implications regarding City Growth

After estimating the suburbanization equations, we combined them with the estimated SMSA growth equations to examine the determinants of city growth; this is described in chapter 6. The functional forms used in the suburbanization equations implied nonlinear relationships between the determinants of SMSA growth and city growth.

POPULATION GROWTH. Two variables representing the density gradient hypotheses were included in the population suburbanization equation. The two variables were both defined as $-(1 - p)\Delta M$, where p is the initial share of population contained in all the SMSA's central cities and ΔM is the SMSA five-year population growth rate; one was "on" if SMSA population growth was positive and zero otherwise, the other was "on" if SMSA growth was negative. Thus, when we add the SMSA growth and suburbanization equations, the coefficient on ΔM must be added to one and multiplied by the set of variables that determine SMSA population growth. That is, we estimated

$$\Delta M = a_0 + a_1X_1 + a_2X_2 + \ldots$$

and

$$\begin{aligned}\Delta C - \Delta M &= b_0 + b_1[-(1 - p)]z\,\Delta M \\ &\quad + b_2[-(1 - p)](1 - z)\Delta M + b_4X_4 + \ldots \\ &= b_0 + [b_1z + b_2(1 - z)](p - 1)\Delta M + b_4X_4 + \ldots\end{aligned}$$

Hence, the combined equation for city growth is

$$\begin{aligned}\Delta C &= \Delta M + (\Delta C - \Delta M) \\ &= b_0 + \{[b_1z + b_2(1 - z)](p - 1) + 1\} \\ &\quad \times (a_0 + a_1X_1 + a_2X_2 + \ldots) + b_4X_4 + \ldots,\end{aligned}$$

where ΔC is the five-year percentage change in city population, the a's and b's are coefficients estimated in the original equations, z is a variable equal to one when SMSA population growth is positive and zero otherwise, and the X's are the explanatory variables in those equations. Each coefficient from the SMSA growth equation is multiplied by the expression in braces, { }, to obtain the estimated effects of each SMSA growth variable on city growth. Since z and p vary across the sample of cities, the effects of SMSA factors do too. See footnote 3 of chapter 6 for some simple examples of how the final coefficient depends on p and z.

INCOME GROWTH. The density gradient hypotheses were not relevant to relative city growth in real per capita income, so the effects of SMSA income factors on city income growth are not nonlinear. However, all the SMSA coefficients are multiplied by a constant. That is, if

$$\Delta M = a_0 + a_1X_1 + a_2X_2 + \ldots$$

and

$$\Delta C - \Delta M = b_0 + b_1\,\Delta M + b_2X_3 + \ldots$$

then

$$\begin{aligned}\Delta C &= \Delta M + (\Delta C - \Delta M) \\ &= b_0 + [1 + b_1]\,(a_0 + a_1X_1 + a_2X_2 + \ldots) + b_2X_3 + \ldots,\end{aligned}$$

where ΔC and ΔM are the percent change in city and SMSA real per capita income, respectively, the a's and b's are the estimated coefficients from the original equations, and the X's are the explanatory variables in those equations. Brackets, [ ], surround the multiplicative constant used to transform all the SMSA coefficients. Because the estimated coefficient on SMSA income change (b_1) in the second equation is -0.124, each of the SMSA coefficients is reduced by 12.4 percent in the combined city income equation shown in table 6-5.

EMPLOYMENT GROWTH. In the case of job suburbanization, there is only one SMSA growth variable included, defined as $G = -(1 - p)\Delta M$, where p is the city's initial employment share, and ΔM is the SMSA employment growth rate. When we add the SMSA growth and suburbanization equations together, the coefficient on each determinant of SMSA employment growth is multiplied by $XX = \{b_1 [-(1 - p)] + 1\}$, where b_1 is the estimated coefficient on G. We estimated $b_1 = 0.43085$, so a city containing one-third of SMSA jobs has 71 percent of the SMSA growth rate influences transmitted to it, while a city containing two-thirds of SMSA jobs grows at 86 percent of the SMSA rate, when the other variables in the equation are held constant. See also the discussion in chapter 6.

Appendix C: The Role of Industry Mix in Metropolitan Employment Change

It is sometimes claimed that metropolitan areas specializing in manufacturing are doomed to economic stagnation by the relative decline in importance of manufacturing in the U.S. economy. This is commonly thought to explain much of the migratory shift from the Northeast and North Central states to other parts of the country. Much of the recent interest in "reindustrialization" policies to revive American manufacturing capabilities presumes that this will automatically help older metropolitan areas.

Several investigators have commented on weaknesses in this argument, particularly the glossing over of great differences among metropolitan areas in their manufacturing growth experience.[30] One way to assess the importance of national industry trends is through the "shift-share" technique of disaggregating employment changes.[31] This procedure facilitates a com-

30. For example, Pravin Varaiya and Michael Wiseman, "Reindustrialization and the Outlook for Declining Areas," in J. Vernon Henderson, ed., *Coupe Papers on Public Economics*, vol. 3: *Research in Urban Economics* (Jai Press, forthcoming).

31. For a clear explanation, see Edgar S. Dunn, *The Development of the U.S. Urban System* (Johns Hopkins University Press for Resources for the Future, 1980), chap. 9. Earlier

parison between the actual employment change in a given area and that which would have occurred had each industry in the area grown at the national rate for that industry. The latter change can be further divided into a "national growth effect," equal to the employment growth which would occur if the entire region grew at the national rate, plus an "industry mix effect," equal to the growth above or below the national average rate which would have been predicted on the basis of the area's employment distribution by industry at the start of the period. The difference between the actual change and the sum of these two effects is due to changes in the share of U.S. employment in various industries held by the area in question; it is termed the "regional share effect." The question of whether an unfavorable industrial specialization has contributed much to a given metropolitan area's failure to grow at the national rate, therefore, is answered simply by comparing the industry mix and regional share effects; if the former is smaller, the industrial composition is relatively less important than intermetropolitan shifts.

This appendix reports three uses of this disaggregation technique. For several metropolitan areas, we calculated the components, using a reasonably detailed industry breakdown, and compared their size. These results are reported immediately below. We then performed a similar comparison, using only four industry groups, for 59 SMSAs for which we had 1960–70 data. Third, we included in our cross-section SMSA employment growth regressions a variable measuring how much local employment would have grown if each of the four industry groups had grown at national average rates for those industries.

Detailed Calculations for Individual Areas

Shift-share analyses using a nine-sector industry breakdown for the period 1968–73 are shown in tables 5-15 and 5-16 for the Cleveland and San Jose metropolitan areas. Cleveland and San Jose are surprisingly similar in their industrial composition, with both specializing more in durable and less in nondurable manufacturing than the nation as a whole. While the Cleveland SMSA's mix is indeed somewhat unfavorable to its growth, this can account for only 9,300 of the 87,000 difference between its actual

applications include Harvey S. Perloff and others, *Regions, Resources and Economic Growth* (Johns Hopkins University Press for Resources for the Future, 1960); Lowell D. Ashby, "The Geographical Redistribution of Employment: An Examination of the Elements of Change," *Survey of Current Business*, vol. 44 (October 1964), pp. 13–20.

Table 5-15. *Shift-Share Analysis for Cleveland SMSA*

Industry sector	SMSA employment: 1968 Percent of employment	SMSA employment: 1968 Thousands employed	SMSA employment: 1973 (thousands)	SMSA employment: 1968–73 growth (percent)	U.S. employment: 1968 (percent)	U.S. employment: 1968–73 growth (percent)	Components of SMSA change (thousands): National growth	Industry mix	Regional share	Total
Mining	0.2	1.5	1.4	−6.7	0.89	6.27	0.20	−0.10	−0.19	−0.1
Construction	4.3	36.4	30.3	−16.8	4.87	21.45	4.79	3.02	−13.91	−6.1
Durable manufacturing	27.8	233.7	212.2	−9.2	17.11	1.83	30.75	−26.48	−25.78	−21.5
Nondurable manufacturing	9.4	78.9	75.2	−4.7	12.00	0.91	10.38	−9.67	−4.42	−3.7
Transportation and utilities	6.0	50.2	48.7	−3.0	6.34	7.72	6.61	−2.73	−5.38	−1.5
Wholesale and retail trade	20.5	172.8	191.8	11.0	20.75	18.27	22.74	8.83	−12.57	19.0
Finance, insurance, and real estate	4.7	39.4	43.8	11.2	4.98	21.00	5.19	3.09	3.87	4.4
Services	14.9	125.1	149.2	19.3	15.63	22.59	16.46	11.80	−4.16	24.1
Government	12.3	103.9	113.1	8.9	17.43	15.97	13.67	2.92	−7.39	9.2
Total nonagricultural wage and salary employment	100.0	841.9	865.7	2.8	100.00	13.16	110.79	−9.32	−77.67	23.8
As percent of 1968 total	...	...	...	...	...	...	13.16	−1.11	−9.23	2.83
Alternative total when disaggregated into 32 industry sectors	...	...	...	...	...	...	110.79	−9.49	−77.50	23.8

Sources: U.S.: Bureau of Labor Statistics, *Employment and Earnings, United States, 1909–75*, Bulletin 1312-10 (GPO, 1976). SMSA: BLS, *Employment and Earnings, States and Areas, 1939–74*, Bulletin 1370-11 (GPO, 1975).

growth and its proportional share of total U.S. employment expansion in 1968-73. Most of its failure to grow at the national rate is explained by its loss of national share in every one of the nine sectors, the most dramatic being durable manufacturing, construction, and wholesale and retail trade. San Jose, in contrast, started the period with an industrial mix essentially neutral in its growth potential, but the region gained in its share of national employment in all but three sectors.

It may be that a finer industry breakdown would reveal important specializations within these nine sectors which would explain more of the growth histories of these two SMSAs. If so, the sources used were insufficiently detailed to reveal it. In San Jose, electronics has been a spectacular growth industry; in fact, the subsector "Electrical Equipment and Supplies" (Standard Industrial Classification code 36) accounts for 99 percent of the region's growth in durable manufacturing. Yet distinguishing that subsector makes only a trivial difference. Even if *all* of San Jose's employment in this subsector is assumed to be in that component which is growing most rapidly nationally, namely "Electronic Components and Supplies" (SIC code 367), the regional share effect still dominates the explanation for San Jose's differentially high growth rate. In fact, none of the three-digit industries within electrical equipment and supplies experienced a national growth rate as high as the local total for all industries, so San Jose's specialization in that industry cannot explain its growth. Similarly, a thirty-two-industry classification for Cleveland (the finest available) yielded results, shown in the last row of table 5-15, essentially identical to the nine-sector results.

Perloff and others also examined a disaggregated manufacturing sector in their study of regional growth.[32] They chose nine manufacturing industries with higher-than-average U.S. growth rates and computed the fraction of each state's manufacturing employment which was in these high-growth industries in 1950. They found this fraction to be *negatively* correlated with employment growth in the period 1939–54! This was due in part to the fact that, contrary to popular preconceptions, the highly diversified economies of the Northeastern and manufacturing-belt states contained a mix of manufacturing industries which favored higher-than-average growth.

Our analyses of other metropolitan areas (New Orleans, Hartford, Memphis) and other time periods (1960–70, 1970–75, 1973–77) revealed similar results: industry mix does not explain growth differences to any great

32. Perloff and others, *Regions, Resources and Economic Growth*, p. 69. See also Dunn, *The Development of the U.S. Urban System*, chap. 11; because agriculture is included, and because the areas differ greatly in their degree of specialization in this slow-growth industry, industry mix effects in Dunn's work tend to be larger than in the tables shown here.

Table 5-16. *Shift-Share Analysis for San Jose SMSA*

	SMSA employment				U.S. employment		Components of SMSA change (thousands)			
	1968									
Industry sector	*Percent of employ-ment*	*Thousands employed*	*1973 (thousands)*	*1968–73 growth (percent)*	*1968 (percent)*	*1968–73 growth (percent)*	*National growth*	*Industry mix*	*Regional share*	*Total*
Mining	0.0	30.1	30.1	0.0	0.89	6.27	0.01	−0.10	−0.01	0.0
Construction	4.7	16.7	19.2	15.0	4.87	21.45	2.20	1.38	−1.08	2.5
Durable manufacturing	28.1	99.3	118.5	19.3	17.11	1.83	13.07	−11.25	17.38	19.2
Nondurable manufacturing	7.3	25.9	25.6	−1.2	12.00	0.91	3.41	−3.17	−0.54	−0.3
Transportation and utilities	34.1	14.6	17.7	28.1	6.34	7.72	1.92	−0.79	2.97	4.1
Wholesale and retail trade	18.0	63.4	84.9	33.9	20.75	18.27	8.34	3.24	9.92	21.5
Finance, insurance, and real estate	3.4	12.2	18.2	50.4	4.98	21.00	1.59	30.95	3.56	6.1
Services	19.0	67.2	89.8	33.6	15.63	22.59	8.84	6.34	7.42	22.6
Government	15.2	53.5	67.3	25.8	17.43	15.97	7.04	1.50	5.26	13.8
Total nonagricultural wage and salary employment	100.0	352.8	442.3	25.4	100.00	13.16	46.43	−1.81	44.88	89.5
As percent of 1968 total	...	...	...	...	...	...	13.16	−0.51	12.72	25.4
Alternative[a]										
Total durable manufacturing	...	...	...	...	...	...	13.07	−11.10	17.22	19.2
Total employment	...	...	...	...	...	...	46.43	−1.66	44.73	89.5
Alternative[b]										
Total durable manufacturing	...	...	...	...	...	...	13.07	−8.04	14.17	19.2
Total employment	...	...	...	...	...	...	46.43	1.40	41.67	89.5

Sources: Same as table 5-15.

a. Partially disaggregating durable manufacturing into electrical equipment and supplies and others.

b. Assuming electrical equipment and supplies all in SIC 367 (electrical components and supplies).

extent. We conclude from all these cases that other factors are primarily responsible for the failure of certain large metropolitan areas to keep pace with national employment growth.

Four-Sector Analysis for 59 SMSAs

Similar shift-share analyses using a four-sector industry breakdown were performed for 59 SMSAs for the period 1960–70. The four sectors were (1) durable manufacturing, (2) nondurable manufacturing, (3) finance, government, and services, and (4) "other," a category including retail and wholesale trade, transportation, contract construction, mining, and public utilities. Over the decade, these four industry groups showed widely different growth rates, from 11.2 percent growth in durables to 51.1 percent in finance, government, and services, with an overall national employment growth rate of 30.8 percent. Yet among the 59 metropolitan areas for which we made these calculations, in only 7 was the industry mix component even as large as the regional share effect. In the other areas, changes in regional share dominated the area's growth path; in fact, the regional share effect was over twice as large as the industry mix effect in 45 of the 59 SMSAs.

Inclusion of Industry Mix Variable in SMSA Regressions

For all 97 SMSAs included in the 1960–70 regression analysis, we calculated a prediction of total employment growth based on the local distribution of 1960 employment among the four industry groups described above and 1960–70 national growth rates of those four industry groups. For the 121 SMSAs in the 1970–75 analysis, we did the same thing based on local industry mix in 1970 and U.S. industry growth rates for 1970–75. We included these variables in the SMSA employment change equations for each period. If, other things equal, local industries tended to grow at rates reflecting national demand factors, the coefficient on this variable would be one; the other included variables would capture the important regional share factors. When multiplier effects are accounted for, the coefficient could even be greater than one.

The results do indicate a contribution of industry mix. However, when we examine the range of growth variation across metropolitan areas, we again find that industry mix is only one of many factors, and by no means the most important.

6

Anatomy of City Decline and Growth, 1960–75

HAVING examined the determinants of SMSA growth and of a city's growth relative to its SMSA, we now combine these results to analyze city growth. The first and second sections of this chapter sort out the important determinants of 1970–75 growth of city population and real per capita income, based on the estimates in chapter 5. The third traces the major influences on city employment growth during the 1960s. The final section is a summary.

The way we decomposed city growth in population, employment, and per capita income into SMSA growth and suburbanization components allows us to examine city growth by simply adding together two equations reported in chapter 5. We can then examine which component is most important in the total change, as well as the relative importance of individual variables in each component. We are particularly interested in the relative contribution of SMSA and intrametropolitan factors because appropriate policy responses depend critically on the geographic scale of relevant behavior.

It is worth repeating that the analysis in this chapter, as in the previous one, can examine variations among areas in growth rates, but not overall urbanization and suburbanization trends. Birth rates, flows from farms, wars, and technological changes affect city growth in ways our analysis does not explain, since all the cities we studied are similarly affected. Likewise, the nationwide pattern of slower growth in real incomes in cities than in SMSAs (table 5-2) cannot be explained by our analysis here.

Changes in City Population, 1970–75

The 121 cities in our sample averaged an 0.8 percent population loss between 1970 and 1975, when the effects of annexation were not included. However, individual cities varied widely from this average, from a loss of 16 percent in Dayton to 28 percent growth in Colorado Springs.

Table 6-1 reports the result of adding together the equations for SMSA population growth and population suburbanization.[1] The equation is not re-estimated, but this indirect estimation explains city population growth quite well, accounting for over two-thirds of the observed variation among our 121 central cities.

The city relative to SMSA population change equation contained two variables formed by a nonlinear combination of the SMSA population growth rate and the initial central city share of SMSA population. So all the coefficients from the SMSA population growth equation appear in this city growth rate equation multiplied by a factor involving the city's initial share.[2] The resulting coefficient indicating the quantitative effect of each variable on city growth therefore varies across the sample as a function of the initial central city share and whether the SMSA is growing or declining. This reflects the fact that determinants of SMSA growth contribute more strongly to city growth the more of the SMSA is contained in the city.[3] It is the mean values of the coefficients for these "SMSA growth factors" which are reported in table 6-1.[4] The table also reports for all variables, the mean effect of the variable (coefficient multiplied by variable value), and the standard deviation of that effect, the latter indicating the range of effects within the sample. These standard deviations are the best indicators

1. The equation estimates are shown in appendix A to chapter 5, tables 5-4 and 5-7.

2. See appendix B to chapter 5 for derivation.

3. SMSA growth determinants are also more important to city growth in declining than in growing SMSAs. This is because we found a systematic tendency for SMSA growth to be focused in the suburbs (density gradients flattened as SMSA population grew) but no similar systematic focusing in declining SMSAs. (See appendix B to chapter 5.) Our estimates indicate that 40 percent of SMSA growth forces would be transmitted to a single central city containing one-third of a growing SMSA's population, but 85 percent of SMSA decline forces would be transmitted to the same city in a declining SMSA. If the city contained two-thirds of the area's population, it would grow at 70 percent of its SMSA's rate or decline at 93 percent of its SMSA's rate—depending on whether its SMSA was growing or declining—when all the other variables in the combined equation are held constant.

4. Mean coefficients, by definition, indicate the central tendency of coefficients varying across the sample.

Table 6-1. *City Population Change, 1970–75: Combined City-Relative and SMSA Equations*

Dependent variable: Percent change in city population in 1975 boundaries, 1970–75[a]

Explanatory variable	*Mean coefficient*	*Mean effect*[b]	*Standard deviation of effect*[b]
SMSA growth factors[c]			
Percent change in SMSA population through natural increase, 1970–75	0.149[d]	0.60	0.51
Percent change in SMSA employment in 1975 boundaries, 1970–75	0.295[d]	3.27	3.39
SMSA unemployment rate, 1970 (percent)	−0.541[d]	−2.29	0.96
Percent Spanish population in city, 1970[e]	0.0636[d]	0.40	0.75
Mean January temperature (degrees Fahrenheit)	0.0615[d]	2.26	1.00
SMSA factors in suburbanization			
Percent change in SMSA real income per capita, 1970–75, inside 1975 boundaries	−0.127	−1.26	0.62
SMSA automobiles per capita, 1970	−9.88	−4.07	0.41
Percent Spanish population in SMSA, 1970[e]	0.0995	0.52	0.94
Intrametropolitan factors			
City minus SMSA percent 1970 housing built before 1940	−0.224	−2.14	2.07
City minus SMSA percent black population, 1970	−0.111[f]	−0.83	1.14
Constant and South dummy	4.56[f]	4.56	1.03
City minus SMSA local government taxes per capita, 1971 (thousands of dollars)	−9.92	−0.50	0.74
School district serving city serves larger area as well, 1971	2.79	0.46	1.04
Number of municipalities in SMSA as defined in 1975	−0.0148	−0.84	1.02
Transformation[g] of city share of SMSA population	−1.31	−0.84	0.24

a. Fraction of variance in dependent variable explained by combined set of explanatory variables = 0.6846.

b. Mean (standard deviation of) effect is sample mean (standard deviation) of [coefficient times variable].

c. If we included SMSA population growth in this table instead of its determinants, its mean coefficient would be 0.637; mean effect = 3.24; standard deviation of effect = 5.01.

d. This coefficient varies as a function of city's share of SMSA population; estimated coefficient (shown in table 5-4) is multiplied by the expression in braces in note g below.

e. The full effect of local concentrations of Spanish population is calculated by combining the city and SMSA coefficients. The mean combined effect is 0.92, and standard deviation of effect is 1.67, third largest among included variables.

f. This coefficient varies as a function of city's region. Constant and South dummy is 3.18 in the South and 5.32 outside the South; the coefficient on city-SMSA percent black differential is −0.16 in the non-South and virtually zero (−0.02) in the South.

g. Transformation is $\{[0.907z + 0.218(1 - z)](1 - p)(-1) + 1\}$, where z is a dummy variable equal to 1 if SMSA population is growing, and 0 otherwise, and p is the share of SMSA population contained in all the central cities in the SMSA. The numbers 0.907 and 0.218 are coefficient estimates from the population suburbanization equation, as shown in table 5-7.

of the strength of individual factors in explaining variations in city growth rates.[5]

Among the SMSA determinants of city growth, variations in SMSA employment growth are by far the most important.[6] In addition, differences in concentrations of black and Hispanic populations, climate, city-SMSA tax disparity, number of municipalities in the SMSA, and geographic scope of the city's school district also contribute substantially to variations in population growth rates among the sample cities.

Tables 6-2 and 6-3 report the estimated effects of all these factors on the population growth of nine individual cities. It is interesting to compare two cities of roughly equal size to see why the equation predicts different growth rates for them. For example, if we compare Houston and Baltimore, both of which were among the ten largest cities in 1970, the difference between their SMSA employment growth rates accounts for 8 of the 14.3 points of difference in rate of population growth. Baltimore's relative concentration of old housing (20.6 percentage points more than the SMSA average) as compared to Houston's (only 2.1 points difference) accounts for four points, and the colder climate in Baltimore is associated with another 1.6 points. Houston's Spanish population in city and SMSA adds

5. The larger the standard deviation, the stronger the effect. The mean effect is not a good indicator of the strength of a given variable in explaining variations in city growth, because it reflects the reference point from which the variable is measured rather than differences actually observed from one city to another. For example, the mean effect of automobile ownership looks misleadingly large because it gives the hypothetical effect of raising autos per capita all the way from zero to its average value (0.4). On the other hand, the mean effect is instructive when it is conceptually meaningful to consider a value of zero for the variable in question. For example, a uniform geographic dispersal of the average SMSA's black population would be expected to add 0.83 percentage point to its central city's five-year growth (however, it would be less in the South and more elsewhere—see footnote f to table 6-1).

6. We earlier modeled the factors that explain variations in employment growth, one of which is SMSA population growth. In fact, the structural equations explaining SMSA employment growth, population growth, and changes in real income per capita could be used to calculate full "reduced form" equations for each of the dependent variables in that equation block. Such equations would express each endogenous variable as a function of all the exogenous variables in the system. That is, in terms of figure 5-1, they would express each element in "block 1 of estimated equations" as a function of "SMSA factors" by netting out the effects of the double arrows representing the relationships among the three elements of block 1. We could have used the reduced-form equation for SMSA population growth here, but did not because we believe the structural equation (which includes other endogenous variables) is more illuminating in this context. A policy to equalize employment growth across areas would indeed have an equalizing effect on population growth rates, as the coefficient displayed in the table implies. However, to design a policy to do this, one would have to take account of the causes of employment growth variations which we identified earlier.

Table 6-2. *Factor Contributions to Five Large Cities' Deviations from Average Population Growth, 1970–75*[a]

Variable	*Sample average*[b]	*Houston*	*Baltimore*	*Cleveland*	*San Francisco*	*Memphis*
1970 population size	422,630	1,233,535	905,787	750,879	715,674	623,988
Actual population growth rate, 1970–75 (percent)	−0.84	8.29	−5.97	−14.93	−7.15	0.66
Actual rate minus average	. . .	9.13	−5.13	−14.09	−6.31	1.50
SMSA growth factors						
SMSA natural increase	0.60	0.36	−0.24	−0.14	−0.31	0.23
SMSA employment change	3.27	5.85	−2.15	−3.27	−2.02	1.96
SMSA unemployment rate	−2.29	0.60	0.83	−0.31	−0.03	−1.01
City percent Hispanic	0.40	0.40	−0.35	−0.23	0.27	−0.37
Mean January temperature	2.26	1.02	−0.61	0.13	−0.05	0.98
SMSA factors in suburbanization						
SMSA income change	−1.26	−0.65	−0.36	0.65	0.26	−1.17
SMSA autos per capita	−4.07	0.15	0.47	−0.36	−0.18	0.72
SMSA percent Hispanic	0.52	0.55	−0.43	−0.42	0.65	−0.46
Intrametropolitan factors						
City minus SMSA percent old housing	−2.12	1.66	−2.48	−4.03	−4.63	1.98
City minus SMSA percent black population	−0.83	0.67	0.26	−2.70	0.38	0.79
Constant and South dummy	4.56	−1.38	−1.38	0.76	0.76	−1.38
City minus SMSA local taxes per capita	−0.50	0.65	0.49	0.26	−1.00	0.20
Extensive school district	0.46	−0.46	−0.46	−0.46	−0.46	−0.46
Number of municipalities in SMSA	−0.84	−0.42	0.64	−1.09	−0.03	0.46
Transformation of city share of SMSA population	−0.84	−0.03	0.19	−0.31	0.22	−0.22
Unmeasured exogenous factors (residual)	−0.16	0.17	0.46	−2.57	−0.14	−0.77

a. All entries except the top three rows are deviations from first-column averages.

b. The sample averages shown in column 1 repeat the "mean effects" of table 6-1. For each factor, the table shows the contribution to each city's population growth arising from the *differences* in the value of that factor between that particular city and the average for all cities in our sample.

Table 6-3. *Factor Contributions to Four Medium-sized Cities' Deviations from Average Population Growth, 1970–75*[a]

Variable	Sample average[b]	Newark	El Paso	Grand Rapids	Mobile
1970 population size	422,630	381,930	322,261	197,649	190,026
Actual population growth rate, 1970–75 (percent)	−0.84	−11.09	19.68	−4.91	3.38
Actual rate minus average	...	−10.25	20.52	−4.07	4.22
SMSA growth factors					
SMSA natural increase	0.60	−0.10	2.17	−0.21	0.13
SMSA employment change	3.27	−3.64	4.64	−1.30	0.97
SMSA unemployment rate	−2.29	−0.34	−1.72	0.23	−0.19
City percent Hispanic	0.40	0.20	4.86	−0.33	−0.35
Mean January temperature	2.26	0.35	1.50	−1.27	0.56
SMSA factors in suburbanization					
SMSA income change	−1.26	0.52	0.15	0.55	−1.00
SMSA autos per capita	−4.07	−0.22	0.74	−0.24	0.06
SMSA percent Hispanic	0.52	−0.32	5.14	−0.39	−0.45
Intrametropolitan factors					
City minus SMSA percent old housing	−2.12	−1.67	2.17	−1.86	1.57
City minus SMSA percent black population	−0.83	−4.81	0.84	−0.27	0.69
Constant and South dummy	4.56	0.76	−1.38	0.76	−1.38
City minus SMSA local taxes per capita	−0.50	0.57	0.89	0.19	−0.32
Extensive school district	0.46	−0.46	−0.46	−0.46	2.33
Number of municipalities in SMSA	−0.84	−0.67	0.80	−0.01	0.56
Transformation of city share of SMSA population	−0.84	−0.26	−0.35	0.28	0.11
Unmeasured exogenous factors (residual)	−0.16	−0.16	0.54	0.28	0.92

a. All entries except the top three rows are deviations from first-column averages.

b. The sample averages shown in column 1 repeat the "mean effects" of table 6-1. For each factor, the table shows the contribution to each city's population growth arising from the *differences* in the value of that factor between that particular city and the average for all cities in our sample.

1.7 points to the gap, but the Baltimore area's less fragmented local government arrangements offset one point of the difference.

San Francisco lost about 7 percent of its 1970 population over the ensuing five years, while Memphis, a similarly sized city, gained two-thirds of a percent. Their growth rates are attributable to different factors, the most important being San Francisco's greater concentration of old housing in the city, 30 points difference between city and SMSA, as compared to virtually zero in Memphis.

El Paso and Newark showed a large difference in growth rates—over 30 percentage points. The most important source of difference is the majority Spanish population in El Paso as compared to much lower fractions in the SMSA and city of Newark; the combined effects of the two measures of Spanish population account for over 10 percentage points of the city growth rate difference. The SMSA employment growth rate, 18.8 in El Paso and minus 1 percent in Newark, retarded Newark's population growth by another 8.8 points. Differences in the cities' relative concentration of old housing and black population account for 3.8 and 5.6 points of the gap, the latter reflecting both Newark's 35-point difference between city and SMSA and El Paso's southern location, where such differences do not affect suburbanization.

Grand Rapids' population growth rate lagged 8 points behind Mobile's over the first half of the 1970s. Accounting for almost half that gap (3.4 points) was the greater concentration of old housing in Grand Rapids (a difference of 18 percentage points between city and SMSA, as compared to Mobile's 2.5 percentage points of difference). The fact that Mobile's school district extended beyond city boundaries enhanced its growth by 2.8 percentage points.

These comparisons convey several important impressions. First, SMSA employment growth was a critical determinant of city population growth. If wide regional divergences in economic growth persist in the future, intercity differences in population growth will also persist. The relative concentration of old housing in city and SMSA was another important determinant of city growth less subject to short-run change. Hispanic population, climate, and the local fiscal situation were all important sources of difference in selected cases. In many cases, several factors *all worked together* to produce differences between specific cities, even though this phenomenon is certainly exaggerated by examining cities at opposite ends of the growth spectrum, as we did.

Table 6-4 identifies the three factors having the largest effects on each of the 121 cities' population growth during the early 1970s.[7] For example, Buffalo lost 12 percent of its 1970 population by 1975, 11.2 percentage points more than the average city lost. This is largely explained by Buffalo's above-average unemployment and concentration of old housing in the central city, and below-average employment growth. In contrast, Cincin-

7. See table 6-2, footnote b. Table 6-4 thus contains a pared-down version for all cities of the information contained for a few cities in tables 6-2 and 6-3. Tables 6-2 and 6-3 report the contribution of every factor; table 6-4 is restricted to the most important three for each city.

nati's greater-than-average population loss resulted mostly from city-SMSA disparities in racial composition and taxes and from local government fragmentation. The table entries reinforce the importance of SMSA employment growth and the relative concentration of old housing in explaining variations in city growth. However, they also illustrate the great diversity among large U.S. cities in growth experience and its apparent causes.

Changes in City Per Capita Income, 1970–75

The 121 cities in our sample averaged 8.3 percent growth in real income per capita over the 1970–75 period. But the experience of individual cities varied from a loss of 5 percent in Honolulu to a gain of 21 percent in Nashville. Table 6-5 reports the coefficients for city income growth rates derived by adding together the SMSA per capita income change equation and the equation for the difference between the city and SMSA changes.[8]

The standard deviation of effects shown in table 6-5 and the individual city effects shown in table 6-6 indicate important determinants of variation in city per capita income growth rates. SMSA income growth is by far the strongest determinant of differences among cities' income growth rates. Among the determinants of that, just as for the population equation, SMSA employment growth is most important. We can further examine the sources of variation by comparing pairs of cities in table 6-6.

Cleveland and Miami both began the decade with a relatively large disparity between city and SMSA income levels—average city income per capita was about 80 percent of SMSA. Per capita real income in Cleveland subsequently grew only 3.4 percent, while Miami's increased over 16 percent.

Six percentage points of this difference are attributable to unknown factors not included in our equations. However, Cleveland's lack of employment growth (as compared to Miami's 14 percent) gave Miami a three-

8. The estimated equations are shown in appendix A to chapter 5, tables 5-6 and 5-8. The functional forms used in estimating the two equations are not nonlinear as they were in the population equations, so the combined results are simpler: SMSA income growth enters the city-minus-SMSA equation as an explanatory variable, so that coefficient is used to transform all the coefficients estimated in the SMSA equation (see appendix B to chapter 5). One other adjustment is made because SMSA employment change affects both SMSA income growth and the relative growth of city income; so the effect reported in table 6-5 is a combination. Unlike the population results, these coefficients do not vary over the sample. But obviously, the importance of any variable in a given city's income growth depends on its value for that city. The mean effects are shown along with the coefficients in table 6-5.

Table 6-4. *Why Cities' Population Growth Rates Differed, 1970–75*

Three most important factors and size of effect for each city

City	City deviation from mean growth	Factor contributions[a]: SMSA growth: SMSA employment change	SMSA growth: SMSA unemployment rate	SMSA growth: Temperature	Suburbanization: South–non-South dummy	Suburbanization: City minus SMSA old housing	Suburbanization: City minus SMSA percent black	Suburbanization: Extensive school district	Residual	Other important factors
Akron, Ohio	−7.8	−2.4	. . .	. . .	. . .	−1.3	. . .	. . .	−1.9	. . .
Albany, N.Y.	−3.9	−2.6	(+)	−1.4	. . .	−1.7	. . .	. . .	. . .	. . .
Albuquerque, N.M.	15.5	7.2	. . .	. . .	. . .	(+)	. . .	(+)	−3.8	3.4[b]
Allentown, Pa.	−2.1	−1.6	1.5	−1.1	. . .	. . .	. . .	. . .	. . .	. . .
Amarillo, Tex.	10.1	5.4	. . .	. . .	(−)	2.1	. . .	. . .	1.9	. . .
Anaheim, Calif.	17.2	4.5	. . .	. . .	. . .	2.4	. . .	. . .	7.7	. . .
Atlanta, Ga.	−11.1	(−)	(+)	. . .	−1.4	. . .	. . .	. . .	−4.7	−2.1[c]
Austin, Tex.	18.5	8.6	. . .	(+)	(−)	2.0	. . .	. . .	. . .	3.2[d]
Baltimore, Md.	−5.1	−2.2	. . .	. . .	−1.4	−2.5	. . .	. . .	. . .	. . .
Baton Rouge, La.	9.1	7.9	. . .	(+)	(−)	(+)	. . .	2.3	−2.4	. . .
Beaumont, Tex.	−2.4	. . .	. . .	. . .	−1.4	1.2	. . .	. . .	−3.7	. . .
Birmingham, Ala.	−8.8	. . .	. . .	. . .	−1.4	. . .	. . .	. . .	−5.3	−1.3[e]
Boston, Mass.	0.2	−5.1	. . .	. . .	. . .	. . .	−1.0	. . .	8.4	. . .
Bridgeport, Conn.	−7.8	−4.2	. . .	. . .	. . .	−1.6	. . .	. . .	−2.3	. . .
Buffalo, N.Y.	−11.2	−4.5	−1.2	. . .	. . .	−4.7	(−)	. . .	. . .	. . .
Canton, Ohio	−6.6	−2.5	(+)	−1.3	. . .	−2.2	. . .	. . .	. . .	. . .
Cedar Rapids, Iowa	−0.6	1.3	. . .	. . .	. . .	1.9	. . .	. . .	−3.1	. . .

Charlotte, N.C.	3.3	. . .	. . .	. . .	−1.4	2.1	. . .	2.3	. . .	. . .
Chattanooga, Tenn.	−2.1	(−)	(+)	. . .	−1.4	−1.5	. . .	. . .	2.6	. . .
Chicago, Ill.	−7.2	−3.0	. . .	. . .	. . .	(−)	(−)	. . .	2.3	−4.7[f]
Cincinnati, Ohio	−8.2	. . .	. . .	. . .	. . .	. . .	−1.8	. . .	. . .	−2.9[c]
	. . .	. . .	. . .	. . .	. . .	. . .	. . .	. . .	. . .	−1.5[f]
Cleveland, Ohio	−14.1	−3.3	. . .	. . .	. . .	−4.0	−2.7	. . .	(−)	. . .
Colorado Springs, Colo.	28.6	. . .	. . .	. . .	. . .	1.1	0.8	. . .	26.2	. . .
Columbia, S.C.	−0.9	(+)	1.2	. . .	−1.4	. . .	. . .	. . .	. . .	−1.2[e]
Columbus, Ga.	−3.5	. . .	(−)	(+)	(−)	2.6	. . .	2.3	−6.3	. . .
Columbus, Ohio	0.0	. . .	. . .	. . .	0.8	1.1	. . .	. . .	. . .	−1.2[f]
Corpus Christi, Tex.	5.9	(+)	. . .	(+)	(−)	2.7	. . .	. . .	−6.8	3.9[b]
Dallas, Tex.	−1.7	. . .	. . .	. . .	(−)	2.0	. . .	. . .	−2.9	−1.7[f]
Dayton, Ohio	−14.9	−4.4	. . .	. . .	. . .	(−)	−2.3	. . .	−4.5	. . .
Denver, Colo.	−5.0	2.7	. . .	. . .	. . .	−1.2	. . .	. . .	−6.4	. . .
Des Moines, Iowa	−2.8	1.7	. . .	−1.0	. . .	. . .	. . .	. . .	−4.7	. . .
Detroit, Mich.	−11.0	−2.7	(−)	. . .	. . .	−3.4	−3.2	. . .	(+)	. . .
Duluth, Minn.	−5.7	−3.0	−3.2	(−)	. . .	. . .	. . .	. . .	4.1	. . .
El Paso, Tex.	20.5	4.6	(−)	(+)	(−)	(+)	. . .	. . .	. . .	5.1[b]
	. . .	. . .	. . .	. . .	. . .	. . .	. . .	. . .	. . .	−4.9[g]
Erie, Pa.	−0.2	−0.5	. . .	−0.9	0.8	. . .	. . .	. . .	. . .	. . .
Evansville, Ill.	−2.9	−1.5	. . .	. . .	. . .	. . .	. . .	2.3	−4.5	. . .
Flint, Mich.	−9.0	−2.9	. . .	(−)	. . .	. . .	−1.7	. . .	−2.8	. . .
Ft. Lauderdale, Fla.	10.4	2.9	. . .	. . .	(−)	(+)	. . .	2.3	5.5	. . .
Fort Wayne, Ind.	1.0	−1.7	0.8	. . .	. . .	. . .	. . .	2.3	. . .	. . .
Fresno, Calif.	6.3	2.3	. . .	. . .	. . .	1.7	. . .	. . .	(+)	2.0[b]
Gary, Ind.	−10.2	−2.1	. . .	. . .	. . .	. . .	−4.8	. . .	−4.8	. . .

Table 6-4 *(continued)*

City	City deviation from mean growth	Factor contributions[a]: SMSA growth: SMSA employment change	SMSA unemployment rate	Temperature	Suburbanization: South–non-South dummy	City minus SMSA old housing	City minus SMSA percent black	Extensive school district	Residual	Other important factors
Grand Rapids, Mich.	−4.1	−1.3	. . .	−1.3	. . .	−1.9	. . .	. . .	. . .	. . .
Greensboro, N.C.	6.2	(−)	(+)	. . .	(−)	3.2	. . .	2.3	3.5	. . .
Hartford, Conn.	−11.7	−2.5	(+)	(−)	. . .	−4.0	(−)	. . .	−3.4	. . .
Honolulu, Hawaii	12.7	4.3	. . .	4.7	. . .	(+)	. . .	2.3	(−)	. . .
Houston, Tex.	9.1	5.8	. . .	(+)	−1.4	1.7	. . .	. . .	. . .	. . .
Huntsville, Ala.	−1.2	. . .	. . .	. . .	−1.4	3.7	. . .	. . .	−2.3	. . .
Indianapolis, Ind.	−1.2	. . .	. . .	. . .	. . .	2.0	. . .	. . .	−1.7	−1.4[f]
Jackson, Miss.	3.4	3.4	. . .	. . .	−1.4	1.6	. . .	. . .	. . .	. . .
Jacksonville, Fla.	7.2	5.0	. . .	2.4	(−)	2.1	. . .	. . .	. . .	. . .
Jersey City, N.J.	−5.5	−7.5	−1.2	. . .	. . .	1.8	. . .	. . .	. . .	. . .
Kansas City, Mo.	−6.0	−1.4	. . .	. . .	. . .	−0.9	. . .	. . .	−2.2	. . .
Knoxville, Tenn.	5.9	. . .	. . .	. . .	−1.4	. . .	. . .	. . .	7.2	−0.8[e]
Lansing, Mich.	−2.7	. . .	. . .	−1.1	. . .	. . .	. . .	. . .	−1.2	−1.0[c]
Las Vegas, Nev.	16.9	4.1	. . .	. . .	. . .	(+)	. . .	2.3	6.7	. . .
Lexington, Ky.	7.6	4.1	. . .	. . .	−1.4	(+)	. . .	2.3	. . .	. . .
Lincoln, Neb.	7.7	5.2	. . .	. . .	. . .	2.2	0.8	. . .	. . .	. . .
Little Rock, Ark.	7.4	3.4	. . .	. . .	−1.4	. . .	. . .	. . .	5.5	. . .
Los Angeles, Calif.	−2.2	. . .	−2.4	2.4	. . .	. . .	. . .	. . .	−4.5	. . .
Louisville, Ky.	−6.3	−2.4	. . .	. . .	(−)	−2.1	. . .	. . .	1.4	. . .
Lubbock, Tex.	10.5	4.9	. . .	. . .	−1.4	2.5	. . .	. . .	. . .	. . .

Macon, Ga.	−0.2	. . .	. . .	. . .	−1.4	. . .	. . .	2.3	−1.7	. . .
Madison, Wis.	−1.3	. . .	. . .	−1.2	. . .	2.4	. . .	. . .	−4.2	. . .
Memphis, Tenn.	1.5	2.0	(−)	. . .	−1.4	2.0	. . .	. . .	. . .	. . .
Miami, Fla.	9.9	. . .	(+)	. . .	(−)	(−)	. . .	2.3	6.6	1.8[b]
Milwaukee, Wis.	−6.3	−2.0	. . .	−1.1	. . .	. . .	. . .	. . .	−2.9	. . .
Minneapolis, Minn.	−12.1	. . .	(+)	(−)	. . .	−4.4	. . .	. . .	−3.2	−3.2[f]
Mobile, Ala.	4.2	. . .	. . .	. . .	−1.4	1.6	. . .	2.3	. . .	. . .
Montgomery, Ala.	10.3	(+)	. . .	. . .	(−)	2.2	. . .	2.3	4.0	. . .
Nashville-Davidson, Tenn.	0.6	(+)	. . .	. . .	−1.4	2.2	. . .	. . .	−1.5	. . .
New Bedford, Mass.	−0.8	−4.0	. . .	. . .	0.8	. . .	. . .	. . .	2.3	. . .
New Haven, Conn.	−7.0	−4.5	. . .	. . .	. . .	−2.6	−1.5	. . .	. . .	. . .
New Orleans, La.	−4.8	. . .	. . .	. . .	−1.4	−1.3	. . .	. . .	−4.5	. . .
New York, N.Y.	−4.4	−13.8	. . .	. . .	. . .	. . .	. . .	. . .	6.9	1.6[h]
Newark, N.J.	−10.3	−3.6	. . .	. . .	. . .	−1.7	−4.8	. . .	. . .	. . .
Newport News, Va.	1.3	3.5	. . .	. . .	(−)	1.9	. . .	. . .	−4.3	. . .
Norfolk, Va.	6.1	2.1	. . .	(+)	(−)	. . .	. . .	. . .	−9.3	1.5[h]
Oklahoma City, Okla.	0.2	. . .	. . .	. . .	−1.4	1.0	. . .	. . .	−0.9	. . .
Omaha, Neb.	4.5	. . .	. . .	−0.8	. . .	1.4	. . .	. . .	1.5	. . .
Paterson, N.J.	−5.2	−5.5	. . .	. . .	. . .	−3.8	(−)	. . .	4.1	. . .
Peoria, Ill.	0.1	−1.3	(+)	−1.2	. . .	. . .	. . .	. . .	3.2	. . .
Philadelphia, Pa.	−6.0	−3.7	. . .	. . .	. . .	(−)	(−)	. . .	5.4	−4.1[f]
Phoenix, Ariz.	13.7	5.1	. . .	. . .	. . .	1.8	. . .	. . .	2.1	. . .
Pittsburgh, Pa.	−11.0	−2.5	. . .	. . .	. . .	−2.4	(−)	. . .	. . .	−3.7[f]
Portland, Ore.	−5.9	. . .	. . .	. . .	0.8	−2.5	. . .	. . .	−2.4	. . .

Table 6-4 *(continued)*

City	City deviation from mean growth	Factor contributions[a]								
		SMSA growth			Suburbanization					
		SMSA employ-ment change	SMSA unem-ployment rate	Tempera-ture	South–non-South dummy	City minus SMSA old housing	City minus SMSA percent black	Extensive school district	Residual	Other important factors
Providence, R.I.	−5.5	−3.2	. . .	. . .	. . .	−3.3	. . .	. . .	1.8	. . .
Raleigh, N.C.	10.1	3.7	(+)	. . .	(−)	(+)	. . .	2.3	2.6	. . .
Richmond, Va.	−5.8	. . .	1.3	. . .	−1.4	(−)	. . .	. . .	−2.5	. . .
Riverside, Calif.	8.4	−1.2	. . .	. . .	. . .	(+)	. . .	. . .	4.9	1.1[b]
Rochester, N.Y.	−8.6	−2.4	(+)	−1.4	. . .	−3.8	. . .	. . .	(−)	. . .
Rockford, Ill.	−0.5	−2.1	. . .	. . .	. . .	0.9	. . .	. . .	1.1	. . .
Sacramento, Calif.	2.3	. . .	. . .	. . .	0.8	. . .	. . .	. . .	1.8	0.7[f]
St. Louis, Mo.	−14.8	3.5	(−)	. . .	. . .	−5.1	−3.1	. . .	(+)	. . .
Salt Lake City, Utah	−2.6	6.0	. . .	(−)	. . .	−2.9	. . .	. . .	−6.7	. . .
San Antonio, Tex.	10.0	(+)	. . .	(+)	(−)	(+)	. . .	. . .	−4.5	3.9[b]
	. . .	. . .	. . .	. . .	. . .	. . .	. . .	. . .	. . .	3.9[g]
San Diego, Calif.	11.9	2.4	. . .	. . .	. . .	1.0	. . .	. . .	5.3	. . .
San Francisco, Calif.	−6.3	−2.0	. . .	. . .	. . .	−4.6	. . .	. . .	. . .	−1.0[c]
San Jose, Calif.	21.3	2.1	. . .	. . .	. . .	(+)	. . .	. . .	11.9	2.2[c]
Savannah, Ga.	−5.9	(−)	(−)	2.3	(−)	. . .	. . .	2.3	−6.4	. . .
Scranton, Pa.	−5.8	−3.7	. . .	−1.3	. . .	. . .	. . .	. . .	−1.9	. . .
Seattle, Wash.	−7.4	(+)	−3.8	. . .	. . .	−1.8	. . .	. . .	−3.7	. . .
Shreveport, La.	2.8	(+)	. . .	. . .	−1.4	(+)	. . .	2.3	−1.7	. . .

South Bend, Ind.	−6.9	−1.1	−1.2	. . .	. . .	. . .	. . .	. . .	−4.2	. . .
Spokane, Wash.	2.7	0.9	−1.4	. . .	. . .	. . .	. . .	. . .	2.6	. . .
Springfield, Mass.	5.0	−1.7	. . .	. . .	. . .	. . .	. . .	. . .	6.3	0.8[e]
Springfield, Mo.	10.4	2.6	. . .	. . .	. . .	2.3	. . .	. . .	4.6	. . .
Stamford, Conn.	−2.5	. . .	. . .	. . .	. . .	2.6	. . .	. . .	−7.8	1.5[e]
Stockton, Calif.	7.8	. . .	. . .	. . .	0.8	. . .	. . .	. . .	5.4	1.3[b]
Syracuse, N.Y.	−6.6	−2.6	. . .	(−)	. . .	−2.1	. . .	. . .	−1.9	. . .
Tacoma, Wash.	−1.2	−1.4	. . .	. . .	. . .	(−)	. . .	. . .	3.2	−1.5[c]
Tampa, Fla.	1.8	3.3	. . .	. . .	(−)	. . .	. . .	2.3	−2.5	. . .
Toledo, Ohio	−3.2	−1.9	. . .	−0.9	. . .	. . .	. . .	. . .	. . .	−1.0[f]
Topeka, Kans.	−3.8	2.9	. . .	. . .	. . .	(+)	. . .	2.3	−11.6	. . .
Trenton, N.J.	−2.4	(−)	(+)	. . .	. . .	−5.2	−2.5	. . .	5.8	. . .
Tucson, Ariz.	11.7	9.2	. . .	(+)	. . .	2.0	. . .	. . .	−5.5	. . .
Tulsa, Okla.	1.3	2.1	. . .	. . .	(−)	3.0	. . .	. . .	−1.4	. . .
Washington, D.C.	−5.1	. . .	(+)	. . .	(−)	−3.6	. . .	. . .	4.6	−3.0[c]
Waterbury, Conn.	−0.1	−2.9	. . .	−0.9	. . .	. . .	. . .	. . .	2.4	. . .
Wichita, Kans.	−3.4	4.7	−3.4	. . .	. . .	(+)	. . .	. . .	−6.9	. . .
Worcester, Mass.	−2.0	−3.5	. . .	−1.0	. . .	. . .	. . .	. . .	1.2	. . .
Youngstown, Ohio	−5.3	−2.5	. . .	(−)	. . .	−2.7	(−)	. . .	2.9	. . .

a. (+) and (−) mean that effect was greater than one percentage point change in five-year city population growth rate, although not one of the three largest effects for this city; sign indicates direction of effect.

b. Percent of SMSA population Spanish.

c. City-SMSA disparity in taxes per capita.

d. SMSA rate of population growth through natural increase.

e. SMSA rate of income growth.

f. Number of jurisdictions in SMSA.

g. Percent of city population Spanish.

h. SMSA automobiles per capita (however, auto registrations for Virginia SMSAs may be underestimated because of boundary problems with independent cities).

Table 6-5. *City Per Capita Income Change, 1970–75: Combined City-Relative and SMSA Equations*

Dependent variable: Percent change in city per capita income, 1970–75[a]

Explanatory variable[b]	*Coefficient*	*Mean effect*[c]	*Standard deviation of effect*[c]
Constant	30.4	30.41	0.00
SMSA growth factors			
Percent change in SMSA employment in 1975 boundaries, 1970–75	0.234	2.73	2.53
Percent change in SMSA population through migration, 1970–75	−0.0744	−0.12	0.50
Percent change in SMSA population through natural increase, 1970–75	−0.361	−1.44	1.00
SMSA unemployment rate, 1970 (percent)	−0.561	−2.38	0.73
Percent SMSA jobs in construction, trade, transportation, utilities, and mining, 1970	0.137	4.67	0.79
Percent SMSA jobs in durable manufacturing, 1970	−0.00251	−0.04	0.03
Percent SMSA jobs in nondurable manufacturing, 1970	0.00280	0.03	0.02
SMSA 1970 income per capita inside 1975 boundaries (thousands of dollars)	−2.15	−10.09	1.55
Estimated SMSA cost of living, 1970 (household budget, thousands of dollars)	−0.881	−12.92	1.00
Percent change in SMSA real cost of living, 1970–75	0.390	1.39	0.78
City growth factors			
Estimated percent change in city per capita income attributable to annexation, 1970–75	0.693	−0.02	1.00
Percent change in city population through annexation, 1960–70	0.0129	0.17	0.36
Percent change in city population inside 1975 boundaries, 1970–75	−0.131	0.11	1.09
Intrametropolitan factors			
City minus SMSA percent change in manufacturing employment, 1967–72	−0.0118	0.04	0.24
1970 city fraction of SMSA jobs	2.45	1.45	0.45
City/SMSA ratio percent housing units in single-family structures, 1970	4.35	3.62	0.78
City/SMSA ratio per capita income, 1970	−8.83	−8.75	0.83
City percent black population, 1970[d]	−0.136	−2.54	1.94
SMSA percent black population, 1970[d]	0.173	1.98	1.63

a. Fraction of variance in dependent variable explained by combined set of explanatory variables = 0.6501.

b. If we included SMSA income change in this table instead of its determinants, its mean coefficient would be 0.876; mean effect = 8.65; standard deviation of effect = 4.28. Note that the items listed as SMSA growth factors do not sum to this total SMSA income growth effect because the coefficient on SMSA employment growth includes its effect on city minus SMSA income growth.

c. Mean (standard deviation of) effect is sample mean (standard deviation) of [coefficient multiplied by variable].

d. The net effect of the difference between city and SMSA racial composition is calculated by combining the city and SMSA coefficients. The mean combined effect is −0.56, and standard deviation of effect is 1.10, third largest among included variables.

point boost. In addition, Miami's more favorable industry mix, lower cost of living, and lower percent black population in the city each contributed about two points. Offsetting these factors, Cleveland's average income benefited from its population decline in both city and SMSA.

Newark and Savannah had relatively low per capita incomes in 1970, yet their subsequent growth differed by about fifteen percentage points. Most of this difference (almost ten points) is attributable to differences in SMSA income growth; per capita income in the Newark SMSA rose by less than 6 percent, while Savannah's SMSA income grew by almost 17 percent from 1970 to 1975. Among the factors responsible for the SMSA income growth difference, the initial income level (almost $2,000 higher in the Newark SMSA) and cost of living combined contributed 7.5 percentage points. In addition, the industry mix in the Savannah SMSA was particularly favorable to income growth: it had half Newark's fraction of employment in durables, and one and a half times Newark's concentration in construction, retail and wholesale trade, utilities, and transportation. Several intrametropolitan factors also contributed to the gap, especially the difference in relative city-suburb concentration of single-family homes—the city of Savannah had almost the same single-family percent as its suburbs. In addition, Newark displayed more city-suburb disparity in racial concentration, which contributed almost four percentage points to its slower growth in per capita income. Offsetting about three points of Savannah's advantage was a convergence tendency our estimates revealed—Newark's initial city-suburb income disparity was considerably greater than Savannah's.

These comparisons and the other results shown in tables 6-5 and 6-6 provide several insights. First, the dominance of *SMSA* factors in the determination of city income changes is striking. Among these are the rate of growth of SMSA employment, the SMSA industry mix, and the initial level of SMSA income and cost of living. Using the estimates shown in table 6-5, we find that in the absence of SMSA income growth and city annexation activities, the average city would have lost approximately 0.3 percent of real per capita income between 1970 and 1975, and the range of growth rates would have been only about nine percentage points (from −5 to +4). This slight loss was offset by an average *gain of 8.6 percent* in city income because of SMSA income growth averaging 9.9 percent, and the range of variation is greatly increased due to the latter factor.

For the average city, SMSA income growth was by far the dominant factor in determining city income growth. Among intrametropolitan factors,

Table 6-6. *Factor Contributions to Five Cities' Deviations from Average Per Capita Income Growth, 1970–75*[a]

Variable	Sample average	Cleveland	Miami	St. Louis	Newark	Savannah
Actual increase in per capita income, 1970–75 (percent)	8.30	3.43	16.37	9.25	−0.12	15.23
Actual minus average	. . .	−4.87	8.07	0.95	−8.42	6.93
SMSA growth factors						
SMSA employment increase	2.73	−2.74	0.56	−2.86	−2.95	−1.99
SMSA inmigration	−0.12	0.64	−0.76	0.48	0.52	0.63
SMSA natural increase	−1.44	0.61	0.81	0.33	0.51	−0.88
SMSA unemployment rate	−2.38	0.42	0.30	−0.37	0.30	−0.03
SMSA industry mix	4.66	−0.40	1.37	−0.08	−0.35	1.70
SMSA income, 1970	−10.09	−1.42	−0.74	−0.27	−2.44	1.87
SMSA cost of living	−12.92	−0.74	1.35	0.04	−1.90	1.29
Increase in SMSA living costs	1.39	−1.22	0.26	−0.89	0.18	1.46
City growth factors						
City annexation, estimated income impact, 1970–75	−0.02	0.02	0.02	0.02	0.02	0.02
City annexation, 1960s	0.17	−0.17	−0.17	−0.17	−0.17	−0.17
City population growth in fixed boundaries	0.11	1.85	−1.29	1.94	1.34	0.78
Intrametropolitan factors						
City minus SMSA manufacturing growth	0.04	0.09	0.22	0.10	0.24	−0.67
City share of SMSA jobs	1.45	−0.14	−0.45	−0.43	−0.81	0.48
City/SMSA percent single-family units	3.62	−0.83	−0.10	−1.36	−2.76	0.46
City/SMSA per capita income, 1970	−8.75	1.92	1.49	1.41	3.20	0.27
City and SMSA percent black population	−0.56	−1.86	0.05	−2.22	−3.57	0.31
Unmeasured exogenous factors (residual)	0.00	−0.87	5.15	5.25	−3.15	0.72

a. All entries except rows 1 and 2 are deviations from first-column averages.

the contemporaneous rate of city population growth was important, though in comparing individual cities, this factor generally operated with a sign *opposite* to the overall difference. That is, cities that had many other factors working for them had their relatively fast population growth reducing their per capita income growth, and conversely. Annexation was also a big source of variation in city income growth rates. For example, we estimate that Chattanooga added about 4 percent to city income by annexing higher-income territory, while Columbus (Georgia) reduced the city's average income by a little more than 1 percent by annexing lower-income territory. And when blacks were more concentrated in the city than the suburbs, city income growth was slower.

Table 6-7 reports the three most important factors in each city's growth in per capita income during the early 1970s. SMSA factors stand out, especially SMSA employment growth, income, and cost of living. Contemporaneous city population growth and percent black population also contributed substantially to differences in city income growth. Yet for individual cities, other factors were quite important. For example, Allentown's real per capita income growth (8 percent) was close to the average, but seems to have resulted from nontypical traits offsetting each other: below-average unemployment, and a below-average concentration in the broad employment category including construction, mining, retail and wholesale trade, transportation, and utilities.

City Employment Growth, 1960–70

We were unable to estimate an equation for employment suburbanization during the early 1970s; so we used our 1960–70 SMSA growth and suburbanization equations to examine the determinants of city employment growth.[9] During the 1960s, it varied widely across the eighty-seven cities included in the analysis, but average growth was 1 percent.

9. The estimated equations are shown in appendix A to chapter 5, tables 5-10 and 5-13. Just as for population, the functional form we used in the employment suburbanization equation implies a nonlinear relationship between the determinants of SMSA employment growth and city employment growth. Thus each coefficient from the SMSA employment equation is multiplied by a factor involving the city share of SMSA jobs. Also adjusted were coefficients on two SMSA growth variables that enter both equations; we report combined effects. Population and income growth in the SMSA enter both equations—employment suburbanization is affected by the difference between city and SMSA growth rates, and SMSA employment growth is directly affected by SMSA growth in the other two factors.

Table 6-7. *Why City Income Grew at Different Rates, 1970–75*

Three most important factors and size of effect for each city

City	City deviation from mean growth	Factor contributions[a]: SMSA employment change	SMSA income	Cost of living	Change in cost of living	City population change	City and SMSA percent black	Residual	Other important factors
Akron, Ohio	−3.5	−2.3	. . .	. . .	−1.2	1.0	. . .	. . .	. . .
Albany, N.Y.	−6.7	−1.9	. . .	−1.2	. . .	. . .	. . .	. . .	−1.3[b]
Albuquerque, N.M.	1.0	4.2	(+)	. . .	. . .	−2.0	. . .	−1.6	. . .
Allentown, Pa.	−0.3	. . .	. . .	. . .	. . .	. . .	. . .	−0.9	1.1[c]
	. . .	. . .	. . .	. . .	. . .	. . .	. . .	. . .	−1.1[d]
Amarillo, Tex.	8.6	2.2	. . .	. . .	. . .	(−)	. . .	4.8	−1.6[e]
Anaheim, Calif.	−6.4	6.0	(−)	. . .	. . .	−2.3	. . .	−4.1	. . .
Atlanta, Ga.	−1.7	. . .	. . .	(+)	1.5	(+)	−2.6	−4.0	. . .
Austin, Tex.	0.3	5.7	. . .	(+)	. . .	−2.4	. . .	. . .	−6.8[e]
Baltimore, Md.	3.6	−1.6	. . .	. . .	. . .	. . .	−1.6	4.8	. . .
Baton Rouge, La.	1.1	4.8	(+)	(+)	. . .	(−)	1.7	−6.2	. . .
Beaumont, Tex.	5.5	. . .	1.2	1.1	. . .	. . .	. . .	2.7	. . .
Birmingham, Ala.	8.2	(+)	1.6	1.3	1.5	(+)	. . .	. . .	. . .
Boston, Mass	−8.4	−3.8	(−)	(−)	(+)	. . .	. . .	−2.8	−2.2[b]
Bridgeport, Conn.	−5.6	−3.3	−1.7	(−)	. . .	(+)	. . .	(+)	−1.8[b]
Buffalo, N.Y.	−6.8	−3.4	. . .	(−)	. . .	1.5	. . .	−1.9	. . .
Canton, Ohio	−0.2	−1.6	. . .	. . .	−1.2	. . .	. . .	2.3	. . .
Cedar Rapids, Iowa	0.5	. . .	. . .	. . .	. . .	. . .	. . .	−1.6	0.6[f]
	. . .	. . .	. . .	. . .	. . .	. . .	. . .	. . .	0.6[b]
Charlotte, N.C.	3.6	. . .	. . .	. . .	0.7	. . .	. . .	1.2	0.9[c]
Chattanooga, Tenn.	4.7	. . .	1.6	(+)	(+)	. . .	(−)	−2.7	4.1[g]
Chicago, Ill.	−5.8	−2.5	−1.9	. . .	. . .	. . .	. . .	. . .	−1.4[b]

Cincinnati, Ohio	−1.1	−1.2	...	...	...	(+)	−1.3	...	−1.1[b]
Cleveland, Ohio	−4.9	−2.7	(−)	...	(−)	(+)	−1.9	...	1.9[h]
Colorado Springs, Colo.	−0.9	...	...	...	...	−3.8	...	3.7	−1.0[e]
Columbia, S.C.	8.2	2.7	1.8	(+)	1.5	...	(+)	...	...
Columbus, Ga.	8.0	(−)	2.2	(+)	(+)	...	2.0	1.5	...
Columbus, Ohio	−1.8	...	...	...	−0.8	...	...	−4.9	2.0[d]
Corpus Christi, Tex.	2.5	...	2.4	(+)	...	...	...	(−)	−1.6[e]
	...	...	...	...	...	...	...	...	1.6[d]
Dallas, Tex.	−2.0	...	...	0.8	...	...	...	−3.7	1.0[d]
Dayton, Ohio	−9.5	−3.4	(−)	...	...	2.0	(−)	−5.5	...
Denver, Colo.	9.2	3.1	−0.9	...	...	...	...	6.5	...
Des Moines, Iowa	0.3	1.0	...	...	...	...	...	−3.4	0.8[c]
Detroit, Mich.	−4.6	−2.4	−1.5	...	(+)	(+)	−2.2	...	...
Duluth, Minn.	2.8	−2.6	(+)	...	...	...	...	3.7	−1.7[c]
El Paso, Tex.	−0.1	(+)	2.7	(+)	...	−2.7	...	(−)	−3.3[e]
Erie, Pa.	0.4	...	1.2	−1.0	...	...	...	1.1	...
Evansville, Ill.	0.7	−1.1	1.3	...	...	...	...	−1.7	...
Flint, Mich.	−5.1	−2.3	...	...	1.3	(+)	(−)	−2.6	...
Ft. Lauderdale, Fla.	6.3	4.1	(−)	(+)	...	(−)	...	2.8	−2.7[i]
Fort Wayne, Ind.	−2.1	−1.3	...	...	−0.8	...	...	−1.3	...
Fresno, Calif.	1.9	3.3	1.4	...	(−)	...	...	...	−2.1[c]
Gary, Ind.	−1.6	−1.7	...	...	...	(+)	−3.6	3.4	...
Grand Rapids, Mich.	−3.7	...	...	−1.0	...	...	...	−1.3	−0.8[c]
Greensboro, N.C.	2.2	−0.9	...	...	...	...	...	3.6	−1.3[h]
Hartford, Conn.	−12.7	(−)	−2.3	(−)	...	(+)	...	−6.4	−2.6[b]
Honolulu, Hawaii	−13.6	(+)	...	−2.7	...	−1.7	...	(+)	−8.6[g]
Houston, Tex.	4.0	4.2	...	(+)	...	(−)	...	−1.9	1.5[d]
Huntsville, Ala.	−3.7	...	(+)	(+)	...	...	(+)	−4.5	−2.3[h]
	...	...	...	...	...	...	...	...	−1.7[d]

Table 6-7 *(continued)*

City	City deviation from mean growth	Factor contributions[a]							
		SMSA employment change	SMSA income	Cost of living	Change in cost of living	City population change	City and SMSA percent black	Residual	Other important factors
Indianapolis, Ind.	−2.8	−0.9	...	...	−1.4	...	...	−1.4	...
Jackson, Miss.	11.4	2.4	2.1	(+)	...	...	(+)	6.4	...
Jacksonville, Fla.	12.0	2.1	(+)	(+)	...	...	(+)	1.9	2.2[j]
Jersey City, N.J.	−3.7	−5.2	...	−1.9	...	...	...	2.1	...
Kansas City, Mo.	−2.5	−1.3	...	...	−0.9	...	...	−1.7	...
Knoxville, Tenn.	1.3	1.3	1.6	(+)	...	...	...	−3.0	...
Lansing, Mich.	−6.4	...	...	...	1.3	...	...	−6.0	−1.3[d]
Las Vegas, Nev.	−6.0	4.6	(−)	...	(−)	−2.2	...	−5.7	...
Lexington, Ky.	8.2	2.7	...	...	...	...	...	−2.1	4.8[g]
Lincoln, Neb.	3.9	1.9	...	...	...	−1.0	...	1.3	...
Little Rock, Ark.	1.8	2.5	(+)	(+)	...	...	...	−4.2	−1.4[h]
Los Angeles, Calif.	−9.0	−1.2	−2.1	...	...	...	...	−3.3	...
Louisville, Ky.	−0.2	−1.8	...	...	...	0.8	−0.6	...	...
Lubbock, Tex.	5.9	2.2	1.5	...	...	(−)	...	1.9	...
Macon, Ga.	5.1	...	1.7	1.3	1.5	...	...	...	...
Madison, Wis.	−3.7	...	...	−1.0	...	...	...	−4.1	0.9[e]
Memphis, Tenn.	8.4	...	1.8	(+)	...	...	1.8	2.7	...
Miami, Fla.	8.1	...	...	(+)	...	(−)	...	5.1	1.5[h] 1.4[d]

Milwaukee, Wis.	1.0	−1.6	...	−1.0	...	...	...	3.2	...
Minneapolis, Minn.	1.9	...	−1.1	...	...	1.6	...	1.1	...
Mobile, Ala.	10.3	1.1	2.6	(+)	...	...	...	6.1	...
Montgomery, Ala.	4.5	(+)	2.2	(+)	...	−1.3	2.1	...	...
Nashville, Tenn.	12.8	...	...	1.1	...	...	...	5.6	2.2[j]
New Bedford, Mass.	−3.7	−3.3	(+)	(−)	1.9	...	...	−1.9	...
New Haven, Conn.	−8.6	−3.9	(−)	(−)	...	...	...	−2.4	−1.9[b]
New Orleans, La.	2.4	...	1.3	1.1	...	...	...	...	1.6[d]
New York, N.Y.	−9.0	−8.3	−2.2	−1.9	...	...	...	(+)	...
Newark, N.J.	−8.4	−3.0	(−)	(−)	...	(+)	−3.6	...	3.2[h]
Newport News, Va.	7.2	1.5	...	...	...	...	1.1	3.6	...
Norfolk, Va.	4.4	...	1.3	...	...	...	1.0	−1.0	...
Oklahoma City, Okla.	0.4	0.8	...	...	...	...	...	−2.5	0.6[c]
Omaha, Neb.	2.8	...	...	...	−0.9	...	...	2.2	0.9[d]
Paterson, N.J.	−11.4	−4.0	...	(−)	...	...	−2.1	...	−2.4[b]
Peoria, Ill.	4.4	...	−0.5	...	...	...	...	5.8	0.6[c]
Philadelphia, Pa.	−1.6	−3.0	...	...	...	...	−1.0	...	0.9[h]
Phoenix, Ariz.	4.6	3.9	...	...	...	−1.8	...	3.1	...
Pittsburgh, Pa.	−1.2	−2.3	...	...	...	1.4	...	...	1.0[e]
Portland, Ore.	0.9	1.0	...	...	...	...	...	1.5	−1.0[c]
Providence, R.I.	−3.5	−2.7	...	(−)	1.9	...	...	...	−1.8[i]
Raleigh, N.C.	4.2	3.5	...	...	...	(−)	1.3	−1.6	...
Richmond, Va.	8.8	...	...	...	...	...	−0.8	7.3	1.1[c]
Riverside, Calif.	−4.4	...	...	...	−1.1	−1.1	...	−3.1	...
Rochester, N.Y.	−8.8	−1.5	−1.3	(−)	...	(+)	...	−4.9	...
Rockford, Ill.	−2.4	−2.1	...	...	...	...	...	2.2	−1.2[d]
Sacramento, Calif.	−3.6	1.9	...	...	...	...	...	−1.8	−1.7[c]
St. Louis, Mo.	0.9	−2.9	...	...	...	(+)	−2.2	5.3	...
Salt Lake City, Utah	4.1	8.7	...	...	...	...	...	−3.6	−1.9[e]
San Antonio, Tex.	2.3	...	2.0	1.7	...	(−)	...	−3.7	...

Table 6-7 *(continued)*

City	City deviation from mean growth	Factor contributions[a]							
		SMSA employment change	SMSA income	Cost of living	Change in cost of living	City population change	City and SMSA percent black	Residual	Other important factors
San Diego, Calif.	−2.3	2.4	...	...	...	−1.6	...	...	−1.2[c]
San Francisco, Calif.	−3.1	−1.4	−2.8	...	...	...	...	2.5	...
San Jose, Calif.	0.6	2.9	(−)	...	...	−2.8	...	3.6	...
Savannah, Ga.	6.9	−2.0	1.9	(+)	(+)	...	...	(+)	1.7[d]
Scranton, Pa.	−1.7	−3.3	1.5	...	...	...	...	(−)	1.7[e]
Seattle, Wash.	−1.9	...	−2.0	...	...	...	...	2.2	−2.2[c]
Shreveport, La.	1.0	(+)	2.2	...	...	...	1.6	−3.8	...
South Bend, Ind.	−2.6	−1.5	...	−0.7	...	0.9	...	...	...
Spokane, Wash.	−0.5	0.6	...	...	...	...	...	...	1.5[c]
	...	...	...	...	...	...	...	...	0.8[d]
Springfield, Mass.	−4.5	(−)	...	−1.8	1.9	...	...	−2.6	...
Springfield, Mo.	0.4	(+)	1.5	...	...	−1.4	...	−1.8	...
Stamford, Conn.	−4.5	...	−9.9	(−)	...	...	...	3.5	2.1[h]
Stockton, Calif.	1.9	1.4	...	...	...	(−)	...	4.0	−2.2[c]
Syracuse, N.Y.	−11.3	−1.9	...	−1.0	...	...	...	−6.9	...
Tacoma, Wash.	−0.2	...	...	...	...	...	...	3.2	−2.3[c]
									−0.7[e]

Tampa, Fla.	8.4	3.9	. . .	(+)	. . .	. . .	. . .	. . .	2.2[e]
	. . .	. . .	. . .	. . .	. . .	. . .	. . .	. . .	−1.8[i]
Toledo, Ohio	−3.8	−1.5	. . .	. . .	1.3	. . .	. . .	−4.8	. . .
Topeka, Kans.	4.4	. . .	. . .	. . .	−0.9	. . .	0.7	. . .	0.9[c]
Trenton, N.J.	−3.7	. . .	(−)	. . .	. . .	. . .	−1.7	−1.6	2.1[h]
Tucson, Ariz.	4.9	5.3	. . .	. . .	. . .	−1.5	. . .	. . .	−1.4[i]
Tulsa, Okla.	1.8	1.5	. . .	. . .	. . .	. . .	. . .	(−)	1.2[h]
	. . .	. . .	. . .	. . .	. . .	. . .	. . .	. . .	1.2[d]
Washington, D.C.	1.2	. . .	−3.3	. . .	. . .	. . .	−4.8	8.7	. . .
Waterbury, Conn.	−6.7	−2.4	. . .	−1.9	. . .	. . .	. . .	. . .	−1.2[d]
Wichita, Kans.	4.6	1.5	. . .	. . .	. . .	. . .	. . .	2.5	−1.6[c]
Worcester, Mass.	−6.5	−3.0	. . .	−1.2	. . .	. . .	. . .	−2.2	. . .
Youngstown, Ohio	3.2	−1.8	. . .	. . .	−1.2	. . .	(−)	7.5	. . .

a. (+) and (−) mean that effect was greater than one percentage point change in five-year city per capita income growth rate, although not one of the three largest effects for this city; sign indicates direction of effect.

b. City/SMSA ratio percent of single-family housing units

c. SMSA unemployment rate.

d. Industry mix.

e. SMSA rate of population growth through natural increase.

f. City fraction of SMSA jobs.

g. Estimated income effect of annexation.

h. City/SMSA ratio per capita income.

i. SMSA rate of population growth through migration.

j. Increase in city population through annexation during 1960s.

Table 6-8. *City Employment Change, 1960–70: Combined City-Relative and SMSA Equations*

Dependent variable: Percent change in city employment in 1960 boundaries, 1960–70[a]

Explanatory variable[b]	*Mean coefficient*	*Mean effect*[c]	*Standard deviation of effect*[c]
Constant	43.5	43.49	0.00
SMSA growth factors			
SMSA population growth, 1960–70 (percent)	0.216[d]	3.92	3.05
Percent change in SMSA real per capita income, 1960–70	−0.514[d]	−16.06	3.27
SMSA income per capita, 1960 (thousands of dollars)	1.82[d]	6.68	0.93
Urbanized area density, 1950 (thousands of people per square mile)	−0.804[d]	−3.97	1.28
Industry mix prediction of SMSA employment growth rate, 1960–70	0.280[d]	8.66	1.14
SMSA local taxes per capita (thousands of dollars)	−0.0237[d]	−6.56	1.68
City growth factors			
City population growth, 1960–70 (percent)	0.520	−0.50	7.24
Percent change in city real per capita income, 1960–70	0.712	18.95	6.74
Percent change in city population through annexation, 1960–70	−0.381	−4.42	11.42
Intrametropolitan factors			
City minus SMSA unemployment rate	−3.87	−2.19	3.38
Transformation[e] of city share of SMSA jobs	−11.0	−9.12	0.78
Logarithm of SMSA employment	3.06	−37.94	2.54

a. Fraction of variance in dependent variable explained by combined set of explanatory variables = 0.6721.

b. If we included SMSA employment growth in this table instead of its determinants, its mean coefficient would be 0.832; mean effect = 15.24; standard deviation of effect = 13.35. Note that the items listed as SMSA growth factors do not add to this total SMSA employment growth effect because the coefficients on SMSA population and income growth include suburbanization responses to the difference between these and city growth.

c. Mean (standard deviation of) effect is sample mean (standard deviation) of [coefficient times variable].

d. This coefficient varies as a function of city's share of SMSA jobs; function described in footnote e.

e. Transformation is $[(-1)(0.43085)(1-p) + 1]$, where p is city share of 1960 SMSA jobs.

The coefficients for the combined equation are reported in table 6-8. The equation resulting from this indirect estimation explains city employment growth fairly well, accounting for about two-thirds of the observed variation among the eighty-seven sample cities.

We set aside the annexation effect because it should be interpreted as a correction for the dependent variable rather than a determinant of city employment growth. The relative sizes of the standard deviations of effect for the other variables imply that the largest source of differences among sample cities' employment growth rates was variations in city population growth. Other critical factors included differences in city income growth, SMSA population and income growth rates, and unemployment rates. SMSA size and tax levels were also important. Table 6-9 reports the employment growth effects of all the variables for five individual cities, providing some examples of divergent growth.

Atlanta and Buffalo, approximately the same size in 1960, offer an interesting contrast. Atlanta gained over 40,000 jobs during the ensuing decade, while Buffalo lost almost the same number. Four major sources account for most of the 33 percentage point difference: Atlanta's faster growth of city income and population and of SMSA population, and Buffalo's greater city unemployment disparity (1.9 point difference between city and SMSA). Unmeasured factors not included in our equation also worked in Atlanta's favor. However, Atlanta's faster growth in SMSA income reduced the size of the growth disparity.

Albuquerque and Bridgeport, with about 73,500 jobs in 1960, also changed in opposite directions during the decade.[10] Faster growth of employment in the city of Albuquerque is largely attributable to its faster population growth, lower relative unemployment rate, and slower income growth in its SMSA. Bridgeport had slower SMSA population growth, over half its employment concentrated in manufacturing, and higher local taxes, all tending to slow city job growth. Offsetting these factors was Albuquerque's below-average income growth during the 1960s (only 16.6 percent—fifth lowest among the eighty-seven cities).

These comparisons focus attention on the importance of contemporaneous city population growth in determining employment change. The deterrent effects of slow SMSA growth and high unemployment on city job growth are also apparent, the latter presumably reflecting an unsuitable city labor pool. In addition, income growth in city and SMSA, working in opposite directions, appeared to be substantial contributors to divergent employment growth rates.

Table 6-10 reports the three most important sources of differing employment growth rates for each of the eighty-seven cities. In this table, we made the correction implied by the estimated annexation effect. A "corrected" estimated growth in city jobs inside constant boundaries for each city was calculated as the sum of the original estimate of constant

10. The annexation correction suggests the "true" gap was almost two percentage points larger than we measured.

Table 6-9. *Factor Contributions to Five Cities' Deviations from Average Employment Growth, 1960–70*[a]

Variable	*Sample average*	*Atlanta*	*Buffalo*	*Birmingham*	*Albuquerque*	*Bridgeport*
1960 employment size	221,530	268,853	251,083	149,287	73,552	73,440
Actual employment growth rate, 1960–70 (percent)	1.03	16.35	−16.90	2.52	18.37	−2.93
Actual rate minus average	. . .	15.32	−17.93	1.50	17.34	−3.96
SMSA growth factors						
SMSA population growth	3.92	5.10	−3.30	−3.29	2.08	−0.66
SMSA income growth	−16.06	−6.29	2.99	−2.77	7.54	−1.78
SMSA income level	6.68	0.06	−0.07	−1.13	0.52	0.68
Urbanized area density	−3.97	−0.07	−2.19	0.24	−0.26	0.51
SMSA industry mix	8.66	0.57	−0.91	0.16	2.87	−1.38
SMSA local taxes	−6.56	0.52	−0.47	2.68	2.30	−0.25
City growth factors						
City population growth	−0.50	1.15	−6.32	−5.97	8.99	0.43
City income growth	18.95	2.28	−4.88	2.57	−7.14	2.31
Annexation[b]	−4.42	4.30	4.42	4.14	2.58	4.42
Intrametropolitan factors						
Unemployment rate difference	−2.19	1.80	−5.16	1.41	3.35	−2.84
Transformation of city share of SMSA jobs	−9.12	−0.40	0.27	−0.43	−0.97	0.00
SMSA size	−37.94	−1.44	−1.93	0.40	3.02	2.13
Unmeasured exogenous factors (residual)	0.09	7.73	−0.38	3.49	−7.53	−6.52

a. All entries except the top three rows are deviations from first-column averages.
b. The mean effect of this variable was, as shown, −4.42. Therefore, all cities with no annexation during the 1960s show a deviation from mean of 4.42.

Table 6-10. *Why Cities' Employment Growth Rates Differed, 1960–70*

Three most important factors for each city.

City	City deviation from mean growth[a]	Factor contributions[b]: City population change	SMSA population change	City income change	SMSA income change	City minus SMSA unemployment	Residual	Other important factors
Akron, Ohio	−22.5	−2.2	. . .	−2.8	. . .	. . .	−18.0	. . .
Albany, N.Y.	8.7	−5.4	. . .	5.9	. . .	(+)	8.6	. . .
Albuquerque, N.M.	14.8	9.0	. . .	(−)	7.5	(+)	−7.5	. . .
Allentown, Pa.	−4.6	. . .	−2.9	. . .	−3.2	. . .	. . .	−2.7[c]
Atlanta, Ga.	11.0	. . .	5.1	. . .	−6.3	. . .	7.7	. . .
Baltimore, Md.	−11.8	. . .	. . .	−2.9	. . .	−2.5	. . .	−2.8[d]
Beaumont, Tex.	9.7	. . .	−3.4	. . .	. . .	4.9	. . .	2.6[d]
Birmingham, Ala.	−2.6	−6.0	−3.3	. . .	. . .	. . .	3.5	. . .
Boston, Mass.	−12.8	−3.7	−3.0	. . .	. . .	. . .	. . .	−4.3[d]
Bridgeport, Conn.	−8.4	. . .	. . .	2.3	. . .	−2.8	−6.5	. . .
Buffalo, N.Y.	−22.3	−6.3	(−)	−4.9	. . .	−5.2	. . .	. . .
Canton, Ohio	−10.7	−5.3	−2.4	. . .	. . .	−3.6	. . .	. . .
Charlotte, N.C.	25.7	(+)	5.2	(+)	−4.9	. . .	12.4	. . .
Chattanooga, Tenn.	−1.5	−8.4	. . .	. . .	−2.5	. . .	6.0	. . .
Chicago, Ill.	−22.2	. . .	. . .	−6.2	(+)	. . .	−5.0	−6.9[d]
Cincinnati, Ohio	−12.9	−4.8	. . .	−3.3	3.1	. . .	. . .	. . .
Cleveland, Ohio	−23.4	−6.9	. . .	(−)	(+)	−5.9	−4.4	. . .
Columbia, S.C.	3.6	−6.2	. . .	(+)	−10.3	. . .	7.4	. . .
Columbus, Ohio	7.7	5.1	2.2	. . .	2.4	. . .	. . .	. . .
Dallas, Tex.	31.2	12.2	6.6	(+)	. . .	. . .	7.2	. . .

Table 6-10 *(continued)*

City	*City deviation from mean growth*[a]	*Factor contributions*[b]						
		City population change	*SMSA population change*	*City income change*	*SMSA income change*	*City minus SMSA unemployment*	*Residual*	*Other important factors*
Dayton, Ohio	2.2	−3.8	...	...	−2.2	...	13.0	...
Denver, Colo.	5.5	−3.3	4.1	...	...	...	4.7	...
Des Moines, Iowa	8.7	...	...	...	3.1	...	7.5	−3.0[e]
Detroit, Mich.	−29.2	(−)	...	...	(−)	−5.9	−6.8	−5.0[d]
Duluth, Minn.	0.9	...	−4.6	−3.5	...	7.6	...	...
Erie, Pa.	4.5	...	...	−3.4	...	...	9.3	3.3[d]
Flint, Mich.	0.3	...	...	...	−2.9	2.2	...	1.9[d]
Ft. Lauderdale, Fla.	25.2	17.3	(+)	11.5	−11.0	(+)	(−)	...
Fort Worth, Tex.	2.3	4.3	4.9	...	(−)	...	−8.0	...
Fresno, Calif.	−2.7	...	...	−8.0	(+)	7.6	−8.6	...
Gary, Ind.	−17.3	...	−2.7	−3.0	...	...	−11.9	...
Grand Rapids, Mich.	−9.1	−5.0	...	2.7	...	...	−8.4	...
Hartford, Conn.	−13.9	...	...	−6.6	...	−4.8	−1.4	...
Honolulu, Hawaii	9.1	5.9	...	13.3	(−)	(+)	−17.4	...
Houston, Tex.	32.8	14.9	8.2	...	...	...	6.8	...
Indianapolis, Ind.	−12.0	−3.7	...	6.5	...	...	−15.7	...
Jacksonville, Fla.	19.9	−9.0	...	10.0	...	...	17.2	...
Jersey City, N.J.	−23.8	...	−4.0	...	2.9	...	−16.2	...
Knoxville, Tenn.	9.3	(+)	...	15.3	−4.8	...	−3.8	...
Lansing, Mich.	2.5	...	...	...	−3.7	3.3	−6.4	...
Los Angeles, Calif.	−6.4	7.4	...	−4.9	(+)	...	(−)	−7.1[d]

Louisville, Ky.	7.7	−5.1	. . .	4.9	. . .	. . .	12.7	. . .
Memphis, Tenn.	−2.6	. . .	. . .	5.6	−3.4	. . .	−7.3	. . .
Miami, Fla.	−1.0	8.2	. . .	−3.1	. . .	−4.0	. . .	. . .
Milwaukee, Wis.	18.4	. . .	. . .	−4.5	4.6	. . .	−7.7	. . .
Minneapolis, Minn.	−10.5	−4.7	. . .	−2.4	. . .	. . .	. . .	−2.5[d]
Mobile, Ala.	−12.6	. . .	. . .	−4.5	. . .	3.3	−12.7	. . .
Nashville, Tenn.	20.5	−9.6	. . .	42.7	(−)	. . .	−6.2	. . .
New Haven, Conn.	−16.0	−4.4	. . .	−4.5	. . .	. . .	−7.2	. . .
New Orleans, La.	−8.0	−2.3	. . .	−2.1	. . .	. . .	−8.9	. . .
New York, N.Y.	−14.1	. . .	. . .	. . .	. . .	. . .	. . .	−8.7[d]
	. . .	. . .	. . .	. . .	. . .	. . .	. . .	−6.0[c]
	. . .	. . .	. . .	. . .	. . .	. . .	. . .	−4.8[e]
Newark, N.J.	−19.3	. . .	. . .	−11.4	. . .	−12.1	10.3	. . .
Norfolk, Va.	10.0	. . .	. . .	. . .	−2.4	2.2	6.3	. . .
Oklahoma City, Okla.	25.7	5.7	3.2	. . .	. . .	. . .	7.6	. . .
Omaha, Neb.	−5.7	−4.0	. . .	(−)	4.1	. . .	−5.9	. . .
Paterson, N.J.	−21.2	. . .	−3.3	. . .	. . .	−11.0	. . .	−3.0[c]
Peoria, Ill.	−6.8	−4.1	. . .	8.7	. . .	. . .	−8.8	. . .
Philadelphia, Pa.	−18.9	. . .	. . .	. . .	. . .	−4.0	−4.7	−5.7[d]
Phoenix, Ariz.	32.4	9.7	7.2	. . .	. . .	. . .	11.9	. . .
Pittsburgh, Pa.	−5.2	−6.7	−3.9	. . .	. . .	. . .	10.9	. . .
Portland, Ore.	0.9	. . .	1.3	−2.5	. . .	1.8	. . .	. . .
Providence, R.I.	−12.2	−6.6	. . .	5.6	(−)	. . .	−4.4	. . .
Richmond, Va.	−3.4	−3.7	. . .	2.0	. . .	. . .	−3.9	. . .
Riverside, Calif.	17.5	8.1	. . .	(−)	. . .	9.1	6.2	. . .
Rochester, N.Y.	−6.5	−3.3	. . .	. . .	. . .	−2.8	. . .	−2.9[f]
Sacramento, Calif.	15.3	. . .	. . .	−12.6	5.4	. . .	17.5	. . .
St. Louis, Mo.	−20.7	−8.4	. . .	−4.5	. . .	. . .	. . .	−3.4[d]
Salt Lake City, Utah	10.0	−3.4	. . .	. . .	3.1	. . .	4.7	. . .

Table 6-10 *(continued)*

City	City deviation from mean growth[a]	Factor contributions[b]						
		City population change	SMSA population change	City income change	SMSA income change	City minus SMSA unemployment	Residual	Other important factors
San Antonio, Tex.	39.6	5.1	...	6.0	...	...	25.9	...
San Diego, Calif.	7.4	10.8	(+)	(−)	4.5	...	−8.0	...
San Francisco, Calif.	−3.0	...	...	...	...	...	6.2	−4.5[d]
	...	...	...	...	...	...	...	−2.1[f]
San Jose, Calif.	28.3	41.6	5.0	...	...	(−)	−10.9	...
Seattle, Wash.	−1.4	−1.9	3.1	...	...	...	−3.8	...
Shreveport, La.	−13.9	...	...	−5.3	3.9	(+)	−16.2	...
Spokane, Wash.	0.6	(−)	−3.1	−5.3	4.8	...	...	...
Springfield, Mass.	−14.8	−2.6	−2.9	...	...	...	−10.1	...
Syracuse, N.Y.	−16.8	(−)	...	−7.0	...	4.5	−10.5	...
Tacoma, Wash.	6.4	2.7	...	...	...	...	−3.7	2.3[d]
Tampa, Fla.	42.1	17.3	...	...	−3.7	...	24.1	...
Toledo, Ohio	−1.8	−2.6	...	1.4	...	...	1.7	...
Trenton, N.J.	15.1	(−)	...	−8.7	...	−4.4	33.7	...
Tucson, Ariz.	41.1	7.3	4.2	(−)	(+)	...	23.8	...
Tulsa, Okla.	7.0	−4.1	...	−3.9	...	(+)	6.8	...

Washington, D.C.	−4.8	. . .	4.7	. . .	. . .	. . .	. . .	−3.6[d]
	. . .	. . .	. . .	. . .	. . .	. . .	. . .	2.9[c]
Wichita, Kans.	4.3	(−)	−3.4	. . .	3.8	. . .	6.9	. . .
Worchester, Mass.	−4.7	. . .	−2.7	5.0	. . .	. . .	−3.4	. . .
Youngstown, Ohio	−32.5	−7.5	−3.0	. . .	. . .	. . .	−20.2	. . .

a. This column reports deviation of each city from mean "corrected" city employment growth 1960–70 in constant boundaries. "Corrected" figure equals initial constant-boundary job growth figure minus annexation effect (coefficient times variable). The sample mean "corrected" city employment growth 1960–70 was 5.4 percent.

b. (+) and (−) mean that effect was greater than three percentage points change in ten-year city employment growth rate, though not one of the three largest effects for this city; sign indicates direction of effect.

c. Industry mix.

d. SMSA size (employment, 1960).

e. Urbanized area density, 1950.

f. SMSA local taxes per capita.

boundary employment growth plus the annexation effect. The first column reports each city's deviation from the mean "corrected" job growth.

The dominant determinant of city employment growth was contemporaneous population growth in the city—it is one of the top three factors for fifty-one of the eighty-seven cities. Reflecting the more moderate explanatory power of this equation, the residual (reflecting unknown excluded factors) is listed even more often. City income growth also appears in the top three for over half the cities. Yet an equally important implication of this compilation is the great diversity among individual cities' conditions.

Conclusion

City growth and decline are clearly the products of both inter- and intrametropolitan factors, as we hypothesized at the start of this analysis. Our decomposition of city growth into these two parts allowed us to examine the determinants of growth and suburbanization in detail, and to obtain a balanced estimate of their contributions to city growth and decline. For income growth, it appeared that intrametropolitan factors were relatively unimportant, with a few individual exceptions. Both inter- and intrametropolitan factors contributed greatly to variations in city population and employment growth.

The strong effects of SMSA growth variables on city growth confirm the importance of the city-SMSA relationship first noted in chapter 3 regarding both descriptive and functional decline. Among intrametropolitan decline factors, relationships were stronger during the 1960s than the 1970s, perhaps partly because the city employment element is missing for the later period.

Thus, to ignore either inter- or intrametropolitan influences would be to overlook important determinants of a city's situation. Ascribing city decline only to intrametropolitan factors implies that city residents and their governments have both more responsibility and more power to change their situations than our findings suggest. This is especially true of cities that do not comprise a dominant fraction of their metropolitan areas. Real income change (one of the indicators of functional decline) in particular seems outside the control of local actors. On the other hand, to ascribe city decline only to metropolitan or national problems is to ignore the important role played by disparities between cities and their suburbs in such factors as old housing, minority population concentration, and unemployment.

7

Neighborhood Change and Urban Decline

A WIDELY PERCEIVED symptom of urban decline is the physical deterioration and social loss of status of individual neighborhoods within big cities or older suburbs. Examples include New York's South Bronx, Cleveland's Central neighborhood, and the Watts area of Los Angeles. Conversely, a recent, enthusiastically heralded sign of urban revitalization has been the renovation and upgrading of some parts of the same cities. Both types of neighborhood change are rooted in the overall urban development process within each metropolitan area.[1]

How the American "Trickle-down" Process Copes with Rapid Population Growth

United States urban development is dominated by the "trickle-down" or "filtering" process. No one person or group consciously designed that process; it evolved from separate decisions made and actions taken by millions of households, developers, local governments, federal agencies, home-builders, lenders, and politicians. It has succeeded in providing excellent housing and high-quality residential environments for a majority of households in U.S. metropolitan areas, in spite of their huge growth since 1945. However, it has also generated dire problems for millions of the poorest households in these areas.

1. This chapter summarizes an analysis presented in more detail in another book written as part of the same overall study. See Anthony Downs, *Neighborhoods and Urban Development* (Brookings Institution, 1981).

In the development of urban areas around the world, most new construction occurs on vacant land at the edges of built-up areas. Therefore, urban population growth is accommodated (except in wartime) by construction of new peripheral housing. In most of the world, some of this housing consists of high-quality units occupied by the affluent; more consists of good-quality units occupied by middle- and moderate-income households; and still more consists of low-quality units occupied by the very poor. The latter are often shacks built by the poor themselves on expropriated land.

But in the United States, construction of new low-quality housing is prevented by rigorous enforcement of zoning laws and building codes that require high-quality units. Therefore, *new* housing is too expensive for most moderate-income and all low-income households to occupy without direct subsidies. Such households are in effect legally excluded from all new-growth areas. So they are virtually compelled to concentrate in older housing units close to the historic center of each metropolitan area, sometimes in long-established suburbs. Most of these units were originally built in neighborhoods then on the urban periphery, and initially occupied by middle- or upper-income households. But as they got older, and new growth moved out beyond them, they gradually "trickled down" through the income distribution. They were successively occupied by groups with relatively lower incomes. During most of their history, these housing units provided good-quality dwelling for their occupants. But in many cases, they eventually became occupied by households too poor to maintain them or to pay rents sufficient to induce landlords to maintain them.

The stages of relative and then absolute decline these neighborhoods went through as this process unfolded are typical of U.S. neighborhood change. From the viewpoint of each neighborhood, such change is usually perceived as undesirable decay. But from an area-wide perspective, this decline is a necessary part of accommodating growth of the low-income population. For reasons just described, large numbers of poor rural or foreign inmigrants cannot settle in peripheral new-growth areas, so they usually arrive in centrally located "entry-port" neighborhoods containing the oldest, most deteriorated housing in the entire metropolitan area. As the total number of such households increases, densities in these "entry-port" areas rise, and soon the households there begin spilling over into surrounding neighborhoods. This causes transition of nearby neighborhoods from moderate-income to lower-income occupancy, and induces the initial occupants to locate farther out.

Under these conditions, it is difficult to create neighborhood stability in most central parts of the metropolitan area. They experience constant changes in the characteristics, as well as the identity, of their residents. Such continuous neighborhood change could be greatly reduced if poor newcomers were allowed to move directly into brand-new neighborhoods on the urban periphery. However, this mixing of new low-income neighborhoods with the new neighborhoods also being built on the urban periphery for high- and middle-income households has been unacceptable to those households in the United States up to now.

One possible reason for this viewpoint is the nature of U.S. public schools. Most high- and middle-income parents want their children to attend schools where other children from similar households predominate, partly because such schools usually provide the most effective academic training. Yet they also want to use public schools rather than private ones, since the former are less costly. The only way they can guarantee both these conditions is to live where there are very few low-income neighborhoods nearby. Thus, the nature of U.S. public schools transforms the desire of high- and middle-income households for *neighborhood* socioeconomic segregation—which is quite common throughout the world—into a desire for *regional* socioeconomic segregation—which is rarer. This conclusion is partly confirmed by our empirical finding that large cities served by public school districts extending into surrounding suburbs tend to grow faster, relative to their suburbs, than those served by school districts ending at city boundaries.

Recent court decisions mandating the busing of children to schools other than the ones nearest their homes tend to reinforce this desire for regional separation by income groups as well as race. If a household's children may attend schools with children living in neighborhoods quite far away, the only way to ensure that its children will attend schools dominated by children from other high- and middle-income households is to live out of practical busing range, or in a different school district, from low- and moderate-income neighborhoods.

Rapid population growth within U.S. metropolitan areas does not always generate widespread neighborhood change. If an SMSA is expanding mainly through net inmigration of households with incomes high enough so they can afford brand-new housing, many newcomers can move directly into newly built subdivisions at the urban periphery or into the middle ring of neighborhoods.[2] Older neighborhoods closer to the area's center will experience normal turnover, but they need not undergo constant

2. Why large numbers of migrants enter some SMSAs but not others is analyzed in chapter 5.

transition of average income or status levels. Such less socially traumatic increases in area-wide population have sometimes taken place in parts or all of rapidly expanding metropolitan areas in the South and West during the past two decades.[3]

An Alternative Theory of Urban Poverty Concentration

A different explanation of why poor households concentrate near the center of each metropolitan area has been suggested by Richard Muth and Edwin Mills.[4] Centrally located land is more accessible to large clusters of jobs than farther-out land; so the average time and money costs of commuting between downtown and far-out land are higher. To make up for this disadvantage, land prices per acre tend to fall with distance from downtown, other things equal. This relationship has been well established empirically by studies of many large urban areas around the world. Where land is more expensive, it is used more intensively. Hence residential and other densities are normally higher on the costlier land close to each area's center than farther out.

Because housing consumption tends to rise with income, middle- and upper-income households want to occupy bigger homes on larger lots than poor households. Therefore, these economists argue that more affluent households live relatively far out where land costs per acre are lower. That leaves poor households concentrated in higher-density housing closer in, where they occupy much less land per household and hence spend less on land in spite of its higher cost per acre.

But there is a countervailing argument to this reasoning even within

3. One type of neighborhood change not resulting from low-income inmigration derives from pressure for intensified land use. Its most common cause is the original growth or later expansion of a commercial district, such as the downtown business district, an outlying shopping district, or a planned shopping center. Such expansion generates demands for relatively intensive use of nearby land, partly because the district attracts large traffic flows that create markets for other activities. A second cause of intensified land use is the creation of medium-rise or high-rise residential structures along a waterfront or other amenity in an area formerly occupied mainly by single-family residences. This has occurred along Lake Shore Drive and Lincoln Park on Chicago's North Side, for example, in parts of La Jolla, California, and along much of South Florida's coastline. Intensification of land use almost always drastically changes the character of those neighborhoods where it occurs. Moreover, such changes are unfavorable to effective continuation of the original use—especially if it was single-family homes.

4. See Richard F. Muth, *Cities and Housing: The Spatial Pattern of Urban Residential Land Use* (University of Chicago Press, 1969), pp. 29–34, 311–13; and Edwin S. Mills, *Urban Economics* (Scott, Foresman, 1972), pp. 71–72, 85–88.

the downtown-centered city model itself. Empirical studies suggest that a major element of commuting cost is the self-perceived value of the time required. This value appears to rise with income, thereby creating an incentive for high-income workers to choose central residential locations. Thus, the theoretical location of various income groups in long-run equilibrium depends upon how fast the demand for housing rises with income, compared to how fast transportation costs (including time value) rise with income.[5] Muth and Mills argue that the former increases faster than the latter; therefore the transportation-cost theory of land use successfully explains the observed tendency of higher-income households to locate farther out.

But more recent evidence on housing demand casts doubt upon their argument.[6] Data from the Experimental Housing Allowance Program—the largest empirical study of housing markets ever undertaken—indicate that most households do not increase their spending on housing anywhere near proportionally to increases in their incomes.[7] Furthermore, recent writings have stressed the positive role of other downtown amenities in the trade-off between space and accessibility. Households may *increase* the proportion of their incomes they spend on some amenities as their incomes rise.[8] If the frequency of downtown trips therefore rises with income, households will shift more toward downtown locations as their incomes rise. Still other evidence indicates that the relation between location choice and income is different among small and large households. In the New York area, 1970 census figures show that high-income families tended to live farther from downtown Manhattan than low-income families, but the reverse was true for unrelated individuals.[9] Moreover, this theory assumes all households ignore neighborhood effects—that is, the nature of surrounding households and environments—in choosing where to live.

5. Formally, the issue rests upon a comparison between the income elasticities of housing demand and transportation cost.

6. See A. Mitchell Polinsky, "The Demand for Housing: A Study in Specification and Grouping," *Econometrica*, vol. 45 (March 1977), pp. 447–61; and Stephen K. Mayo, "Theory and Estimation in the Economics of Housing Demand," *Journal of Urban Economics*, vol. 10 (July 1981), pp. 95–116.

7. See Eric A. Hanushek and John M. Quigley, "Consumption Aspects," in Katharine L. Bradbury and Anthony Downs, eds., *Do Housing Allowances Work?* (Brookings Institution, 1981), pp. 185–240.

8. For evidence supporting this conclusion, see Douglas Diamond, "Income and Residential Location: Muth Revisited," *Urban Studies*, vol. 17 (February 1980), pp. 1–12.

9. Clifford R. Kern, "Private Residential Renewal and the Supply of Neighborhoods," in David Segal, ed., *The Economics of Neighborhood* (Academic Press, 1979), pp. 121–46.

But recent studies of household behavior indicate such effects are important influences upon residential choices.[10]

Thus, it does not appear that transportation-cost theories of land use can explain the spatial pattern of income-group residences observed in U.S. metropolitan areas. Nor is it likely that the trade-off between housing prices and transportation costs to the city center is the primary factor accounting for the concentration of poor households in inner-city locations. This conclusion is strengthened by the fact that, in many urban areas around the world where zoning and other land-use controls are not strongly enforced, poor people live at all distances from the urban center, not mainly clustered near it. Hence the central concentration of poverty in U.S. urban areas results to a significant extent from the deliberate exclusionary policies embodied in our urban development process.

The Spatial Hierarchy of Neighborhoods

In nearly every large urban area throughout the world, a spatial hierarchy of residential neighborhoods has arisen. It contains many separate neighborhoods with differing average levels of household income and social status, but relative homogeneity of these traits within each neighborhood. Such hierarchies rarely result from a deliberate ranking process or conscious overall plan of urban development. Rather, they reflect the widespread preference for neighborhoods where most nearby households have similar incomes, social status, and sometimes ethnic character.

In U.S. metropolitan areas, most of the lowest-ranking neighborhoods are close to the older core of the area; most—but usually not all—of the highest-ranking neighborhoods are close to the outer periphery; and most of the middle-ranked neighborhoods are somewhere between.[11] In big metropolitan areas containing large black populations, there are often two spatially separate hierarchies: one mainly white, and one mainly black. Except in a few cities like Los Angeles, other ethnic submarkets are not

10. See David L. Birch and others, *The Behavioral Foundations of Neighborhood Change* (Joint Center for Urban Studies of the Massachusetts Institute of Technology and Harvard University, 1977). About 1,900 households living in four metropolitan areas were interviewed over the period 1971 through 1976 concerning their residential location choices. When asked what had been most important in selecting their existing neighborhoods, they cited twelve factors, eight of which involved neighborhood effects rather than distance from downtown or characteristics of the housing unit chosen. These eight neighborhood factors were cited as most important by 43 percent of the respondents; whereas other factors were cited by 57 percent.

11. See Downs, *Neighborhoods and Urban Development*, chap. 4.

usually large enough to form a third hierarchy, although individual neighborhoods may have a distinct ethnic character.

The lowest-ranking neighborhoods in an SMSA are not necessarily in bad condition in an absolute sense. Some metropolitan areas are so new, so prosperous, so well maintained, or so fast-growing that even their worst neighborhoods are in good condition compared to "slums" elsewhere. This seems to be true of Seattle, for example. These areas are not undesirable places to live. Yet because they are the *least* desirable around, they are also the most susceptible to future decline if overall housing demand in that metropolitan area weakens in relation to overall supply for any long period.

Differential Code Enforcement by Neighborhoods

Very low-income households cannot afford to acquire or occupy relatively high-quality housing without large public subsidies. Hence some substandard housing—deteriorated, overcrowded, poorly built, or lacking complete plumbing—is present in every large metropolitan area in the world except those few with extensive subsidized housing programs, as in Stockholm. Nearly all U.S. metropolitan areas contain significant amounts of such substandard housing.

This situation poses a dilemma for local governments. They want housing codes in all neighborhoods that help eliminate health and safety hazards. But their higher-income residents also want regulations to maintain housing to high standards in neighborhoods occupied by middle- and upper-income households so it cannot deteriorate into low-quality but nonhazardous housing.

Resolving this dilemma requires maintaining high-quality housing standards in middle- and upper-income neighborhoods, moderate standards in moderate-income neighborhoods, and low standards that rule out only serious hazards in very poor neighborhoods. Hypothetically, this could be done by (1) adopting different legally required standards in different parts of each community; (2) adopting a single high-quality standard, but enforcing it to varying degrees; or (3) dividing the metropolitan area into separate legal jurisdictions and adopting different standards in each.

The democratic ideal of equal treatment before the law makes it politically unacceptable for a community to adopt different legally required housing standards for the affluent and the poor, though it may do so for new versus existing housing. Also, recent court decisions mandating equal-quality services in all parts of a government's jurisdiction make it more difficult to adopt a single standard but enforce it differently. Hence, from the viewpoint of middle- and upper-income households, the only method available to resolve this dilemma is to maintain legally separate communities, each fully controlling housing standards and land uses within its boundaries. By politically dominating many of these small communities, middle- and upper-income households can ensure maintenance of high-quality housing standards where they live—even though they could not similarly dominate the entire area if it were within a single jurisdiction. Then socioeconomic segregation can be achieved through legal means, rather than just market forces.

Such *municipal* separation thus concentrates most poor people within each metropolitan area jurisdictionally as well as spatially—usually within the central city. In 1976, all U.S. central cities contained 9.5 million poor persons, or 15.8 percent of their total populations—up from 14.9 percent in 1969. All suburbs contained 5.7 million poor persons, or 6.9 percent of their populations—down from 8.1 percent in 1969.[12]

The Different Benefits of the Trickle-down Process

The U.S. urban development process has produced good neighborhood and community environments for nearly all high-income and most middle-income households. It has also provided reasonably good environments for many moderate-income and some low-income households. These beneficiaries constitute a vast majority of all households in U.S. metropolitan areas, who provide strong political support for maintaining the institutional and legal structures on which the process is based.

But this same process also produces disastrous results for many of the lowest-income households by compelling them to concentrate together in the oldest neighborhoods. These households include many of the least capable, least self-confident, least resourceful, least hopeful people in the entire urban area. As a result, undesirable conditions such as high rates of unemployment, public dependency, crime, vandalism, delinquency, arson, housing abandonment, drug addiction, and broken homes proliferate.

Some observers believe that concentration of poverty alone cannot account for these conditions. They contend that concentrations of the poor

12. Department of Housing and Urban Development, *The President's National Urban Policy Report, 1980* (HUD, August 1980), p. 4-2. See also data for changes in the 1960s reported in chapter 3, above, tables 3-6, 3-7, and 3-8.

in U.S. cities during the late nineteenth and early twentieth centuries were less subject to such social problems. Based upon the evidence of somewhat different, but equally deleterious, conditions cited by contemporary observers, we are skeptical that conditions were any better in earlier concentrated-poverty areas of U.S. cities.[13] Violent crime rates may have been lower, though no accurate data concerning them exist. But exploitation of child labor, sanitation, housing, nutrition, working conditions, and absolute standards of living were all probably worse than those in present urban poverty concentrations within the United States.

On the other hand, there can be little doubt that concentrations of poverty in some other nations have not generated the same conditions. Anyone who has visited urban slums in different parts of the world soon learns that behavior in each is influenced more by the locally prevailing culture than by overcrowding, poverty, or high density. Moreover, certain negative conditions in U.S. urban poverty concentrations are statistically associated with particular ethnic groups. For example, the incidence of serious crimes is relatively high among blacks, even after allowing for differences in income, and they also have relatively high proportions of single-parent households with children.[14] This suggests that the long history of racial discrimination and unequal treatment of American blacks adversely influences behavior in many urban poverty concentrations where blacks predominate. Long-term remedies are therefore more complex than just deconcentrating the poor. Nevertheless, such deconcentration is probably a prerequisite if other remedies are to work.

Another group has also been injured by disruptive neighborhood change: people who would have preferred to remain in older city neighborhoods had change been more gradual and not accompanied by extreme deterioration. Many have felt forced to move and have viewed the whole process as a great hardship.

Thus, arrangements that have enabled the majority of households in

13. The Report to the National Commission on the Causes and Prevention of Violence indicates that levels of crime and violence were probably higher in earlier periods of American history than they are now. See Richard Maxwell Brown, "Historical Patterns of Violence in America," pp. 75–76, and Roger Lane, "Urbanization and Criminal Violence in the 19th Century: Massachusetts as a Test Case," pp. 468–84, in Hugh Davis Graham and Ted Robert Gurr, eds., *The History of Violence in America* (Bantam Books, 1969).

14. See the President's Commission on Law Enforcement and Administration of Justice, *The Challenge of Crime in a Free Society* (GPO, 1967), pp. 44–45; Edwin M. Schur, *Our Criminal Society: The Social and Legal Sources of Crime in America* (Prentice-Hall, 1969), pp. 125–31; and James Q. Wilson, *Thinking About Crime* (Basic Books, 1975), pp. 13–20, 73.

metropolitan areas to separate themselves from undesirable conditions also impose severe social and economic costs on others. These costs are closely intertwined with the nation's most serious urban problems, such as unemployment, crime, physical deterioration, and even much personal disorder and despair.

Fundamental policies that would alleviate the worst urban problems would require major changes in the entire structure of urban areas. In particular, they would decrease the spatial concentration of the poorest households by providing them with opportunities to live elsewhere. But the majority that now benefits from the hierarchical and exclusionary structure of neighborhoods created by the urban development process resists such changes.

What Happens When Metropolitan-Area Population Growth Slows or Stops

From the viewpoint of most urban households, the U.S. urban development process successfully copes with rapid metropolitan-area population growth, even though it unfairly imposes heavy social costs on certain groups. However, when metropolitan-area population growth slows or stops, this same process produces other socially undesirable results. These results are especially likely when the growth slowdown occurs among the poor. True, a drop in low-income inmigration usually improves the welfare of a metropolitan area's poor population considered as a whole. There are fewer poor households competing for existing lower-cost housing and available jobs than there would be with continued rapid growth. Yet for residents of very poor neighborhoods, this causes a shift from the maladies of overcrowding to those of depopulation. Upwardly mobile households continue to move out of the lowest-income neighborhoods as better housing becomes available elsewhere. Hence the total population of these areas falls sharply, and serious housing abandonment begins. Moreover, as the most mobile depart, the remaining population consists to an even greater extent of households either unable or unwilling to upgrade themselves. Thus neighborhood decline can result either from heavy net inmigration of poor households or from the complete absence of inmigration.

Two questions arise: why do builders continue creating new housing if there is an overall surplus within the metropolitan area, and why don't they locate the new housing on the inner-city land vacated by housing abandonment? Relatively affluent households with rising real incomes prefer more modern, more spacious accommodations to their present quarters. Hence there is a market for new peripheral units. Since the developers of new housing are not the owners of the old housing, they are willing to profit by actions that undermine the demand for more centrally located housing. Builders do not create many new units on inner-city sites because most households affluent enough to afford newly built housing either prefer more modern, more spacious accommodations or are unwilling to live in proximity to poverty.

Consequently, the "emptying out" of older inner-city neighborhoods results from continued operation of the basic U.S. urban development process after the rapid population growth it originally arose to cope with has stopped. Some urban experts contend there is no reason to impede further peripheral growth because the whole process is a form of technological progress, in which modern, spacious dwelling units and neighborhoods replace obsolete, crowded ones. From this perspective, slowing suburban growth to "save" central cities is halting the march of progress.

There is truth in this view, but it ignores two crucial facts. Certain social policies may have biased the choice facing consumers in favor of new suburban units compared to older city housing. In addition, the buyers of new suburban housing often do not pay the full social costs of the units they enjoy. The public costs of creating the new streets, sewers, water systems, parks, and schools in their subdivisions are spread over all the taxpayers in their communities, not just those buying homes in that subdivision.[15] Allowing households to enjoy the benefits of new suburban housing without paying all its social costs causes an inefficient allocation of resources. Trying to remedy this inefficiency by taxing sales of new suburban housing and using the proceeds to aid declining cities would be neither practical nor politically feasible. However, this situation does justify federal and state financial aid to declining cities funded through income and other taxes that fall disproportionately on suburban residents.

Slower growth of metropolitan-area low-income population also has

15. Partly as a result of reductions in local property taxes mandated by Proposition 13, many California communities have already shifted much of the marginal cost of furnishing added public infrastructures for new subdivisions onto their developers—and therefore, ultimately their new or potential residents. This has been done by means of high building permit fees, land contribution requirements, utility hook-up fees, and other direct costs.

important positive results. Reduced competition for low-wage jobs and low-cost housing raises wages and lowers housing prices for many poor households. Reduced expansion of an area's total low-income population also decreases the "inside-outward" pressure for neighborhood change to accommodate more poor households. This raises the probability that some inner-city neighborhoods can be stabilized in character, or revitalized. Stabilization is being attempted with some success in the South Shore area of Chicago by a locally owned bank focusing upon neighborhood development. In fact, the recent nationwide rise in political significance of the "neighborhood movement," which reflects the concern of its members in maintaining their neighborhood status quo, is probably related to the sharp decline in low-income population growth within large cities.

Two types of neighborhood revitalization can be identified. Both involve improved physical condition of structures and increased property values, but they differ concerning who occupies the rehabilitated structures. *Gentrification* occurs when more affluent newcomers buy and refurbish homes in run-down neighborhoods, displacing many of the poorer initial residents. *Incumbent upgrading* occurs when the initial low- or moderate-income residents rehabilitate deteriorated areas themselves. Revitalization can occur in response to metropolitan, city, or neighborhood characteristics, such as widespread suburban traffic congestion or architecturally interesting old housing in specific neighborhoods. Other factors important during the 1970s included rising energy costs and easy availability of mortgage credit (except since 1979). All these factors generated much more neighborhood revitalization in the nation's large cities during the 1970s than ever before.

Gentrification may have negative effects for low-income residents displaced by higher-income newcomers. In areas initially occupied by homeowners, most displacement is voluntary, and does not harm those displaced since they reap a capital gain upon selling their houses. But when the initial residents are poor renters, displacement may harm some who are compelled to move. Since nearly 40 percent of all renters move each year in the normal course of events,[16] not all renters who move out of a reviving neighborhood are truly displaced by revitalization. But for those who would

16. The figure was 38.9 percent in 1977. U.S. Departments of Commerce and Housing and Urban Development, *Annual Housing Survey: 1977, Part D, Housing Characteristics of Recent Movers* (GPO, 1979), p. 1. Not all 38.9 percent moved out of the neighborhood in which they started; however, this figure does not include multiple moves by households who moved more than once in the twelve months preceding the survey.

otherwise have remained, revitalization imposes displacement costs including moving expenses, disruption of long-established social networks, and in some cases inability to find equally satisfactory housing elsewhere. One recent study of the Prospect Hill neighborhood in Cincinnati found that about one-fourth of the households leaving the area over a two-year period were involuntarily displaced by reinvestment activities, and that one-fifth of those displaced felt their new home and neighborhood were inferior to what they had left.[17]

Conclusion

The socioeconomic and ethnic segregation deeply embedded in U.S. urban development strongly contribute to physical decay and population losses in many older big-city neighborhoods. Many poor urban households become concentrated in such neighborhoods because fragmented suburban jurisdictions adopt public policies that deliberately exclude them. These arrangements load central city governments with a disproportionate share of the social and fiscal burdens of coping with the nation's poverty. Moreover, this outcome is neither accidental nor caused by the operation of free markets. Rather, it results at least in part from public policies that are hard to change because they benefit a majority of urban households.

17. Michael Schill, "Neighborhood Reinvestment and Displacement," working paper (Princeton Urban and Regional Research Center, Princeton University, 1981), table 5. Schill's study is currently being extended to five other cities.

8

Forces Affecting the Future of Cities

URBAN AREAS are the most complex of all mankind's inventions. It is virtually impossible to forecast their future within a single, comprehensive model incorporating all the key relationships among the variables identified earlier. Will the past influences of these variables continue unchanged? These influences can be altered if future events either change the *magnitude* of a factor or shift its *relationship* to city growth or decline. For example, the relationship between city growth and net migration from SMSAs to nonmetropolitan areas is unlikely to change, but the *magnitude* of that outflow might increase in the 1980s. On the other hand, the past *relationship* between an area's containing a state capital and its attaining faster-than-average growth may change as the expansion of state and local governments slows.

An Approach to the Future of Urban Areas

Here we aim at assessing the overall net strength of the forces likely to be exerted on central cities in various categories. We defer our conclusions about how those forces will affect urban growth and decline. In this chapter we identify the specific factors we found to be important determinants of urban decline, and consider the future of each in light of the underlying economic, social, and political trends most likely to affect it. These trends are treated as exogenous; our assumptions about them are explained in the appendix to this chapter. The specific factors are grouped according to which population or employment flow they most directly affect. Within each group, we have listed them roughly in order of estimated importance, based where possible on their relative strength in explaining city growth rate differences as indicated by the last column of table 6-1 or 6-8.

Overall Metropolitan Population Growth

Two sets of factors primarily affect the population growth of all U.S. metropolitan areas combined.

NATIONAL POPULATION GROWTH. Rapid national population growth produces absolute increases in almost all metropolitan areas, even if some are experiencing heavy outmigration. This condition of "a rising tide floating all boats" prevailed in the United States from 1945 through about 1965. Thereafter the nation's population growth rate slowed. Whether total future population growth will be fast or slow will depend especially on fertility rates, the number of women of childbearing age, and immigration.

1. Fertility rates have fallen about 40 percent from their postwar high in 1957. Nevertheless, demographers disagree about their future course. Some believe the smaller number of workers entering the labor force in the 1980s will produce higher real wages per male worker, thereby freeing more women to stay home and rear children and causing fertility rates to rise sharply again.[1] Others contend that recent fertility declines reflect longer-run shifts in attitudes: young people wanting to spend many of their most fertile years enjoying high living standards before having children, women wanting to establish permanent careers, and widespread beliefs that big families contribute to population and environmental problems.[2]

Fertility rates have important impacts upon estimates of future urban population growth.[3] A lifetime fertility rate (that is, the average number of children ever born to 1,000 women) of 2,100 would exactly replace the existing population in the absence of any net immigration. Since 1945, lifetime fertility rates in the United States have varied from a high of about 3,700 in the late 1950s to a low of just under 1,800 in the late 1970s. We believe future fertility rates will not return to anything like their high levels

1. Richard A. Easterlin, *Birth and Fortune: The Impact of Numbers on Personal Welfare* (Basic Books, 1980), p. 134.

2. William P. Butz and Michael P. Ward, "The Emergence of Countercyclical U.S. Fertility," *American Economic Review*, vol. 69 (June 1979), pp. 318–28.

3. Census Bureau projections show that a lifetime fertility rate of 2,700 children ever born per 1,000 women would produce a total 1990 population 18.4 million (7.8 percent) higher than a rate of 1,700, and 11.2 million (4.4 percent) higher than a rate of 2,100. *Statistical Abstract of the United States, 1979*, p. 8.

of the late 1950s. An assumed rate of 1,800 seems reasonable for the next two decades, and consistent with the recent leveling off of both actual fertility and intentions stated in surveys.

2. The number of women of childbearing age will rise in the 1980s. The number of U.S. women aged fourteen to forty-four rose steadily from 35.4 million in 1950 to 37.5 in 1960, 44.7 in 1970, and 52.1 in 1978. It is expected to increase further to 56.9 million in 1985 and 58.0 million in 1990, and then level off in the 1990s.[4] Therefore, the number of births will probably be somewhat higher in the 1980s than in the 1970s, averaging over 3.5 million per year.

3. In the 1970s, the annual rate of *legal* immigration into the United States averaged about 400,000, the highest rate since 1920. Most Census Bureau projections assume a continuation of this rate. However, these projections ignore *illegal* immigration. Since 1977, over one million persons have been apprehended *each year* trying to enter the nation illegally; most observers presume the number who succeed in crossing U.S. borders undetected is substantial.[5] However, the number leaving the country surreptitiously each year is also unknown; so *net* illegal immigration is extremely difficult to estimate accurately, with estimates ranging from 116,000 to 800,000.[6]

If such immigration continues unabated, it will increase the nation's future population well above current Census Bureau projections.[7] Most illegal immigrants are from Mexico, and pressure for continued illegal entry from there is not likely to decline. The Mexican economy needs an outlet for its many unemployed, and the United States needs Mexican oil. Moreover, there may be a relative shortage of unskilled labor in some parts of the United States toward the end of the 1980s because of the smaller number of young people entering the labor force. Therefore, a significant amount of illegal immigration will take place over the next two decades. We have tried to compensate for this error by using a Census Bureau

4. Ibid., pp. 8–9.

5. *Immigration to the United States*, Hearings before the House Select Committee on Population, 95 Cong. 2 sess. (GPO, 1978), pp. 1, 12–32.

6. One of the most careful studies estimated that there was a cumulative total of 4.2 million illegal immigrants in the United States as of April 1973. But its authors said the total could range from 2.9 million to 5.7 million and still be consistent with their data. Ibid.

7. If new illegal immigration averaged 400,000 persons per year, and legal immigration and fertility conformed to the Census Bureau's Series II projections, then we calculate that the total population would exceed those projections by 6.1 million in 1990 and 11.4 million in 2000 (an error of 4.4 percent in that year).

projection based on a higher fertility rate than we believe will actually occur. Hence we use the Series II projections, which ignore illegal immigration but assume a lifetime fertility rate of 2,100, rather than the 1,800 we believe is more likely.[8]

Another implication of illegal immigration is that urban areas containing large Hispanic communities will grow more rapidly, or decline more slowly, than will be forecast by official sources. This tendency has already been borne out from 1970 to 1975 by our statistical analysis, even though it is based on population figures that probably exclude most illegal immigrants. Hispanic immigrants will continue to settle where other Hispanics are already established, concentrating more in large cities than suburbs. We expect that only after the 1980s will the Hispanic population start suburbanizing, as the black population did in the 1970s.

METROPOLITAN SHARE OF NATIONAL POPULATION GROWTH. The 121 large SMSAs described in chapter 3 captured 67.3 percent of all national population growth from 1960 to 1970, but only 43.2 percent from 1970 to 1975. The 279 areas classified as SMSAs in 1975 encompassed 91.1 percent of all population growth from 1960 to 1970, but just 62.5 percent from 1970 to 1977.[9] The future size of this share will depend mainly on two things: metropolitan spillover growth into surrounding counties and migration to areas not in or adjacent to SMSAs.

1. The remarkable reversal of net migration to metropolitan areas in the 1970s is partly an illusion. Counties both adjacent to SMSAs and having over 20 percent of their employed residents commuting into SMSAs grew faster from 1970 to 1975 than any other group of U.S. counties except large fringe counties within SMSAs.[10] As industries, shopping centers, offices,

8. The Series II projection for 2000 is 14.5 million (5.9 percent) higher than the Series III projection, which assumes a lifetime fertility rate of 1,700; thus interpolation indicates that a projection using a rate of 1,800 would be about 10.9 million lower than the Series II projection. This implies annual average growth from 1980 to 2000 about 545,000 higher under the Series II projection than under a projection based upon an 1,800 lifetime fertility rate. We believe that average annual divergence is a good approximation of the combined effect of both net illegal immigration each year—which we estimate will average about 400,000 persons—and the subsequent natural increase generated by such immigration. (Note that the Census Series II–X projection, which excludes the 400,000 net legal immigrants assumed in Series II, predicts a 1980–2000 growth which is 10 million less than Series II; *Statistical Abstract of the United States, 1979*, p. 7.)

9. Ibid., p. 19.

10. Peter A. Morrison, *Current Demographic Change in Regions of the United States* (Rand Corp., November 1977), p. 7; and Kevin F. McCarthy and Peter A. Morrison, *The Changing Demographic and Economic Structure of Nonmetropolitan Areas in the 1970s* (Rand Corp., January 1978), pp. 26–27.

and other employment sources moved farther out from central cities, more and more workers moved outside SMSAs and commuted into them, despite higher gasoline prices. This dispersion was also encouraged by lower housing costs[11] and less regulation of land uses in nonmetropolitan areas. Ironically, increased land-use regulation within SMSAs—partly aimed at compelling more compact settlement patterns to save energy—might cause even greater dispersion of both homes and workplaces in the future. We expect such spillover growth to continue, probably at about the same rate as in the recent past.

2. Population growth of nonmetropolitan areas had markedly different characteristics in the 1970s from such growth in the past.[12] It was not confined to SMSA spillovers or to consolidation in medium-sized "growth centers," but also occurred in rural counties not adjacent to SMSAs and containing no sizable urban communities. Moreover, the main economic supports underlying nonmetropolitan growth seem to have shifted from manufacturing and government to retirement and recreation.

In our opinion, the spreading of population growth across more nonmetropolitan areas results partly from a gradual homogenization of U.S. culture and amenities. This very long-term cultural and economic process began with the extension of railroads throughout rural areas in the late nineteenth and early twentieth centuries and continued with rural electrification in the 1920s and 1930s, followed by nearly universal possession of radios. Then came massive building and improvement of rural highways, construction of the Interstate Highway System, and a virtual "explosion" of automotive vehicle use after 1950.[13] Enormous gains in farm productivity increased the average size of remaining farms and required greater sophistication and education among those operating them. In recent years, television, the building of shopping centers and modern health-care facilities in small cities, more widespread use of air travel, and many other changes have further integrated even the most spatially isolated communities into the national culture.

11. For example, in the Washington, D.C., area in 1979, a builder was offering the exact same house on two sites, one twenty miles farther from downtown than the other—and $17,000 less expensive. The extra gasoline cost of driving that additional 9,600 miles per year would be $960—assuming gasoline costs $1.50 per gallon, the commuter's car gets fifteen miles per gallon, and the commuter has ten paid holidays and two weeks vacation. In contrast, a 12 percent, twenty-five-year home mortgage for the additional $17,000 cost of the closer-in home would require payments of about $2,150 per year.

12. McCarthy and Morrison, *The Changing Demographic and Economic Structure*.

13. For a discussion of the last factor, see Anthony Downs, "The Automotive Population Explosion," *Traffic Quarterly*, vol. 33 (July 1979), pp. 347–62 (Brookings Reprint 353).

Thus, differences in quality of life between rural and urban areas have greatly diminished, especially over the past three decades. Furthermore, the shift away from large families has created millions of relatively "footloose" households not tied to specific communities or residences. Finally, the proportion of the population on farms has fallen so low (3.7 percent in 1978) that migration from farms cannot continue its past role as a substantial contributor to metropolitan growth. Even the net outflow of 301,000 per year from farms during the 1970–77 period was reversed in 1978.[14]

Under these circumstances, we believe the fundamental thrust of urban decentralization that first expressed itself in suburban growth, and more recently in nonmetropolitan growth, will continue. As a result, metropolitan areas will continue to capture a much smaller share of total population growth than they did in the 1950s and 1960s. Our best guess is that the 279 areas defined as SMSAs in 1975 will capture close to 65 percent of total national population growth in the 1980s, the same as from 1970 to 1977. Combined with our estimate of national population growth, this implies that they will gain 14.3 million additional residents during the 1980s, slightly more than occurred during the 1970s, but still well below growth in the 1960s.

Population Growth of Particular Metropolitan Areas

This section analyzes how future trends will affect the factors influencing the population growth of individual SMSAs, either directly or by affecting employment growth.

CLIMATE AND RECREATIONAL ATTRACTION. A warm climate was associated with faster SMSA growth, other things equal. Areas with mild climate and high recreational amenities should continue to draw residents, especially as real incomes rise.

SMSA UNEMPLOYMENT RATE. The higher an SMSA's unemployment rate relative to the national average, the slower its population growth. During the recessions of 1970–71 and 1974–75, unemployment rates averaged higher in the Northeast and North Central regions than in the South and West. For example, in 1975, the average statewide unemployment rate was 9.7 percent among the nine Northeastern states, and 8.1 percent among the seventeen Southern states. During recovery periods, these regional differentials declined: in 1978, the average statewide unemploy-

14. *Statistical Abstract of the United States, 1979*, p. 681.

ment rate was 6.1 percent in both Northeastern and Southern states.[15] Consequently, migration flows responding to unemployment rate differences during the recessions caused further metropolitan decline in Northeastern and North Central SMSAs. If future business cycles continue to have this effect, more migration along these regional lines can be expected. Moreover, within each region, those SMSAs with wide cyclical fluctuations in unemployment rates (such as Detroit and Pittsburgh) will tend to grow more slowly than those with relatively low, stable unemployment rates (such as Minneapolis-St. Paul and Omaha).

However, there is a tendency for regions with long-depressed economies to gradually shift their employment emphasis to more dynamic activities. For example, New England lost many labor-intensive apparel, shoe, and manufacturing industries, but has slowly evolved into a center for higher education and for electronic and high-technology industries. Moreover, high cyclical unemployment rates are associated with heavy manufacturing industries, which comprise a declining share of total U.S. employment. As more and more SMSAs reduce their dependence upon such industries, the differential regional impact of recessions should decrease. But the impact of recessions will then be focused more sharply than ever upon those few SMSAs still heavily dependent upon highly cyclical activities. Sketchy evidence indicates this may be the case in the 1980 recession, particularly in areas specializing in automobiles, automobile parts, and steel.

Altogether, we expect SMSA unemployment to remain an important influence upon city population growth, but to have a less differentiating impact upon such growth over the next two decades.

HISPANICS AS A PROPORTION OF CENTRAL CITY POPULATIONS. A high concentration of Hispanics in a central city appears to increase the growth rate both of the surrounding metropolitan area and of the city relative to its metropolitan area. We expect that Hispanic populations will continue to play an important role in directing immigration from abroad into those SMSAs and central cities that already contain large Hispanic communities.

SMSA RATE OF NATURAL POPULATION INCREASE. Nearly all individual SMSAs have positive rates of natural increase. SMSAs with high fractions of elderly population (like Tampa-St. Petersburg) have low rates of natural increase that slow their overall population growth; whereas those experiencing recent employment growth (like San Jose) tend to have younger families and higher rates of natural increase. These relationships seem unlikely to change much in the future.

15. Ibid., p. 405.

TOTAL SMSA EMPLOYMENT. Large total size is associated with somewhat slower employment growth, probably because of diseconomies of scale or congestion. Since this relationship evolves slowly over time, its effects in the future will not differ much from those in the recent past. However, many areas now growing rapidly will eventually become large enough so that their size will tend to slow their growth.

TYPES OF INDUSTRIES IN THE SMSA. Metropolitan areas specializing in industries with high national growth rates tend to grow more rapidly. We expect some reduction in the specialization of older metropolitan areas in manufacturing and other slow-growing industries. Nevertheless, those SMSAs currently dominated by such industries and unable to attract a diversified economic base will continue to grow more slowly.

One industry found to encourage employment growth is state government: SMSAs containing a state capital tended to grow faster. However, this association is likely to diminish in the future. The rapid growth of state government employment relative to other industries ended in about 1975, and is not likely to recur during the 1980s at anything like its earlier pace.

REAL INCOME PER CAPITA. Employment grows more rapidly in metropolitan areas with high per capita income but low and slowly rising living costs. Wages and incomes are rising faster in the South and more slowly in the Northeast than in other regions. From 1970 to 1978, per capita personal income in current dollars rose 87.1 percent in the Northeast, but it rose 19.0 percent faster in the North Central region, 26.8 percent faster in the South, and 19.4 percent faster in the West.[16] This was only partly compensated for by the cost of living. During the same period, the consumer price index for urban consumers, which increased 65.6 percent in the Northeast, rose 1.6 percent faster in the North Central region, 8.9 percent faster in the South, and 7.3 percent faster in the West.[17] Since incomes corrected for living costs are already higher in Southern SMSAs and cities than in Northeastern ones, their faster escalation will increase the gap. That will tend to accelerate the migration of jobs from the Northeast to the South.

Population Growth of Central Cities Relative to Metropolitan Areas

We now turn to the major factors identified earlier as influencing the growth of cities *relative* to their SMSAs.

16. Ibid., p. 445. Regional averages were obtained from the data in this table by weighting each subregion with its 1978 population as set forth in ibid., p. 30.

17. Ibid., p. 485.

SMSA POPULATION GROWTH. Fast-growth SMSAs generally have larger *differentials* between their overall growth rates and those of their central cities—even though *absolute* central-city growth rates are higher than in slow-growing SMSAs. This relationship should remain basically the same in the future, since we have forecast a continuation of current SMSA population growth rates.

INTRAURBAN EMPLOYMENT DECENTRALIZATION. One determinant of relative population growth is relative employment growth: job suburbanization encourages population suburbanization somewhat. The technological trends we anticipate will not greatly slow intraurban decentralization of employment. Manufacturing firms will continue to find lower-density sites more suitable as old plants and equipment are retired.[18] The increasing proportion of economic activity in services will favor central locations, but this will be offset by communications improvements that facilitate decentralization of many such services. Energy-saving technological improvements will offset much of the higher energy costs that suburban locations might otherwise incur for travel and home heating and cooling. Expansion of air travel will continue to draw activities to the vicinity of suburban airports.

Because of the overall increase in communications, and the importance of face-to-face meetings for a certain portion of it, central business districts will continue to thrive as employment centers. At present, such jobs are filled by a high proportion of suburban residents. Nevertheless, those jobs are well served by mass transit and so could provide the city with some attraction as a place to live, especially cities not served by high-speed transit lines to suburban areas.

OLD HOUSING. The higher the city-suburb disparity in the fraction of housing built before 1940, the lower the city's relative growth. This relationship has strong impacts upon city-SMSA population growth differentials, which we expect to continue. True, higher energy costs will cause some shift of future housing investment into more "in-fill" construction and rehabilitation of older buildings within large cities. Older cities with little vacant land tend to have more old housing than their suburbs, and continued housing construction in the suburbs just increases the difference.

Hence central cities containing large amounts of vacant land or able to annex either vacant land or growing suburbs will be able to maintain growth

18. See Andrew Hamer, *Industrial Exodus from Central City: Public Policy and the Comparative Costs of Location* (D. C. Heath, 1973), for computations of typical city-suburban cost differences in the Boston area.

rates much closer to those of their SMSAs. Cities in the Northeast and North Central regions are more fully built up than most of those in the South and West, and also have greater obstacles to annexing surrounding land. This relationship will aggravate the weaker positions of Northeastern and North Central cities relative to their SMSAs.

Over a long period, several developments will eventually reduce city-SMSA disparities in the concentration of older housing. One is continued abandonment and eventual removal of many old housing units in once dense Northeastern and North Central cities. Also, relatively low suburban housing construction in slowly growing or shrinking SMSAs will cause their suburban inventories to age faster. Rapid growth in newer cities will gradually fill their remaining vacant areas and spill over into surrounding territory. If they cannot annex that territory, they will find themselves in the same quandary that many large Northeastern and North Central cities face today. Already cities like Dallas and Denver that once expanded aggressively into surrounding territory are confronted on all sides by incorporated communities that vehemently resist absorption—even by changing state annexation laws. It seems likely that many large Southern and Western cities will encounter increasing difficulty when they try to annex surrounding territory. The faster they grow now, the sooner that day will arrive.

BLACK POPULATION. In most SMSAs, the central city contains a higher percentage of blacks than the suburbs.[19] The larger this differential, the slower the growth of both population and income in the central city relative to its SMSA. This seems to confirm that some whites withdraw from central cities to avoid living with blacks, as suggested in chapter 7.

Although neighborhood racial segregation in U.S. urban housing markets declined slightly from 1960 to 1970, it remains high.[20] True, suburbanization of black middle-class households is accelerating: a recent study reports net movements of blacks from central cities to suburbs during 1974, 1975, and 1976 in fourteen of nineteen major SMSAs analyzed.[21] Yet disparities between black and white settlement patterns were *increasing* in seven of

19. In our 121-SMSA sample, there were 8 exceptions in 1970: Anaheim-Santa Ana-Garden Grove, Baton Rouge, Columbus (Georgia), El Paso, Honolulu, Huntsville, Lubbock, and Montgomery.

20. Annemette Sørensen, Karl E. Taeuber, and Leslie Hollingsworth, Jr., "Indexes of Racial Residential Segregation for 109 Cities in the United States, 1940 to 1970," *Sociological Focus*, vol. 8 (April 1975), pp. 125–42.

21. Kathryn P. Nelson, *Recent Suburbanization of Blacks: How Much, Who, and Where?* (Department of Housing and Urban Development, February 1979).

the nineteen SMSAs analyzed,[22] largely because net outmovement of whites from many central cities was occurring at an even faster rate. Consequently, we think this relationship will remain operative in the 1980s and beyond, despite black suburbanization.

Some observers believe that racial desegregation of schools has hastened the withdrawal of whites from many central cities, thereby increasing this differential;[23] whereas others have found no such effect.[24] Our analysis does show that central cities with school districts that extend beyond the city boundaries tend to grow faster than those with entirely separate districts. This is consistent with the idea of "white flight" from racially integrated big-city schools, but does not prove it. We suspect that the ability of white parents to move away from big-city school systems containing high percentages of minority-group students does contribute to continued racial segregation in housing, and that this relationship will not change much in the future.

SCHOOL QUALITY. Although we could not test this variable directly in our empirical analysis, we found indirect evidence supporting the widespread belief that the quality of central-city public schools affects relative population growth. The future of school quality seems so heavily dependent on public policies toward school finance, desegregation, teachers' salaries, and other matters that we do not hazard a prediction of the future course of this factor.

CRIME RATES. Our statistical analysis failed to detect any influence of crime rates on population suburbanization. But this may have been due to a lack of comparability in data from different jurisdictions or a lack of correlation between actual interarea variations and a general *perception* that city rates are higher than suburban rates. We think higher crime in central cities is a factor motivating households to move, though it is perhaps not as important as is commonly believed.

Crime rates are much higher among males aged fourteen to twenty-four than among other sex and age groups and among blacks and Hispanics than among whites.[25] One of the reasons for past rises in crime rates has

22. Ibid., p. 27.

23. James S. Coleman, Sara D. Kelley, and John A. Moore, "Trends in School Segregation, 1968–73" (Urban Institute, August 1975); Charles T. Clotfelter, "Urban School Desegregation and Declines in White Enrollment: A Reexamination," *Journal of Urban Economics*, vol. 6 (July 1979), pp. 352–70.

24. William H. Frey, "Central City White Flight: Racial and Nonracial Causes," *American Sociological Review*, vol. 44 (June 1979), pp. 425–48.

25. Marvin E. Wolfgang, Robert M. Figlio, and Thorsten Sellin, *Delinquency in a Birth Cohort* (University of Chicago Press, 1972), p. 54.

been the increasing proportion of the population in these categories. Demographic trends, however, will reduce or eliminate this factor in the 1980s and 1990s. The proportion of the population consisting of fourteen- to twenty-four-year-old males rose from 10.1 to 10.6 percent between 1970 and 1978, but is projected to be 7.9 percent in both 1990 and 2000. The proportion consisting of black males in that age range rose from 1.3 percent to 1.6 percent during the same years, but will decline to between 1.4 and 1.5.[26] Thus, there are good prospects that crime rates will at least stop rising as fast as in the recent past. However, this might not happen in cities receiving large number of immigrants.

BIASED FEDERAL POLICIES. Another theory we did not test directly is that locational incentives facing households and firms are distorted by federal tax and expenditure policies, which have therefore restrained central city population growth. Most such biases developed as by-products of specified policy goals still thought to be important, such as encouraging capital formation; many, such as homeowner tax deductions, affect very large interest groups. Thus we do not expect any major overhaul of programs affecting urban areas.[27] Even the modest step of requiring "Urban Impact Statements" in order to detect such biases is likely to receive less emphasis under the Reagan administration.

TRANSPORTATION COSTS. There is widespread theoretical and empirical evidence that the dramatic lowering of real transportation costs over the last century has been a powerful factor in the decentralization of metropolitan areas. However, it seems likely that this long cost decline has ended with the sharp rises in oil prices in the 1970s. Energy price increases may raise the cost of automobile commuting somewhat, though we expect this to be largely offset by technological advances and shifts to more fuel-efficient engines. Thus, although transportation costs are not likely to *rise* enough to affect suburbanization greatly, one important factor causing decentralization in the past will no longer be operating.

FRAGMENTATION OF SMSA GOVERNMENTS. The more municipalities there are within an SMSA, the more slowly its central city grows in relation to the SMSA as a whole, other things equal. We speculate that this relationship arises from two different causes. Where numerous suburban communities exist, households can choose among many different combinations of service levels, tax rates, and neighborhood environments. Then the central city's particular "package" of services, taxes, and neighborhood

26. *Statistical Abstract of the United States*, 1979, p. 32.

27. For a similar view, see James S. Coleman, "Can We Revitalize Our Cities?" *Challenge*, vol. 20 (November/December 1977), pp. 23–34.

environments is less likely to be the preferred choice of as many households as when it must compete with only a few alternatives.[28] In addition, a multiplicity of separate communities makes it politically easier for suburban households to adopt and enforce exclusionary housing regulations. The tendency for urban population growth to extend beyond current SMSA boundaries will increase the number of separate municipalities within each large urbanized area in the future.

TAX BURDENS. The greater a city's tax burden relative to that in surrounding suburbs, the slower the city's relative population growth. We see little reason for this relationship to change in the future. In fact, even more big cities will probably experience serious fiscal difficulties. Central cities can offset these effects only by tax-base sharing with their suburbs, obtaining larger transfer payments from other governments, cutting back on their services, or producing those services with greater productivity or lower wages for city workers. They will undoubtedly try all these tactics, but they are not likely to prevent their relative tax rates from rising.

FRACTION OF SMSA POPULATION INSIDE THE CENTRAL CITY. The larger the initial fraction of SMSA population within the central city, the faster city population and per capita income grew relative to those in the entire SMSA. Cities long unable to annex nearby territory tend to contain small fractions of their total SMSA populations. For many years, most SMSA growth has occurred outside their boundaries, partly because their own territory was fully built up earlier. We believe more Southern and Western cities will find their borders frozen; hence they will gradually contain smaller and smaller fractions of their total SMSA populations.

Assessment

It is difficult to draw general conclusions concerning the future population, employment, and income growth of U.S. cities from the specific factors analyzed in this chapter. Yet some overview can be derived by examining their net impact upon four patterns which have been evident in the recent past.

Net Migration from Metropolitan to Nonmetropolitan Areas

We believe this tendency will continue unabated. The rising cost of urban housing (aggravated by suburban land-use controls), along with the

28. Charles M. Tiebout, "A Pure Theory of Local Expenditures," *Journal of Political Economy*, vol. 64 (October 1956), pp. 416–24.

suburbanization of jobs, will motivate many households to move farther out onto less expensive land, while still commuting to jobs within SMSAs. Greater numbers of retired persons seeking low-cost environments will prefer nonmetropolitan areas. More use of air travel and more recreation orientation will increase the attraction of remote areas. So will development of energy sources in some areas, especially in the West.

Net Migration from Northeast and North Central Areas to the South and West

Overall, this flow is likely to continue, and probably accelerate. Mild climates will continue to attract residents. Business cycles will keep on producing higher unemployment rates during recessions in the Northeast and North Central regions, so that migration from high- to low-unemployment SMSAs will have a strong regional component. Large-scale illegal immigration from Mexico will stimulate faster growth in SMSAs near the Mexican border or already containing large Hispanic populations. Higher cost-of-living-adjusted incomes in Southern than in Northeastern SMSAs will further encourage the trend.

Net Migration from Central Cities to Surrounding Suburbs

Future trends have ambivalent implications for this tendency. Some factors will clearly encourage continued outflows. These include "white flight" from cities with high percentages of black residents; greater city-suburban differences in the age of the housing stock; continued fragmentation of local government; and increasing fiscal difficulties for many large cities that will force them to maintain high tax rates. Further decline in the importance of manufacturing will weaken the role of cities in which older, more obsolete industrial facilities are located. Slower growth of government jobs will also hurt cities. Annexation will be available to fewer and fewer cities as a means of keeping a share of the more rapidly growing residential areas.

Other factors will tend to slow this process. These include higher costs of commuting, relatively lower land prices in declining central cities, higher costs of new home construction, further shifts of jobs to office space suitable for downtown locations, increased desire for public transportation among two-earner households, and continued growth of relatively small households. Moreover, the rapid growth of the Hispanic population will strengthen cities relative to suburbs. So will major medical centers, which will receive greater future emphasis in the nation's health-care system. Also, slower real income growth will reduce the ability of households to move into more expensive suburban housing. And slower inmigration of low-income households to older cities will promote neighborhood stabilization and upgrading.

The net result is that many large cities will experience strengthened housing demand in some of their older neighborhoods, as well as job growth in their downtown areas. At the same time, the forces causing suburbanization will predominate, though perhaps less than during the 1970s.

Regional Differences in City-SMSA Relationships

Several factors will weaken the relative positions of Southern and Western cities within their SMSAs, thus making them more like many Northeastern and North Central cities. Most important is increasing resistance to annexation of suburban territory. More growth in Southern and Western SMSAs will occur outside city boundaries, thereby decreasing the cities' ability to keep their percentages of older housing close to those in surrounding suburbs. On the other hand, Southern city public school districts are more likely to extend beyond their municipal limits, and such districts are associated with faster relative city growth. Hispanic population growth will continue to be strong in the South and West and, for a time at least, to concentrate in central cities. Northeastern and North Central cities are more likely to experience fiscal difficulties compelling them to raise their tax rates faster than their suburbs do. The withdrawal of whites from cities with higher fractions of blacks than their suburbs appears to remain more likely in the Northeast region, since city versus suburb racial segregation is greater there.[29]

Over the very long run, we expect region-wide differences among *cities* to decline, though those among *SMSAs* may continue. In fact, suburbanization does not vary systematically by region, whereas growth relationships among SMSAs do. Hence regional differences among cities spring largely from regional differences in the characteristics and growth rates of their metropolitan areas. Nevertheless, we do not expect regional differences

29. In our 153 cities, the average difference between the percentage black population in a city and that of its SMSA was 5 percentage points in 1970. For the 28 cities in the Northeast region, it was 9 percentage points; for the 32 Western cities it was 2 percentage points. North Central and Southern cities were about average on the difference measure, although the percentage black in city *and* suburbs was considerably higher in the South (see table 4-3).

in the relative strength and growth prospects of large cities to disappear during the 1980s or even the 1990s.

Appendix: Trends Relevant to the Future of Urban Areas

Economic Trends

1. Real income *per household* will continue to rise in the future, but more slowly than in the 1950s or 1960s. Median family income in 1978 dollars rose at compound annual rates of 3.25 percent from 1950 to 1960, 2.96 percent from 1960 to 1970, and 0.79 percent from 1970 to 1978. Continued difficulties in raising productivity are likely to keep its rise during the 1980s at the lower end of this range.

Real income *per capita* will also continue to rise and will increase more slowly than in the past two decades, but faster than real income per household. Per capita disposable personal income in 1972 dollars rose at compound annual rates of 1.23 percent from 1950 to 1960, 2.98 percent from 1960 to 1970, and 2.47 percent from 1970 to 1979. However, it rose only 1.76 percent per year from 1973 to 1979, including a decline from 1973 to 1974.[30]

Average household size will decline somewhat (see Demographic Trends).

2. The consumer price index (CPI) will continue to rise at an average annual rate of over 6 percent in the 1980s, with cyclical fluctuations in annual rates related to movements of the general business cycle. The CPI increased at average annual compound rates of 2.09 percent in the 1950s, 2.75 percent in the 1960s, and 7.85 percent in the 1970s. From 1976 through 1980, it rose at 9.78 percent per year compounded.[31]

3. The national unemployment rate will also move in a cyclical pattern, but its annual average over a whole cycle will decline somewhat in the late 1980s because of a smaller number of young persons entering the labor force. The average annual unemployment rate for the entire nation was 4.51 percent in the 1950s, 4.78 percent in the 1960s, and 6.19 percent in the 1970s.[32]

30. *Economic Report of the President, January 1980*, pp. 232, 229.

31. *Statistical Abstract of the United States, 1979*, p. 483; U.S. Department of Labor, Bureau of Labor Statistics *News*, "The Consumer Price Index—June 1980" (July 23, 1980).

32. Bureau of the Census, *Historical Statistics of the United States: Colonial Times to 1970*, pt. 1 (GPO, 1976), p. 135; *Statistical Abstract of the United States, 1979*, p. 392; Council of Economic Advisers, *Economic Indicators—June 1980*, p. 12.

4. Although tax rates, living costs, and wage rates in the South will all rise faster than those in other regions, they will remain well below the latter throughout the 1980s and 1990s.

5. Rising international competition will increase the pressure on manufacturing firms to locate where operating costs are lowest. This means more manufacturing activity will shift to the South.

6. Manufacturing employment will continue to decline as a percentage of total employment. The fraction of all nonagricultural employed persons working in manufacturing was 33.7 percent in 1950, 30.9 percent in 1960, 27.3 percent in 1970, and 23.4 percent in 1979.[33]

7. The percentage of all jobs located in offices will continue to rise.

8. The cost of energy—especially of petroleum products—will rise somewhat faster than the cost of living generally, but not as fast as in 1979. Intermittent shortages of gasoline may occur.

9. Ownership and use of automotive vehicles in the United States will continue to expand rapidly, though perhaps somewhat more slowly than in the early 1970s. The number of such vehicles in use grew at an average annual rate of 2.4 million in the 1950s, 3.0 million in the 1960s, and 4.3 million from 1970 through 1978.[34] This will be possible, in spite of rising gasoline costs, because of continued improvements in average fuel economy.

10. The percentage of total personal income consisting of total transfer payments will continue to rise, but at a slower rate than the average during the past ten years. Transfer payments constituted 6.7 percent of total personal income in 1950, 7.2 percent in 1960, 10.0 percent in 1970, and 13.1 percent in 1979.[35] Thus, in the 1970s, personal income rose 10.2 percent per year compounded, compared to 27.2 percent per year compounded for total transfer payments.

11. The percentage share of gross national product (GNP) devoted to spending by state and local governments will remain relatively stable or even decline slightly, in sharp contrast to its steady and significant increase from 1950 to about 1977. In those twenty-seven years, state and local government expenditures increased from 10.5 percent of GNP to 15.4 percent, rising at a compound rate of 9.5 percent per year, compared to 7.5 percent for GNP.[36]

33. *Statistical Abstract of the United States*, 1970, p. 218; *Statistical Abstract of the United States*, 1979, p. 408.

34. Anthony Downs, "The Automotive Population Explosion," *Traffic Quarterly*, vol. 33 (July 1979), p. 348 (Brookings Reprint 353).

35. *Statistical Abstract of the United States*, 1979, p. 443.

36. Ibid., p. 283.

12. The percentage of GNP devoted to health care will remain at least as high as it was in the late 1970s, and will probably rise significantly over time. This will occur because of the increasing percentage of elderly in the population, plus some type of broader public funding of health care. National health care expenditures constituted 4.5 percent of GNP in 1950, 5.2 percent in 1960, 7.6 percent in 1970, and 9.1 percent in 1978.[37]

13. Real interest rates paid to savers will be higher in the 1980s than they were in the 1970s, especially for capital used in real estate finance. Such increases will be necessary to call forth the savings needed for investment in housing and other capital goods. This means nominal interest rates will be higher in relation to prevailing rates of inflation than in the 1970s.

14. The cost of newly built housing will continue rising faster than the cost of living generally, although the average size of new units will decline somewhat. The median price of new private single-family homes sold in the United States rose from $20,000 in 1965 to about $65,000 in 1979, or at a compound annual rate of 8.7 percent, compared to 6.1 percent for the CPI in that period.[38] Housing prices will rise because land prices will increase as population and real incomes go up, and because local regulations will cause major delays in new development. Real mortgage interest rates will rise as savers and lenders adjust to expected inflation.

15. Consumer demand for mobile homes as permanent housing will remain strong in the 1980s, but the actual extent of their use will depend upon how restrictive local governments are about permitting it.

16. Major capital investments will be made in developing new sources of energy (such as shale oil), and in more intensively using certain existing sources (such as coal and natural gas). This will stimulate local economies where such resources are located.

Demographic Trends

17. The total population of the United States will rise by about 21.3 million (9.6 percent) in the 1980s, and 16.9 million (6.9 percent) in the 1990s. These estimates are based on the Census Bureau's Series II projections, and indicate a continued slowing in the relative rate of population growth.

18. The number of persons aged sixty-five and over will rise about 18.6

37. Ibid., p. 100.

38. Ibid., pp. 792, 483; and *Economic Report of the President, January 1980*, pp. 259–60.

percent in the 1980s, twice as fast as the population as a whole. The growth of this group can be reliably forecast because all its members are already alive, and death rates change relatively slowly. This increase of 4.1 million elderly persons will constitute about 22 percent of the total population gain, although the elderly made up only 11.3 percent of the total population in 1980.[39]

19. The number of persons aged twenty-five to forty-four will also rise rapidly in the 1980s. It will increase by about 16.1 million, or 26.2 percent—a rate almost triple that for the population as a whole.[40]

This will cause a continued high level of household formation. The Census Bureau forecasts an average net addition of about 1.68 million households per year from 1980 to 1990. However, that forecast does not take changes in housing costs into account, even though such costs influence the ease of forming separate households. Because of higher real housing costs in the 1980s than in the 1970s, the actual figure will be slightly less than this. The total number of households rose 0.91 million per year in the 1950s, 1.03 million per year in the 1960s, and 1.64 million per year from 1970 through 1978.[41]

Large numbers of households will be shifting from early-married status to the stage at which they will be starting to have and rear children. This will cause many to seek single-family homes (though a higher fraction of such homes will be townhouses and other attached types than in the past).

The number of persons entering the labor force each year will decline in the 1980s, especially after 1985, because of the lower number of young persons. This will occur despite a continuing rise in female labor force participation rates. The annual average growth in the labor force will be about 1.5 million in the 1980s, compared to 2.1 million in most of the 1970s.[42]

20. The number of persons under fourteen will remain roughly constant until about 1985, and then grow until about 1995; most of this growth will be in the number under six. Although fertility rates will remain low, the number of women of childbearing age will rise in the 1980s because of

39. *Statistical Abstract of the United States, 1979*, pp. 6, 8. Series II projections were used for 1990 estimates of total population, and the 1980 population was assumed to be 222.2 million for the entire nation, and 25.148 million for those sixty-five and over.

40. Ibid.

41. Ibid., p. 46.

42. *Domestic Consequences of United States Population Change*, House Select Committee on Population, 95 Cong. 2 sess., committee print (GPO, 1978), p. 51.

high birth levels in the 1950s and early 1960s. Hence the number of children born will be larger in the 1980s than in the 1970s. The number aged fourteen to twenty-four will decline among whites throughout the 1980s, but will stabilize among nonwhites.[43]

This will end recent declines in the number of children attending primary schools. That number will stabilize until about 1985, and then rise until about 1995.

Enrollments in secondary schools and in colleges and universities will be falling in the 1980s.

21. The percentage of racial minorities in the total population will rise gradually in the future because their birth rates will remain higher than those for whites, and their death rates lower (because of lower average age).

22. Gross annual inflows of Hispanics will continue at high levels, especially by means of illegal immigration across the Mexican border. They will form an important fraction of total annual population growth.

23. The number of immigrants legally entering the United States will remain at a level of at least 400,000 per year, and may be higher in response to various refugee movements, or to labor shortages in the United States emerging in the late 1980s.

24. The percentage of women working outside their homes will continue to rise.

The number of households with no adult males will rise faster than the total number of households.

The number of households containing more than one person working outside the home will also rise faster than the total number of households.

The fraction of all employed persons working part-time will rise, and a greater variety of part-time working arrangements will be more widely available from both private-sector and public-sector employers.

25. Families that have children will have a smaller number, on the average, than in the 1950s, 1960s, or even the 1970s. Also, a higher percentage of married couples will not have any children.

26. The number of households consisting of persons of opposite sex living together without being married will rise sharply, especially among persons in their twenties and early thirties. However, the percentage of persons who eventually marry will remain almost as high as it was in the 1970s.

43. *Statistical Abstract of the United States*, 1979, p. 8.

27. The net movement of persons from farms to urban areas will remain quite low in the 1980s and 1990s, similar to that in the 1970s.

Social Trends

28. The average amount of leisure time per worker will rise, but will be partly offset by continued "moonlighting" by many workers.

29. Rates of early retirement among workers will slow compared to the 1970s. However, the number of retired persons will still rise somewhat faster than the number of persons sixty-five and over.

30. Crime rates among members of a given age-sex-race category will remain at their current levels; however, the proportion of people in the most crime-prone categories will go down in most areas.

31. Many young people will continue to live apart from their parents for a time before forming "permanent" households, although the higher real cost of housing will cause this to happen less often than in the 1970s.

32. Racial segregation of neighborhood residential areas will decrease slightly but remain the dominant pattern, although it will be easier for individual minority-group households to move into predominantly white areas almost everywhere than it was before 1975.

33. Most households at all income levels will continue to want to live in neighborhoods occupied mainly by other households with roughly the same socioeconomic status as their own. This may be somewhat less true of households at the lowest income levels, many of whom will wish to avoid living in areas of concentrated poverty.

34. As real incomes rise, the demand for amenities thought to be associated with "quality of life" (such as climate, attractive environment, and recreational pursuits) will rise more rapidly than that for goods and services.

35. Expressed American preferences for small-town living styles will continue among a majority of households, though a significant minority will seek high-urbanity life-styles.

More and more households—especially those with children—will move to smaller communities, both inside and outside metropolitan areas, as their real incomes rise.

According to recent surveys, about 10 percent of all U.S. households are *high-urbanity* households who prefer living in large cities near major activity centers. Many have no school-age children. These households will tend to move *closer* to big-city downtown areas as their real incomes rise—contrary to the behavior of the majority of households.[44]

36. In many cities, neighborhood organizations will grow stronger and seek to play larger roles in influencing the delivery of city services to their territories. They will also encourage more participation in local decision-making. That will cause the negotiation process associated with major decisions to become more complex and time-consuming.

Technological Trends

37. Improvements in communications will:

—Reduce the economies of scale caused by agglomeration of many producing industries. This will allow them to disperse more of their facilities than in the past to lower-density areas.

—Make it possible to separate corporate headquarters from lower-level productive facilities in the same firm. This will permit dispersal of non-top-level office functions outside large cities and metropolitan areas.

—Increase the total amount of communication and interaction carried out. This will expand employment in communications industries. It also implies that the total impact of better communications will not be experienced as reduced costs of the same amount of interaction as before, but will involve more interaction too.

—Cause some increases in productivity among office workers.

—Not markedly reduce the total need for face-to-face communication, because total interaction will rise and more participants will be brought into most decision-making processes. Hence travel to achieve face-to-face meetings will *rise*—or at least remain stable—rather than declining.

38. Energy-saving innovations in automobiles, industry, home heating and cooling, and other sectors will check the growth of demand for energy without drastically altering existing patterns of working and living.

39. There will be no major breakthroughs in mass transit technology within feasible cost ranges.

40. In some cities, renovation of older structures will become a large enough "industry" so that more efficient processes will develop; scarcities of skilled workers will not remain serious constraints to rehabilitation.

44. Paul K. Mancini and Martin D. Abravanel, "Signs of Urban Vitality and of Distress: Citizen Views on the Quality of Urban Life," in U.S. Department of Housing and Urban Development, Occasional Papers in Housing and Community Affairs, vol. 4 (HUD, July 1979), p. 23.

41. Continued expansion and greater use of air travel service throughout the United States will help integrate urban areas—including relatively remote communities—into the national economy and culture.

Public Policy Trends

42. In spite of the need for metropolitan-area-level institutions with decision-making powers, most metropolitan areas will not create such institutions. Therefore, decision-making powers—including those governing land use—will remain fragmented.

43. Local policies that limit population growth and other real estate development, or impose time-consuming delays upon them, will expand in nearly all jurisdictions. This will cause a slower response-capacity by the housing and general real estate development industries to increases in demand, even in most fast-growing metropolitan areas.

However, there will be little coordination of such policies in overall growth-control strategies at the metropolitan level.

Regional differences in growth-control policies will persist, with some states retaining relatively permissive attitudes (for example, Texas) and others highly restrictive attitudes (for example, California).

44. Federal taxation and regulatory policies will gradually shift toward favoring investment and savings more than in the past, in relation to consumption.

45. Political struggles between environmentalists and energy extraction industries will slow down the exploitation of natural resources related to energy. This will raise the cost of producing and using energy products, especially those involving coal or nuclear power.

46. Enforcement of antipollution regulations will curtail slightly the growth of highly polluting activities in large cities with high current levels of air pollution or even in those few entire metropolitan areas with high pollution levels near their edges.

47. Rising costs of developing and occupying housing, plus the inability to produce rental housing that is economically feasible, will lead to more public interference with the rental market. This will take the forms of local rent controls, tenant-landlord bills favoring tenants' rights, condominium conversion statutes giving tenants some rights of occupancy in existing units, and more pressure for expanded public subsidies to renters—especially the elderly.

48. Federal spending on defense will rise significantly in relation to

both total federal spending and total GNP. This will benefit the economies of many communities specializing in defense activities.

49. A continuing "fiscal squeeze" on large cities losing population will require them to reduce personnel and cut back on long-term capital investments, possibly including maintenance of their existing infrastructure. This will reduce the quality of public services offered in many such cities, though it will be partly offset by improved productivity.

50. The present ability of many large cities—especially in the South and West—to annex surrounding territory will be reduced. Increasing resistance from residents of potential "target" areas will often involve changing state annexation laws.

51. Citizen demands for local government services will rise faster in many Southern communities that now provide relatively low levels of such services. This will cause faster increases in state and local taxes and employment in these communities than elsewhere.

9

General Conclusions about the Future of Cities

THE last chapter assessed the future strength of various trends likely to influence urban decline. However, additional properties of urban areas as dynamic systems must be considered before conclusions can be drawn about the probable future extent of their decline. The first three sections of this chapter analyze some of these dynamic elements. We then present conclusions concerning the overall prospects for reversing urban decline, the likelihood of decline or revitalization in particular neighborhoods, and the major problems that declining cities will probably encounter.

Dynamics of Urban Decline

Once decline in a city's population or employment has begun, what course will it follow? The answer depends upon whether it was started by one-time or continuing changes, and whether it triggers self-limiting or self-reinforcing effects.[1]

1. Many of the ideas in this section are taken from Katharine L. Bradbury, Anthony Downs, and Kenneth A. Small, "Some Dynamics of Central-City Suburban Interactions," *American Economic Review*, vol. 70 (May 1980, *Papers and Proceedings, December* 1979), pp. 410–14. For related arguments, see W. E. Oates, E. P. Howry, and W. J. Baumol, "The Analysis of Public Policy in Dynamic Urban Models," *Journal of Political Economy*, vol. 79 (January–February 1971), pp. 142–53; Tatahiro Miyao, "Dynamic Instability of a Mixed City in the Presence of Neighborhood Externalities," *American Economic Review*, vol. 68 (June 1978), pp. 454–63; and Martin T. Katzman, "The Quality of Municipal Services, Central City Decline, and Middle-Class Flight," Research Report R78-1 (Department of City and Regional Planning, Harvard University, February 1978), chap. 1.

Economists traditionally view change as an adjustment from one equilibrium to another in response to a one-time shift in conditions. For example, when transportation costs fell, people and firms did not have to locate as close together. So the denser parts of metropolitan areas thinned out, and central cities with fixed boundaries experienced falling population and employment. Such a process of adjustment, examined in isolation, is inherently self-limiting. When the lower density appropriate to the new transportation prices was reached, the decline presumably stopped. This stabilization operates through the land market, which balances the revised demand for space with the supply through changes in price.

However, the changes resulting from such adjustments, or from external shocks, may set in motion other forces that do not have the same self-limiting character. The reactions of households and firms to the initial change may serve either to dampen or to amplify that change. We call these two possibilities "self-limiting" and "self-reinforcing" processes.[2] Self-limiting forces do not necessarily reverse the initial change; they merely limit its extent. In contrast, self-reinforcing forces continuously intensify the initial change, which may or may not arrive at a new equilibrium. These forces may cause an overshooting of the most socially desirable state.

For example, consider a stable, racially integrated neighborhood initially containing twenty minority households, seventy majority households, and ten vacant units.[3] Suppose all households prefer racial integration to complete neighborhood segregation, but majority households will not live in an area if the proportion of minorities in their immediate vicinity rises above 30 percent. At the outset, it is below 30 percent everywhere in the neighborhood. Now assume ten additional households move into the vacant units, half of them minority. The new neighborhood composition is twenty-five minority households and seventy-five majority ones, providing a racially integrated condition desired by all residents there. But if the new minority households all locate close together because the vacancies happen to be

2. In different contexts, others have described these processes as negative and positive feedback or cumulative causation. See Thomas Vietorisz and Bennett Harrison, "Labor Market Segmentation: Positive Feedback and Divergent Development," *American Economic Review* (May 1973, *Papers and Proceedings, December 1972*), pp. 366–76; Gunnar Myrdal, *Rich Lands and Poor: The Road to World Prosperity* (Harper, 1957); Eric E. Lampard, "The History of Cities in the Economically Advanced Areas," *Economic Development and Cultural Change*, vol. 3, no. 2 (1955), pp. 81–136; and Alfred J. Watkins, *The Practice of Urban Economics* (Sage Publications, 1980), chaps. 1, 5, and 6.

3. This example draws heavily upon the ingenious work of Thomas C. Schelling in *Micromotives and Macrobehavior* (Norton, 1978), especially chap. 4.

clustered, the minority proportion next to nearby majority-occupied units will rise above 30 percent. Alternatively, the new minority households might be widely scattered, but the sudden change might set up an *expectation* that more minority households will soon follow. In either case, enough majority households may be induced to move out to bring the overall minority percentage above 30. This accelerates majority outmovement and raises the minority percentage among remaining residents still higher. Eventually, either the neighborhood will have high vacancies, or those vacancies will gradually fill up with other minority households—resulting in complete racial segregation that no one prefers.

Self-reinforcing forces are only one possible reason for a city to continue declining once it has started. Decline may be sustained for a while, but at decreasing speed or intensity, as part of a self-limiting process that is still working itself out. For example, an initial drop in an area's population usually leads to falling employment, which in turn causes a further decline in population. But if that first population drop is the only basic change in the initial situation, successive decreases in population and jobs will become smaller and smaller as the city asymptotically approaches a new equilibrium size. Or an initial decline can continue because the underlying cause continues to change. For example, average real household incomes may rise in a given year, and then continue rising each year thereafter. The movement of city households to newer suburban homes stimulated by the first year's income rise would be followed by additional suburbanization caused by subsequent increases. Equilibrium will be reached, in such cases, only when the underlying causes themselves stop changing.

It is important to distinguish among these three types of dynamism both in forecasting city futures and in designing appropriate policy responses. If continuing decline is an interim result of self-limiting forces, it will not persist unless the underlying causes keep changing too. Hence public policy should probably not intervene except to ease transitional injuries. If such decline results from ongoing shifts in underlying causes that are considered desirable in themselves, such as rising real incomes, then again public intervention to alter the results is probably unwise. These two cases appear to underlie most of the recommendations of the President's Commission for a National Agenda for the Eighties.[4] But if continuing decline

4. President's Commission for a National Agenda for the Eighties, *A National Agenda for the Eighties* (GPO, 1980); see also the more detailed report of its Panel on Policies and Prospects for Metropolitan and Nonmetropolitan America, *Urban America in the Eighties: Perspectives and Prospects* (GPO, 1980).

results from self-reinforcing elements, it is likely to keep intensifying unless public policies intervene.

Self-Reinforcing Elements

The following self-reinforcing processes, several of which were discussed in chapter 2, are important to the future of U.S. cities.

Differential Migration by Race and Income

An especially large net outflow of high- and middle-income households, particularly those with children, has been typical of large cities experiencing population losses. Once such an outmovement has begun, it tends to reinforce itself for several reasons, described earlier. Also, as high- and middle-income households leave the city, the percentage of children in the city's public schools from such families declines. But many high- and middle-income parents want their children to attend schools in which the other children are from similar homes. As classroom or school dominance by children from such families becomes less common in a city, more of these families move to suburbs where their dominance is nearly universal. This intensifies the condition that caused them to leave, stimulating still others to follow them.

Local Taxes and Government Services

As explained in chapter 2, total costs for many local government services do not fall proportionally as a city's population declines. Thus, per capita costs for the remaining residents rise. In addition, if the local tax structure is progressive, outmigration of high- and middle-income people raises per capita taxes for all remaining residents. Furthermore, the cost of providing some city services varies inversely with residents' incomes. Hence the departure of high- and middle-income households causes costs per capita to rise, and taxes per capita to rise even more. These changes are likely to create or increase a disparity between household tax burdens within the city and those in surrounding suburbs. Higher tax disparities generate greater suburbanization of population.

Finally, selective departure of high- and middle-income groups erodes the political influence of such groups upon the city government. This can shift public activities toward those valued by the poor and away from those valued by high- and middle-income groups, making the city less attractive to the latter.

Similar forces affect the locational decisions of firms, which also pay local taxes and consume local government services.

City-Suburban Disparities in Percentage of Older Housing

Cities with much higher percentages of old housing than their suburbs tend to grow relatively more slowly. Hence their suburbs are likely to capture a relatively greater share of SMSA new housing construction, thereby causing the city-suburb disparity in percentage of old housing to widen further.

Ghetto Culture

The way young people grow up in many big-city concentrated-poverty areas often creates negative attitudes and capabilities concerning work that reinforce their initial poverty.[5] From early family life through school experiences to their "street life" with peer-group members, their whole environment discourages development of the skills and work habits conducive to traditional employment: "the awareness is likely to be that hard work has few rewards, that illicit activity and corruption may pay better, and that one is not a part of the predominant society and has no obligation to it."[6] This attitude prevents these young people from passing on positive attitudes toward traditional employment to their own children. Therefore, the distinctive culture found in many big-city concentrated-poverty neighborhoods acts in a self-reinforcing manner to prevent the upward mobility that would relieve some of the worst social problems there.

Agglomeration Economies among Firms

Most U.S. cities evolved because private firms found it profitable to operate near suppliers, customers, or other firms engaged in similar activities. Such "agglomeration economies" grow with the number of other relevant firms in the vicinity, at least until congestion becomes a problem.

5. Garth L. Mangum and Stephen F. Seninger, *Coming of Age in the Ghetto: A Dilemma of Youth Unemployment* (Johns Hopkins University Press, 1978), chap. 4.

6. Ibid., p. 82.

If a city begins to lose firms because of factors other than agglomeration, each departure reduces opportunities for interaction for the remaining firms. As departures create expectations of further departures, a beneficial network of business interrelationships built up over many decades can be destroyed.

Critical Mass Activities

A fall in patronage of decreasing-cost activities such as mass transit,[7] specialized restaurants and retail outlets, and cultural activities causes average costs to rise. This forces price increases or service cutbacks, or else calls forth a public subsidy which (unless externally financed) creates a negative feedback through the fiscal system.

Maintenance of Residential Property

The market value of a housing unit is affected by the condition of nearby units. If one unit is severely damaged by an accident or left vacant for long, it detracts from the desirability of the entire neighborhood. The subsequent fall in housing demand reduces the profitability of landlords' maintenance efforts on all properties in the area. Additional units will become run down, and may even be abandoned. Physical blight and abandonment are contagious through a process of self-fulfilling negative expectations. The fragmented ownership of real estate in each neighborhood makes this a self-reinforcing process. Once it has begun, no one owner can stop it by improving his or her own property. The recovery of such an area requires a reversal of each owner's negative expectations about the behavior of others. That in turn necessitates concerted action among property owners that is difficult to accomplish—though it can be done.[8]

Neighborhood revitalization can become a similar self-reinforcing process in the opposite direction. Once a few "pioneering" households begin

7. For a careful argument that mass transit is subject to long-run decreasing average costs once service quality is taken into account, see Herbert Mohring, "Optimization and Scale Economies in Urban Bus Transportation," *American Economic Review*, vol. 62 (September 1972), pp. 591–604.

8. One of the most successful programs for achieving such concerted action is the Neighborhood Housing Services program, now operating in dozens of cities across the nation. For a description of this program and its effectiveness, see Roger S. Ahlbrandt, Jr., and Paul C. Brophy, *Neighborhood Revitalization: Theory and Practice* (Lexington Books, 1975), chap. 9.

to renovate run-down housing in a deteriorated but well-located neighborhood, the whole community may shift expectations about the area's future. Positive expectations then become "self-fulfilling" prophecies encouraging fragmented owners to upgrade their properties.[9]

Political Power of Cities

As cities lose population, they also lose political power within their SMSAs and in state and national arenas. Moreover, they lose resources distributed by state and federal governments on a per capita basis. To the extent that city governments are major channels through which income redistribution to the poor is carried out, this loss tends to place the burden for such redistribution yet more heavily on local taxpayers.

If city population decline involves all the above self-reinforcing elements, what will slow it down or stop it once it has started? Will it continue until these cities disappear? Or will self-limiting factors eventually stabilize their populations? And if most large U.S. cities were once growing rapidly in population but are now declining, what factors caused them to reverse direction? Will those factors halt the future growth of large U.S. cities that are still expanding? Answering these questions requires examining key self-limiting elements relevant to city population changes.

Self-Limiting Elements

Some self-limiting elements important to the future of U.S. cities are as follows.

SMSA Unemployment Rate

Metropolitan areas with relatively low unemployment rates tend to have faster population growth than those with high rates, and vice versa. This limits population changes caused by factors other than changing economic

9. However, experience indicates that not all blighted neighborhoods which appear "ripe" for revitalization actually "take off" in a process of renovation and rising property values. A study by the Federal National Mortgage Association of eighteen such areas in St. Louis revealed significant renovation activity in only six of them after a period of a year from the initial surveys. See Joseph Hu, "The Demographics of Urban Up-Grading," FNMA Seller-Servicer (November–December 1978), pp. 30–37.

opportunities. For example, if people leave a metropolitan area because of its undesirable climate, the unemployment rate will fall, thereby increasing the area's attraction both to existing residents and to potential inmigrants. Similarly, the drawing power of areas with good climates such as San Diego is reduced below what it would otherwise be by the high unemployment that results from rapid inmigration.[10]

Total SMSA Size

The larger an SMSA's total employment, the slower its rate of employment growth. But larger total employment also implies larger total population. Thus, as an SMSA grows larger in total employment and population, its rate of further growth tends to decrease.[11]

10. But an opposite second-round effect also occurs. As inmigration responds to unemployment rates, employment shifts in response to the resulting population change. Thus, low unemployment leads to greater inmigration, which creates more jobs; whereas high unemployment slows population growth and therefore job growth. These impacts are self-reinforcing, rather than self-limiting.

Quantifying both types of effects indicates the self-limiting one is dominant. Suppose the 1970 unemployment rate in the average SMSA in our study rose by one percentage point, i.e., the number of jobless workers increased by 4,058. (The calculations that follow are based upon an average SMSA population of 997,191, and employment of 388,593. The average unemployment rate was 4.24 percent. These figures imply an average labor force of 405,800 and a ratio of labor force to population of 0.407. The reasonableness of this result is corroborated by *Statistical Abstract of the United States, 1978*, pp. 8, 400, which show a ratio of labor force to population for the entire United States of 0.42 in 1970.) Our equation (chapter 5) implies this rise in unemployment would decrease population growth over the next five years by 0.85 percentage point, or 8,476 persons (including 3,450 labor-force participants). Hence the original increase in unemployment of 4,058 would be reduced to 609 by this self-limiting effect. But this decline in net inmigration would simultaneously reduce SMSA employment growth by 0.52 percent, or 1,761 jobs over five years, according to our employment growth equation. Thus, a net rise of 2,370 jobless persons results over five years from an initial increase of 4,058 in such persons. Though these calculations are only approximate, they indicate that the initial unemployment increase would be reduced by 42 percent over the five-year period, rather than increased, because of the dominance of self-limiting responses over self-reinforcing ones.

11. We did a simple calculation to compare the relative magnitudes of this self-limiting effect and the self-reinforcing effect discussed earlier. Suppose the average SMSA experienced a 10 percent increase in employment over five years for some reason. According to our 1970–75 estimates, this would increase population there by 4.6 percent. That would in turn augment employment by an additional 2.8 percent, just in the first round of impacts. The 10 percent increase in employment would at the same time reduce subsequent employment growth by 0.2 percent (at the mean) through its effect upon employment size. Thus, the self-limiting process is considerably weaker than the self-reinforcing relationship between employment growth and population growth. This example illustrates the importance of quantifying the interrelationships among variables discussed in this chapter and the preceding one before drawing any broad conclusions from their directions of impact alone.

Land and Housing Prices

We have defined severely declining cities as those which are losing both population and households. Hence the total demand for housing in severely declining cities is shrinking. This causes a relative decline in the prices of land and housing, compared to prices in nearby suburban communities or in growing cities. The expanding amounts of vacant and abandoned land within some large cities should eventually depress land prices enough so that developers will buy sites there and build new structures on them.

We discussed earlier why this has not happened very often up to now. The main obstacle is the unwillingness of households or firms that can afford newly built structures to locate in areas still surrounded by low-income households and neighborhood decay. However, falling relative land prices will eventually make themselves felt. That conclusion is affirmed by the frequent renovation of neighborhoods in very old European cities. Many have experienced immense changes, including market collapses, physical destruction, and racial transitions; yet individual neighborhoods within them have survived over the centuries. They have either been continuously maintained in good condition or gone through cycles of prosperity, decline, decay, and renovation. It may take several decades to "resurrect" a heavily deteriorated neighborhood, but historically this has almost always occurred unless the entire city was abandoned. Hence we believe this self-limiting element will eventually be important to now declining cities in the United States.

Congestion

As a city grows more populous, congestion often rises in such public facilities as highways, parks, court systems, museums, and schools. Such crowding usually makes these facilities less desirable, thereby exerting some restraint upon the city's further growth. This may in fact be a reason for our finding that total SMSA size tends to be self-limiting. Conversely, when a city loses population, congestion declines, making these facilities more attractive.

Except for land prices, these self-limiting elements appear much more powerful restraints upon the *growth* than the *decline* of city population. For declining cities in the United States at present we think these self-limiting elements are weaker than self-reinforcing ones. However, it is difficult to confirm these conclusions empirically because both types of elements are so hard to quantify. Moreover, the self-limiting factor of lower land and housing prices in declining cities could eventually exert enough positive influence upon future property development to halt population losses there.

Is Decline Reversible?

City population and job losses are rooted in powerful, long-established forces such as rising real incomes, expanding use of automotive vehicles, widespread preferences for low-density living, and technological advances in communications and industrial processes. Many of these forces benefit millions of people—often a majority of urban residents. Their current and likely future strength was underscored by the analysis in chapter 8. Also, this chapter shows that once population and job decline has begun, a number of self-reinforcing elements tend to perpetuate it, even if the initial underlying cause is removed. It thus seems extremely likely that population decline will continue in most large cities for at least the next decade or two, and almost as likely that job decline will continue in most of them.

This suggests that public policies aimed at reversing declines would require such enormous expenditures of money and effort to become effective that they must be considered infeasible in reality. The case study described in chapter 11 confirms this conclusion. Therefore, *we believe that current population declines in most large U.S. cities are irreversible in the near future.*

However, this does *not* mean those cities are going to disappear. Large cities still perform many social functions that will remain vital in the future, such as higher education, health care delivery, office-based activities, and government administration. They still contain enormous inventories of useful buildings and infrastructure; given the high cost of new construction, these assets are too valuable to abandon. Furthermore, housing demand is still rising in some large cities losing population, because of falling average household size. Eventually, these factors will make low-priced central-city land attractive enough to redevelop, though probably with much lower-density uses than in the past. When that happens, several of the self-reinforcing forces discussed previously will diminish in strength, and city populations will tend to stabilize.

Neighborhood Decline and Revitalization

Whether or not a given city continues to lose population, the quality of life there will be greatly affected by the amount of neighborhood decline and revitalization that occurs. Neighborhood revitalization can take place relatively independently of neighborhood decline in the same city. For example, about half of Boston's dwelling units in 1975 were in stable neighborhoods, just over one-third were in revitalizing neighborhoods, and about one-sixth were in declining neighborhoods.[12]

Neighborhood *decline*, whether through "emptying out" or "overcrowding," involves increasing physical deterioration, worsening quality of environment, reduced social status, greater incidence of social pathologies, and a loss of confidence among investors and property owners in the area's future economic viability. As argued in chapter 7, neighborhood decline in one form or another can take place under nearly all metropolitan housing conditions, so it is difficult to predict its future extent. Equally difficult is associating neighborhood decline with specific neighborhood traits, and then accurately predicting where those traits will exist.[13] Nevertheless, empirical studies have isolated some traits that seem to make a neighborhood more susceptible to decline: very low incomes, old housing, proximity to deteriorating neighborhoods, absentee landlords, low rates of owner-occupancy, absence of strong community organizations, and presence of noisy traffic, to name a few. There is also a growing body of literature concerning how to measure the developmental stages of individual neighborhoods, how to forecast their future conditions accordingly, and what micro-level policies to adopt under various conditions.[14]

Neighborhood *revitalization*, whether "gentrification" or "incumbent upgrading," involves rehabilitation of older housing. Usually starting in run-down neighborhoods occupied mainly by low-income households, it entails improved physical condition of structures, rising property values,

12. Rolf Goetze, *Building Neighborhood Confidence* (Ballinger, 1976), p. 36.

13. The complex dynamics of neighborhood decline are analyzed in more detail in Anthony Downs, *Neighborhoods and Urban Development* (Brookings Institution, 1981).

14. U.S. Department of Housing and Urban Development, *Neighborhood Conservation and Property Rehabilitation: A Selective Bibliography* (HUD, October 1979); HUD, *Neighborhood Preservation: A Catalog of Local Programs* (HUD, February 1975); Downs, *Neighborhoods and Urban Development;* Rolf Goetze, *Understanding Neighborhood Change* (Ballinger, 1979); and HUD, *The Dynamics of Neighborhood Change*, report prepared for HUD by the Real Estate Research Corporation (GPO, 1976).

more attractive local environments, declining crime rates, and increased confidence by investors and property owners. It does not necessarily entail increasing population.

Greater housing demand in an area is one of the preconditions for revitalization. It can result from nationwide factors (such as rapid formation of small households containing young adults), from metropolitan-wide factors (such as large physical distances, as in New York, or inmigration of wealthy households, as in Santa Barbara), from city-wide factors (such as greater downtown employment, as in Baltimore), or from neighborhood factors (such as location near downtown, good public transit, and architecturally attractive older housing, as in Philadelphia's Rittenhouse Square). The likely trends described in chapter 8 indicate that many of these factors will remain significant during the next decade or longer. Hence, we believe neighborhood revitalization will become more widespread in the 1980s. Its extent within each city will depend on both how many favorable factors exist there and how strongly local government policies encourage it.

However, gentrification also creates problems when low-income residents are displaced by higher-income newcomers. As noted in chapter 7, the total extent of such displacement has been relatively small in recent years. However, it will probably increase if revitalization expands in the 1980s. Nevertheless, city governments have good reasons to encourage gentrification. It raises property values, attracts or retains high- and middle-income households, and improves the physical attractiveness of neighborhoods.

Thus, we anticipate that the number of revitalizing neighborhoods will increase in most large cities, but neighborhood decline will not disappear. It may even expand into some areas now in fairly good condition. Consequently, it would be a mistake to observe what is happening in a few neighborhoods in any large older city and then generalize that condition as dominant throughout the city. In fact, the simultaneous occurrence of revitalization and decline in different parts of the same city is likely to become increasingly common.

Future Problems in Declining Cities

If the overall population decline of most large cities is irreversible, many will be unable to perform some of their social functions as well as they have in the past. The problems of city *governments* should be distinguished from those of city *residents*. For example, fiscal difficulties are government problems, whereas unemployment and crime are resident problems. Residents' problems are more fundamental, since the government is an intermediary serving the needs of residents and of society generally.

Some of the major problems facing central city governments will be reductions in intergovernmental aid,[15] increased average costs for many public services, loss of taxable resources, and continued difficulty in coping with social problems and unrest. Problems facing central city residents will include the negative effects of these government problems on tax rates and public services, and also physical deterioration in declining neighborhoods, some displacement from revitalizing neighborhoods, and a continued stagnation of many city economies as providers of income and upward mobility.

The heaviest burdens of these problems are likely to fall upon poor residents. Furthermore, those cities with the highest percentages of poor residents are the most likely to experience decline. In fact, large cities have become specialized locations for coping with the nation's poverty. In 1979, households with incomes under $7,000 comprised 27.4 percent of all central-city households, compared to only 14.8 percent of all suburban households.[16] Moreover, the concentration of poor households in central cities increased during the past decade. It is unlikely to decrease in the future, since neither socioeconomic nor racial segregation shows signs of diminishing significantly,[17] and central cities will contain higher fractions of the nation's oldest housing.

One of the most important social functions of large cities has always been helping poor households upgrade themselves. Performance of this function has recently been made more difficult by movement of many low-skilled manufacturing jobs out of such cities. Of 229 large U.S. central cities, 54 percent lost manufacturing employment from 1967 to 1972.[18]

15. See John L. Goodman, Jr., "Federal Funding Formulas and the 1980 Census," *Urban Institute Policy and Research Report*, vol. 10 (Winter 1980), pp. 7–9, for a more detailed discussion of how population affects federal aid to cities.

16. *Annual Housing Survey, 1979, Part C: Financial Characteristics of the Housing Inventory* (GPO, 1980), pp. 1–35.

17. Within 109 cities, residential segregation by race declined slightly during the 1960s, after rising during the previous two decades. See Annemette Sørensen, Karl E. Taeuber, and Leslie Hollingsworth, Jr., "Indexes of Racial Residential Segregation for 109 Cities in the United States, 1940 to 1970," *Sociological Focus*, vol. 8 (April 1975). Note, however, that these indexes do not allow us to draw conclusions about the degree of segregation *between* cities and suburbs.

18. Department of Housing and Urban Development, *The President's National Urban Policy Report, 1980* (GPO, 1980), p. 3-3.

This drop in low-skilled jobs has been only partly offset by the growth of service and government employment. Nevertheless, activities within large cities are still helping millions of poor persons upgrade their status by providing them with jobs, training, formal education, housing, health care, and cultural opportunities.

This upgrading function will remain important partly because of the clustering of minority groups in large cities. Though outmigration of some middle-class blacks and Hispanics into surrounding suburbs is under way in many SMSAs, in 1977, 59.4 percent of all black households and 50.9 percent of Hispanic households lived in central cities, compared to 25.4 percent of all non-Hispanic white households.[19] This minority concentration in cities will tend to perpetuate poverty concentration there too.

This analysis implies that combating poverty should be a central component of any strategy aimed at aiding *residents* of declining cities. Yet local governments have very limited means for combating poverty. If they try major redistributive programs, selective outmigration of the more affluent will remove resources from their jurisdiction. Major income redistribution financed by taxes within local jurisdictions is impossible when taxpayers are mobile. Thus, eliminating or even greatly reducing poverty is not within the power of city governments (or perhaps of any governments). To the extent that society decides to address poverty problems through public action, these actions must be considered primarily state and federal responsibilities. All a city government can do is cope with some of the public problems poverty generates, and help its residents make the most of whatever opportunities they face. Various strategies for doing this are discussed in chapter 13.

Conclusions

Most large U.S. cities that severely declined in population during the 1970s will continue to do so in the 1980s. The self-limiting factors that might halt further population losses do not seem as strong as many powerful self-reinforcing factors. However, these cities will not disappear. Eventually, vacant areas created by building abandonment will become sufficiently inexpensive and isolated from surrounding blight to entice developers to build new, lower-density structures on them.

19. See Kathryn P. Nelson, *Recent Suburbanization of Blacks: How Much, Who, and Where?* (Department of Housing and Urban Development, 1979), p. 1.

Some rebuilding and renovation have already begun in cities still losing population. Nevertheless, in severely declining cities, it will take many years—even decades—for population losses to be transformed into stability.

Self-reinforcing factors in many *growing* cities will encourage further population growth. However, one growth-limiting factor—inability to annex surrounding territory—will increasingly inhibit their future expansion. Hence in the face of continued slow national growth, even more large U.S. cities are likely to be losing population in the 1990s.

These conclusions indicate that any programs designed to reverse population declines are not likely to work. Most cities would be better off trying to adapt themselves to a smaller size. Furthermore, population loss is not necessarily injurious to city residents, whose welfare is the ultimate test of any city's "success." Their welfare is more threatened by the way U.S. urban development isolates the poor from other groups. Such concentration occurs regardless of whether the cities are gaining or losing population. However, a city's ability to provide upgrading opportunities for its poorest residents does appear to be diminished by continued population decline. This conclusion strongly implies that federal and state policies attacking poverty directly should be important components of any strategy designed to assist people in urban areas—even taking precedence over attempts to combat urban decline itself.

10

Energy Scarcity and Urban Development Patterns

WILL energy scarcities or high prices reverse postwar trends toward decentralization of U.S. urban development? Some urban planners think so. If fuel is costly or hard to obtain, they say, central locations and high densities will become more attractive as people seek to shorten trips, use mass transit, and reduce home heating and cooling costs. Anecdotes in the real estate news already suggest home buyers are more concerned about such factors. But more reliable empirical evidence is needed to answer this question.

In this chapter, we will consider two scenarios. In the *high-cost scenario,* growing world scarcity leads to commercial development of expensive extraction methods and synthetic fuels, producing a stable supply at much higher prices than those prevailing in the late 1970s. The *severe-shortage scenario* involves unstable supply, with intermittent disruptions over a long period.

Energy scarcity can exert its full influence on urban concentration only over a period long enough to permit capital stock adjustment. Changes in vacancy rates and building abandonment can quickly absorb only a limited increase in demand for city locations. Therefore, much of any short-run demand shift would be capitalized into higher prices for city properties. Nevertheless, in and near declining cities, the *rates* at which continual outmigration, building abandonment, and suburban construction occur can change almost instantaneously. Such changes would provide strong signals about likely future centralization. Furthermore, property price increases immediately improve the city's fiscal health through lower tax delinquency and, following reassessment, a larger tax base.

The biggest incentives for readjusting urban locations involve automobile transportation and residential heating and cooling. These two items account for 13.1 and 11.9 percent, respectively, of all U.S. energy consumption, according to estimates for 1973.[1] Since all other residential uses amounted to only 8.6 percent, these two together account for a large part of the typical urban household's energy budget. Industry and commerce absorb more than half of all U.S. energy consumption, but their dominant end uses—process steam, process heat, and electric motive power (together absorbing 32.3 percent of all consumption)—cannot be reduced much by location changes.

Adjustment Mechanisms

Changes in urban location are but one of many possible adjustments households can make to reduce energy consumption. To assess how much location shifting might occur, we need to understand not only the strength of each primary incentive (high price or a supply shortage), but also how extensively these other adjustments will occur. If gasoline and heating fuel consumption can be easily reduced by suburban residents, they will have only weak incentives to become city residents to save fuel.

Several adjustment mechanisms are set forth in table 10-1. They are listed roughly in order of the length of time for which a household is committed to use each, once started. The first entries involve simple adjustments in day-to-day behavior, such as slower and smoother driving or lower winter thermostat settings. The last entries involve changes in long-lived capital stock. Entries in between involve equipment purchases or shifts in daily routines. Each requires start-up costs, such as obtaining information about potential carpools or transit service, or the purchase of extra equipment for automobiles or furnaces. This ordering does not indicate the ultimate strength of each adjustment. Given time, many people might prefer long-term capital stock adjustments to altering cherished habits of comfort or convenience.

We know a lot about the potential for achieving energy savings through these mechanisms. For example, one study found that an increase in multipurpose trips occurred during the 1973–74 gasoline shortage.[2] A 1974

1. Sam H. Schurr and others, *Energy in America's Future: The Choices Before Us*, a study by the staff of the Resources for the Future National Energy Strategies Project (Johns Hopkins University Press for RFF, 1979), p. 75.

2. Robert L. Peskin and others, *The Immediate Impact of Gasoline Shortages on Urban Travel Behavior* (Federal Highway Administration, April 1975).

Table 10-1. *Some Adjustment Mechanisms Available to Households for Reducing Energy Consumption*

Automobile transportation	*Home heating/cooling*
Driving habits (speed, acceleration, etc.)	Domestic habits (thermostat settings, use of curtains, etc.)
Discretionary trips	Retrofit of existing house (furnace insulation, etc.)
Multipurpose trips	Housing type—attached or multi-family—existing units
Carpools	House design for energy efficiency—new units
Transit	Housing type—attached or multi-family—new units
Purchase of fuel-efficient cars	Move to warmer climate
Residential location choice—existing units	
Residential location choice—new units	
Move to more compact metropolitan area	

survey revealed that 89 percent of respondents claimed to "frequently" drive more slowly in order to save gasoline, and 31 percent reduced shopping and recreational trips.[3] Similarly, home heating fuel consumption fell from 1973 to 1976 by about 9 to 13 percent through adjustments in thermostat settings and other living habits, plus some "retrofitting" of homes.[4]

Several authors have concluded that the most potent way to reduce energy consumption in surface transportation is to improve motor vehicle fuel economy.[5] Legal regulation, rising gasoline prices, and intermittent shortages have already raised the fuel economy of newly purchased U.S. domestic cars by more than 40 percent between 1974 and 1978, through design modification and downsizing. The 27.5-mile-per-gallon standard now mandated for model 1985 cars would be an additional 50 percent improvement. Market incentives may push actual achievements even higher. General Motors has announced its intention to reach a fleet average of 31 miles per gallon by 1985.[6] Smaller but substantial improvements are also possible in truck design.[7]

3. Office of Technology Assessment, *Energy, the Economy, and Mass Transit* (OTA, 1975).

4. Schurr and others, *Energy in America's Future*, pp. 141–42.

5. See particularly Alan Altshuler, with James P. Womack and John R. Pucher, *The Urban Transportation System: Politics and Policy Innovation* (MIT Press, 1979), chap. 5; and Schurr and others, *Energy in America's Future*, pp. 143–59.

6. *Wall Street Journal*, July 10, 1980.

7. National Academy of Sciences, *Alternate Energy Demand Futures to 2010*, Report of the Demand and Conversion Panel to the Committee on Nuclear and Alternate Energy Systems (NAS, 1979), pp. 168–69.

A similar picture emerged from the Ford Foundation's Energy Policy Project. Its report compared a "zero energy growth scenario," in which transportation energy consumption was reduced from 43 quadrillion to 19 quadrillion BTUs ("quads"), with a baseline scenario of total energy growth at the 1950–70 rate of 3.4 percent per year. Of the hypothetical 24-quad reduction, 36 percent was in the airline industry and another 13 percent in trucking and rail. About 49 percent was to result from improving average fuel economy to 33 miles per gallon by 2000. Only 0.8 percent would result from putting 6 percent of the population in new communities in which auto travel would be halved.[8]

For the high-price scenario considered in this chapter, statistical evidence confirms that gasoline savings would come mainly from changes in auto fuel efficiency. The price elasticity of demand for gasoline shows the percentage by which gasoline consumption would fall because of a 1 percent rise in price. Overall, this elasticity was computed by James Sweeney to range from 0.22 over one year to 0.78 in the long run.[9] Of this 0.78 percent reduction in gasoline consumption, only 0.06 percent would be due to reduced driving; the remainder would result from higher average fuel economy. Similarly, from a 1976 sample of individual households purchasing new cars, Lave and Train estimated a gasoline price elasticity of 0.41 just from shifts among different size classes.[10]

Technological possibilities for saving fuel in space heating and cooling are also striking.[11] A Resources for the Future study concluded that simple alterations in furnaces can reduce consumption of heating fuel by at least 20 percent. Modifications economical under modest tax incentives plus a total price of $5.40 per million BTUs in 1977 prices (about 75 cents per gallon of fuel oil—well below 1980 prices) would reduce consumption by 64 percent in existing and 77 percent in new structures.[12]

8. Energy Policy Project of the Ford Foundation, *A Time to Choose: America's Energy Future* (Ballinger, 1974), pp. 57–58, 100–01.

9. As reported in John F. Kain, "The Future of Urban Transportation: An Economist's Perspective," discussion paper D79-12 (Department of City and Regional Planning, Harvard University, 1979), pp. 21–22.

10. Computed from Charles A. Lave and Kenneth Train, "A Disaggregate Model of Auto-Type Choice," *Transportation Research*, vol. 13A (1979), table 4, p. 8; data on fuel economy of the various size classes were kindly supplied by the authors.

11. See Arthur D. Little, Inc., *Residential and Commercial Energy Use Patterns, 1970–1990*, vol. 1 of U.S. Federal Energy Administration, *Project Independence Blueprint*, 1974; Hittman Associates, Inc., *Residential Energy Consumption: Detailed Geographic Analysis*, Report HIT-650-11, prepared for Department of Housing and Urban Development, 1977; Schurr and others, *Energy in America's Future*, pp. 125–43.

12. Schurr and others, *Energy in America's Future*, pp. 130, 139, 141.

Thus, several avenues are available to reduce energy consumption with minimal expense and inconvenience in those sectors most strongly affected by energy scarcity. These mechanisms could greatly reduce the impact of scarcity upon other aspects of life, including inter- and intrametropolitan location. Given the great strength of those forces underlying recent migration patterns, changes in those patterns resulting from energy scarcity would therefore be relatively minor. Before accepting this conclusion, however, we need to consider in more detail the locational incentives likely to result from the two basic scenarios described earlier.

High-Cost Scenario

It is by no means certain that real energy costs will continue rising over the next one or two decades. At present, those costs are heavily influenced by an international cartel of oil-exporting nations, OPEC. Various projections of crude oil prices, under either free market or monopoly conditions, show them to be quite sensitive to the timing and eventual cost of alternative sources of power. These include synthetic fuels, nuclear breeder reactors, solar, nuclear fusion, and extraction of low-grade sources of conventional fuels.[13] Favorable developments in any of these areas might turn restrictive policies by OPEC against its members' long-term advantage. In addition, any big new oil discoveries such as recent ones in Mexico would increase the potential for instability in the cartel, weakening its ability to determine the world price.

Nordhaus convincingly argues that oil price increases need not be inexorable just because oil supplies are finite.[14] He contends that a profit-maximizing cartel would not necessarily raise its price gradually. Rather, under certain circumstances closely resembling those in the 1970s, it would raise the price to just below the ceiling set by alternative technologies, holding it there until crude oil reserves were exhausted. If a start-up time were required for competing technologies, the monopolist might even

13. See, for example, William D. Nordhaus, "The Allocation of Energy Resources," *Brookings Papers on Economic Activity*, 3:1973, pp. 529–76; Symposium on the Economics of Exhaustible Resources, *Review of Economic Studies* (special issue, 1974); Y. R. Benari, "Depletable Resource Pricing and Output Strategies in Light of a Possible Future Substitute" (Ph.D. dissertation, Princeton University, 1976); H. Houthakker and M. Kennedy, "Long-Range Energy Prospects," discussion paper 634 (Harvard University Institute of Economic Research, 1978); W. D. Nordhaus, *The Efficient Use of Energy Resources* (Yale University Press, 1979).

14. Nordhaus, *Efficient Use of Energy Resources*.

raise the price considerably above this long-run limit, then gradually lower it. This tactic is especially likely if short-run demand elasticity is low because of lags in adjusting use patterns. The anticipation of a new technology can therefore depress the price of oil well before that technology is actually adopted. Moreover, dramatic reductions in oil consumption have occurred in response to recent price increases. The more the world's energy users learn to conserve oil, either by substituting other fuels or by cutting their energy use altogether, the greater the constraint on future price rises.

Nevertheless, if favorable developments do not occur, recent oil price increases may continue. But how fast? Since we are trying to analyze impacts on long-term investments, the relevant consideration is not the temporary world-market disequilibria reflected in 1979's high and erratic spot-market prices. Rather, it is the long-term price dictated by considerations of world reserves and demand. An upper limit on that price should be set by the world's ability, within a few decades, to develop large amounts of synthetic fuels, including shale oil. The cost of these technologies are uncertain, but most estimates place them below $40 per barrel in 1977 prices—roughly four times the 1977 average U.S. domestic oil price.[15] With around 38 gallons of refined products produced per barrel of crude oil, the real costs of those products will probably not rise by more than $0.75 per gallon.[16] In addition, government policy might single out gasoline for special taxes to curtail consumption or to subsidize other oil uses like home heating.

What is a reasonable limit for the rise in the long-term price of liquid fuels when supply is stable? We will consider it an increase of $1 per gallon for gasoline and of $0.75 per gallon for fuel oil, in 1977 prices. We assume that natural gas would rise in price by the same amount as fuel oil, per unit of heat value, and that electricity would be generated from fuel oil, with its price rise based upon a straight pass-through of fuel costs. All calculations shown below are proportional to these increases; so the results can easily be adjusted to fit alternative assumptions.

15. Schurr and others, *Energy in America's Future*, found that "liquids and gases from coal and oil shale appear to be producible at costs about twice the 1978 prices of petroleum and natural gas" (p. 5). Costs could be well under that: specific estimates, all in 1977 prices, are $15–$19 per barrel for liquefied coals (p. 263), $23–$37 for surface-mined shale oil, and $50 for in-situ shale oil (p. 254).

16. An increase in crude petroleum price does not result in a proportional increase in the retail price of refined products, since a substantial fraction of the latter is composed of refining and distribution costs. For example, in 1977 the weighted average price of imported and domestic oil was $10.56 per barrel, which accounted for approximately one-half of the retail price of gasoline at that time (approximately $0.55 per gallon). Computed from *Statistical Abstract of the United States, 1978*, pp. 488, 765.

As noted earlier, many likely adjustments to such price increases would reduce incentives to relocate. For example, multipurpose auto trips could cut auto travel about proportionally from all residential locations, thereby decreasing absolute travel-cost differences by location. Nevertheless, we will compute cost increases resulting from higher fuel prices *in the absence of any such adjustments*. This places an upper bound on the incentives to alter locations likely to result from long-term energy price increases.[17]

We first compute differential cost increases arising from the higher prices at alternative locations, assuming that technological and behavioral patterns of energy use are those prevailing in the 1970s.[18] We do this for work travel, nonwork travel, and residential space heating and cooling. We then estimate the effects of these intraurban cost differentials on rates of migration into and out of central cities.

Work Trips

The argument that higher gasoline prices will cause greater centralization of urban development rests on two assumptions. One is that travel destinations are more centralized than residences, so people can reduce their auto use by living closer in. With respect to work trips, this is less true than commonly believed. Census data for 1975 indicate that 47.4 percent of all jobs in metropolitan areas were located outside central cities, compared to 58.9 percent of household residences.[19] Only 18.6 percent of metropolitan jobs were held by suburban residents commuting to central cities; nearly half that fraction commuted in the opposite direction. Thus, almost 70 percent of all commuting to metropolitan jobs occurs *within* the central city or *within* the suburbs, rather than between them. A more detailed breakdown does show that much intrasuburban commuting is

17. If the extent of all the relevant adjustments could be estimated, computations using the post-price-rise consumption quantities would then provide a lower bound on such cost differentials, because they would ignore the additional cost or inconvenience incurred as part of these adjustments. This is an example of the more general index number problem: the true loss of real purchasing power due to a price rise is somewhere between the losses computed based on quantities consumed at old and new prices.

18. We have made two exceptions to the use of technological factors from the 1970s. For automobile fuel economy and residential heating and cooling efficiency, as already noted, substantial changes probably will occur due to price rises already in effect by 1977. We thus assume 20 miles per gallon, the standard now mandated by law for 1980 model cars, as the average fuel consumption for commuting vehicles. We assume an improvement of fuel efficiency in home heating/cooling of 20 percent. The Resources for the Future study indicates this amount could be achieved by low-cost improvements in existing structures.

19. Bureau of the Census, *Current Population Reports*, Series P-23, no. 99, "The Journey to Work in the United States, 1975" (GPO, 1979), table A.

Table 10-2. *Percentage Distribution of All Workers Living and Working in Same SMSA and Not Working at Home, 1975*

Location of residence	Location of employment		
	City	*Suburb*	*Total*
City	34.8	8.1	42.9
Suburb	19.5	37.7	57.1
Total	54.2	45.8	100.0

Source: U.S. Bureau of the Census, *Current Population Reports*, Series P-23, no. 99, "The Journey to Work in the United States, 1975" (GPO, 1979), table F.

inward; nevertheless, the naive view that huge numbers of workers must move to the city to live closer to their jobs is inaccurate.

The second assumption is that residences, rather than jobs, will be relocated. Yet many employers try to situate their workplaces near concentrations of labor.[20] If higher energy costs made workers more resistant to commuting long distances, this tendency would be reinforced, and suburban locations would become even more attractive to firms. Hence the net effect could be *decentralizing*.

Thus, even the *direction* of the net locational changes resulting from higher energy costs is unclear without some quantification. To assess the magnitudes and directions involved, we use recent census data on the modal shares and mean trip lengths for commuters by location of residence and workplace. We first compute the fuel consumed on work trips by a household with an average number of workers and an average distribution of workplaces, located at alternative residences. This provides a picture of how large the incentives to centralize might be. Similarly, the difference in total commuting costs to an average firm, depending on its location in city or suburbs, measures the relocational incentive arising from its desire to reduce commuting costs for its potential workforce.

Data are from the Travel-to-Work Supplement to the Annual Housing Survey, conducted by the Census Bureau in 1975, based on answers by a national sample of 136,800 respondents. Table 10-2 shows the percentage distribution of all U.S. workers living and working within the same SMSA and not working at home, by origin-destination possibilities. Table 10-3 reports the corresponding percentages of trips made by driving an auto, and average trip lengths for auto drivers. The resulting average annual cost

20. See, for example, Rodney A. Erickson and Michael Wasylenko, "Firm Relocation and Site Selection in Suburban Municipalities," *Journal of Urban Economics*, vol. 8 (July 1980), pp. 69–85.

Table 10-3. *High-Energy-Cost Scenario: Work Travel, 1975 National Sample*

Location of residence	Location of employment: City	Location of employment: Suburb	Weighted average per household[a]
City			
Auto drivers[b]	64.0	80.5	...
Auto trip length[c]	5.6	10.1	...
Average cost increase[d]	86.0	195.0	160
Suburbs			
Auto drivers	375.8	79.8	...
Auto trip length	11.5	7.4	...
Average cost increase	209.0	142.0	210
Weighted average cost increase per employee[e]	156.0	165.0	...

Source: "The Journey to Work in the United States, 1975," tables F, H, 1.

a. Average cost increase per household (1 household = 1.18 employed workers), assuming 54.2 percent work in city and 45.8 percent work in suburbs (see table 10-2).

b. Percent of commuters who drive to work (assumes average carpool contains 2.5 persons).

c. One-way average trip length for auto drivers, in miles (assumes 2.5 persons per carpool).

d. Cost increase per worker, in dollars per year, resulting from added cost per auto driver of 5 cents a mile (assumes 240 round trips per year).

e. Average cost increase per employee, assuming firm draws 42.9 percent of its workers from city and 57.1 percent from suburbs (see table 10-2).

increase per worker due to a rise of $1 per gallon of gasoline is also shown for each of these categories.

The absolute cost increases are quite small in comparison to total incomes or housing costs. Differences among these categories of workers are even smaller. The largest difference is between suburban and city residents who work in the city. Suburban commuters into cities could reduce auto use for commuting by an average of over 50 percent by moving to a city residence. Yet such a move would cut thc added cost from a $1 per gallon gasoline price rise by only $123 per year. In contrast, among people with suburban jobs, those commuting from city homes travel farther on the average than those commuting from suburban homes. So the gasoline price rise would create a net $53 per year incentive for the former to move to the suburbs. On the average, a household choosing between a city and suburban residence would have to add extra commuting costs of $160 per year if it located in the city, versus $210 if in the suburbs. Many households would face larger incentives to centralize, and a lot of shifting would probably occur. But much of it would cancel out; so the $50 differential ($210 minus $160) is a reasonable measure of the net incentive toward centralization. Yet adjustments like smaller cars, more carpooling, and more transit use would reduce this incentive even more; so it must be regarded as very weak.

A similar computation for the average metropolitan *firm* is shown in the last row of table 10-3. More workers live in the suburbs than in the city, but the larger proportion of transit use among city dwellers cancels almost exactly the advantage that would otherwise accrue from a firm's choosing a suburban workplace. Hence the net effect of the gasoline price rise on firm locations would be negligible.

Another possible influence of higher gasoline prices on firms would stem from the increased cost of trucking. Cheap truck transportation was a major factor encouraging suburbanization of employment.[21] Yet increased fuel prices would probably not reverse this trend. For one thing, the fuel costs of the *urban* portion of freight shipments is very small for typical firms. A shift to rail for *intercity* freight shipments might occur, but it would probably be accommodated through more use of "piggyback" operations rather than relocations of firms. Trucks would not be eliminated altogether because they have inherent service advantages for local pickup and delivery.

To study these locational incentives in more detail, we performed a similar analysis for the Cleveland metropolitan area, as shown in tables 10-4 and 10-5. This area is typical of many fairly spread-out, medium-sized metropolitan areas with dispersed job locations.[22] We divided the Cleveland SMSA into three residential zones and four workplace zones, creating twelve origin-destination categories. The distribution of commuter flows among them for the year 1976 is shown in table 10-4. Auto-driver mode share and trip length are shown in table 10-5, along with the implied increases in commuting cost for the "average" worker due to a $1 per gallon gasoline price rise. This more detailed view reveals substantial cost differences between close-in suburbs (within Cuyahoga County) and those farther out. The few workers commuting from outer counties to Cleveland would experience such large increases in annual commuting costs that

21. Leon Moses and Harold Williamson, Jr., "The Location of Economic Activity in Cities," *American Economic Review*, vol. 57 (May 1967, *Papers and Proceedings, December 1966)*, pp. 212–22.

22. For example, Cleveland's urbanized area population density, as defined by the Census Bureau, was 3,033 per square mile in 1970. This compares with 2,696 for Atlanta, 3,314 for Cincinnati, 3,577 for Denver, 3,115 for Houston, 3,095 for Pittsburgh, 3,148 for San Diego, 2,297 for Seattle, and 3,376 for all urbanized areas. Cleveland's median work-trip distance of 7.8 miles in 1976 compares with 8.8 for Baltimore, 8.4 for St. Louis, 7.3 for Indianapolis, 7.4 for Denver, and 7.7 for Louisville. Bureau of the Census, *Current Population Reports*, Series P-23, no. 72, "Selected Characteristics of Travel to Work in 20 Metropolitan Areas, 1976" (GPO, 1978), p. 8; and *County and City Data Book, 1972* (GPO, 1973), table 6.

Table 10-4. *Percentage Distribution of All Workers Living and Working in Cleveland SMSA, 1976*

	Location of employment				
Location of residence	*Central business district*	*Balance of city*	*Balance of Cuyahoga County*	*Balance of SMSA*	*Total*
City of Cleveland	3.2	16.5	8.5	0.5	28.7
Balance of Cuyahoga County	6.4	16.4	27.8	1.8	52.4
Balance of SMSA	0.8	2.6	4.2	11.3	18.9
Total	10.5	35.4	40.5	13.6	100.0

Source: Bureau of the Census, unpublished preliminary tabulation from the 1976–77 Travel-to-Work Supplement to the Annual Housing Survey. Based on first one-third of households surveyed (approximately 1,667 households). Figures are rounded.

some would relocate inward. However, these figures are upper bounds. Moreover, such commuters constitute only 18 percent of the workers living in those outer counties, and only 3.4 percent of all SMSA workers.

As before, the net influence of the price rise on location decisions can be assessed by considering a household with an average number of workers at various job locations, and a firm with an average number of employees at various residential locations. The average Cleveland SMSA *household* had 1.26 employed workers in 1976, with workplaces distributed according to the bottom row of table 10-4.[23] Its increase in commuting cost depends on its residential location, as shown in the last column of table 10-5. The average *firm* drew its employees from various locations, as shown in the last column of table 10-4. The commuting costs of its average employee would vary with the firm's location, as shown in the bottom row of table 10-5. In footnotes e, g, and h of that table, the figures are aggregated to city and suburb levels by using appropriate weights from table 10-4, for comparison with the earlier national results.

The net change in city-suburb locational incentives in the Cleveland area caused by the gasoline price rise is larger than that calculated for the national sample, but still modest. The typical household has a $140 per year incentive to choose a city location ($279 minus $139). For the typical firm, the incentive is $33 per year per worker ($207 minus $174) to move farther out of the city. For both households and firms, incentives to avoid

23. That is, 860,000 nonagricultural wage and salary employees divided by 681,200 year-round occupied housing units. Bureau of Labor Statistics, *Employment and Earnings*, May 1978; and Bureau of the Census, *Current Housing Reports, Annual Housing Survey, 1976, Housing Characteristics for Selected Metropolitan Areas: Cleveland, Ohio Standard Metropolitan Statistical Area* (GPO, 1978).

Table 10-5. *High-Energy-Cost Scenario: Work Travel, Cleveland SMSA*

	Location of employment				
Location of residence	*Central business district*	*Balance of city*	*Balance of Cuyahoga County*	*Balance of SMSA*	*Weighted average per household*[a]
City of Cleveland					
Auto drivers[b]	32.6	52.0	70.0	60.0	...
Auto trip length[c]	7.4	4.6	7.3	17.4	...
Average cost increase[d]	58.0	58.0	123.0	250.0	139.0
Balance of Cuyahoga County					
Auto drivers	38.0	71.3	71.8	89.9	...
Auto trip length	13.2	11.0	5.5	13.2	...
Average cost increase	121.0	188.0	94.0	284.0	197.0[e]
Outer suburbs					
Auto drivers	81.4	77.9	87.3	63.3	...
Auto trip length	28.7	27.6	17.3	5.9	...
Average cost increase	561.0	516.0	363.0	89.0	505.0[e]
Weighted average cost increase per employee[f]	186[g]	213[g]	153[h]	238[h]	...

a. Average cost increase per household (1 household = 1.26 employed workers), assuming distribution of workplaces as in last row of table 10-4.

b. Percent of commuters who drive to work (assumes average carpool contains 2.5 persons).

c. One-way average trip length for auto drivers, in miles (assumes 2.5 persons per carpool).

d. Cost increase per worker, in dollars per year, resulting from added cost per auto driver of 5 cents a mile (assumes 240 round trips per year).

e. Annual cost increase for average suburban residential location is (0.524 × \$197 + 0.189 × \$505)/(0.524 + 0.189) = \$279 per household.

f. Average cost increase per employee, assuming distribution of residences as in last column of table 10-4.

g. Annual cost increase for average city workplace location is (0.105 × \$186 + 0.354 × \$213)/(0.105 + 0.354) = \$207 per employee.

h. Annual cost increase for average suburban workplace location is (0.405 × \$153 + 0.136 × \$238)/(0.405 + 0.136) = \$174 per employee.

the outer suburbs are considerably larger. Hence there might be some shift in suburban growth from far-out areas to older suburbs closer in.

Nonwork Trips

Suburban residents drive more than city residents for nonwork purposes. Not all of this divergence is due to differences in such characteristics as age and family composition; some represents inherent differences between city and suburban living patterns. Therefore, higher gasoline prices should produce some tendency toward more centralized residences.

Table 10-6. *Some Determinants of Average Automobile Use for Nonwork Purposes per Driver*

Description	*Regression coefficient*
Increment to autos per household arising from	
Single-family rather than multi-family home	0.138
Owner-occupied rather than rented home	0.192
Suburban rather than central-city location	0.202
Increment to daily nonwork auto-miles per driver arising from	
One additional auto per household	7.450
Suburban rather than central-city location	1.685

Source: Douglas P. Sharp, "Projections of Automobile Ownership and Use Based on Household Lifestyle Factors" (Ph.D. dissertation, School of Engineering, University of Pittsburgh, 1978), pp. 57, 82.

We can place an upper bound on this incentive by determining the average number of additional vehicle-miles per household associated with suburban residence. Using early 1970s data, Douglas P. Sharp developed several statistical models of automobile ownership and use.[24] Holding key demographic traits constant, he distinguished the influence of housing type, housing tenure, and residence location. The relevant regression coefficients are shown in table 10-6. To determine the total cost differential between a suburban and a city residence, we apply the average proportions of each housing structure and tenure type found in U.S. suburbs and central cities, as shown in table 10-7. This indicates that a suburban residence is associated with an additional 2,260 vehicle-miles per year for the average household.[25] At 20 miles per gallon, the suburban-city differential in annual cost for nonwork auto travel would rise by $113 if gasoline prices rose $1 per gallon.

24. "Projections of Automobile Ownership and Use Based on Household Lifestyle Factors" (Ph.D. dissertation, School of Engineering, University of Pittsburgh, 1978).

25. From table 10-7, a typical household contemplating alternative metropolitan locations has a probability of choosing a single-family home which is 0.223 larger if it locates in the suburbs rather than a central city and a probability of owner-occupancy 0.190 larger. When these differences are applied to the first two coefficients in table 10-6, the average number of additional autos owned by such a household if it lives in the suburbs rather than the city is $(0.138 \times 0.223 + 0.192 \times 0.190 + 0.202) = 0.269$. From the last two coefficients, this implies an additional $(7.45 \times 0.269 + 1.685) = 3.69$ daily vehicle-miles per driver for nonwork purposes. The number of drivers per household was approximately 1.68 in 1975, based on the distribution of households among life-cycle stages shown in Sharp's dissertation, p. 109 (definitions are on p. 40).

Table 10-7. *Housing Characteristics of Central City and Suburban Location, U.S. Metropolitan Areas, 1976*

Location of residence	*Type of unit as percent of all housing units*	
	Single-family	*Owner-occupied*[a]
All metropolitan areas	61.9	64.6
City	49.8	53.3
Suburb	72.1	72.3
Suburb-city	22.3	19.0

Source: *Statistical Abstract of the United States*, 1978, pp. 789, 793.
a. Refers to whites only.

Residential Heating and Cooling

One reason people move to the suburbs is that single-family homes are more prevalent there, and most American households prefer such homes. But when energy is costly, this attraction is weakened, because single-family homes use two-thirds more energy per square foot of living area for space heating than multi-family units.[26] If fuel oil prices were to rise by 75 cents per gallon (and gas and electricity by the same amount per heat value), annual heating costs would increase by $610 in the average single-family home, compared to $366 for a comparable multi-family unit.[27] This seems to create a notable incentive toward relocating from single-family to multi-family units, though other forms of adjustment might make the actual incentive much smaller. Moreover, applying the proportions of structure types in cities and suburbs shown in table 10-7, the average increase in heating costs would be $542 in the suburbs and $487 in central cities, for a difference of only $55. Thus, the incentive to change housing types would be felt mainly *within* cities and suburbs; it would have only a minor net effect on each city's housing market as a whole.

We also made a more detailed analysis, not shown here, of prototype housing units in the four major census regions of the nation, based on engineering studies.[28] It shows annual city-suburban cost differentials averaging $93, ranging from $63 in the South to $136 in the Northeast,

26. Schurr and others, *Energy in America's Future*, p. 128.

27. Based on an average assumption per housing unit of 122 million BTUs (ibid., p. 128); 5.8 million BTUs per 42-gallon barrel of oil (ibid, p. 226), with a 20 percent reduction assumed through efficiency improvements (see text).

28. See Kenneth A. Small, "Energy Scarcity and Urban Development Patterns," *International Regional Science Review*, vol. 5 (Winter 1980), pp. 97–117.

Table 10-8. *Upper-Bound Impacts of High-Energy-Cost Scenario*
1977 dollars per year

Description	*Increase in suburban relative to central-city annual costs*
Households (per household)	
Work trips	50
Nonwork trips	113
Residential heating/cooling	93
Total	256
Firms (per employee)	
Work trips	9

Source: Table 10-3 and text.

resulting from a 75-cent-per-gallon price increase in fuel oil (or its equivalent in natural gas or electric utility rates). These are small inducements for changing from suburban to city living. Differences *within* cities and suburbs, in this case between attached and detached dwellings, are more significant; hence they might result in a noticeable increase in demand for higher-density living in both locations.

A Perspective on Magnitudes

The upper bounds on city-suburban cost differentials arising from energy price increases, as computed above, are summarized in table 10-8. One way to place these differentials in perspective is to compare them to other cost differentials currently facing households and firms. For example, the suburban growth of the 1970s took place despite considerably higher average house values in suburban locations: $44,000 as compared to $34,000 in central cities in 1977.[29] This difference of about $1,000 per year in annual housing cost (annualizing at 10 percent) reflects, of course, many differences in size and quality of units as well as neighborhood characteristics. Thus, the maximum likely energy-caused increases in the average city-suburban housing cost differential are not large relative to those caused by other factors affecting housing markets.

Perhaps a more useful comparison is with other determinants of intraregional migration rates. The responsiveness of households to tax disparities

29. Bureau of the Census, *Current Housing Reports, 1977, Part A: Median Values of Owner-Occupied Houses* (GPO, 1979), table A-2.

has been estimated by William H. Frey.[30] In a multiple-regression analysis of thirty-nine SMSAs, he found people were more likely to move out to the suburbs if taxes there were much lower than in the city. His results imply that an increase of 0.1 in the ratio of suburban to city per capita taxes (holding constant the quality of public services) causes a decrease of 1.2 in the percentage of city movers who choose a suburban destination. This change represents a reduction of 0.24 percent in the annual rate of outmigration from cities, and it could be brought about by a change of approximately $110 in the average city-suburb tax differential.[31] If households reacted to the energy cost increases summarized in table 10-8 in the same way as Frey's analysis says they would to comparable tax increases, net outmigration from cities would decrease by an average of 0.56 percentage point per year. This is well within the range of uncertainty about likely changes in migration rates caused by the many other forces affecting cities discussed in earlier chapters. It compares to 1970–78 average annual net outmigration rates of 2.5 percent for St. Louis, 1.8 for Baltimore and Washington, D.C., 1.5 for New York, 1.4 for Philadelphia, and 1.2 for San Francisco.[32] Thus, rising energy costs will—at most—have locational impacts comparable to those of other uncertain factors.[33]

A rough analysis can also be made of the impact upon total gasoline

30. "White Flight and Central-City Loss: Application of an Analytic Migration Framework," *Environment and Planning A*, vol. 11 (January 1979), pp. 129–47. Frey also examined suburb-to-city and nonmetropolitan-to-city migration, but obtained statistically insignificant (and wrong-signed) coefficients on tax variables in those cases (ibid., p. 141, and private correspondence).

31. Census figures from the 1976 Annual Housing Survey show that 20 percent of central city households move within their SMSA each year. The average taxes in Frey's sample were $258 per capita in central cities and $190 in suburbs in 1970 (U.S. Advisory Commission on Intergovernmental Relations, *City Financial Emergencies*, Report A-42 [ACIR, 1973], app. B, table B-18). Strictly speaking, the change in the ratio depends on whether the differential is added to suburban taxes or subtracted from city taxes; to avoid this anomaly, we average these two figures, obtaining $224. Multiplying by an average household size of 3.13 (*Statistical Abstract of the United States, 1978*, pp. 17, 789) and inflating to 1977 prices give $1,100 as an average household tax burden from which to compute changes in the ratio.

32. Computed from Bureau of the Census, *Current Population Reports*, Series P-25, no. 873, "Estimates of the Population of Counties and Metropolitan Areas: July 1, 1977 and 1978" (GPO, 1979). Migration figures for cities not coinciding with a county equivalent are unavailable.

33. Will energy-induced incentives for relocation be offset by capitalization of the new energy cost differentials into property values and rents? Yes, eventually—but only after urban densities have adjusted to new equilibrium levels. Until then, capitalization will cause the increased demands for energy-efficient locations to generate increased residential density there, thus permitting the induced net migrations to occur.

usage of suburb-to-city relocations caused by higher gasoline prices; this ignores for the moment any rise in heating costs. Average gasoline consumption per metropolitan household in 1977 would have been about 620 gallons per year at a fuel efficiency of 20 miles per gallon.[34] According to table 10-8, a rise in gasoline price of $1 per gallon over 1977 levels, or about 150 percent, would produce a city-suburb cost differential of $163 (in 1977 dollars). When Frey's coefficient of 0.24 percentage point is applied to the migration rate for each $110 differential, this would change the central city's total households by 7.1 percent in twenty years. The net result would be a total reduction in gasoline consumption by metropolitan residents of only 0.81 percent from a 150 percent increase in price[35]—an implied gasoline price elasticity of 0.005! Clearly any back-to-the-city movement spurred by higher gasoline prices will hardly conserve much gasoline.

Severe-Shortage Scenario

In the 1970s, several relatively sudden gasoline shortages occurred that were not fully dealt with through market mechanisms, but involved complex formal and informal rationing. If domestic synthetic fuels are developable at the prices considered in the previous section, such shortages are not likely to last long enough to affect the location of buildings with long lifetimes. Prolonged shortages would indicate extreme short-sightedness, foreign policy disasters, or totally unforeseen obstacles to development of domestic fuel resources. If such disruptions nevertheless take place, their frequency and extent will be unpredictable. They will probably call forth emergency measures whose details are also difficult to guess in advance. Still, we can make some observations about whether central cities would benefit from such prolonged shortages by capturing more resources from suburbs.

34. Assuming 1.29 cars per metropolitan household and 9,600 miles per car, from *Statistical Abstract of the United States*, 1979, pp. 643, 650.

35. From table 10-2, central cities contain about 42.9 percent of all SMSA households, so the 7.2 percent increase in central-city households represents a shift of 3.1 percent of *all* metropolitan households from suburb to city. Each of these thereby saves 50 gallons on work trips and 113 gallons on nonwork trips annually, according to previous analysis summarized in table 10-8. The total reduction is therefore $0.031 \times 163 = 5$ gallons per household, or 0.8 percent.

Gasoline Rationing

The primary public response to a severe supply disruption would probably be gasoline rationing, especially since a standby plan has been approved by Congress. How would such rationing affect urban locational incentives?

The type of rationing adopted in the U.S. standby plan in 1980 allows a legal "white market" for coupons. This scheme is equivalent to a rise in the price of gasoline equal to the resulting free-market coupon price, plus an income redistribution to those receiving coupons.[36] Thus, persistent "white market" rationing would provide locational incentives exactly like those analyzed in the previous section. Their size would be determined by the rise in the effective consumer price (gasoline price plus coupon price).

On the other hand, many individuals favor gasoline rationing like that in World War II, which prohibited the sale of coupons. Then the amount of gasoline each individual could have would be set uniformly but arbitrarily by regulation—though with the many exceptions that so greatly complicated the wartime system. This would create a greater incentive to avoid very long commuting, since additional coupons could not be purchased (legally). However, ride-sharing and the use of fuel-efficient cars would still remain strong competitors to relocation as means of coping.

The dominant feature of any rationing system would be uncertainty concerning how long it would last. Hence both households and firms would seek flexibility to adapt to varied circumstances. This creates the strongest case for relocating, since a centralized location close to one's job provides maximum options for both work and nonwork travel. On the other hand, most location decisions are fairly long-term commitments, especially for owner-occupants. They might suffer capital losses on city properties if anticipated rationing failed to materialize or did not last long. In contrast, ride sharing, use of suburban transit, and cutting back discretionary trips could all reduce gasoline consumption quickly without committing the household to a decision that would be unattractive if the shortage were short-lived. Thus, with somewhat less confidence, we still believe there would be no dramatic changes in existing location trends unless very severe and prolonged shortages occurred.

36. See Randall J. Pozdena and Kenneth A. Small, "Balancing the Gains and Losses from the Gasoline Shortage," in Joseph W. Garbarino, ed., *Policy Options for the Gasoline Shortage* (Berkeley: University of California, Institute of Business and Economic Research, 1974), pp. 45–57.

Land-Use Controls

Public policy might respond to energy shortages and higher prices by changing land-use controls, rather than relying solely upon atomistic household behavior shifts. Could major changes in such controls cut energy use enough to make the difficulties of implementing them worthwhile?

One possible policy would be channeling future suburban growth into narrow, relatively high-density corridors served by public transit. Suppose this succeeded in raising development density for one-half the suburban growth that would otherwise occur. Cheslow and Neels found "savings of more than 40 percent in annual transportation energy use per household, when relatively high density, centrally-located development was compared to low density fringe development in the same metropolitan region, after control for household and other characteristics."[37] A similar cut in fuel use for heating and cooling could result from a shifting from detached to attached dwellings. Yet the short-run impacts of such controls would be relatively small because they would affect only additional growth. In a slow-growing metropolitan area like Cleveland, only about 5.2 percent of the households in the Cuyahoga County suburbs and 18.7 percent in the outer suburbs will have been added from 1980 to 1990. Residents of these suburbs now contribute about 50 and 35 percent, respectively, of all vehicle-miles for work trips within the SMSA. So this hypothetical growth-control policy would reduce total auto use for work trips by only 1.8 percent in a decade.[38]

True, energy consumption in faster-growing metropolitan areas could be more affected by land-use controls. Consider an area the size of Cleveland with suburban households growing 8 percent per year cumulatively and accounting for 85 percent of all vehicle mileage. Such an area could cut driving mileage nearly 20 percent in a decade if one-half the added households were induced to reduce driving by 40 percent through stringent land-use controls. Yet even this cut is rather modest in relation to how severe the supply shortage would have to be to produce such land-use regulations. Most suburbanites would regard those regulations as depriving

37. Melvyn D. Cheslow and J. Kevin Neels, "The Effect of Urban Development Patterns on Transportation Energy Use," paper presented at the 59th annual meeting, Transportation Research Board, January 1980, p. 37. Similar but somewhat smaller magnitudes can be derived from Boris S. Pushkarev and Jeffrey M. Zupan, *Public Transportation and Land Use Policy* (Indiana University Press, 1977), chap. 2.

38. The fraction of metropolitan travel attributable to new growth in the absence of controls would be $(0.52 \times 0.50 + 0.187 \times 0.35) = 0.091$, and 20 percent of this is the postulated saving.

them of valued freedom of locational choice, hence terribly burdensome. Thus, the potential for using land-use controls to conserve energy by changing locational patterns is quite limited.

Conclusion

Neither higher energy prices nor energy shortages are likely to alter the fate of central cities in the next two decades. Both technical possibilities and consumer preferences favor widespread use of other means of reducing energy consumption, rather than changes in workplace or home locations. Even without such nonlocational adaptations, differences in energy consumption between city and suburban sites are relatively modest, so they create only small incentives for individuals or firms to alter their locations. The differential costs introduced by higher energy prices or energy shortages are much smaller than other sources of value divergence between suburban and city residences. Even if supplies were highly uncertain, other means of adjustment would be more flexible and less disruptive than large-scale reversal of postwar decentralization.

If higher energy costs cause any change at all in development patterns, it will probably be greater nucleation in both suburbs and cities. Relative energy-cost differences between low- and high-density developments, between transit-accessible and highway-oriented developments, or between close-in and far-out suburbs are much greater than the average differences between central cities and suburbs. Furthermore, average work trips could be shortened notably if suburban workers switched homes within the suburbs to be closer to their jobs, without any net increase in population concentration. These internal shifts deserve more attention than given here; they might greatly affect future travel patterns. But they do not change our basic conclusion that higher energy costs in themselves will not stimulate any major revitalization of central cities.

11

Alternatives for One Declining Area: Cleveland, Ohio

THE Cleveland metropolitan area provides a useful case for studying trends and policies concerning urban decline. Its population fell 5.7 percent from 1970 to 1977, while the city of Cleveland lost 19 percent of its population. The city's population drop was accompanied by increasing crime and housing abandonment, plus well-publicized fiscal crises. The city ranks in the lowest quintile among the 153 largest U.S. cities in 1970–75 per capita income growth, and the highest quintile in 1970 percent of housing old, 1969 percent of families in poverty, 1975 unemployment rate, 1975 violent crime rate, 1970–75 increase in violent crime rate, and 1972–76 increase in city government debt burden.[1] Yet Cleveland is unusual only in degree; in many ways, it is typical of large, older urban areas throughout the Northeast and Midwest. It has a diverse industrial mix with a moderately greater proportion of manufacturing than the United States as a whole (33 percent versus 26 percent in 1973). One study divided 125 large U.S. cities into ten groups using cluster analysis on variables representing growth, economic prosperity, demographic composition, and city-suburban disparities. It found Cleveland the city most representative of the cluster containing 15 large, older cities in the Northeast and Midwest. That study also classified Cleveland as most typical of 31 "big cities" constituting one of a four-group categorization.[2]

1. See chapters 3 and 5.

2. Emmett Keeler and William Rogers, *A Classification of Large American Urban Areas* (Santa Monica: Rand Corp., May 1973). See also footnote 22 in chapter 10 concerning Cleveland's population density.

We began our analysis of the Cleveland area with projections of employment, population, income, housing, travel patterns, and tax bases. These were made through 1990, assuming continuation of basic underlying trends. We then estimated the impacts, relative to this "Base Case," of several antidecline "policy packages." Each exemplifies a major but feasible public policy intervention in a particular area. The impacts considered include (1) the immediate effect on those factors primarily addressed by the policy (for example, on tax rates for the fiscal equalization policy); (2) the direct responses of employers and households to resulting incentives to change locations *within* the metropolitan area; (3) secondary (multiplier) effects on other locational decisions; and (4) the "indirect" effects of the altered employment and population distribution on other key variables. In each case, separate estimates were made for the city of Cleveland, the "inner suburbs" (the remainder of Cuyahoga County), and the "outer suburbs" (the other three counties in the SMSA). Also, in the case of jobs and travel patterns, the central business district (CBD) was distinguished from the rest of the city.

To quantify such complex phenomena, we had to make hundreds of assumptions, most minor, but some crucial, and all subject to uncertainty. These assumptions and their results are summarized in this chapter and described fully in another volume.[3] However, our judgments were designed to assess the relative orders of magnitude of forces we believe are important in many metropolitan areas; so these judgments are in no way meant to be specific planning guidelines of policies for the Cleveland area.

Recent Growth and Decline

The Cleveland metropolitan area shared in the nation's rapid urban growth during and after World War II. Its population peaked at just over two million in 1968, and has declined slightly since then. Employment grew rapidly through the 1960s, but much more slowly thereafter. Much of the area's growth went into the suburbs, leaving the city in 1980 with only two-thirds of its 1950 peak population. Salient facts are shown in table 11-1.

Both the growth and decentralization of this area mirror the experience of many older urban centers. Immigration from abroad had been an im-

3. Katharine L. Bradbury, Anthony Downs, and Kenneth A. Small, *Futures for a Declining City: Simulations for the Cleveland Area* (Academic Press, 1981).

Table 11-1. *Cleveland Area Growth and Decline, Selected Years, 1940–77*
Thousands

Year	Population: City	Population: SMSA	SMSA wage and salary employment
1940	878	1,320	n.a.
1950	915	1,533	n.a.
1960	876	1,909	700[a]
1970	751	2,064	855
1977	609	1,947	859

Sources: Population, U.S. Bureau of the Census, *Statistical Abstract of the United States*, selected years; and *Current Population Reports*, series P-25 and P-26, selected issues. Employment, U.S. Bureau of Labor Statistics, *Employment and Earnings, States and Areas, 1939–74*, Bulletin 1370-11 (GPO, 1975), p. 563; and *Employment and Earnings*, vol. 26 (May 1979).

n.a. Not available

a. Excludes Geauga and Medina counties, which contained 5.9 percent of the four-county SMSA's population in 1960.

portant factor in the early decades of the twentieth century, but it tapered off in the postwar period. By 1960, the city's foreign-born population was down to 11 percent, with another 20 percent second-generation immigrants.[4] In contrast, significant migration of blacks from other parts of the United States into the city of Cleveland continued until about 1965. The city's black population rose from 10 percent of the total in 1940 to 38 percent in 1970. This inflow occurred mainly east of the Cuyahoga River, with blacks still accounting for only 2 percent of the west side's population as of 1970.[5] Real incomes rose rapidly in the SMSA, paralleling the United States as a whole; incomes in the city also rose but much more slowly. Good highways and increasing automobile use facilitated suburban development, with per capita automobile ownership rising 49 percent between 1960 and 1975.[6] Female labor force participation among the city's working age population, starting from a higher rate than in the United States as a whole (34 percent versus 27 percent in 1940), rose dramatically, reaching 50 percent by 1970.[7] Federal grants accounted for about 2 percent of total general revenue for the city throughout the 1960s, but soared in 1970 and continued upward to 32 percent in 1976 and 1977.[8]

4. U.S. Bureau of the Census, *County and City Data Book, 1962* (GPO, 1963), p. 546.

5. Unpublished data from Cleveland City Planning Commission.

6. Data from R. L. Polk Company.

7. Cleveland City Planning Commission, *Jobs and Income*, vol. 1 (February 1978), p. 91.

8. Bureau of the Census, *City Government Finances*, selected years.

Tables 6-2, 6-6, and 6-7 show the strength of various factors accounting statistically for the city's low 1970–75 growth experience relative to other cities. The major traits explaining its nearly 15 percent population loss were its high concentration of old housing (73 percent over thirty years old in 1970, up from 66 percent in 1950); lagging SMSA employment growth; and the city's racial composition (low in Hispanics and, more important, high in blacks). The area's fragmentation into more than 130 separate municipal and township governments also encouraged suburbanization. As shown in table 6-10, the city's employment loss during the 1960s was largely attributable to three factors: a big population loss and slow income growth over the same period, and 2.1 percentage points difference between city and SMSA unemployment rates in 1960.

Cleveland's experience is consistent with many of the theories of decline described in chapter 4. Violent crime in the city is unusually high, as are both racial and income disparities in the SMSA. Loss of manufacturing jobs has hurt the economic bases of both city and SMSA. The city's labor force is predominantly blue-collar, while its growing employment sectors are those providing services. Furthermore, its notoriously severe lakeside climate may be a more important negative factor than indicated by our simple winter temperature measure (on which Cleveland is about average).

Yet not all of the area's traits should affect its growth adversely. The city is not unusually dense, nor were its taxes particularly high at the beginning of the 1970s. As discussed in appendix C to chapter 5, the area's high specialization in manufacturing cannot itself account for much of its relative lag in employment growth. Nearly 90 percent of this lag is caused by the Cleveland area's loss of share of U.S. employment in its major industries, rather than slower national growth of those industries. Furthermore, unemployment in both the city and the SMSA has been *below* average for comparably sized areas during the last decade. Even the city's 9.5 percent rate in 1976 was exceeded by many cities, including Boston, Baltimore, San Francisco, and Phoenix. Thus Cleveland should not be viewed as a place where all the worst problems besetting American cities have converged simultaneously.

Future Trends: Base Case Projections

Since intermetropolitan employment and population changes are mutually reinforcing, an ideal method of projection should consider them simultaneously. Instead, we projected employment first, then population based upon employment. We did so partly to simplify the problem, and partly to make use of a study by the Northeast Ohio Areawide Coordination Agency (NOACA) based upon this procedure.

Employment was projected by NOACA at the SMSA and county level with a "shift-share" technique that extrapolated past changes in each county's share of national employment in a given industry. These projections therefore reflect both existing industry mix and past migration history of particular industries. They were then made consistent with our own expectations regarding national economic conditions. For the latter, we used recent projections by the Bureau of Labor Statistics[9] (BLS), adjusting them to reflect an assumed 6 percent U.S. unemployment rate. We also extrapolated past decline in Cleveland's share of Cuyahoga County employment. Cleveland's central business district, on the other hand, has held its own or even grown slightly; so we projected employment there as constant at its mid-1970s level of about 150,000.[10] We assumed 6 percent unemployment in the SMSA and 8.5 percent in the city throughout the 1980s.

We further assumed SMSA population would continue its gradual fall relative to employment, paralleling the overall U.S. trend embodied in the BLS projections. Within this total, we accepted NOACA's percentage allocation of population to the four counties and the city of Cleveland. These allocations accord well with our own analysis in chapters 8 and 9 of the underlying forces tending to disperse population. The results portray continued outmigration from both the city and the SMSA as a whole, though at rates about half those observed in the first half of the 1970s. To derive *households* from population, we assumed the long-range trend toward smaller average household size would continue. For *per capita income* in various parts of the Cleveland SMSA, we extrapolated the 1959–74 trend in the ratio of per capita income there to that in the entire United States, using projections of the latter made by the Bureau of Labor Statistics.

The resulting projections, summarized in table 11-2, are thus based mainly on extrapolation of underlying trends. Hence they are not predictions of what will actually happen in Cleveland, but rather estimates of what would happen if no major changes took place other than those

9. Norman C. Saunders, "The U.S. Economy to 1990: Two Projections for Growth," *Monthly Labor Review*, vol. 101 (December 1978), pp. 36–46.

10. Based on estimates compiled by the Greater Cleveland Growth Association.

Table 11-2. *Base Case Projections for the Cleveland Metropolitan Area, 1975, 1980, and 1990*

Description	1975 (actual)	1980 (projected)	1990 (projected)	Change, 1980–90: Number or amount	Change, 1980–90: Percent
Population					
City	638,800	574,500	469,700	−104,800	−18.2
Suburbs	1,336,000	1,360,600	1,372,900	+12,300	+0.9
SMSA	1,974,800	1,935,100	1,842,600	−92,500	−4.8
City ÷ SMSA	0.323	0.297	0.255	. . .	. . .
Households					
City	233,700	216,200	192,800	−23,400	−10.8
Suburbs	442,300	482,300	532,400	+50,100	10.4
SMSA	676,000	698,500	725,100	+26,600	+3.8
City ÷ SMSA	0.346	0.310	0.266	. . .	. . .
Jobs					
City	404,500[a]	380,200	314,500	−65,700	−17.3
Suburbs	448,900[a]	529,300	616,000	+86,700	+16.4
City ÷ SMSA	0.474	0.418	0.338	. . .	. . .
Per capita income[b]					
City	6,157	6,268	7,515	+1,247	+19.9
Suburbs	8,406	9,320	11,661	+2,341	+25.1
SMSA	7,678	8,414	10,604	+2,190	+26.0
City ÷ SMSA	0.802	0.745	0.709	. . .	. . .

Source: Katharine L. Bradbury, Anthony Downs, and Kenneth A. Small, *Futures for a Declining City: Simulations for the Cleveland Area* (Academic Press, 1981).

a. Estimate based on trend in city's share of employment for sectors included in economic census of 1967 and 1972.

b. In 1977 dollars.

mentioned above.[11] The results show just how severe a decline Cleveland could experience in the 1980s: losses of nearly 20 percent of its jobs and population and 10 percent of its households. These results also provide a yardstick against which we can measure the impacts of various policies.

Several other variables pertinent to housing, transportation, and fiscal conditions were also projected: new housing units constructed, number and length of various auto trip types, tax bases and rates, and so forth. These were based on very detailed assumptions plus analyses of local data sources. They sought to trace the consequences of basic trends, while

11. Nevertheless, our population projections for 1980, made well before the 1980 census figures were available, came quite close to the actual counts of 573,822 and 1,898,720 for city and SMSA, respectively. Bureau of the Census, "Final Population and Housing Unit Counts: Ohio," *1980 Census of Population and Housing: Advance Report*, PHC 80-V-37 (GPO, 1981).

accounting for a few changes known to have occurred locally (such as increased service levels mandated when the regional transit authority was formed).

Policy Impacts

We considered five separate policy packages, plus an "all-out revitalization package" combining all five.

1. A "job stimulus package" consists of several private employment incentives plus federally subsidized public employment targeted on the city of Cleveland, modeled after the CETA (Comprehensive Employment and Training Act) program and the once-proposed National Development Bank. Using recent CETA and UDAG (Urban Development Action Grant) experience on costs, leveraging, and displacement,[12] we estimate that this package's $63 million per year in federal aid would add 3,100 new primary jobs in the city, and move 3,740 existing jobs to the city from other parts of the metropolitan area.

2. A "housing rehabilitation package" includes $59.2 million per year in capital subsidies to increase rehabilitation and new construction within the city of Cleveland by 2,650 units per year. We assumed one-third would attract households that would not otherwise locate in the city.

3. A "fiscal equalization package" includes consolidation of all municipal and township governments within Cuyahoga County; a school district tax-base-sharing plan; and an increase in state aid to local governments to bring Ohio more in line with other states.

4. A "transit improvement package" consists of $260 million in capital improvements to the transit system. They include thirty-seven miles of new exclusive busways, a CBD loop subway, and a 60 percent increase in vehicle-miles of transit service offered at a cost of $36 million per year. This immediately adds 1,080 jobs to the city, and exerts other direct effects on migration discussed below.

5. A "suburban growth control package" postulates constraints on new suburban housing construction that reduce the 1980–90 growth in suburban

12. See Susan J. Jacobs and Elizabeth A. Roistacher, "The Urban Impacts of HUD's Urban Development Action Grant Program," in Norman J. Glickman, ed., *The Urban Impacts of Federal Policies* (Johns Hopkins University Press, 1980); Georges Vernez and Roger J. Vaughan, "Counter-Cyclical Public Works Programs," paper prepared for a conference held by the Economic Development Administration, June 1978; and Robert F. Cook, "Fiscal Implications of CETA Public Service Employment," paper prepared for the same conference.

Table 11-3. *Hypothesized Direct Impacts of Policy Packages after Ten Years*

	Impact in 1990 (relative to Base Case)							
	Jobs in city		*Households in city*		*City-suburb disparity in typical annual taxes paid*[a] *(dollars)*		*City-suburb differential in annual travel cost including time value*[a] *(dollars)*	
Policy package	*Number*	*Percent of 1990 Base Case*	*Number*	*Percent of 1990 Base Case*	*Firm (per employee in city)*	*Household*	*Firm (per employee in CBD)*	*Household*
Immediate impact of policies								
1. Job stimulus	+6,840	+2.2	...	...	...	...	...	...
2. Housing rehabilitation	...	...	+8,830	+4.6	...	...	...	...
3. Fiscal equalization[b]	...	...	...	...	−211	−316	...	...
4. Transit improvement	+1,080	+0.3	...	...	...	...	−193	+22
5. Suburban growth control	...	...	+10,020	+5.2	...	...	...	...
6. All-out revitalization	+7,920	+2.5	+13,985	+7.3	−211	−316	−193	+22
Direct impact of cost differentials on migration[c]								
3. Fiscal equalization	+4,430	+1.4	+9,015	+4.7	...	...	...	...
4. Transit improvement	+4,350	+1.4	−900	−0.5	...	...	...	...
6. All-out revitalization	+8,780	+2.8	+8,115	+4.2	...	...	...	...

a. Cost figures are at 1977 prices (the overall U.S. consumer price index is used as an inflator or deflator where appropriate).

b. The fiscal impacts shown are for 1985. They are somewhat smaller in 1980 and somewhat larger in 1990.

c. Cumulative impact by 1990. The impacts are assumed to cumulate over ten years for the fiscal equalization package but begin at a smaller level than that implied by the 1985 disparities shown above; impacts are assumed to cumulate over only 7.5 years for the transit improvement package because of its more gradual implementation.

households by 25 percent compared to Base Case projections of 500 per year. Four-fifths of this suburban reduction shifts into the central city; the rest moves outside the SMSA.

For packages 1, 2, and 5, the immediate impacts on the location of households and jobs, summarized in table 11-3, essentially define the scope of each package. In contrast, packages 3 and 4—the fiscal and transit packages—also have immediate impacts on tax rates and transportation costs (in addition to direct job creation within the transit program). Cost differentials between pre- and post-program conditions for packages 3 and 4 were laboriously estimated from many data sources about relations between tax bases, revenue needs, average travel times, transit trip shares, and so forth, on the one hand, and the policies in the program packages, on the other. Some of the most important assumptions are listed in appendix A to this chapter. We believe the estimated changes in cost differentials shown in table 11-3 are both reasonable for each package and suitable for comparison with packages 1, 2, and 5—all intended to be about equally "strong."

The next step was to estimate the effects of the cost differentials in packages 3 and 4 on intrametropolitan migration rates. For household movements, we used the estimate by Frey[13] of how migration rates respond to tax disparities, described in chapter 10. For the 1980s, Frey's calculations imply a reduction in outmigration of about 0.21 percentage point (430 households per year) for each $120 change in the city-suburb tax differential.[14] We assume households would respond the same way to a travel-cost differential related to their place of residence as to a tax differential.

For firm movements, we used Hamer's estimates of city-suburban average cost differentials for manufacturing firms in the Boston area, plus his observation that about 2 percent of manufacturing employment was leaving the city each year.[15] From these findings, we interpreted firm migration as a disequilibrium phenomenon. City-suburban cost differentials create an incentive for firms to outmigrate. The percent that do so is proportional to the size of the cost differential. Hamer's evidence suggests

13. William H. Frey, "White Flight and Central-City Loss: Application of an Analytic Migration Framework," *Environment and Planning A*, vol. 11 (January 1979), pp. 129–47.

14. Average taxes per household are projected to be about $1,200 per year in the city in 1985, and 17.5 percent of city households move to somewhere within the metropolitan area each year. The calculation stated in the text is not exact, since the change in the ratio depends on how a reduction in disparity is divided between a decrease for the city and an increase for the suburbs.

15. Andrew M. Hamer, *Industrial Exodus from Central City: Public Policy and the Comparative Costs of Location* (Lexington Books, 1973).

that about 2 percent of manufacturing jobs leave the city each year for each \$1,000 per employee cost differential between city and suburban locations.[16] These assumptions are admittedly tenuous, but they provide the best available quantitative estimate concerning the response of employment to changes in the profit potential of locating in a central city.

The cumulative direct impacts on population and employment under these assumptions are shown for 1990 in the lower panel of table 11-3. All the packages also have "secondary" effects of two types: changes in residences caused by desires to live closer to (changed) workplaces; and the multiplier effects of a new geographical distribution of spending by relocated firms and households. We estimated the first type by assuming the distribution of homes for all workers at a given workplace (CBD, balance of city, inner suburbs, or outer suburbs) is unchanged. This distribution can be determined for 1976 from unpublished Census Journey-to-Work data (see table 10-4). Thus, newly relocated jobs are soon filled with workers whose distribution of residences is typical for all jobs in the same area. This occurs through either changes in unemployment rates (for one-fourth of the implied change in residential locations) or changes in migration rates (for the other three-fourths). The other secondary effect consists of "indirect" and "induced" jobs from altered spending patterns of firms and households. Quantifying these required estimating both the metropolitan-wide employment multiplier and the intrametropolitan *distribution* of indirect and induced jobs by workplace and household location, respectively. Based on evidence for the St. Louis SMSA by Hirsch, we assumed the metropolitan multiplier to be 2.25.[17] Since there is no empirical evidence on the distribution, we used our best judgment to choose parameters falling between logical extreme boundaries.[18] The result is the "preferred values" in table 11-7, below.

16. Hamer's figures of \$416 to \$856 for a plant with 400 square feet of floor space per employee (p. 89) have been updated to 1977 prices and averaged to get the approximate figure of \$1,000. In the case of tax differentials, we apply this only to "primary" employment engaged in producing goods or services purchased from outside the city itself, assumed to constitute one-third of the city's projected 1985 employment of 350,000. In the case of travel cost differentials (applicable to the CBD only), the incentive is assumed effective on *all* firms (150,000 CBD employees), since improved accessibility actually enlarges the market area a "local" firm can serve from the affected location.

17. Werner Z. Hirsch, "Interindustry Relations of a Metropolitan Area," *Review of Economics and Statistics*, vol. 41 (November 1959), pp. 360–69.

18. At one extreme, denoted by Alternative A in table 11-7, all of the 0.40 indirect jobs associated with a given "primary" job are located in the same ring as the primary job, and all 0.85 jobs associated with the spending of a "primary" worker are in the same ring as the

Table 11-4. *Impacts of Policy Packages on City of Cleveland, 1990*
Thousands

Description	*Jobs*	*Households*	*Population*
Base Case			
1980 value	380.2	216.2	574.5
1980–90 change	−65.7	−23.4	−104.7
Impact relative to Base Case (1990)			
Job stimulus	10.0	2.0	5.0
Housing rehabilitation	4.1	8.8	22.4
Transit improvement	7.0	0.2	0.4
Fiscal equalization	9.3	9.6	24.4
Suburban growth control	4.4	10.0	25.5
All-out revitalization	32.6	25.7	65.4
Income transfer	1.8	0.5	1.4

Total household and job shifts resulting from a given policy also influence such variables as tax disparities, travel patterns, per capita income, unemployment, housing construction, and housing quality.

Results

The estimated impacts of the five packages on employment, households, and population[19] in the city of Cleveland, including secondary effects, are shown in table 11-4. Some packages are more effective at retaining households; others have a greater impact on jobs. Each policy's *total effect* is greater for that factor on which its *immediate impact* was largest (compare tables 11-3 and 11-4). In addition, policies acting directly on *households* had a more balanced final impact upon both housing and labor markets than policies focused directly on *jobs.* Fiscal equalization affects both households and jobs similarly, partly because it had immediate impacts on both. The tendency for jobs to follow households within a metropolitan area more strongly than vice versa also appeared in our regression analyses for 1960–70 in chapter 5.

worker's residence. At the other extreme, Alternative B, the geographical distribution of indirect and induced jobs is independent of the location of the associated sources of spending, and is thus identical to the distribution of all jobs in the SMSA, taken to be that predicted by our 1980 Base Case projections.

19. Population follows from households simply by assuming that average size for those households whose locations are affected by a policy is the same as that for the entire SMSA.

Table 11-4 also shows the all-out revitalization package. It is defined as a combination of all the others, with some adjustments for interactions among them.[20] Taken together, these packages would have a major impact on the city of Cleveland. They would halve its severe job erosion projected for the 1980s, and reverse its projected fall in number of households (though not in population, since average household size decreases). To implement this strong combination of policies, many of which would face severe political and financial obstacles, would strain the ability of the Cleveland area's already fractious political structure to achieve a working consensus. The combined impacts shown must therefore be regarded as a highly optimistic upper bound on how much public policy could offset the economic and demographic forces currently at work.

Even all five policies combined would be unable to reverse either employment or population decline in the city. True, both the extent of such decline in the Base Case and the impacts of these policies are uncertain, yet these calculations indicate it is very unlikely that Cleveland's decline could actually be fully arrested through any feasible policies. Thus, our first major lesson from the case study is that, *in severely declining cities, feasible public policies can only slow, not reverse, descriptive decline over the next decade or so.*

Another vital question is whether policies aimed mainly at retaining jobs or households in the city will automatically have strong and desirable side effects. Would they help with such problems as fiscal health, housing quality, energy consumption, and the viability of public transit systems? To address this question, we estimated the indirect effects of these employment and population shifts on such variables. The results can be compared either with the changes in those variables contained in the Base Case, or with the direct impacts upon those variables of the three packages (fiscal equalization, transit improvement, and housing rehabilitation) aimed specifically at them.

The fiscal effects of location changes are shown in table 11-5. They are based on four critical assumptions: (1) additional (or lost) households and firms in any jurisdiction have SMSA average amounts of real property, payroll earnings, and income; (2) public expenditures per capita are un-

20. Both the suburban growth control and the housing rehabilitation packages were assumed to be less effective in absolute terms in the presence of the other packages: in the former case because other policies would already be reducing suburban growth, thereby making some of the controls redundant, and in the latter because of constraints on the construction industry's ability to expand rapidly.

Table 11-5. *Comparison of Fiscal Effects of Policy Packages in 1990*
1975 dollars unless otherwise specified

Description	*Base Case*	*Almost all-out*[a]	*Fiscal equalization*	*All-out revitalization*
Tax burdens				
Annual taxes paid by typical SMSA household to all local governments				
Cleveland	1,413	1,365	1,150	1,135
Inner suburbs	917	923	1,010	1,012
Outer suburbs	855	850	940	938
Annual taxes paid by typical SMSA firm to all local governments, per employee				
Cleveland	1,115	1,071	952	937
Inner suburbs	754	751	842	841
Outer suburbs	538	532	591	588
Tax disparity between city and average suburban location				
Household tax	515	463	162	145
Business tax per employee	419	374	178	163
Change in disparity compared to Base Case (percent)				
Household tax	. . .	−10	−68	−72
Business tax per employee	. . .	−11	−58	−61

a. "Almost all-out" consists of the four elements of all-out revitalization other than fiscal equalization.

affected by changes in population, except that additional residents above the city's Base Case population projection cost a smaller amount per capita because they help prevent underutilization of existing capital stock; (3) intergovernmental revenues cover the same fraction of total expenditures as in the Base Case; and (4) all tax rates levied by each government are changed by identical proportions to meet revised local revenue requirements.

As shown in the last two lines of the table, the all-out revitalization package generates a striking reduction in city-suburb fiscal disparities. However, this is almost entirely due to the fiscal equalization package; no more than one-fifth of the city's fiscal improvement comes from the major economic and demographic shifts described above. The four other packages together reduce the city's 1980–90 job loss by over a third, and its household loss by three-fourths; yet they reduce the city's tax on a typical household or firm by only 3 to 4 percent. In contrast, the fiscal equalization policies alter the tax variables by reorganizing local government financing methods.

Only this reorganization, not economic growth from revitalization, seems able to undo the adverse fiscal results of fragmented local government.

Transportation effects of the all-out revitalization package are summarized in table 11-6. Impacts due solely to the locational shifts are computed assuming no *behavioral* change by workers with given residential and workplace combinations. That is, we assume all workers added to any geographical category change their modal choices and average trip lengths to conform with those of other persons in that category. Similarly, we assume households added to each residential ring make the same number of nonwork transit trips as other households there. However, the "modal share shifts" shown in the third column are behavioral changes attributable directly to the better services in the transit improvement package. They assume elasticities of transit share of 0.5 with respect to both vehicle-miles of service offered[21] and transit in-vehicle travel time.[22] That is, a 1 percent improvement in either of the latter raises public transit's share of all trips by one-half percent. The table shows that declining transit ridership is strongly affected by the locational shifts resulting from the all-out revitalization package. The 9.2 percent increase in transit work trips results largely from the assumed concentration of added jobs in the transit-oriented CBD. Yet this is less than the increase in transit work trips attributable to a larger transit modal share. Furthermore, even in this transit-oriented city, transit's share of work trips is so small that improvements in it have a negligible impact on energy consumption for work travel. Such improvements reduce the share of workers driving automobiles by only a small fraction, and leave average work-trip distance almost exactly the same as before (8.7 miles). The reduction in work trips from outer suburbs is offset by an increase in the number of (also relatively long) work trips from inner suburbs to the CBD.

Since we did not formally model housing quality, we are restricted to

21. This elasticity has been measured at 0.95–1.32 by Gary R. Nelson. See "An Econometric Model of Urban Bus Transit Operations," in John D. Wells and others, *Economic Characteristics of the Urban Public Transportation Industry*, Institute for Defense Analyses for the U.S. Department of Transportation (GPO, 1972). However, Cleveland recently undertook a major expansion of transit service, increasing vehicle-miles by a projected 30 percent between 1975 and 1980. It is with respect to this higher level of service that the additional changes in the transit improvement package were estimated. Thus, we felt that Cleveland would have a higher initial transit share and a lower elasticity than the representative member of Nelson's sample.

22. This approximates the findings reported in Daniel McFadden, "The Measurement of Urban Travel Demand," *Journal of Public Economics*, vol. 3 (November 1974), pp. 303–28.

Table 11-6. *Comparison of Travel Effects*

Description	*Base Case, 1980–90 change (percent)*	*All-out revitalization, 1990 impact as percent of 1980 Base Case*		
		Locational shifts	*Modal share shifts*	*Total*
Work trips, SMSA				
Total	+2.3	+1.0	0	+1.0
Transit	−5.9	+9.2	+10.3	+19.5
Auto driver	+3.4	−0.6	−1.3	−1.9
Auto vehicle-miles	+1.0	−0.7	−1.5	−2.2
Transit rides, SMSA				
Nonwork	−12.9	+6.2	+13.4	+19.6
Total	−8.6	+8.0	+11.6	+19.6

cruder comparisons of direct and indirect policy impacts concerning housing. One such comparison is the increase in value of housing stock at fixed prices arising from higher incomes on the one hand and from public subsidies on the other. Base Case per capita incomes in the city are projected to be 71 percent of the SMSA average in 1990 (down from 80 percent in 1975). The all-out revitalization package shifts 65,400 more people to the city (14 percent of its Base Case 1990 population), as indicated in table 11-4. If they have SMSA average per capita incomes, then the city's per capita income would be 5.0 percent higher than in the Base Case. In addition, lower city unemployment (falling from 8.5 to 6.8 percent) increases incomes by 1.6 percent, based on the difference between unskilled wages and typical transfer payments to the unemployed. If the income elasticity of housing demand is 0.5, each 1 percent rise in income would increase spending on housing by one-half percent.[23] Hence these improvements in city incomes would result in a 3.3 percent rise in housing "quality." If price effects are taken into account, the housing-quality response would be even smaller, although we cannot estimate by how much. In comparison, the housing rehabilitation package includes $592 million in publicly sub-

23. This is higher than the estimated income elasticities emerging from the Experimental Housing Allowance Program. See Eric A. Hanushek and John M. Quigley, "Consumption Aspects," in Katharine L. Bradbury and Anthony Downs, eds., *Do Housing Allowances Work?* (Brookings Institution, 1981), pp. 184–246, for a summary of these results. But it is slightly below the *permanent* income elasticity (0.57) estimated by A. Mitchell Polinsky and David T. Ellwood, "An Empirical Reconciliation of Micro and Grouped Estimates of the Demand for Housing," *Review of Economics and Statistics*, vol. 61 (May 1979), pp. 199–205.

sidized housing improvements over ten years. They would increase the average value of the city's occupied housing stock by 10.3 percent. This outcome is based on the 1977 average value of about $20,000 per housing unit[24] and accounts for the net addition of 8,830 units from this package (table 11-3). This shows again that *particular "target" variables in a city are much more powerfully affected by incentives aimed directly at them than by the indirect effects of incentives or actions that improve the city's general economic health.*

Thus, our second lesson from this policy simulation is that attracting households and firms to a declining city, or retaining them there, will not cure its other difficulties. *Even if descriptive declines in population and jobs can be greatly reduced, many associated functional problems in declining cities can only be remedied by policies focused directly upon them.* Sound municipal finances, horizontal and vertical tax equity, clean air, energy conservation, transit accessibility, and decent shelter are proper goals of public policy under certain circumstances. Achieving them will require actions directed at them, no matter what else is done to increase the attractiveness of the city to potential firms and residents.

Conversely, policies aimed only indirectly at attracting firms or households to the city are not very effective at doing so. This conclusion is confirmed by the results of other policies we simulated for the Cleveland area. We computed the effects of giving the $63 million of federal money in the job stimulus package directly to residents currently on welfare, in addition to what they receive now. This "income transfer package" is more than twice as effective as the job stimulus package at raising city per capita incomes. Yet its effects on retaining jobs and households in the city are extremely weak, as shown in the last row of table 11-4. Thus, while direct income transfers do aid the poor, they do not help much in correcting the adverse dynamic forces besetting the city—and contributing to poverty there. Similarly, when we "targeted" funds in our job stimulus program on unemployed city residents, the city's unemployment rate was reduced far more than by any other single policy package; yet only slightly more jobs and households were retained in the city than by the untargeted version.

24. In 1976, the median owner-occupied unit was valued at $23,900, and the median renter-occupied unit at $13,400, if we accept the rule of thumb that value is 100 times monthly gross rent. Since 47 percent of the city's 230,800 occupied housing units were owner-occupied, these average to $18,300, to which an inflation factor has been added to approximate the value in 1977 prices.

Conclusion

Cleveland is similar enough to many other severely declining U.S. cities that key conclusions drawn from our Cleveland policy simulations also apply to them. Such transferability is especially appropriate for severely declining cities in declining metropolitan areas.

Any of the major policy packages we tested could, if fully applied, greatly affect the extent to which a city like Cleveland would continue to decline, both descriptively and functionally. All five packages combined, if fully applied, could even halt future declines in the city's households, though not in jobs, population, or the fiscal health of the city government. However, it would be difficult to apply any of these policies fully, because doing so would be expensive or politically unpopular, or both. Therefore, the possibility of applying all five policy packages at the same time—or others with similarly powerful effects—must be considered remote. We conclude that it is highly unrealistic to expect any severely declining city to stop declining either descriptively or functionally in the near future. Not enough households or businesses would change locations in response to any feasible revitalization policies.

Nevertheless, some of the policy packages we analyzed may still be worth implementing, at least in part. The policies aimed at reducing fiscal disparities between cities and suburbs seem especially promising. They have the strongest impacts on both household and employer location decisions; so they help maintain a healthy balance of activities within the central city. Moreover, they were the *only* policies we tested that had much positive effect on the city government's fiscal health. Unfortunately, outright governmental consolidation has almost no political support, as discussed further in chapter 12. But some politically more feasible partway measures, such as tax-base sharing and power equalizing, would have similar effects; they are also discussed in chapter 12.

The other policy we considered that requires little added public outlay is suburban growth controls. However, as in fiscal resource sharing, easily identifiable groups would lose financially; hence they strongly oppose such policies. Moreover, growth controls distort development patterns in haphazard and probably harmful ways, and may not be constitutional. So we do not regard growth controls as a promising approach.

The remaining policy packages all require major added public spending.

Therefore, their political feasibility must be judged in relation to that of *any* large increase in federal and state urban programs. If funds can be obtained, two relatively promising approaches are subsidies to central-city employers targeted on the unemployed, and subsidized central-city housing rehabilitation. Both might suffer some "leakage" of subsidy funds to people who are not "truly needy," but this could be limited by careful program design.

Transit system improvements should not be viewed primarily as urban revitalization tools, even though they have important side effects. The positive effects of radial transit improvements on downtown business tend to be offset by greater ease of getting downtown from suburban homes. Such improvements add downtown jobs, but reduce the city's population and secondary employment. These negative impacts can be minimized by concentrating transit resources on improving circulation *within* the city's core, and between the core and in-city neighborhoods.

In summary, urban decline is a multifaceted phenomenon that generates problems requiring multifaceted policy responses. No one "fundamental" improvement in cities—even locating more jobs there—will solve a multitude of urban problems simultaneously. Those problems arise because the dynamics of decline prevent achievement of many legitimate public policy goals concerning city life. Such goals include attractive housing, good transit service, energy conservation, sound government finance, personal safety and security, and many others. Addressing each goal requires aiming specific policies directly at it, rather than relying on the indirect effects of policies aimed at other goals. Hence the most effective mix of policies and programs in each city will depend on that city's particular characteristics and problems.

Appendix A: Some Assumptions Underlying the Estimates of City-Suburban Cost Differentials

Fiscal Equalization Package

We assume the reorganization does not induce governments to change service levels per capita. This assumption allows us to measure correctly the net benefits (and losses) to individual jurisdictions of the redistribution implicit in the reorganization entirely through the tax side, even if individual governments should eventually change their expenditures in response, provided those changes were valued by residents at cost.

City of Cleveland government consolidated with all municipal and township governments in Cuyahoga County

All municipal functions taken over by consolidated government; service levels unchanged.

Personnel costs "level up"—average cost of servicing inner suburbs rises by 10 percent.

Federal intergovernmental transfers decline to sum of Base Case suburban total plus 90 percent of city Base Case.

As a result of the above changes, total municipal revenue needs in county are approximately 10 percent higher than Base Case.

Revenue mix: property tax and "other" taxes same as county total municipal levies in Base Case; income tax absorbs extra revenue needs.

Metropolitan-wide school fund sharing plan

Uniform SMSA-wide property tax levied to raise $900 per student, distributed to districts.

Districts levy additional local property taxes to maintain Base Case spending levels.

State aid becomes less redistributive because of base-equalizing—half distributed as in Base Case, half equally per student.

As a result of these changes, local revenue needs (including SMSA-wide levy) of Cleveland city school district fall by approximately 10 percent and those of inner suburb districts rise by approximately 8 percent.

State aid to all local governments increased by 35 percent

Increases to each government in proportion to Base Case aid.

Financed by SMSA-wide levies on all tax bases.

Transit Improvement Package

Value of travel time (1985)	$4.15 per hour (1977 prices)
Total time saving:	
Transit trips	7.0 million passenger-hours per year
Auto trips	2.3 million passenger-hours per year
Time saving on trips to CBD:	
Transit trips	5.6 million passenger-hours per year
Auto trips (work)	1.4 million passenger-hours per year

Average time saving per one-way trip:

Transit to CBD	8.5 minutes (26 percent of average trip time)
Transit, non-CBD	
Work	3.2 minutes (10 percent of average trip time)
Nonwork	5.8 minutes (29 percent of average trip time)
Auto to CBD (work)	2.3 minutes

Fraction of average time saving invariant with respect to residential location: 0.25.

Fraction of average time saving which varies proportionally to line haul distance: 0.75.

Average line haul distance to CBD:

From residence in city	4.44 miles
From residence in suburbs	12.02 miles

Resulting time saving per work trip to CBD:

Transit, from city	6.34 minutes
Transit, from suburbs	13.54 minutes
Auto, from city	1.73 minutes
Auto, from suburbs	3.70 minutes

Transit modal share for CBD work trips, without package:

From residence in city	57 percent
From residence in suburbs	36 percent

Average number of CBD workers per household, entire SMSA, 1985: 0.21.

Number of round trips per year per worker between home and workplace zones:

Work purposes	240
Nonwork purposes	24

Appendix B: Secondary Impacts

Table 11-7. *Percentage Distribution of Indirect or Induced Jobs, by Location of Directly Affected Job or Residence*

Workplace or residence location	*Location of indirect or induced job*				
	Central business district	*Rest of city*	*Rest of Cuyahoga County*	*Outer suburbs*	*All locations*
Central business district					
Alternative A	100	0	0	0	100
Preferred value	60	15	20	5	100
Alternative B	17	25	45	13	100
Rest of city					
Alternative A	0	100	0	0	100
Preferred value	15	55	25	5	100
Alternative B	17	25	45	13	100
Rest of Cuyahoga County					
Alternative A	0	0	100	0	100
Preferred value	10	20	60	10	100
Alternative B	17	25	45	13	100
Outer suburbs					
Alternative A	0	0	0	100	100
Preferred value	8	12	30	50	100
Alternative B	17	25	45	13	100

12

Policies to Deter Urban Decline, Part One

WHAT public policies should be adopted in response to U.S. urban decline? This chapter and the next deal with that sweeping question, emphasizing federal policies, though treating all levels of government. We indicate what policy postures, directions, and strategies should be adopted, instead of making detailed recommendations about specific programs. Such generality is necessary because of the many forces affecting all cities, the enormous diversity of U.S. urban conditions, and the rapid rate of change in our society.

Our recommendations are not all equally grounded in the empirical analysis presented in this study. Some are directly derived from that analysis; others can be clearly justified by empirical studies made by other urban analysts. A third group represents our best judgments, but cannot be unequivocally justified by any empirical studies we know of. We provide all three types of recommendations because we wanted to suggest policy responses to most of the major problems identified earlier, and doing so required including some recommendations based largely upon our own judgments. In fairness to readers, we try to clearly distinguish among them.

Why Public Policies Should Respond to Urban Decline

If big-city population decline is irreversible, why should public policies try to stop it, or counteract its effects? If it results from "free market forces," why not let them run their course? There is nothing sacred about any particular levels of population or employment in large cities. In fact, the suburbanization causing city population and job losses has clearly been an upgrading process, so why not let it continue unabated?

The answers to these questions consist of both general principles and specific justifications for public policies. In general, public policy intervention in markets is justified by economists as promoting either *equity* (fairer distribution of the costs and benefits of public and private actions) or *efficiency* (achievement of greater total outputs from given resource inputs). These two principles underlie all the policy recommendations in this chapter.

They also underlie two major corollaries concerning *externalities* and *mobility*. Some public intervention is often required to cope with direct relationships among people that do not flow through markets. Such externalities usually involve one group of people imposing costs upon another group without either obtaining the consent of or compensating the latter. Examples are a factory polluting the air in surrounding residential areas, and a new high-rise apartment generating traffic that congests nearby streets. Since externalities are not based upon voluntary transactions, they often create inequitable or inefficient effects that free markets cannot handle without public policy intervention. Externalities are especially pervasive in urban areas, where so many people live and work close together; hence many of our policy recommendations deal with them. Also, we believe public policies should try to reduce obstacles to individual, household, and business mobility whenever possible. Changes in spatial economic organization are mediated efficiently by markets only when economic agents can adjust quickly.

Even when equity or efficiency considerations imply intervention is appropriate, it need not be aimed at reversing or slowing city population or job losses. In some cases, intervention should focus on alleviating or reversing inequitable or inefficient outcomes. Thus the policies advanced in this chapter include not only attempts to remove some causes of population or job losses, but also methods of adapting to declining city size. We particularly stress policies that address the most serious aspect of city decline: neighborhood concentrations of poor families and individuals.

Removing Policy Biases against Big Cities

Some urban studies show that biased public policies have contributed to recent big-city losses of population and jobs.[1] These are public policies

1. Statement of George E. Peterson in *Federal Tax Policy and Urban Development*, Hearing before the Subcommittee on the City of the House Committee on Banking, Finance and Urban Affairs, 95 Cong. 1 sess. (GPO, 1977), pp. 10–34.

that distort the market prices or incentives confronting firms, households, and individuals so they are more likely to choose suburban or nonmetropolitan locations than big-city sites. Such biases cause choices of consumers and investors to diverge from the most efficient possible uses of resources. Insofar as these policies cause decline, they also increase the need for costly fund transfers to cities through the federal government.

Most such distortions were not deliberately designed to make cities less attractive; rather, they were accidental results of decisions made for other purposes. For example, tax benefits were designed to encourage building new housing units during a national shortage. But no comparable benefits were provided for renovating older housing. That distorted the incentives facing real estate investors, furthering the growth of suburbs compared to large older cities.

Just how much such biases have affected the decline of big cities has not been empirically established. Our analysis showed that a large city-suburban disparity in age of housing tends to encourage suburbanization, but we cannot determine how much of that disparity is due to biased policies. But most goals that inspired biased policies can be pursued in other ways that do not harm large cities. So "urban impact" analyses should be applied to all such policies, and only those biases necessary to achieve critical goals should be retained.

Specifically, we recommend the following changes to remove anti-city biases.

1. Provide identical federal and local tax benefits—including depreciation treatment—for renovating existing property and for new construction.

2. Make federal sewer-and-water-assistance grants usable for renovating existing systems as well as building new ones.

3. Provide the same fraction of federal funding for public transit and highway maintenance and renovation as for new highway construction.

4. Reduce the relative investment advantages of owning expensive homes compared to owning less expensive ones or renting. This can be done by substituting a tax credit at one standard rate for present homeowners' deductibility of mortgage interest and property taxes from federally taxable income.[2] Central cities have higher proportions of both rental units

2. Existing rules provide larger tax benefits per dollar deducted to homeowners in high tax brackets than to those in low tax brackets, thereby encouraging ownership of expensive homes by high-income households. Using a tax credit would give the same aid per dollar deducted to all homeowners, regardless of their tax brackets (assuming they paid taxes), and would therefore increase the relative flow of tax benefits into central cities.

and low-cost owner-occupied homes than suburbs. Therefore, policies favoring ownership of expensive homes encourage further suburban expansion and discourage adequate maintenance of rental structures in older cities.[3]

5. Eliminate the federal tax exemption of interest on industrial revenue bonds.[4]

6. Enact a federal prohibition of local rent controls, or federal penalties against cities that adopt them, because such controls greatly inhibit new investments in rental properties—including maintenance of older existing buildings. Big cities have higher proportions of rental housing than suburbs; so rent controls discourage investments in those cities more than elsewhere.

7. Direct higher fractions of federal job growth toward residents of central cities rather than residents of suburbs through recruiting practices.[5]

8. Whenever feasible, attack racial segregation in public schools with policies other than large-scale mandatory movements of children away from their own neighborhoods. Some recently imposed desegregation plans do not clearly benefit anyone, though they create major transportation and disruption costs and probably speed up the withdrawal of middle-class whites to nearby suburbs.[6]

3. See George S. Tolley and Douglas B. Diamond, "Homeownership, Rental Housing, and Tax Incentives," in *Federal Tax Policy and Urban Development,* Hearing, pp. 114–95. This has become a much more significant source of bias in recent years, because the tax advantages of homeownership rise greatly in times of inflation. See also George E. Peterson, "Federal Tax Policy and the Shaping of Urban Development," in Arthur P. Solomon, ed., *The Prospective City* (MIT Press, 1980), pp. 399–425.

4. See Congressional Budget Office, *Small Issue Industrial Revenue Bonds* (CBO, April 1981), for a discussion of the origins and current volume of IRB use as well as a discussion of policy alternatives.

5. The number of federal civilian employees in all metropolitan areas increased by 24,247 from 1966 to 1976, but the number in central cities fell by 41,726. See Diane Devaul, "The Location of Federal Civilian Employees: Policies, Procedures, and Practices," paper prepared for the Office of Community Planning and Development, Northeast-Midwest Institute 3 (Department of Housing and Urban Development, March 1979).

6. See William H. Frey, "Central City White Flight: Racial and Nonracial Causes," *American Sociological Review,* vol. 44 (June 1979), pp. 425–48; and Karl E. Taeuber, "Housing, Schools, and Incremental Segregative Effects," *The Annals of the American Academy of Political and Social Science,* vol. 441: *Race and Residence in American Cities* (January 1979), pp. 157–67. See also Gary Orfield, *Must We Bus? Segregated Schools and National Policy* (Brookings Institution, 1978), for a reasoned critique of current policies and suggestions for more effective methods of implementing busing and other aspects of school desegregation plans. See also Charles T. Clotfelter, "School Desegregation as Urban Public Policy," in Peter Mieszkowski and Mahlon Straszheim, eds., *Current Issues in Urban Economics* (Johns Hopkins University Press, 1979), pp. 359–87.

Regional Impacts of Policy Choices

Some observers believe many declining cities have been hurt by federal policy biases concerning *regions*, as well as those favoring suburbs over central cities. There is some consensus that federal tax and spending policies redistribute resources toward the South and West away from the Northeast and North Central regions.[7] The former two regions have been growing much faster than the latter two for several decades for many reasons discussed earlier. In fact, the South and West captured almost 90 percent of the nation's population growth in the 1970s, even though they contained only 52 percent of total population in 1980.[8] Consequently, most severely declining cities (including twenty-five of the thirty-four in our sample) are in the Northeast and North Central regions. If federal policies are indeed redistributing resources away from those two regions because of biases, that would aggravate the urban decline already occurring there for other reasons.

Most public policies that redistribute resources among the four major regions do so incidentally in pursuit of other goals. Such redistribution may be entirely appropriate if it results from an agreed-upon schedule of taxes, a consensus "targeting" of expenditures to needs, and competitive contracting of government purchases. The federal government performs many functions, most of which require behavior that neither aims at nor achieves "fiscal neutrality" among regions. In fact, seeking such neutrality would often prevent its achieving other vital goals. For example, if incomes are higher in the West, that region will contribute more per capita to federal taxes; if much of the retired population migrates to the South, more social security expenditures will be made there. Therefore, the net regional effects of the total federal budget are not really an appropriate policy issue.

However, net regional impacts are a legitimate concern in evaluating proposed policy changes. For example, the budget suggested by the Reagan administration for fiscal 1982 and beyond was hotly contested on regional-impact grounds. Defense spending—which it proposed to raise sharply—

7. See Advisory Commission on Intergovernmental Relations, *Regional Growth: Historic Perspective* (GPO, 1980); Advisory Commission on Intergovernmental Relations, *Regional Growth: Flows of Federal Funds, 1952–76* (GPO, 1980); and Thomas Muller, "Regional-Urban Policy: Should the Government Intervene?" *Challenge*, vol. 24 (March/April 1981), pp. 38–41.

8. Metropolitan areas in the Northeast lost 2 percent of their 1970 population by 1980; 1980 Census data as reported in *New York Times*, March 3, 1981.

tends to be concentrated in the West and South; whereas the Northeast and Midwest would lose substantially through its proposed cuts in human resource programs.[9] Hence some representatives from the Northeast and North Central regions thought their areas would be doubly penalized by this budget. Defenders of these regions were also concerned that proposed tax rate cuts and accelerated depreciation "could encourage manufacturers to close plants in the aging Great Lakes industrial crescent and build new ones in the booming Sun Belt States."[10]

If careful analysis indicates a proposed policy would strongly reinforce current population or job shifts away from the North, that proposal should be reexamined. Its designers should seek alternative measures to accomplish the same national goals without such regionally different results. If such measures cannot be found, the policy's aggravation of Northern decline should be considered a cost to be weighed against achievement of its primary goals.

Another regional bias issue arises from the fact that national recessions typically affect Northern urban areas more strongly than Southern or Western ones. Janet Rothenberg Pack summarizes the evidence as follows:

> For the last 25 years, at least, the Northeast and Midwest economies have been robust only when national growth rates have been high. Other regions continue to grow, sometimes quite rapidly, even during recessions. Regional differences in growth rates have been smaller in periods of strong national expansion and wider during periods of severe economic slowdown.[11]

Because national macroeconomic policies aim at goals other than regional equality, this has limited implications for such policies. One is that programs aimed at countering the ill effects of recessions should be *locally targeted*

9. Dan Bolz, "Administration Moves Abandon Ailing Northeast and Midwest Cities," *Washington Post*, February 23, 1981. "Budget Cut Geography," an editorial in *Washington Post*, May 7, 1981, reports on an Office of Management and Budget study of fiscal year 1982 impacts. Research at the University of Michigan "indicates that the administration's budget . . . will have its severest impact on states that have been experiencing the lowest rates of economic growth and will have the most difficulty in coping with budget reductions." Proposed reductions in grants to state and local governments would be even more concentrated in slower growing states. Reported in "The Geography of the Budget," a letter to the editor of *Washington Post*, May 25, 1981, from James W. Fossett, Kevin L. Kramer, and John Oppenheim, research associates, Institute for Social Research, University of Michigan. New York Governor Hugh Carey "attacked portions of President Reagan's budget program as 'obnoxious' and 'regionally biased' against the Northeast." Robin Herman, "Carey Sees 'Regional Bias' in Reagan Plan," *New York Times*, February 15, 1981.

10. Iver Peterson, "Revitalization Plan Troubling Midwest," *New York Times*, December 1, 1980.

11. ACIR, *Regional Growth: Historic Perspective*, p. 51.

to those areas hit hardest, rather than aimed at the national economy in general. Therefore, the countercyclical assistance programs used to combat the 1975 recession were less "regionally biased" against declining cities than an equivalent increase in general revenue sharing would have been. These programs included emergency local public works, anti-recession fiscal assistance, and expanded public service employment. They used local unemployment rates in their allocation formulas, whereas general revenue sharing allocations are based mainly upon total population.

One clear federal bias is not taking account of regional living-cost variations in calculating transfer payments and taxes. As noted in chapter 3, nominal dollar incomes per capita were higher in Northeastern SMSAs than in the South in the early 1970s, but the reverse was true after correcting for living-cost differences. The higher cost of living in the Northeast implies, for example, that the typical resident of the Boston or Buffalo area pays more federal income taxes than someone at the same standard of living residing in Atlanta or Houston. Similarly, a nationally uniform social security payment supports recipients at a higher standard of living in Orlando or Austin than in New York or Philadelphia.[12] In choosing a policy response to these disparities, a critical issue is the geographic mobility of potential program beneficiaries. In the interests of limiting total system costs, mobile recipients should not receive cost-of-living-adjusted benefits. Rather, uniform benefits should expose them to market incentives to move to lower-cost areas. On the other hand, it hardly seems fair that immobile residents of high-cost areas should receive lower real incomes from national transfer programs. Since it is not possible to discriminate among beneficiaries within a single program, adjustments for cost-of-living differences should be made only in those programs in which recipients are predominantly immobile. The current lack of comparative cost-of-living data for places other than the forty metropolitan areas in the Bureau of Labor Statistics' sample presents some serious implementation difficulties.[13] But

12. Note, however, that to the degree that nominal wages are also higher in high-living-cost areas, retirees who stay in the region where they accumulated their work history will have some reflection of cost of living in their benefit levels.

13. Some federal housing subsidies vary with the local cost of housing. This is accomplished through determination of "fair market rent" standards for each area by a panel of local experts and Department of Housing and Urban Development surveys. Other programs have corrected in a very rough way for cost-of-living differences in determining eligibility (but not subsidy amount) by using some fraction of the local median income as the eligibility cutoff. For a description of some of the conceptual and practical difficulties of making cost-of-living adjustments in transfer program benefit levels, see Janice Peskin, "Geographic Payment Variation in a Federal Welfare System," Technical Analysis Paper 14 (Office of Income Security Policy, Department of Health, Education, and Welfare, January 1977).

the unfairness of the current system argues strongly for expending the necessary resources to make the corrections where feasible.

Altogether, the federal government cannot shape its tax and spending policies primarily to produce fiscal neutrality among regions. Therefore, some net federal redistribution of resources among regions is probably bound to arise. However, the federal administration and Congress should be more sensitive to the differential regional impacts of proposed policy changes than in the past. This implies that some type of "regional impact analysis" ought to be conducted concerning proposals for any major changes in federal taxes or spending. That could be done along with the "urban impact analysis" suggested earlier as a means of reducing federal anti-city biases.

Adapting to Lower Populations and Resources

Although adjusting to lower levels of population and resources is a major strategy we recommend for severely declining cities, we do not present a comprehensive set of tactics for this strategy. Most such tactics would not be derived from this study, so we cannot cover the subject here nearly as well as many recent analyses of "cutback planning" written by specialists in municipal government.[14]

Big-City Poverty, Diversity, and Local Governments

Because many large cities have become specialized as locations for the poor, their governments bear a disproportionate share of the public costs of coping with poverty. It would be inequitable for them and for their tax-paying residents to bear these costs without outside financial aid because poverty is a condition largely generated by the national economy. Moreover, many suburban residents have deliberately erected legal barriers that exclude the poor from their communities. Yet they benefit from the overall economy and from specific arrangements that sustain poverty, such as continuance of low-wage jobs. Hence they should pay a reasonable share of poverty's public costs.

However, the determination of fiscal conservatives to reduce federal

14. For example, see Charles H. Levine, ed., *Managing Fiscal Stress* (Chatham House, 1980), especially Levine's essay, "Organizational Decline and Cutback Management," pp. 13–30.

domestic spending raises the questions, just how much outside aid should cities receive, and in what forms? No general answers to these questions are possible because the burdens of poverty vary so much from one city to another. Nevertheless, those burdens are going to rise relative to the total costs of local government in cities where the total population declines faster than the poor population. Their governments will probably need ever larger infusions of resources from state and federal governments, precisely at a time when those infusions are being reduced. There are two basic sources of relief for these burdens: (1) additional intergovernmental aid, and (2) reductions in either the responsibilities or the "localness" of local governments.

Intergovernmental Aid

Big-city governments already depend heavily on outside help. In 1978 *all* city governments (including those in many suburbs) received 32.2 percent of their total revenues from intergovernmental transfers.[15] The forty-eight largest cities received 42.9 percent of their total revenues from such transfers, including 16.6 percent directly from the federal government.[16]

In recent years, the "targeting" of federal aid to areas with the most intense needs has helped large cities capture somewhat more than equal per capita shares of the total assistance provided in certain federal programs.[17] But political representatives of other areas resent such concentration of aid, even though it can be justified by differing intensity of needs. Hence targeted programs can usually be passed only as part of specific logrolling deals in which nontargeted areas benefit disproportionately from other unrelated legislation.

Furthermore, all determinations of "intensity of needs" are based upon value judgments. Legislators from areas rated as having low intensity of needs by one set of criteria are quick to invent other criteria by which they have very intense needs. Thus, in a democracy, it is difficult to sustain targeted programs over long periods in the face of the inherent pressure to spread all aid roughly in proportion to population. This difficulty will

15. *Statistical Abstract of the United States, 1980*, p. 312.

16. Ibid., p. 313.

17. For studies of the success of targeting in various programs, see Richard P. Nathan, Allen D. Manvel, Susannah E. Calkins, and Associates, *Monitoring Revenue Sharing* (Brookings Institution, 1975), chap. 5; and Richard P. Nathan, Charles F. Adams, Jr., and Associates, *Revenue Sharing: The Second Round* (Brookings Institution, 1977), chap. 3.

be increased by a continuing decline in the overall political power of large cities in Congress and state legislatures as their populations fall, and by the general budget-cutting environment that now prevails.

Federal flexibility in advancing national urban goals under diverse conditions is now maintained through several intergovernmental funding arrangements.

REVENUE SHARING. This involves the distribution of federal or state funds to local governments through some formula based on selected local conditions.[18] Each local government is "entitled" to receive whatever funds the formula allocates to it. The funds can be used for anything permitted by the applicable legislation.

Revenue sharing seeks to combine the federal government's superior ability to collect taxes with state and local governments' superior knowledge of local needs. In contrast to state and local governments, the federal government can tax affluent households and firms without much danger they will "escape" to another jurisdiction. Hence federal taxation is the best foundation for all government action aimed at income redistribution. Moreover, local (and state) government revenues decline in business downturns, while expenditure needs rise, especially in high unemployment areas.[19] This strains local government budgets during recessions, but they cannot respond through prolonged deficit financing, as can the federal government. For these reasons, revenue sharing is superior to shifting both taxation and spending downward to states and localities. Also, revenue sharing allows local priorities to determine the use of federal funds.

However, under revenue sharing, all communities in the universe of funded locations receive assistance, whether or not they really need the money. Moreover, revenue sharing does not require local officials to apply for funds, or to define in advance how they will use them. Hence there are few rewards for careful planning beyond those any government has for use of its own funds, and no incentive to focus upon achieving specific national goals.

BLOCK GRANTS. These were originally mergers of several categorical programs dealing with related activities. As now operated, they involve distribution of funds by formula to entitled jurisdictions, as in revenue

18. The term "revenue sharing" as used here denotes a basic method of funding, not the particular program called "general revenue sharing." The latter, however, is an example of the former.

19. See Advisory Commission on Intergovernmental Relations, *State-Local Finances in Recession and Inflation: An Economic Analysis* (GPO, 1979), for a summary of studies on the cyclical sensitivity of state-local revenues and expenditures.

sharing. However, permissible local uses of funds are restricted to certain activities within the jurisdiction of the funding agency. Also, the formula usually focuses more aid upon areas "most in need" of such activities. Moreover, the funding agency tends to add more detailed requirements as time passes.

CONTINGENT CATEGORICAL PROGRAMS. A *categorical* program makes available federal or state funds only for specified purposes. Funds are awarded only to those local governments whose detailed applications for particular projects win approval. Hence communities are not "entitled" to categorical funds, but must take the initiative to get them. Many such programs use matching grants to encourage local governments to add their own funds to these activities.

A *contingent* categorical program mandates different uses of funds, depending upon local conditions. For example, a community containing many deteriorated, abandoned buildings could be awarded federal code enforcement funds only for demolition; whereas a community with only marginally decaying structures would be allowed to use similar funds only for code enforcement and rehabilitation.

One difficulty with contingent programs is determining exactly what local conditions prevail. For example, whether housing subsidies should help people rent existing units or build new ones logically depends upon whether the local housing market is tight or loose, and why. But no reliable current data exist concerning either the vacancy rate or the duration of vacancies—the two best indicators of housing market tightness.[20] Hence contingent categorical programs often must rely upon the subjective judgments of local officials, which makes them more closely resemble other categorical programs or block grants.

ANNUAL NEGOTIATED AGREEMENTS. On an experimental basis, some local governments have contracted with numerous federal agencies at once, to combine funding for many categorical programs. The local government determines its overall priorities across many possible activities. It then arranges to pool federal funds from several programs to best serve those priorities. The federal agencies agree to fund these activities with money from all the programs selected. This approach seeks to improve coordination of the many federally funded activities within a given city. A recent variation called the "negotiated investment strategy" also involves private sector

20. See C. Peter Rydell, *Vacancy Duration and Housing Market Condition* (Rand Corp., January 1978).

representatives in the initial planning, thereby integrating both public and private resources.[21]

As of fiscal 1975, about 76 percent of federal funds distributed to state and local governments went via categorical grants, 10 percent via block grants, and 14 percent via revenue sharing. However, about 69 percent of all categorical grant funds used formula-based distribution methods; so close to three-fourths of all federal intergovernmental funding was based upon formulas of some type.[22]

Although all these approaches deal in some way with diversity of local conditions and needs, it is useful to contrast them with our version of an "ideal" approach that would incorporate several different funding arrangements. Overall, city officials would exercise major discretion to choose actions best suited to local conditions. But they would also have to shape their actions to effectively serve national purposes. The best way to accomplish these goals *in theory* would be a "menu approach."

A formula based upon relevant local conditions would allocate to each local government a total amount of federal funds usable for a broad range of permissible activities. There could be one large allocation covering many activities under the jurisdiction of several federal departments, similar to general revenue sharing; then the formula establishing "need" would cover broad traits, as does the current formula for the general revenue sharing program. Or several separate allocations could cover somewhat narrower ranges of activities, each under the jurisdiction of a different federal agency. This would resemble several block grants; so the formulas measuring "need" would be defined in more specific terms. Under either arrangement, local officials could decide to allocate funds from any one pool among the eligible activities in any way they wanted.

Once they decided to spend some funds on a specific activity, they would have to follow rules for the relevant program established by the federal operators. Local officials would file a plan with those operators, who would have a fixed time within which to reject that proposal if it was seriously deficient. Otherwise, the proposal would be considered approved, and federal funding would be automatic. Thus, the burden of proof would

21. Harvey Garn and Larry Lederber, "The Negotiated Investment Strategy: A Review of the Concept and Its Implications for Revitalizing Cities" (Committee for Economic Development, November 1980).

22. These estimates are set forth in *The President's National Urban Policy Report, 1980* (GPO, 1980), p. 11-3.

be on federal program specialists who believed a local proposal should be rejected. Federal officials could maintain appropriate leverage over local activities by carefully specifying national objectives and prohibiting certain uses of funds.

In theory, this menu approach would force federal program specialists to compete with each other to "capture" funds for their programs from the broad allocations made to local governments. It thus creates "consumer sovereignty" for local governments. They could spend their funds on any combination of items from the available menu of federal programs within the range of permissible activities. Total funding for each federal program would emerge from the aggregate choices of many local governments. If federal program specialists made their requirements terribly stringent or imposed unpopular rules, few local governments would allocate funds to those programs. On the other hand, local officials would have to allocate the funds to activities the federal government wanted to support.

This menu approach would also allow local governments to adapt funding to the time-sequence requirements of large-scale projects. For example, local officials could concentrate a large amount of funds on a mass transit project in one year, or for several years, while "starving" other programs. When that project was finished, they could "starve" mass transit while focusing on other projects. Such temporal flexibility is difficult to achieve under present arrangements.[23]

The most extreme version of this menu approach would be a radical departure from what happens now. It would resemble a merger of all existing local aid programs into one giant revenue sharing program, with a single formula determining total potential funding for each community. This has the political disadvantage of requiring individual congressional committees now specializing in certain programs to abandon control of the amounts allocated to each program. Less radical versions of the menu approach could be approximated by creating several broadly defined block grant programs, and changing the way localities now spend money under each. Congressional committees might be more willing to accept this approach, since they could still set the total amounts authorized and appropriated for the whole set of activities permitted under each block grant. In either case, in exchange for broadening the scope of existing block grants, or creating new ones by merging related categorical programs,

23. We are indebted to Robert W. Hartman of the Brookings Institution for pointing out this advantage of the menu approach.

Congress would obtain more specific control over the list of permissible activities. The approach has the great advantage of letting individual communities choose among programs but still allowing federal officials to shape each program to serve the national interest.

Annual negotiated agreements also allow local governments to emphasize those particular federal programs they want most, using funds from many programs. Yet each community must negotiate its overall funding by getting many federal agencies to pool their funds. Such negotiations are so complex and time-consuming, and require such great goodwill among many officials, that this approach probably cannot be used for any large number of cities simultaneously.

At present, we believe revenue sharing and expanded block grants modified as discussed above are the best ways to balance national purposes (including income redistribution) and the diversity of local conditions. However, achieving some federal goals would require categorical funding in matching or direct grant form even if the menu approach were adopted.

The federal government should offer open-ended matching grants for specific categories of expenditures for which local governments would otherwise spend less than federal decision makers consider desirable. This is true in particular concerning national purposes that are extremely unpopular locally or involve major innovations. Unpopular programs need categorical funding so local officials can shift the blame to distant federal officials. Examples are building public housing projects and halfway houses for ex-convicts. Innovative programs need categorical funding because most local officials are reluctant to try new and untested arrangements unless they can get added funds by doing so. Once an innovative program has proved successful, it should be folded into some broader block grant arrangement.

Coping with Local Government Fragmentation

A major factor preventing large cities from halting the downward spiral of decline is the division of fiscal authority within each metropolitan area among many local governments. Our case study revealed that county-wide government consolidation combined with other equalizing fiscal measures is a promising approach to alleviating city losses of population, employment, and income. The regression analysis in chapter 5 showed that higher city-suburb tax disparities and greater local government fragmentation both contributed to suburbanization. These findings suggest that regionalization of municipal government might be an effective remedy for the fiscal strains on city governments.

The essential fiscal problem of these governments is a chronic shortage of available resources relative to higher-than-average needs associated with large poverty populations. Most policy responses aim at providing more revenues or taxable resources to city governments, reducing the range of needs they must address, or otherwise promoting a better balance between the two. One approach is spreading the city government's boundaries, or otherwise expanding its access to a broader economic base. Annexation or consolidation of the city with surrounding territory is one form of such regionalization. Others are shifting service responsibilities to higher governments, metropolitan tax base sharing, and some forms of intergovernmental aid.

Such regionalization aids a city only when the surrounding territory has a richer or faster-growing economic base relative to its needs than the city. Chapter 3 showed that average city-SMSA disparities are relatively large for declining cities; so access to average regional resources would indeed improve their fiscal health. However, functionally declining cities are quite likely to be in functionally declining SMSAs; so the benefits of regionalization may decline over time. Also, some growing cities, notably in the South, would *lose* through regionalization because they are better off than their suburbs.

ANNEXATION AND METROPOLITAN GOVERNMENT. Many Southern and Western cities can annex surrounding territory, whereas most Northeastern and Midwest cities cannot. This disparity partly explains the relatively greater economic and fiscal health of the former. True, the social problems associated with concentrated poverty are not alleviated much by annexation. But the city government is strengthened fiscally by spreading the high per capita budget costs of serving poverty areas over a broader economic base. During the 1960s, 85 percent of total population gains in the 153 largest cities were due to annexation. Those cities *lost* population during the first half of the seventies, but would have lost more than twice as much without annexation.[24] However, annexation is unavailable to the circumscribed cities of the Northeast and Midwest, and will probably become less feasible in the future for many of the cities recently using it.

24. Annexation contributed 3,246,000 of the 153 cities' 3,811,000 population growth during the 1960s. The 153 cities lost over 702,000 people between 1970 and 1975, in spite of the addition of almost 785,000 people through annexation.

A more extreme form of regionalization, metropolitan government, removes the fiscal advantage that residents of high-income jurisdictions have gained by insulating themselves from low-income taxpayers. Loss of local control and a decrease in the variety of public service offerings in the metropolitan area are two drawbacks. Also, the shift to metropolitan-wide provision of services may be accompanied by a "leveling-up" of wages and other expenditures. This *raises* total costs of service provision in the area, rather than lowering them through greater efficiencies. Another problem of all metropolitan arrangements is keeping political boundaries congruent with market areas or with the boundaries of regional problems. For all these reasons, metropolitan governments have not been politically popular and are unlikely to become so. Since 1950, only six major city-county consolidations have occurred.[25]

SHIFTING FUNCTIONS TO OTHER GOVERNMENTS. According to the extensive literature on how various functions should be assigned to different levels in our federal system, states or regional bodies should be responsible for services that require broad area planning (such as air pollution control) or involve a substantial state or regional interest (such as higher education).[26] This means some functions now performed by local governments could be shifted "upward" to these other levels. For example, the city of Cleveland shifted its sewer system and some of its parks to county-wide agencies in order to cut its costs. Local governments would benefit from reduced spending needs, especially because the shift of financial responsibility would be total and permanent. The biggest disadvantage is loss of local control over service levels. Minimizing this disadvantage is what usually guides selection of specific functions to shift. City governments are sure to benefit, but city residents may not, depending on how the state or agency finances the service and at what level.[27]

25. The six are the Parish of East Baton Rouge and the city of Baton Rouge, Jacksonville-Duval County (Florida), Lexington-Fayette County (Kentucky), Nashville-Davidson County, Indianapolis-Marion County, and Columbus-Muscogee County (Georgia). Advisory Commission on Intergovernmental Relations, *The Challenge of Local Governmental Reorganization*, vol. 3: *Substate Regionalism and the Federal System* (GPO, 1974).

26. For example, see Dick Netzer, "State-Local Finance and Intergovernmental Fiscal Relations," in Alan S. Blinder and others, *The Economics of Public Finance* (Brookings Institution, 1974), pp. 361–421.

27. The net effects on city governments and city residents of plans for reallocation of responsibilities in several areas were studied by the Urban Observatories. See Roy W. Bahl, ed., "Symposium—State and Regional Government Financing of City Government Services: Tax Burden and Budgetary Implications," *National Tax Journal*, vol. 29 (March 1976), pp. 55–122.

TAX-BASE SHARING. One recent proposal to ease central-city fiscal problems is metropolitan tax-base sharing. As of 1981, this had been implemented only in the Minneapolis-St. Paul metropolitan area, although it has been considered in New Jersey and Maryland as well. The Twin Cities plan allocates 40 percent of any increase in each member city's commercial and industrial tax base to a metropolitan pool. The pool is shared among 195 municipalities and among school districts according to a formula based on population and relative fiscal capacity (as measured by assessed value per capita). The net effect on the tax base of any community depends on (1) how fast its commercial and industrial base is growing, (2) how big its total base is, and (3) its population.

The basic argument favoring the Twin Cities' plan was a reduction in competition among localities to attract taxable business. Such competition was believed to be distorting the locational decisions of firms, and causing underuse of existing sewer, water, and road infrastructures by encouraging growth in undeveloped areas. In addition, tax concessions by local governments transferred resources from all those governments as a whole to local businesses.

The Minnesota plan took effect in 1974, but used 1971 as the base year for determining growth. By 1978, the shared base had grown to 11 percent of the total value of area-wide commercial and industrial property.[28] In spite of the small size of this total, the plan has already reduced disparities in tax bases and rates in the metropolitan area. Rate disparities are decreasing both because access to the base is more nearly equal and because part of the tax on commercial and industrial property is at a uniform area-wide rate. The plan appears to redistribute resources to communities with low fiscal capacity or high concentrations of the poor and elderly, even though service needs are not directly reflected in the distribution formula. The major beneficiaries have been the central cities of Minneapolis and St. Paul, though the total amount of redistribution is still small.[29] That may be a political advantage, since at the program's start it provided only modest—therefore palatable—gains and losses to individual cities. Its incremental nature also greatly aided its political acceptability. An incremental plan is most effective in areas with rapid growth, but inflation causes

28. Andrew Reschovsky, "An Evaluation of Metropolitan Area Tax Base Sharing," *National Tax Journal*, vol. 33 (March 1980), pp. 55–66.

29. Ibid.; Andrew Reschovsky and Eugene Knaff, "Tax Base Sharing: An Assessment of the Minnesota Experience," *Journal of the American Institute of Planners*, vol. 43 (October 1977), pp. 361–70; and Paul A. Gilje, "Sharing of Tax Growth—Redefinitions," *Governmental Finance* (November 1977), pp. 35–40.

a gradual increase in that portion of the total tax base included in the "pool" even in stagnant SMSAs.

Metropolitan tax-base sharing delivers the major advantage promised by metropolitan government without incurring its major disadvantage. It unifies a central city with the entire surrounding market area, allowing the city government access to revenues generated in parts of the area that are still growing. Yet it also retains complete local control over service provision, tax rates, and land use. Also, its operation from year to year is automatic, since the intergovernmental transfers do not require annual legislation. That is a major political and planning advantage. A possible variation on the Minnesota plan is making the sharing formula more redistributive by adding need or cost factors, such as a weight for poverty. That might reduce middle- and upper-income communities' incentives to exclude the poor.

POWER-EQUALIZING STATE AID. One form of aid from states to localities, not discussed earlier, closely resembles regionalization. It is called "power equalizing" because its aid formulas seek to equalize the taxing "power" (or tax base) available to individual jurisdictions in a state. In its purest form, such a formula sets aid equal to the difference between actual local tax revenues and the amount that would be raised with the local tax rate applied to the average (state) tax base per capita (or, for school aid, per pupil).[30] In this form, aid would be negative for jurisdictions with above-average tax bases; hence they would contribute to the pool for distribution to jurisdictions entitled to positive aid. State funds would cover any net difference between contributions and distributions.[31]

The power-equalizing concept was developed partly in response to court decisions invalidating public school financing based on local property taxes.[32] The courts ruled that the quality of a child's schooling should not depend on the wealth of his or her parents or neighbors. Power equalizing effectively "targets" aid at poor jurisdictions. However, the basic formula does not reflect differences in service costs or needs, and takes no account

30. For example, the formula might be

$$A_i = r_i(B_s - B_i),$$

where A_i is the aid per capita to jurisdiction i, r_i is the tax rate in jurisdiction i, B is the tax base per capita, and subscripts s and i refer to the state average and jurisdiction i, respectively.

31. Other forms involve only positive aid, either by setting B_s equal to the highest per capita base in the state or by constraining aid to be nonnegative, thereby "equalizing" only the jurisdictions below the state mean up to the mean. State revenues are then used to fund the aid. More limited forms provide as aid only a fixed fraction of A_i (defined in the preceding footnote); that is, they move a fraction of the way toward full equalization.

32. Examples are *Serrano* v. *Priest* in California and *Robinson* v. *Cahill* in New Jersey.

of competing claims by overlying governments or districts on each local tax base.

Like all forms of matching aid—including tax-base sharing—power-equalizing aid distorts the perceived local cost of government spending versus private expenditure. If one believes poorer governments spend too little because of current fiscal stringency, this is an advantage. Conversely, if one believes the key problem of poorer governments is not inadequate spending but excessive tax rates, then programs that stimulate spending are to be avoided. However, where tax rates are very high, matching aid seems unlikely to generate much added spending.[33]

RECOMMENDATIONS. Federal and state governments should have primary responsibility for redistributive programs aiding poor residents, but cities must provide those residents and others with a full range of local services. We believe metropolitan tax-base sharing is the most promising means of alleviating the fiscal difficulties that accompany that local responsibility. Through careful choice of what bases are contributed to the pool, and of what formula is used to distribute shares among member jurisdictions, such a program can be tailored to each metropolitan area's needs and resources. Also, both the pace of implementation and the ultimate degree of redistribution can be varied to suit local desires.

In view of the advantages of tax-base sharing, why has it been seriously considered up to now only in Minnesota, New Jersey, and Maryland? We believe failure to consider this option more widely has resulted as much from lack of leadership ability at the metropolitan level as from real opposition.[34] Because the plan is incremental, individual areas are "held harmless" when it starts; that is, they do not share their then existing tax bases, though they do share the subsequent growth in the valuation of those bases. Moreover, the nonshared portion of subsequent growth compensates jurisdictions for the service costs they bear. We believe states

33. The degree to which matching grants stimulate spending is still an open question. Martin Feldstein even concluded that power equalizing for schools would go too far in eliminating the correlation between local wealth and school expenditures, creating a *negative* association; see Martin S. Feldstein, "Wealth Neutrality and Local Choice in Public Education," *American Economic Review*, vol. 65 (March 1975), pp. 75–89.

34. A recent analysis of this question by Francine Rabinovitz concluded that adoption of tax-base sharing was easier in the Minneapolis-St. Paul area than elsewhere because it did not contain a large minority-group population seeking to maximize its political power. However, many other metropolitan areas that do not have large minority-group populations have also failed even to consider this device. See Francine Rabinovitz, "Tax Base Sharing: Is It Transferable?" paper written for Land Policy Round Table, February 1981.

should encourage local governments and metropolitan advisory bodies to investigate their areas' potentials as tax-base-sharing sites.[35]

However, metropolitan tax-base sharing should be accompanied by continued state and federal intergovernmental transfers, for two reasons. First, tax-base sharing equalizes only part of local tax bases, and that only gradually. So special needs must still be met, and states or the federal government will still want to support particular services. Second, such plans give local municipalities more equal access only to those resources *within* each metropolitan area. State or federal aid remains the appropriate basic tool for redistributing resources *among* metropolitan areas in recognition of their varying needs and affluence.

35. Metropolitan areas that cross state boundaries pose special problems for base-sharing plans, because municipalities in different states may have different legal rights and obligations. Among the 276 SMSAs defined in 1975, 37 contained parts of more than one state. This statistic is based on SMSA definitions reported in Office of Management and Budget, *Standard Metropolitan Statistical Areas, 1975*, rev. ed. (GPO, 1976).

13

Policies to Deter Urban Decline, Part Two

LOCAL GOVERNMENTS are not the only entities within large cities that need outside assistance; many individuals and households are even more dependent upon such aid. The federal government currently transfers billions of dollars each year to individual residents in the forms of welfare aid, unemployment compensation, food stamps, social security payments, Medicare and Medicaid assistance, housing subsidies, Comprehensive Employment and Training Act (CETA) assistance, and many other benefits.[1] These programs are much more important than payments to city governments in helping poor *residents* of central cities.

Moreover, many programs that aid individuals and households directly are less susceptible to the political problems associated with "targeting" than programs that aid city governments. Examples are social security, food stamps, and unemployment compensation. Almost every congressional district contains many persons receiving such assistance. Consequently, in spite of recent budget cuts in these programs, Congress will probably curtail direct aid to poor people less severely in the long run than programs targeted on big-city governments. Hence, likely future declines in the political power of big-city governments make it advisable to consider switching more federal aid from *empowering governments* to deliver services, to *empowering individuals and households* to purchase services or provide their own.

In this chapter, we analyze how individual empowerment might deal

1. For an estimate of how much such aid went to residents of central cities in a recent year, see Anthony Downs, "Urban Policy," in Joseph A. Pechman, ed., *Setting National Priorities: The 1979 Budget* (Brookings Institution, 1978), pp. 180–85.

with certain problems associated with urban decline. We also discuss the need to undertake revitalization policies at appropriate scales of effort, and present some final conclusions.

Directly Empowering Individuals and Households

Losses of population or jobs within a city are socially undesirable only insofar as they harm individuals and households—not the city's reputation or government in themselves. Therefore, the success of public policies responsive to decline should be ultimately judged by their impacts upon the lives of residents, either in the city or elsewhere. In most cases, aiming public policies *directly* at providing good incomes, jobs, housing, education, and health care to those city residents lacking them is more effective than aiming at counteracting overall city losses in population or jobs. Funds used for *indirect* assistance benefit many other persons, and therefore may not serve the policies' goals at all.

For example, consider a federal tax credit awarded for plant-and-equipment investments in decaying inner-city neighborhoods. Much of the federal cost will subsidize firms claiming tax credits for investments they would have made anyway. Still more will be used to increase the capital intensity of the enterprise rather than to increase the workforce. And many of the jobs that are added will be filled by persons other than unemployed local residents. But providing the unemployed residents with job vouchers that pay their employers a share of the cost of hiring them would concentrate the resulting benefits mainly upon the unemployed. This conclusion was reinforced by the simulations described in chapter 11.

Furthermore, providing people with goods or services can often be best accomplished by giving them more power to choose among competing suppliers. The most desirable way for them to acquire that power is by having well-paying jobs so they can enter the markets for these goods and services. Current publicly financed efforts to aid those who cannot find jobs are of three types. In some programs, such as aid to families with dependent children, the beneficiaries are provided with cash, although how they spend it is sometimes restricted. In others, such as public housing and city-run medical centers, government agencies provide benefits directly. Still other programs involve government agencies paying suppliers, as in the subsidized housing and Medicare programs.

In the last two types, poor households have little or no choice among alternative suppliers, a situation that perpetuates a hallmark of poverty: feelings of dependency, helplessness, and lack of control over one's own destiny. Moreover, a sizable share of the money allocated usually aids the professional "intermediaries," not the poor.[2] To avoid these undesirable traits, we believe as many government programs as possible should provide the poor directly with the means to obtain specific goods and services. Public officials would still decide who was eligible to receive aid, explain the rules, monitor behavior to guarantee the rules were followed, and evaluate each program. But the key choices would be made by the poor themselves. This recommendation is largely based on our own judgment, though it is indirectly supported by our Cleveland area simulations, which showed that funds spent for one primary purpose do not spill over much into solving other problems.

The best way to empower consumers (other than by providing jobs, which we discuss below) is probably through a guaranteed minimum annual income. Then each household could decide for itself how to allocate that aid among available goods and services. However, Congress usually prefers aid tied to the consumption of specific goods or services; this preference reflects partly the political influence of their suppliers and partly an unwillingness to allow tax money to be spent on goods and services that many taxpayers regard as nonessential. Even so, such "earmarked" assistance could be provided to each household as a purchase voucher, as happens now with food stamps. Then the choice among specific suppliers and versions of each item would be left up to the assisted households. This approach also compels suppliers to compete with each other in the market, rather than gaining their business by meeting various bureaucratic criteria. Yet federal officials could still limit the uses of funds by imposing quality requirements, as in the Experimental Housing Allowance Program.[3]

Such *empowering the individual* with added market choices has already proven feasible concerning housing and food. We believe it can also be extended to employment, education, and transportation, although this is a highly controversial judgment. We examine these possibilities in the following subsections. We then discuss why we think empowerment cannot now be successfully used to reduce socioeconomic segregation.

2. For a discussion of these and other negative aspects of professional service-providers, see Ivan Illich, *Toward a History of Needs* (Bantam Books, 1980), pp. 6–45.

3. See U.S. Department of Housing and Urban Development, *Experimental Housing Allowance Program: A 1979 Report of Findings* (GPO, 1979).

Employment

Unemployment is certainly one of the most serious urban problems in the United States. There are at least four strategies for dealing with it.

One is to maintain strong enough aggregate demand in the economy as a whole to keep overall unemployment rates low.[4] However, even when the national unemployment rate was quite low, as from 1967 through 1969 when it was below 4 percent, unemployment rates within many concentrated-poverty neighborhoods remained high.[5] Therefore, reducing unemployment in concentrated-poverty areas to more acceptable levels would require other tactics in addition to maintaining high aggregate demand.

Another way to attack unemployment is to provide low-skilled unemployed persons with training aimed at raising their productivity. In theory, after training has improved their skills, they become productive enough to earn a "decent" wage—or at least the minimum wage.[6] However, this strategy has been tried continuously for over a decade without eliminating high levels of unemployment. It has been especially ineffective at reducing unemployment among black teenagers.[7]

4. Analyzing public policies needed to maintain high levels of aggregate demand is outside the scope of this book. For a discussion of the relationship of such policies to urban unemployment, see Department of Housing and Urban Development, *The President's National Urban Policy Report, 1980* (HUD, 1980), pp. 3-1–3-8. See also Elizabeth A. Roistacher, Margaret C. Simms, and Andrea Mills, "Recession and the Cities: Metropolitan Structure and Unemployment over the Business Cycle," paper presented at the American Economic Association meeting in Chicago, August 30, 1978.

5. In fact, the most widespread peacetime rioting in U.S. history occurred precisely during those three years in hundreds of such neighborhoods. The National Advisory Commission on Civil Disorders concluded that high levels of unemployment in ghetto neighborhoods were among the key causes of that rioting. See National Advisory Commission on Civil Disorders, *Report* (GPO, 1968), pp. 123–31, 19–61.

6. This theory assumes there are enough existing or potential unfilled job openings to absorb all such trained workers. It is true that many job openings go unfilled even during recessions. Yet this theory does not really explain the dynamic process of how training would generate sufficient increases in aggregate demand to absorb all the added workers involved. One author who has attempted to examine this question is Lester C. Thurow, *Generating Inequality: Mechanisms of Distribution in the U.S. Economy* (Basic Books, 1975).

7. See Garth L. Mangum and Stephen F. Seninger, *Coming of Age in the Ghetto: A Dilemma of Youth Unemployment* (Johns Hopkins University Press, 1978). After a careful analysis of ghetto youth unemployment, they conclude that neither training nor any other now-feasible remedies will work: "Redeveloping or breaking up the ghetto and rebuilding the family is the logical policy implication flowing from the facts. But no one seems to have a practical prescription for that set of maladies" (p. 86).

A third strategy is to increase total employment in a given city and hope the city's unemployed will get some of the added jobs. This hope has been used to justify many Economic Development Administration and Urban Development Action Grant projects. However, such a "trickle-down" strategy is usually an inefficient way to help unemployed residents in concentrated-poverty neighborhoods. Many public subsidies provide better jobs for people already employed, or cause firms to operate inefficiently by choosing locations other than those best suited for their activities. This conclusion is confirmed by our analysis of Cleveland. Since nearly 70 percent of the workers in downtown Cleveland live outside the city, most additions to employment there would not aid unemployed city residents. Even most added jobs filled by Cleveland residents would not benefit unskilled, unemployed residents of concentrated-poverty areas.

A more direct and efficient strategy is to target wage subsidies and public employment to unemployed residents of concentrated-poverty areas. Paying employers a premium for hiring unskilled workers would increase the employer's return beyond the market value of whatever marginal product that worker could create. This premium could be either a federal tax credit or a direct federal payment. Because it would let each worker negotiate his or her own subsidized employment, we call such a payment a job voucher.

A recent analysis of such a strategy concluded that "a reduction of one-half to two-thirds percentage point in the aggregate unemployment rate is possible with a targeted employment subsidy costing from $7.5 billion to $29 billion. . . . About 500,000 jobs can be created . . . without generating increased inflation."[8] A wage subsidy through federal tax credits has already been adopted on a limited scale as the Targeted Jobs Tax Credit, aimed at persons on welfare as well as poor youth, poor ex-offenders, Vietnam veterans, and some handicapped persons. A preliminary analysis

8. Robert H. Haveman and John L. Palmer, eds., "Introduction and Summary," *Jobs for Disadvantaged Workers: The Economics of Employment Subsidies* (Brookings Institution, 1982), p. 9; the study referred to is by Donald A. Nichols. See also Robert H. Haveman and Gregory B. Christainsen, "Public Employment and Wage Subsidies in Western Europe and the United States: What We're Doing and What We Know," in *European Labor Market Policies,* Special Report 27 (National Commission for Manpower Policy, September 1978), pp. 259–345; John Bishop, "The Design of Employment Subsidies—Lessons of the U.S. Experience," paper presented at the 36th Congress on Public Finance and Public Employment, International Institute of Public Finance and Public Employment, Jerusalem, 1980; and Isabel V. Sawhill, "Expanding Employment Opportunities in the Central City," paper prepared for the Allied Social Science Associations meetings in Denver, September 5, 1980.

indicates that this tax credit created 400,000 extra jobs in construction and distribution and may have stimulated further jobs in other fields.[9]

The "voucher" approach also supports the recent proposal of creating "enterprise zones" to stimulate additional jobs and investment within big-city concentrated-poverty areas. Enterprise zones as currently proposed in the United States would be narrowly defined areas in which businesses (including operators of rental housing) would receive wage subsidies for eligible low-skilled workers and would have reduced capital gains taxes, faster allowable depreciation for tax purposes, and possibly lower property taxes.[10] Such zones should not try to reverse the long-run tendency for manufacturing and other employment to decentralize, nor should they be considered a substitute for improving the mobility of unemployed persons.[11] But it is unrealistic to assume that most unemployed persons now living in concentrated-poverty neighborhoods could soon move to more economically dynamic areas, even if public assistance for such moves was available. Our analysis of urban development shows that many growing metropolitan areas deliberately create barriers to the entry of low-income households, except into already poor areas. The major purpose of enterprise zones should therefore be providing economic opportunities for individuals trapped in concentrated-poverty neighborhoods.

Consequently, subsidies offered in such zones should focus directly upon the disadvantaged and provide strong enough incentives to overcome the sizable drawbacks of these locations. That probably implies very large wage subsidies. It would also be more fruitful to concentrate subsidies on labor costs rather than on capital costs, especially since firms most suitable for such zones are likely to prefer older structures to costlier new ones. Accelerated depreciation seems an especially inappropriate tool for promoting employment in distressed areas.

9. John Bishop, *Employment in Construction and Distribution Industries: The Impact of the New Jobs Tax Credit*, DP 601-80 (Madison, Wis.: Institute for Research on Poverty, 1980), p. 39.

10. For a description of proposed legislation, see *Congressional Quarterly*, vol. 39 (June 6, 1981), p. 984; and *National Journal*, vol. 13 (June 13, 1981), p. 1081. For a more extended analysis, see Susan S. Jacobs and Michael Wasylenko, "Government Policy to Stimulate Economic Development: Enterprise Zones," paper presented at Conference on Financing State and Local Governments in the 1980s, Chicago, January 16–17, 1981; or Kenneth A. Small, "Geographically Differentiated Taxes and the Location of Firms" (Princeton University, Urban and Regional Research Center, October 1981).

11. That is the basic strategy for dealing with urban unemployment recommended by the President's Commission for a National Agenda for the Eighties; see *Urban America in the Eighties: Perspectives and Prospects* (GPO, 1980), pp. 97–109.

Finally, Congress has often failed in the past to constrain such location-based subsidies to the relatively small areas where they are appropriate, yielding instead to powerful political pressure to spread eligibility ever more widely.[12] If Congress does establish enterprise zones, their effectiveness would be greatly undermined by similarly expanding the territory eligible for aid.

Education

Many big-city public school systems are failing to serve urban children and parents effectively. Evidence includes increasing violence within schools, declining achievement scores, high levels of absenteeism, and greater shifting of relatively bright students from public to private schools.[13] These outcomes have such complex causes that no single set of recommendations can cope with all of them. Nevertheless, we believe increased choices for parents and children could form part of a set of recommendations that would significantly improve present conditions while reaping several of the advantages of individual empowerment programs already discussed.

Many people believe that if a school is attended primarily by children from impoverished homes, especially minority homes, effectively educating those children is virtually impossible. This is based on evidence that educational achievement is rooted primarily in the socioeconomic and parental background of students, not the performance of schools.[14] But several recent studies have discovered many schools attended mainly by disadvantaged children that have attained achievement levels at or above national norms. After analyzing these studies, Ronald Edmonds concluded that such schools all exhibited certain traits that appeared to be responsible

12. A prime example is municipal industrial development bonds exempt from federal income taxes. Originally intended to promote growth in economically depressed areas, they were gradually made available to more and more jurisdictions. By 1980, they had become usable almost everywhere. Hence they were financing new suburban industrial and commercial properties in competition with the very depressed areas they were originally supposed to aid. See Office of Community Planning and Development, Department of Housing and Urban Development, "Industrial Development Bonds," Working Paper on Urban Policy and Evaluation (March 15, 1979), pp. 21–23.

13. See "Why Public Schools Fail," *Newsweek*, April 20, 1981, pp. 62–73.

14. See Christopher Jencks and others, *Inequality: A Reassessment of the Effects of Family and Schooling in America* (Basic Books, 1972), for a detailed presentation of this view. See also Gary Orfield, *Must We Bus? Segregated Schools and National Policy* (Brookings Institution, 1978), p. 69.

for their effectiveness.[15] These were strong leadership from the principal, high-level expectations concerning student performance, a disciplined and orderly atmosphere, emphasis upon improved reading as a key goal, and constant assessment of student performance. Edmonds believes that these traits can be introduced elsewhere with equally positive results. Hence he concluded: "All children are eminently educatable, and . . . the behavior of the school is critical in determining the quality of that education." Moreover, he argued: "In and of itself, pupil family background neither causes nor precludes elementary school instructional effectiveness."[16] Whether such exceptional performance can be repeated on a large scale within big-city school systems remains to be proved. But Edmonds's analysis at least indicates that such systems have the potential of working well.

A major external obstacle to creating disciplined environments within many big-city public schools is the inhibiting rules under which they must now operate. Most public schools cannot expel or severely discipline unruly students, even when they attack teachers physically. Nor can they keep disruptive nonstudents out of their territory.[17] These rules need to be changed if public schools are to be effective, even if state attendance laws have to be altered.

In addition, large bureaucracies rarely change their behavior because of purely internal pressures. They usually reform themselves only in response to outside pressures that threaten their perquisites or their very existence.[18] Therefore, many big-city public school systems will probably not reform themselves unless stimulated by outside pressure. We believe increased competition could provide such pressure.[19]

Furnishing parents with educational vouchers usable in private or public schools would be one way to create such competition.[20] The exact

15. See Ronald Edmonds, "A Discussion of the Literature and Issues Related to Effective Schooling" (Center for Urban Studies, Graduate School of Education, Harvard University), p. 2. See also Michael Rutter and others, *Fifteen Thousand Hours: Secondary Schools and Their Effects on Children* (Harvard University Press, 1979), pp. 106–44, 177–205.

16. Edmonds, "Discussion of the Literature," pp. 27, 29.

17. "Why Public Schools Fail."

18. See Anthony Downs, *Inside Bureaucracy* (Little, Brown, 1967), pp. 167–210.

19. Several methods of increasing competition for public schools are discussed in Anthony Downs, "Competition and Community Schools," in *Urban Problems and Prospects*, 2d ed. (Rand McNally, 1976), pp. 243–69.

20. School vouchers have already been tried in one small-scale experiment in Alum Rock, California. But their use was so restricted by the rules necessary to get permission to try

structure of any voucher program crucially affects how well it would serve public and private educational goals.[21] Financing arrangements, curriculum and attendance regulations, and the information furnished to parents can vary tremendously. We believe educational vouchers should be used only with strict minimum educational standards (including some guarantee of academic freedom), limits on the ability of parents to add private funds to the voucher amounts, and prohibition of discrimination by race or income.

There is a real danger that educational vouchers would cause greater educational segregation of children by socioeconomic class, religious and political beliefs, and perhaps race. Henry Levin is opposed to them for this reason,[22] and we have serious reservations ourselves. Yet Levin's own analysis indicates how at least some safeguards against such outcomes could be built into a voucher system, including those mentioned above. Therefore, we recommend trying such a system on an experimental or demonstration basis. Expansion to a full national program should be contingent on a convincing demonstration that safeguards against increasing segregation are effective.

We do not mean to exclude other innovative mechanisms for expanding parental choice in education, such as "mini-schools" with different teaching styles within existing public school systems, decentralizing the governance of local public schools, or "independent public schools" within existing school districts. Nor do we mean to imply that vouchers or any other innovative program would remove all existing deficiencies from big-city education systems. Moreover, each innovation would have to be introduced gradually, with frequent evaluations comparing it to existing arrangements. But enhancing competition among education "suppliers" by allowing parents to procure some educational services other than from a single assigned public school could create a whole new educational atmosphere in many big cities.

---

them that the results were inconclusive. See Daniel Weiler and others, *A Public School Voucher Demonstration: The First Year at Alum Rock* (Rand Corp., June 1974). Among the restrictions involved was a prohibition against using voucher funds to finance private schools of any kind. Thus, the vouchers broadened students' options only by allowing them to choose among different individual public schools within their school district. Hence this "demonstration" ruled out from the start one of the major goals of most educational voucher proposals: the creation of strong competition for public schools from outside their own system.

21. Henry M. Levin points this out in "Educational Vouchers and Social Policy," in James J. Gallagher and Ron Haskins, eds., *Care and Education of Young Children in America: Policy, Politics and Social Science* (Ablex, 1980), pp. 103–25.

22. Ibid.

Transportation

The voucher approach could also be used to provide transportation services for the handicapped and the elderly. Giving them vouchers for hiring existing taxicab services would be far less costly than physically converting existing facilities or providing all-new accessible facilities. This conclusion is confirmed by the results of a year-long experiment in St. Louis that measured the expense and limited usage of transit buses equipped with wheelchair lifts.[23] One hundred and fifty-seven transit buses (only sixty for the first eight months) were placed in regular service on seventeen routes over a period of nearly two years between 1977 and 1979. These attracted an average of 117 trips per month by people in wheelchairs, at an estimated average *additional* operating cost of $18,691 per month, or $160 per trip.[24] During the first year of operation, only forty different individuals ever used the wheelchair lifts, constituting about 2 percent of all wheelchair-using people living within one-fourth mile of the routes. Of these, three individuals accounted for half the total trips. The estimated extra cost of serving these forty people for twelve and a half months was $205,560, or $5,139 per person.[25] That would have purchased far more taxicab rides for these people than the number of trips they took on specially accessible buses. True, this experiment was hampered by severe equipment reliability problems. Yet among the 98 percent of potential users who did *not* take advantage of the wheelchair lifts, reliability problems ranked only twelfth of seventeen reasons given for not using them. Much more important were two other factors: either the handicapped people already had automobile transportation, or their handicaps prevented them from reaching the fixed routes of the specially equipped buses. This would be a problem with any fixed-route transit also serving large numbers of nonhandicapped people, since its routes cannot be designed to pass close to where the handicapped live. Therefore, the evaluators concluded that "the addition of lift-equipped transit vehicles has only limited value."[26]

23. The following results are taken from a project evaluation of this experiment for the Urban Mass Transportation Administration. See Diego Teixeira, Frank Varker, and Robert Bowlin, *Accessible Bus Service in St. Louis,* Urban Mass Transportation Administration, Transportation Systems Center Project Evaluation Series, Service and Methods Demonstration Program (GPO, 1980).

24. Ibid., p. I-7. This figure includes only "marginal out-of-pocket costs" by the most conservative definition used by the authors, and excludes the large capital costs of equipping the buses.

25. Ibid., p. 9-25.

26. Ibid., p. 8-51.

Some representatives of handicapped groups have insisted that equal access to all public facilities should be a guaranteed right. But the St. Louis example demonstrates that this can be an extraordinarily costly way to solve the immediate problem for the handicapped, which is lack of mobility. Moreover, it reaches only a small fraction of those it is designed to help. Transportation vouchers would provide the elderly and handicapped with superior service and greater individual choice at much lower cost to taxpayers than making traditional transit systems more accessible.

Socioeconomic Segregation

Many of the worst U.S. urban problems result from institutional arrangements that sustain the socioeconomic hierarchy of neighborhoods within each metropolitan area. Those arrangements benefit a majority of metropolitan-area households at the expense of concentrating large numbers of poor households in neighborhoods with very undesirable environments. Should public policies try to abolish socioeconomic segregation and replace it with something better?

Any effective attack on such segregation would require providing many low- and moderate-income households with subsidies so they could move out of concentrated-poverty areas. Hence we discuss this issue under the heading of "empowering individuals."

Even if socioeconomic segregation were abolished, that would not eliminate poverty. Poverty is not primarily caused by such segregation, but rather results mainly from the overall operation of the economy in conjunction with the unequal distribution of skills and abilities. Nevertheless, reduced spatial segregation of poor households would allow many to escape from highly adverse environments. It might also benefit society generally by cutting overall rates of crime, vandalism, drug addiction, broken families, arson, unemployment, and ill health. And it would ameliorate the fiscal problems of those local governments now providing public services to a citizenry containing relatively high fractions of poor persons.

Socioeconomic segregation within U.S. urban areas is marked by two key traits: (1) high-quality housing standards legally required everywhere but differently enforced; and (2) low levels of overall housing subsidy to the poor, with subsidized units concentrated in large cities, especially in minority-group neighborhoods. Only two basic devices are available for spatially distributing poor households more widely within each SMSA. One is using much greater housing subsidies so poor people can occupy high-quality housing outside deteriorated areas (changing the second trait above). The other is allowing housing deterioration to occur in more parts of each SMSA (changing the first trait).

Housing subsidies can be provided as either identifiable projects (such as public housing developments) or invisible payments (such as housing allowances) used by households to help pay rents or ownership costs. The latter are a promising solution to some aspects of housing deprivation.[27] True, identifiable projects are more acceptable to the home-building industry because they usually involve new housing construction. But such projects often arouse vigorous opposition from nearby residents, whereas recipients of invisible payments can be widely scattered within a community without causing much protest.

In theory, units aided with either form of subsidy could be almost uniformly scattered in all neighborhoods, scattered in small clusters in many but not all neighborhoods, or concentrated in a few large clusters. These patterns could arise either spontaneously through the decisions of many individuals who received invisible payments or as a result of overall planning.

Placing subsidized units in high-income areas where extremely high-quality (and high-cost) housing standards prevail is almost never feasible. It would require extraordinarily high subsidies per household or introducing units of much lower quality than prevail there now. Governments and taxpayers are unwilling to pay for the former, and residents of such areas normally have enough political power to prevent the latter. Nor is it certain that many low-income households would want to live in such surroundings. Therefore, dispersal of low-income households into *all* parts of U.S. metropolitan areas cannot be achieved.

At the other extreme, large-scale clustering might reestablish poverty concentrations in suburban locations, especially if it involved massive public housing projects. However, large suburban poverty clusters would be better for their occupants than most existing poverty areas in big cities. Subsidies would enable poor suburban occupants to keep their housing units in good condition; they would have better access to expanding suburban job centers; and their children could more readily attend socioeconomically and racially integrated public schools.

Small-scale scattering would provide the benefits of large-scale clustering, but would avoid concentrating large numbers of the poor in the same

27. See Katharine L. Bradbury and Anthony Downs, eds., *Do Housing Allowances Work?* (Brookings Institution, 1981).

neighborhoods. It could occur as almost uniform dispersal *outside* relatively affluent neighborhoods, or as small clusters in many selected neighborhoods. However, there would be some potential drawbacks for the poor. One is their possible isolation from certain low-cost social services many now use. A second might be reduction of their political power in local government because they would form many small scattered groups. In addition, it would be difficult to serve dispersed poor populations with public transit.

In 1976, there were 4.141 million poor families and unrelated individuals in all U.S. central cities combined, compared to 2.489 million in all suburbs, based on the official U.S. definition of poverty.[28] About 41 percent of the former lived in concentrated-poverty areas.[29] If one-half of them both wanted and were able to move to other areas, that would create a major change in existing economic segregation. The movement of these 846,000 households from concentrated-poverty neighborhoods to suburbs would cause an increase of a third in the number of poor households there, yet increase the total number of suburban households only 3 percent.

Could a politically feasible subsidy program be designed which would spatially disperse households now concentrated in city poverty neighborhoods? Probably not, if that were made its explicit purpose. Such subsidies would be bitterly opposed by most high- and middle-income suburban residents, who form a large percentage of all SMSA residents; whereas only 12.4 percent of all SMSA households were poor as of 1976.[30] They would also be opposed by many nonpoor central-city residents who would be asked to accept new low-income neighbors. Moreover, they would be opposed by central-city politicians fearful of losing some of their established political supporters. Black and other minority-group politicians are especially hostile to scattering a noticeable fraction of their electorate into other jurisdictions. Furthermore, low-income residents of concentrated-poverty areas are highly skeptical of any government promises to improve their lot. Many fear they might lose some services they currently enjoy. So even

28. Bureau of the Census, *Current Population Reports*, Series P-60, no. 107, "Money Income and Poverty Status of Families and Persons in the United States: 1976" (Advance Report) (GPO, 1977), p. 28.

29. The Census Bureau estimated that 911,000 poor families (46.5 percent) and 782,000 poor unrelated individuals (35.9 percent) lived in "poverty areas" within central cities in 1976. That is a total of 1.693 million poor households in such areas, or 40.9 percent of all such households within central cities. A "poverty area" is any Census Tract in which over 20 percent of the residents were poor as of 1970.

30. See Bradbury and Downs, *Do Housing Allowances Work?*

most of the beneficiaries of abolishing socioeconomic segregation would not provide very strong support for doing so in this manner.

There would be greater—though still not dominant—political support for spending more on federal housing subsidies without specifiying whether to use them for dispersing the poor. Then some net movement of poor households out of concentrated-poverty neighborhoods would take place spontaneously. But Experimental Housing Allowance Program data indicate that this effect is small.[31] Therefore, increasing total spending on housing allowances would not reduce the geographic concentration of poverty very much. If more were spent on new construction subsidies, explicit public decisions would have to be made about where to locate those new units. Because of small political support for explicitly reducing poverty concentrations, most such units would be built near areas already poor. Thus, increasing spending on housing subsidies without explicit plans to reduce concentrations of poverty would probably not accomplish that goal.

The other possible method of geographically dispersing poor households—reducing housing quality restrictions to allow deteriorated units in more parts of each SMSA—is even less likely to work. Opposition among residents of good-quality areas to having *any* subsidized housing in their neighborhoods would be strengthened by their desire to avoid low-quality units nearby. They would vehemently oppose allowing deteriorated housing in more neighborhoods, whether scattered or concentrated in a few "slums." True, many older suburban neighborhoods will undergo decline like that experienced by city neighborhoods in the past. But their decline will occur accidentally, not as part of a deliberate strategy of dispersing the poor. Such a change may not reduce poverty concentrations, only move them, although it does disperse the fiscal burdens among more governments.

Thus, at present, there are no politically feasible alternatives to the existing hierarchy of neighborhoods based upon socioeconomic segrega-

31. "Analyses of program data from the Demand Experiment show that the neighborhoods moved to by blacks and hispanics had lower levels of minority concentration and higher average incomes than the ones they started from. These new neighborhoods were also more favorably ranked in subjective assessment—less litter, less crime, more public services, etc. . . . The controls [who received no housing assistance] showed similar changes. Thus, to the extent that allowance and control households move at only slightly different rates and generally move to similar neighborhoods, housing allowances do not significantly effect greater racial and economic integration." HUD, *Experimental Housing Allowance Program: A 1979 Report of Findings*, p. 47.

tion. Some alternatives can be conceived that we believe are economically and socially possible, and would probably provide large added benefits to the poor population and to the nation as a whole. An example is small-scale scattering. But these alternatives would be strongly opposed by a majority of households. Therefore, we do not believe it is practical to recommend an all-out assault on existing socioeconomic segregation at this time. It appears more fruitful to concentrate efforts in the near future upon other ways of dealing with concentrated poverty, as discussed earlier in this chapter and the previous one.

Implementing the "Empowerment" Approach

The individual or household empowerment approach is strongly opposed by certain groups. Many suppliers of services prefer working with government officials to competing on the open market for the patronage of poor households. More vehemently opposed are existing public agencies or labor unions that now monopolize the supply of certain services. Examples are public school administrators, teachers, and transit operator unions. They naturally fear that added competition would reduce their monopoly advantages by forcing them to provide better services at lower costs to consumers. They also believe—with some justification—that new alternative suppliers would have the unfair advantage of freedom from many regulations and obligations built up over the years that restrict their own ability to perform well.

Also opposed to vouchers are competitors of potentially empowered individuals already positioned in the market. For example, unionized workers do not want to compete with unemployed workers seeking jobs with the aid of wage subsidies. They argue that employers will substitute subsidized workers for people already working without subsidies—thereby just shifting unemployment to existing workers. Some such job substitution would probably occur. After examining both Western European and U.S. experience with wage subsidy and public employment programs, Robert Haveman and Gregory Christainsen concluded: "The net jobs created by marginal, targeted wage subsidy programs and low wage public employment programs are likely to range from 20 to 50 percent of the gross employment effect, at least in the first few years of program operation."[32] Thus, substitution effects may be significant, yet they are not likely to wipe out all the benefits of such programs.

32. Haveman and Christainsen, "Public Employment," p. 336.

An analysis of targeted wage subsidies by George Johnson indicates they can benefit both the target group and taxpayers generally *if* the subsidy fully covers members of the problem group, and their unemployment is caused by structural factors or induced by income transfer programs.[33] Therefore, if all members of a structurally disadvantaged group are eligible, including those already working, substitution among them will be minimized. Hence, if such a program is undertaken in a city, we recommend that it be made available to *all* very low-skilled workers living in concentrated-poverty areas with high unemployment rates.

However, the opposition to many forms of empowerment is so strong we believe they should be tried first on an experimental or demonstration scale in several metropolitan areas to test their feasibility, effectiveness, and costs. This has already been done concerning a housing allowance, which proved feasible. We recommend that it also be done concerning employment, education, and transportation as discussed above.

The empowerment approach would focus public responses to urban decline upon those whom it injures most: the residents of big-city concentrated-poverty areas. They are also the people most harmed by the socioeconomic segregation built into U.S. urban development. Such direct aid should be supplemented, as discussed in the previous section, by aid to governments of declining cities that need help in performing their specialized role as service-providers to poor households.

Achieving Effective Scale for Recommended Policies

Most of our recommendations have so many variations, and would have to be applied under such diverse conditions, it is impractical here to quantify how large or costly they should be. However, many would not be effective unless carried out at a certain minimum scale. Both economies of scale and externalities in service provision make many large programs more effective *per dollar* than smaller programs. For example, transit services exhibit economies of scale; hence a major investment produces a more than proportionally greater increment to such services than a smaller one. Similarly, starting a very small housing rehabilitation financing program would not improve overall expectations enough to attract the *private* capital needed to augment the rehabilitation subsidies. True, even a grossly underfunded program usually creates some improvements for a few participants. But it often fails to achieve the larger goals involved.

33. See Haveman and Palmer, *Jobs for Disadvantaged Workers.*

In addition, the side effects of small programs can sometimes undermine their intended benefits. To use an example mentioned earlier, if only a few unemployed residents of concentrated-poverty neighborhoods were eligible for wage subsidies, employers might substitute them for similar persons already working, thus shifting unemployment from one group to another.

Perhaps even more important, failing to provide remedies at sufficient scale is likely to create further skepticism about the overall worth of public policies. Many people already believe government action is usually "too little and too late," or plagued by incompetence and overregulation. It would be undesirable to strengthen those beliefs by adopting our recommended policies at scales too small to be effective. This does *not* mean that the *overall level* of federal efforts in recommended programs must be large. We believe it would be much better for society if the federal government undertook fewer programs aimed at social problems than in the past, but funded those it created with more adequate resources.

Conducting programs at the proper scale is not always just a matter of money; it sometimes involves intensity of change, too, especially in programs aimed at altering long-entrenched behavior. As noted earlier, many young people reared in ghettos have never developed positive attitudes toward, or work habits for, steady employment. Inculcating such attitudes and behavior in them is difficult if they remain living in neighborhoods dominated by "street life" and its values. Removing them to entirely different environments where they encounter many-faceted educational experiences is more likely to produce lasting results. That is what the Job Corps does, and may explain why it appears relatively successful over the long run.[34]

Nevertheless, achieving minimum scale usually requires enough resources to make significant progress toward "solving" the problems concerned. Congress and some state and local legislatures chronically adopt many different programs they fail to fund at an effective scale. Most elected officials want to appear to be "doing something" about every problem raised by any sizable group of their constituents. Congress is especially prone to begin new programs for symbolic reasons, then fail to expand them to effective scales. Sufficient political pressure to produce such expansion is usually mustered for only those few programs that affect either large numbers of people or small numbers of very influential people. The

34. Sar A. Levitan and Benjamin H. Johnson, *The Job Corps: A Social Experiment That Works* (Johns Hopkins University Press, 1975).

programs then mushroom and eventually reduce the legislature's ability to expand funding for other new programs. Examples of such resource-absorbing programs are Medicare, social security, and aid to families with dependent children.

To counteract this tendency, legislatures must specify relative priorities among the many possible responses to urban decline. Since most of our recommendations involve spending money and others involve making controversial changes in the "rules of the game," it is appropriate for us to indicate what we believe their relative priorities should be.

We have argued that the most serious problems associated with urban decline involve the impacts of concentrated-poverty environments upon those living in them. Therefore, we place top priority on policies aimed directly at improving their lot, including the "people empowerment" programs and demonstrations suggested in the preceding section. In some cases, the proper scale for such actions is surprisingly small.[35] In contrast, most efforts to improve the general economic situation of cities with declining populations require enormous resources and should receive the lowest priority. They would be relatively ineffective and would not aid those people with the most intense needs. Intermediate priority should go to increases in fiscal assistance to local governments of declining cities to help them meet the burdens of coping with poverty.

Conclusion

Nearly all U.S. metropolitan areas have failed to reform those institutions and practices that perpetuate or aggravate the problems of urban decline for one reason: too many people benefit from the existing arrangements. That is why radical restructuring of urban areas seems so unlikely. Hence it forms an unsuitable foundation for any realistic program for improving urban conditions.

35. For example, unemployment *rates* among central-city youth, especially blacks, were extremely high in the 1970s. But the total number of unemployed youth in *all* central cities in 1976 was only 536,000, or about 7.3 percent of the 7.3 million unemployed persons in the nation in that year. There were 750,000 CETA jobs in existence at that time, but only about one-fifth involved young people. One-half of all unemployment among central-city youth could have been eliminated through the creation of about 270,000 more CETA jobs, or approximately a one-third expansion of the CETA public job program. That would have cost around $2 billion. Since total youth unemployment was actually lower in 1979 than in 1976, and central-city populations have declined significantly, there are probably not many more unemployed young people in those cities today than there were then. Hence it is certainly

At the same time, American voters are not wholly insensitive to the pressing social needs around them. This was demonstrated by the dramatic if faltering steps taken in the War on Poverty of the 1960s. If a clear case can be made that present arrangements greatly disadvantage certain groups, or impair the efficiency of urban areas in carrying out vital social functions, people can be induced to vote marginal sacrifices for themselves to help correct the situation.

In this book, we have tried to show that there *are* valid reasons for public policy to intervene in the current processes of urban change. The adverse situations in which many cities find themselves are not solely the result of their incompetence or of "natural" market forces working themselves out. Rather, those situations are strongly molded by political institutions, legal regulations, social prejudices, and market imperfections. The process of decline itself sets in motion nonmarket responses which inefficiently aggravate it. Yet market forces are extremely powerful; so it would be folly to try policies that ignored their constructive roles in guiding the form and structure of economic change.

The real challenge is to design policies that address the worst aspects of urban decline without radically assaulting long-entrenched institutional arrangements, that correct the workings of markets without trying to override them wholesale, and that appeal to the sympathetic and enlightened impulses of voters without endangering their confidence in the existing system.

---

within the realm of conceivable policies to fund wage-subsidy or job-creation programs at sufficient scale to cut that unemployment by half or even more. That is the objective of recent youth unemployment legislation, though it was not funded at quite that large a scale as of 1980. Our use of this example is not meant to imply that reducing unemployment among youth should be given higher priority than reducing unemployment among adults; in fact, we support the reverse. However, this example shows that at least some serious urban problems are small enough so that it would be feasible to solve them almost completely.

Appendix: Variable Definitions and Sources

Population

1960 SMSA population inside 1960 SMSA boundaries (SP11).* Unpublished data from Bureau of the Census, "Population Change, and Components of Change: 1960 to 1970"; except New England data from *Census of Population, 1960, Number of Inhabitants: United States Summary,* Final Report PC(1)-A1 (GPO, 1961).

1960 SMSA population inside 1970 SMSA boundaries (SP21). Unpublished data from Bureau of the Census, "Population Change, and Components of Change: 1960 to 1970"; except New England data from *Census of Population, 1970, Number of Inhabitants: United States Summary,* Final Report PC(1)-A1 (GPO, 1971).

1960 SMSA population inside 1975 SMSA boundaries (SP31). Unpublished data from Bureau of the Census, "Population Change, and Components of Change: 1960 to 1970"; except New England data from *Current Population Reports,* Series P-25, nos. 649–98, *Population Estimates and Projections* (GPO, February–April 1977).

1970 SMSA population inside 1960 SMSA boundaries (SP12). Unpublished data from Bureau of the Census, "Population Change, and Components of Change: 1960 to 1970"; except New England data calculated from SP22 and individual city and town figures in *Census of Population, 1970, Number of Inhabitants: United States Summary.*

1970 SMSA population inside 1970 SMSA boundaries. Unpublished data from Bureau of the Census, "Population Change, and Components of Change: 1960 to 1970"; except New England data from *Census of Population, 1970, Number of Inhabitants: United States Summary.*

1970 SMSA population inside 1975 SMSA boundaries (SP32). Unpublished data from Bureau of the Census, "Population Change, and Components of Change:

* Numbers in parentheses are computer file numbers assigned to each variable. They are reported only when they are used elsewhere in this appendix to explain the computation of another variable.

1960 to 1970"; except New England data from *Current Population Reports*, Series P-25, nos. 649–98, *Population Estimates and Projections*.

1975 SMSA population inside 1970 SMSA boundaries (SP23). Calculated from SP33 and county data in Bureau of the Census, *County and City Data Book, 1977* (GPO, 1978); not calculated for New England.

1975 SMSA population inside 1975 SMSA boundaries (SP33). *County and City Data Book, 1977*.

1977 SMSA population inside 1975 SMSA boundaries (SP37). Bureau of the Census, *Current Population Reports*, Series P-25, no. 873, *Population Estimates and Projections: Estimates of the Population of Counties and Metropolitan Areas: July 1, 1977 and 1978* (GPO, 1978).

1960 city population (CP11). *Census of Population, 1960, Number of Inhabitants: United States Summary*.

1970 city population inside 1960 boundaries (CP12). Same as CP22, except for cities with annexation between 1960 and 1970, for which data were obtained from Bureau of the Census, *County and City Data Book, 1972* (GPO, 1973), app. H.

1970 city population (CP22). *Census of Population, 1970, Number of Inhabitants: United States Summary;* and unpublished (revised) figures from Bureau of the Census.

1970 city population inside 1975 boundaries (CP32). Unpublished data from Bureau of the Census, "Estimates of the Population Inside and Outside Central Cities, July 1, 1975, and Components of Change, 1970 and 1975."

1975 city population (CP33). Unpublished data from Bureau of the Census, "Estimates of the Population Inside and Outside Central Cities, July 1, 1975, and Components of Change, 1970 and 1975."

1977 city population (CP77). Unpublished data from the Population Division, Statistical Information Office, Bureau of the Census.

Population inside SMSA but outside central city was calculated by subtracting from SMSA population the population in all cities in the SMSA of over 100,000 population and all "central cities" in the SMSA as designated by the Bureau of the Census.

The above data were used in straightforward ways to calculate percentage changes over time in constant boundaries, through annexation, or total; city share of SMSA population; differences between city and SMSA in percentage change, and so on.

1960–70 percentage increase in SMSA population inside 1970 boundaries through net migration (PSMGA). Unpublished data from Bureau of the Census, "Population Change, and Components of Change: 1960 to 1970."

1960–70 percentage increase in SMSA population inside 1970 boundaries through natural increase (PSNTA). Calculated as the difference between total percentage increase in population and net migration: PSNTA = 100(SP22 − SP21)/SP21 − PSMGA.

1970–75 percentage increase in SMSA population inside 1975 boundaries through net migration (PSMGB). *County and City Data Book, 1977*, table 3.

1970–75 percentage increase in SMSA population inside 1975 boundaries through natural increase (PSNTB). Calculated as the difference between total percentage increase in population and net migration: PSNTB = 100(SP33 − SP32)/SP32 − PSMGB.

Year in which city reached 100,000 population. *Census of Population, 1970, Number of Inhabitants: United States Summary*, table 28.

Dummy variable indicating city gained population faster than the national population growth rate (14.5 percent) over the 1940–50 period. Donald J. Bogue, *Population Growth in Standard Metropolitan Areas, 1900–1950: With an Explanatory Analysis of Urban Areas* (Housing and Home Finance Agency, 1954).

Employment

1960 SMSA nonagricultural wage and salary employment (SEM11). Bureau of Labor Statistics, *Employment and Earnings, States and Areas, 1939–75*, BLS Bulletin 1370-12 (GPO, 1976).

1960 SMSA nonagricultural wage and salary employment in four major industry groups. See appendix C to chapter 6, above, for industries in each group and derivation of industry mix prediction of growth. Bureau of Labor Statistics, *Employment and Earnings, States and Areas, 1939–75*.

1960 employed persons working in the SMSA (SJ11). *Census of Population, 1960*, Subject Report PC(2)-6B, *Journey to Work* (GPO, 1961).

1970 SMSA nonagricultural wage and salary employment (SEM22). Bureau of Labor Statistics, *Employment and Earnings, States and Areas, 1939–75*.

1970 SMSA nonagricultural wage and salary employment in four major industry groups. See appendix C to chapter 6, above, for industries in each group and derivation of industry mix prediction of growth. Bureau of Labor Statistics, *Employment and Earnings, States and Areas, 1939–75*.

1970 SMSA nonagricultural wage and salary employment inside 1975 boundaries (SEM32). Bureau of Labor Statistics, *Employment and Earnings, States and Areas, 1939–75*, with boundary change corrections based on population.

1970 employed persons working in the SMSA (SJ22). *Census of Population, 1970*, Subject Report PC(2)-6D, *Journey to Work* (GPO, 1971).

1970 employed persons working in the SMSA as defined in 1960 (SJ12). Calculated from SJ22 and county data in *Census of Population, 1970, Journey to Work*.

1975 SMSA nonagricultural wage and salary employment (SEM33). Bureau of Labor Statistics, *Employment and Earnings*, vol. 23 (August 1976).

1976 SMSA nonagricultural wage and salary employment (SEM6). Bureau of Labor Statistics, *Employment and Earnings*, vol. 24 (August 1977).

1977 SMSA nonagricultural wage and salary employment (SEM7). Bureau of Labor Statistics, *Employment and Earnings*, vol. 24 (September 1977).

1967–72 percentage change in SMSA manufacturing employment. *County and City Data Book, 1977*.

Dummy variable equal to one if city is state capital.

1960 employed persons working in the city (CJ11). *Census of Population, 1960, Journey to Work*.

1970 employed persons working in the city (CJ22). *Census of Population, 1970, Journey to Work*.

Estimate of 1970 employed persons working in city, inside 1960 city boundaries (CJ12). Calculated from CJ22, subtracting estimate of 1970 jobs in territory annexed

1960–70; estimate assumes annexation increased 1970 jobs by the same proportion as population: $CJ12 = CJ22(CP12/CP22)$.

Just as for population, percentage changes and city share of SMSA totals were calculated from these employment figures in straightforward ways. Nonagricultural wage and salary employment and employed persons data are never combined in a ratio or change measure.

1967–72 percentage change in city manufacturing employment. *County and City Data Book, 1977.*

Income

SMSA income per capita in 1959.† Calculated as [(mean income) (number of recipients)/population] from *Census of Population, 1960, General Social and Economic Characteristics,* Final Report PC(1)-C[number], [*state name*] (GPO, 1961), table 76.

SMSA income per capita in 1969.† *County and City Data Book, 1972,* table 3.

SMSA income per capita in 1974.† *County and City Data Book, 1977.*

City income per capita in 1959.† Calculated as [(mean income) (number of recipients)/population] from *Census of Population, 1960, General Social and Economic Characteristics,* table 76.

City income per capita in 1969.† *County and City Data Book, 1972,* table 6, item 366.

City income per capita in 1974.† *County and City Data Book, 1977.*

Estimated percentage change in city income due to annexation, 1960–70. Calculated assuming that annexed populations have average income of SMSA. Sources are those of population and income noted above.

Estimated percentage change in city income due to annexation, 1970–75. Calculated assuming that annexed populations have average income of non-central-city portion of SMSA. Sources are those of population and income noted above.

Percent of SMSA families below the poverty level in 1959, 1969. *Census of Population, 1970, Poverty Status in 1969 and 1959 of Persons and Families, for States, SMSAs, Central Cities, and Counties: 1970 and 1960,* Supplementary Report, tables 8 and 10.

Percent of city families below the poverty level in 1959, 1969. Ibid., table 8.

SMSA population below the poverty line in 1959. Ibid., table 5.

SMSA population below the poverty line in 1969. *County and City Data Book, 1972,* table 3, item 64.

City population below the poverty line in 1969. Ibid., table 6, item 373.

SMSA cost of living in 1970, 1975.† Defined as annual costs of an intermediate budget for a four-person family. Used size of metropolitan area and geographic proximity to assign data from one of the 40 published areas to each of the 121 SMSAs. Bureau of Labor Statistics press releases.

† Variables expressed in dollars were all inflated (or deflated) to 1975 dollars using the consumer price index. Source: *Economic Report of the President,* selected years.

Land Area

SMSA land area in 1960. Square miles. *County and City Data Book, 1962*, table 3.

SMSA land area in 1970. Square miles. *County and City Data Book, 1972*, table 3.

SMSA land area in 1975. Square miles. *County and City Data Book, 1977*, table 3.

City land area in 1960. Square miles. *County and City Data Book, 1962*, table 6; and *Census of Population, 1960, Characteristics of the Population: United States Summary* (GPO, 1961), table 30.

City land area in 1970. Square miles. *Census of Population, 1970, Characteristics of the Population: United States Summary* (GPO, 1971), table 31.

City land area in 1975. Square miles. 1970 data plus changes as reported in Bureau of the Census, *Boundary and Annexation Survey, 1970–1975*, Series GE-30-2 (GPO, 1978), tables 4–6, 11.

These area figures were used along with population to calculate population density in cities or SMSAs.

Urbanized area population density in 1950 (persons per square mile). Bogue, *Population Growth in Standard Metropolitan Areas, 1900–1950*.

Fiscal

SMSA local government taxes in 1961.† Defined as general revenue from own sources of all local governments in the SMSA. Bureau of the Census, *Census of Governments*, 1962, vol. 5: *Local Government in Metropolitan Areas* (GPO, 1964), table 12.

SMSA local government taxes in 1971.† Defined as general revenue from own sources of all local governments in the SMSA. Bureau of the Census, *Census of Governments, 1972*, vol. 5: *Local Government in Metropolitan Areas* (GPO, 1975), table 12.

SMSA city-equivalent local government taxes in 1971 (defined separately for each city over 100,000 population in SMSA).† Defined as general revenue from own sources of local governments in the SMSA that coincide with the city government functions: (1) all municipalities and townships, plus (2) school districts only if (a) city schools are financed by city government or (b) city school district boundaries coincide with city government boundaries, plus (3) county government only if city has no overlying county government. Calculated from data in ibid., table 13.

City "all-local" taxes in 1971.† Defined as general revenue from own sources of city, plus school district only if boundaries coincide with city boundaries. *Census of Governments, 1972*, vol. 4: *Government Finances*, no. 1, *Finances of School Districts* (GPO, 1974), table 9, and no. 3, *Finances of County Governments* (GPO, 1974), table 4.

Taxes per capita were calculated by dividing the above local tax figures by local population; tax effort was defined as taxes as a percent of local income, and calculated by dividing local taxes per capita by per capita income.

City-SMSA disparities were then calculated as city minus SMSA or ratio of city to SMSA of tax rate measures (taxes per capita or tax effort), using city "all local" taxes compared to SMSA "city-equivalent" taxes.

City government debt burden, 1971 and 1975.† Defined as the two-year average ratio of debt service costs to all city own-source revenues, where debt service costs include interest expenditures, long-term debt retired, and short-term debt outstanding. Bureau of the Census, *City Government Finances*, various years.

Number of municipalities in the SMSA as defined in 1976 (count of municipalities and townships). Bureau of the Census, *Census of Governments, 1977*, vol. 1: *Governmental Organization* (GPO, 1978), table 15.

Dummy variable indicating city school district serves surrounding area as well, equal to one for those areas where city government does not finance public schools and city school district boundaries do not coincide with city boundaries. Based on data in *County and City Data Book, 1972*, table 6; *Census of Governments, 1972*, vol. 5: *Local Government in Metropolitan Areas*, table 13, and vol. 4: *Government Finances*, no. 1, *Finances of School Districts*, table 9; and *Local Government Finances in Selected Metropolitan Areas and Large Counties, 1971–72*, Series GF72, no. 6 (GPO, 1974), table 4.

Housing

Number of SMSA housing units in 1960. *County and City Data Book, 1962*, table 3.

Number of housing units in 1960 inside SMSA as defined in 1970 (SNH21). *County and City Data Book, 1972*, app. B-1.

Number of SMSA housing units in 1970 (SNH22). Ibid.

Number of housing units in 1970 in SMSA as defined in 1975 (SNH32). Calculated from SNH22 assuming boundary change adds same proportion to housing units as to population.

Number of city housing units in 1960, 1970. *County and City Data Book, 1972*, app. B-2.

Number of 1960 housing units built before 1930 in SMSA, city. Bureau of the Census, *Census of Housing, 1960*, vol. 1: *States and Small Areas: United States Summary*, HC(1)-1 (GPO, 1961), table 17.

Number of 1970 housing units built before 1940 in SMSA, city. Bureau of the Census, *Census of Housing, 1970, Detailed Housing Characteristics: United States Summary*, HC(1)-B1 (GPO, 1971), table 39.

Number of units built more than thirty years earlier was divided by total number of units to calculate percentage of units "old."

Percent of 1960 housing units in single-family structures in city, SMSA. *County and City Data Book, 1962;* SMSAs from table 3, item 53; cities from table 6, item 352.

Percent of 1970 housing units in single-family structures in city, SMSA. *County and City Data Book, 1972;* SMSAs from table 3, item 80; cities from table 6, item 379.

Housing units built between 1960 and 1970 in SMSA (SHNA), city (CHNA). (Includes only units in the 1970 stock.) *Census of Housing, 1970, Detailed Housing Characteristics: United States Summary,* table 3.

New housing units built 1970–75 in SMSA as defined in 1975 (SHSB). Measured as number of housing units authorized by building permits and public contracts. Bureau of the Census, *Construction Reports,* C40-[year]-13, *Housing Authorized by Building Permits and Public Contracts* (GPO, 1971–75), table 3-5.

Percentage increase in 1960 SMSA housing stock through new construction, 1960–70 (PNC2A). Calculated as 100(SHSA/SNH21).

SMSA housing construction in excess of population growth, 1960–70. Calculated as PNC2A minus [100(SP22 – SP21)/SP21].

Percentage increase in 1970 SMSA housing stock through new construction, 1970–75 (PNC3B). Calculated as 100(SHSB/SNH32).

Transportation

Automobiles per capita in SMSA as defined in 1975 in 1960, 1970, 1975, from data, by county, provided by R. L. Polk and Company.

Beltway variable indicating fraction of circumference of city encircled by a beltway. Based on highway maps referring to 1972.

Other Local Attributes

Unemployment rate (percent) in 1960 in SMSA, city. *Census of Population, 1960,* vol. 1: *Characteristics of the Population: United States Summary,* chap. B, *General Social and Economic Characteristics* (GPO, 1964); SMSAs from table 142; cities from table 154.

Unemployment rate (percent) in 1970 in SMSA, city. *Census of Population, 1970,* vol. 1: *Characteristics of the Population: United States Summary,* sec. 1 (GPO, 1973); SMSAs from table 184; cities from table 188.

Unemployment rate (percent) in 1975 in SMSA, city. Unpublished data from Bureau of Labor Statistics, "Labor Force Unemployment Statistics for All Cities and SMSAs, Annual Averages for 1975."

Violent crimes in 1960 in SMSA, city. Defined as murder, forcible rape, robbery, and aggravated assault. Federal Bureau of Investigation, *Uniform Crime Reports: Crime in the United States, 1960* (GPO, 1961), table 4.

Violent crimes in 1970 in SMSA, city. Defined as murder, forcible rape, robbery, and aggravated assault. Federal Bureau of Investigation, *Uniform Crime Reports: Crime in the United States, 1970* (GPO, 1971), table 5.

Violent crimes in 1975 in SMSA, city. Defined as murder, forcible rape, robbery, and aggravated assault. Federal Bureau of Investigation, *Uniform Crime Reports: Crime in the United States, 1975* (GPO, 1976), table 5.

Each of the above three sets of crime figures was divided by population and expressed as a rate per 100,000 people.

Mean temperature in January (degrees Fahrenheit). *County and City Data Book, 1972,* table 6, item 488.

Black population in 1960 in SMSA, city. *Census of Population, 1960,* vol. 1: *Characteristics of the Population,* pt. [state number] (GPO, 1961), sec. B, table 21.

Black population in 1970 in SMSA, city. *County and City Data Book, 1972;* SMSAs from table 3, item 10; cities from table 6, item 308.

Percent of 1970 population Spanish in SMSA, city. SMSAs from *County and City Data Book, 1972,* table 3, item 20; cities from *County and City Data Book, 1977,* item 214.

Index

Abravanel, Martin D., 199n
Adams, Charles F., 266n
Agglomeration economies, 206–07
Ahlbrandt, Roger S., Jr., 207n
Air pollution, 101
Allman, T. D., 2n
Altshuler, Alan, 219n
Annexation: advantages, 272; income effects, 95, 102, 149; population effects, 29, 31, 42, 84, 85, 187, 272
Annual negotiated agreements, 268–69, 271
Ashby, Lowell D., 127n
Automobiles. *See* Transportation

Bahl, Roy W., 50n, 273n
Baumol, W. J., 202n
Benari, Y. R., 221n
Biased policy theories, 78, 106
Bishop, John, 282n, 283n
Blacks: crime and, 173, 188, 189; neighborhood segregation, 170, 173; population trends, 25, 74–76, 90, 104, 215, 239; urban change and, 92, 93, 95, 100, 138, 147, 149, 187–88, 192
Blinder, Alan S., 273n
Block grants, 16, 267–69, 271
Bolz, Dan, 263n
Bowlin, Robert, 287n
Bradbury, Katharine L., 77n, 169n, 202n, 238n, 251n, 289n, 290n
Bradford, David F., 100n
Brophy, Paul C., 207n
Brown, Richard Maxwell, 173n
Business. *See* Employment
Butz, William P., 179n

Calkins, Susannah E., 266n
Categorical programs, 16, 268, 269, 271
Cheslow, Melvyn D., 235
Christainsen, Gregory B., 282n, 292
Cleveland case study: area characteristics, 237–38; description, 13–14; growth characteristics, 238–40; growth trends, 240–43; policy impact analysis, 243, 245–52; transportation cost effects, 226–28
Climate, 90, 104, 135, 138, 183, 240
Clotfelter, Charles T., 25n, 261n
Coleman, James S., 25n, 188n, 189n
Commuting. *See* Transportation
Congestion, 210
Consumer empowerment. *See* Empowerment system
Contingent categorical programs, 16, 268
Cook, Robert F., 243n
Cost of living, 46–47, 91, 92, 96, 101, 106, 147, 149, 185, 264
Crime, 43, 48, 61, 100, 173, 188–89, 240
"Critical mass" activities, 27, 207

Demographic trend theories, 78, 106–07
Descriptive decline: defined, 18–19; employment loss, 22–24; functional decline and, 58–59, 61, 108; patterns, 33–35, 42; population loss, 24–27
Devaul, Diane, 261n
Diamond, Douglas B., 169n, 261n
Disamenity avoidance theories, 78, 99–101
Disparity indexes, 62–64
Distress indexes, 48–50, 56–58, 64
Divergence indexes, 62–64
Dommel, Paul, 50n

Downs, Anthony, 3n, 73n, 77n, 165n, 169n, 170n, 182n, 194n, 202n, 212n, 238n, 251n, 278n, 285n, 289n, 290n
Dunn, Edgar S., 126n, 129n

Easterlin, Richard A., 179n
Economic evolution theories, 78, 105
Edmonds, Ronald, 284–85
Ellwood, David T., 251n
Employment: cities, 32, 34, 92–94, 149, 156–57, 164, 214–15; Cleveland case study, 238, 240, 241, 243, 245–46, 248; income and, 91, 92, 94–96, 101, 107, 139, 147, 149, 157, 164, 185; industry mix and, 96, 105, 147, 185; loss, 22–24, 34, 206–07; metropolitan areas, 32–33, 89–91, 96, 101, 104, 135, 181–82, 184, 185, 209; policy options, 243, 248, 281–84; population and, 24, 33–34, 90–91, 94, 103–05, 107–08, 135, 138, 139, 157, 164, 181–82; regional differences, 96; suburbanization, 94, 105, 182, 186, 206; taxes and, 91, 101, 206; transportation and, 223–24, 226, 227; trends, 181–82, 185, 186, 214–15; unemployment and, 72, 94, 105, 106, 157
Empowerment system: description, 16–17, 279–80; employment, 281–84; implementation problems, 292–93; schools, 284–86; socioeconomic segregation and, 288–92; transportation, 287–88
Emptying out decline, 11
Energy scarcity: consumption reduction, 186, 218–21; effects of, 12–13, 217–18; high-cost scenario, 221–33; severe-shortage scenario, 233–36
Enterprise zones, 283–84
Erickson, Rodney A., 224n
Externalities, 14–15, 259

Farm population, 71–72, 74, 183
Federal aid, 15–16, 239, 266–71
Feldstein, Martin S., 276n
Fertility rates, 69, 71, 179–81
Figlio, Robert M., 188n
Fossett, James W., 50n, 263n
Frey, William H., 188n, 232, 233, 245, 261n
Functional decline: defined, 18–19; descriptive decline and, 58–59, 61, 108; employment loss and, 22–24; extent, 42–43, 45–50, 56–59, 61; indexes, 48–50, 56–58, 64; population loss and, 24–27; trends, 42–43, 45

Gallagher, James J., 286n
Garbarino, Joseph W., 234n
Garn, Harvey, 269n
Gasoline. *See* Energy scarcity; Transportation
Gasoline rationing, 234
Gentrification, 176–77, 213
Gilje, Paul A., 274n
Glazer, Nathan, 25n, 26n
Glickman, Norman J., 243n
Goetze, Rolf, 212n
Goodman, John L., Jr., 214n
Gorham, William, 25n, 26n
Graham, Hugh Davis, 173n
Gurr, Ted Robert, 173n

Hamer, Andrew M., 186n, 245, 246n
Hamilton, Bruce W., 19n
Hanushek, Eric A., 169n, 251n
Harrison, Bennett, 203n
Hartman, Robert W., 270n
Haskins, Ron, 286n
Haveman, Robert H., 282n, 292, 293n
Heating and cooling costs, 12, 13, 218–20, 230–31, 235
Henderson, J. Vernon, 126n
Herman, Robin, 263n
Hirsch, Werner Z., 246
Hispanics: crime and, 188; population trends, 74, 76, 90, 104, 181, 184, 215; urban change and, 93, 135, 138, 184
Hollingsworth, Leslie, Jr., 187n, 214n
Housing: cities, 45, 61, 93, 95, 103, 135, 137–39, 147, 149; Cleveland case study, 240, 243, 250–52; code enforcement, 171–72; energy scarcity and, 217, 230–31; income and, 76–77, 95, 96, 106, 147, 168–69, 171–72; neighborhood change and, 10–11, 166–69, 171–72, 174–77, 207–08, 212, 213; policy options, 106, 243, 288–92; population change and, 10–11, 24–26, 93, 106, 135, 137–39; regional differences, 187, 192; suburbanization and, 10–11, 45, 73, 93, 101, 106, 182, 186–87, 206; transportation and, 223–29; trends, 182, 186–87, 192, 210, 212, 213
Houthakker, H., 221n
Howry, E. P., 202n
Hu, Joseph, 208n

Illich, Ivan, 280n
Immigration, 69, 76, 180–81, 238–39
Income: cities, 61–62, 92, 100–02, 139, 147, 149, 157, 164; Cleveland case study, 239, 240; employment and, 91, 92, 94–96, 101, 107, 139, 147, 149, 157, 164, 185; housing and, 76–77, 95, 96, 106, 147, 168–69, 171–72; metropolitan areas, 89, 91–93, 96, 103,

185; neighborhood change and, 167–69, 171–72; population and, 24, 59, 91, 92, 95, 103–04, 107, 149, 183, 205; racial composition and, 95, 96, 100, 147, 149; regional differences, 45–48, 61–62, 96, 100, 185; schools and, 167, 205; suburbanization and, 95–97, 100–03, 192; transportation and, 168–70; trends, 45, 76–77, 185; urban decline and, 81
Incumbent upgrading, 176
Individual empowerment. *See* Empowerment system
Inflation, 72–73

Jacobs, Susan J., 243n
Jacobs, Susan S., 283n
Jencks, Christopher, 284n
Johnson, Benjamin H., 294n
Johnson, George, 293

Kain, John F., 220n
Katzman, Martin T., 202n
Keeler, Emmett, 237n
Kelejian, Harry H., 100n
Kelley, Sara D., 25n, 188n
Kennedy, M., 221n
Kern, Clifford R., 169
Knaff, Eugene, 274n
Kramer, Kevin L., 263n

Lampard, Eric E., 203n
Land-use control, 182, 235–36
Lane, Roger, 173n
Lave, Charles A., 220
Lederber, Larry, 269n
Levine, Charles H., 265n
Levin, Henry M., 286
Levitan, Sar A., 294n
Local government: Cleveland case study, 243; fiscal equalization, 243, 247, 249–50, 253; fiscal problems, 26–27, 72–73, 138, 214, 215; fragmentation, 16, 93, 135, 139, 189–90, 240, 271–77; housing code enforcement, 171–72; intergovernmental aid, 266–71, 277; land-use controls, 182, 235–36; policy options, 15, 243, 247, 249–50, 253, 271–77; regionalization, 271–77; tax rate effects, 26, 47–48, 78, 91, 93, 101–02, 139, 190, 192, 205, 206, 231–32, 248–50
Long, Norton E., 2n

McCarthy, Kevin F., 181n, 182n
McFadden, Daniel, 250n
Mancini, Paul K., 199n
Mangum, Garth L., 206n, 281n
Manvel, Allen D., 266n
Matching funds, 271, 276
Mayo, Stephen K., 169n
Menu approach, 16, 269–71
Mieszkowski, Peter, 261n
Mills, Andrea, 72n, 281n
Mills, Edwin S., 19n, 28n, 102n, 123n, 168
Minorities. *See* Blacks; Hispanics
Miyao, Tatahiro, 202n
Mohring, Herbert, 207n
Moore, John A., 188n
Morrison, Peter A., 2n, 181n, 182n
Moses, Leon, 226n
Muller, Thomas, 26n, 262n
Muth, Richard F., 168
Myrdal, Gunnar, 203n

Nathan, Richard P., 50n, 266n
Neels, J. Kevin, 235
Negotiated investment strategy, 268–69
Neighborhood change: causes, 10–11, 165–67, 212; Cleveland case study, 248–50; housing code effects, 171–72; population change effects, 167–68, 174–77; revitalization, 12, 176, 207–08, 210, 212–13, 248–50; socioeconomic segregation, 170–72, 177, 286, 288–92; transportation cost effects, 168–70; trends, 12, 212–13; urban development effects, 165–67, 172–74
Nelson, Gary R., 250n
Nelson, Kathryn P., 25n, 187n, 188n, 215n
Netzer, Dick, 273n
Nichols, Donald A., 282n
Nonmetropolitan growth, 11, 182, 183, 190–91
Nordhaus, William D., 221
Northeast Ohio Areawide Coordination Agency (NOACA), 241
Norton, R. D., 86n

Oates, Wallace E., 102n, 202n
Oppenheim, John, 263n
Orfield, Gary, 261n, 284n
Overcrowding decline, 10, 26

Pack, Janet Rothenberg, 263
Palmer, John L., 282n, 293n
Pechman, Joseph A., 3n, 278n
Peirce, Neal R., 2n
Perloff, Harvey S., 127n, 129n
Peskin, Janice, 264n
Peskin, Robert L., 218n
Peterson, George E., 26n, 259n, 261n
Peterson, Iver, 263n
Polinsky, A. Mitchell, 169n, 251n
Population change: causes, 8–10; cities, 31, 33–35, 57–59, 84–86, 92–94, 133, 135, 137–

39, 149; Cleveland case study, 238–41, 245, 246, 248; effects of, 18, 24–27; employment and, 24, 33–34, 90–91, 94, 103–05, 107–08, 135, 138, 139, 157, 164, 181–82; historic trends, 29, 31–32, 68–69, 71, 72, 74–76, 179–81; housing and, 10–11, 24–26, 93, 106, 135, 137–39; income and, 24, 59, 91, 92, 95, 103–04, 107, 149, 183, 205; metropolitan areas, 29, 33–35, 59, 86, 89–93, 96–97, 101, 104, 181–85, 209; neighborhood, 167–68, 174–77; racial factors, 93, 135, 138, 139, 181, 184, 187–88; regional differences, 11, 35, 75, 76, 96–97, 184, 191; schools and, 93, 138, 188, 205; self-limiting factors, 208–11; self-reinforcing factors, 205–08; suburbanization, 85–86, 92–94, 106–07, 182, 185–90, 191–92; taxes and, 26, 93, 102, 139, 205, 248–50; transportation and, 182, 232–34; trends, 11–12, 31–32, 35, 179–93, 215–16; unemployment and, 90, 103, 138, 183–84, 208–09
Positive attraction theories, 78, 103–04
Poverty concentration: effects, 25; employment and, 206, 281–84; empowerment aid approach, 17, 279–93; ghetto culture factors, 206; housing and, 77, 166–67, 171–72, 288–92; minority groups, 25, 75, 76; neighborhood change and, 10–11, 165–68, 170–71, 176–77; population change and, 59, 174–76; regional differences, 45–46; schools and, 284–86; transportation and, 168–70, 287–88; trends, 43–44, 61, 214–15; urban development effects, 165–68
Power-equalizing aid formulas, 16, 275–76
Pozdena, Randall J., 234n
Public policies, 108, 204–05, 211, 215, 216; adjustment to decline, 12, 15; aid to cities, 15–16, 266–71, 277; anti-city bias, 15, 78, 106, 189, 259–61; Cleveland case study, 243, 245–52; empowerment approach, 16–17, 279–93; energy scarcity approaches, 234–36; local government fragmentation, 271–77; need for intervention, 19, 258–59; regional bias, 15, 78, 106, 262–65; scale of programs, 17, 293–95
Pucher, John R., 219n
Pushkarev, Boris S., 235n

Quigley, John M., 169n, 251n

Rabinovitz, Francine, 276n
Racial segregation, 74, 187–88, 192
Recreational amenities, 183
Reschovsky, Andrew, 274n
Revenue sharing, 16, 267, 271
Rogers, William, 237n
Roistacher, Elizabeth A., 72n, 243n, 281n
Rutter, Michael, 285n
Rydell, C. Peter, 268n

Saunders, Norman C., 241n
Sawhill, Isabel V., 282n
Schelling, Thomas C., 203n
Schill, Michael, 177n
Schools, 25, 93, 99, 138, 167, 188, 192, 205, 284–86
Schur, Edwin M., 173n
Schurr, Sam H., 218n, 219n, 220n, 222n, 230n
Segal, David, 169
Self-limiting processes, 202–04, 208–11, 215
Self-reinforcing processes, 202–08, 216
Sellin, Thorsten, 188n
Seninger, Stephen F., 206n, 281n
Sharp, Douglas P., 229
Simms, Margaret C., 72n, 281n
Small, Kenneth A., 77n, 100n, 202n, 230n, 234n, 238n, 283n
SMSAs. *See* Standard metropolitan statistical areas
Social functions, 19–22, 213–15
Socioeconomic segregation, 167, 170–72, 177, 286, 288–92
Solomon, Arthur P., 261n
Sørensen, Annemette, 187n, 214n
Standard metropolitan statistical areas (SMSAs), defined, 5
Stanley, David T., 50n
State aid, 275–76
Steinnes, Donald N., 94n
Straszheim, Mahlon, 261n
Sweeney, James, 220

Taeuber, Karl E., 187n, 214n, 261n
Targeted Jobs Tax Credit, 282–83
Tax avoidance theories, 78, 101–02
Tax-base sharing, 16, 274–77
Tax rates: employment and, 91, 101, 206; population change and, 26, 93, 102, 139, 190, 205, 231–32, 248–50; suburbanization and, 190, 205, 231–32; trends, 47–48, 190, 192
Teixeira, Diego, 287n
Thurow, Lester C., 281n
Tiebout, Charles M., 102, 190n
Tolley, George S., 261n
Train, Kenneth, 220
Transportation: Cleveland case study, 239, 243, 250, 254; employment and, 223–24, 226, 227; empowerment system, 287–88; energy scarcity effects, 12–13, 189, 218–20, 234; gas rationing, 234; income and,

168–70; neighborhood change and, 168–70; nonwork trip patterns, 228–29; population change and, 182, 232–34; suburbanization and, 99–100, 104, 182, 186, 189, 239; trends, 73–74, 186; work trip patterns, 223–28
Trickle-down process, 100, 165–66

Unemployment: cities, 42–43, 61, 72, 138, 149; Cleveland case study, 240; employment and, 72, 94, 105, 106, 157; empowerment approach to, 281–84; income and, 91, 149; metropolitan areas, 42, 90, 91, 183–84; population and, 90, 103, 138, 183–84, 208–09; regional differences, 47, 48, 61, 72, 183–84; trends, 42–43, 61, 72, 183–84
Urban decline: case study, 13–14; causes, 8–10, 77–79, 81, 83; defined, 4, 18; effects of, 202–05; energy scarcity effects, 12–13, 236; extent, 4–5, 8, 64; historic trends and, 68–69, 71–77; neighborhood deterioration, 10–11; overview, 1–3; policy impact analysis, 248, 252–54; policy recommendations, 12, 14–17, 19, 260–61, 265, 271, 276–77, 279–80, 282–88, 291–92; problems of, 213–15; reversibility, 211; self-limiting processes, 202–04, 208–11; self-reinforcing processes, 202–08; trends, 11–12, 35
Urban development, 77, 100, 165–67, 172–75

Varaiya, Pravin, 126n
Varker, Frank, 287n
Vaughan, Roger J., 243n
Vernez, Georges, 243n
Vietorisz, Thomas, 203n
Voucher system. *See* Empowerment system

Ward, Michael P., 179n
Wasylenko, Michael, 224n, 283n
Watkins, Alfred J., 203n
Weiler, Daniel, 286n
Wells, John D., 250n
Wheaton, William C., 65n
Williamson, Harold, Jr., 226n
Wilson, James Q., 173n
Wiseman, Michael, 126n
Wolfgang, Marvin E., 188n
Womack, James P., 219n

Zupan, Jeffrey M., 235n